The Other Orlando

What To Do When You've Done Disney & Universal

Kelly Monaghan

The Other Orlando

What To Do When You've Done Disney & Universal

Published by The Intrepid Traveler
P.O. Box 531, Branford, CT 06405

Copyright © 2007 by Kelly Monaghan
Fourth Edition
Additional research by Alexis Elder
Printed in Canada
Book Jacket: George Foster, Foster & Foster, Inc.
Maps designed by Evora Taylor
ISBN: 978-1-887140-66-9

Publisher's Cataloguing in Publication Data. Prepared by Sanford Berman.

Monaghan, Kelly

The other Orlando: what to do when you've done Disney & Universal. Branford, CT: Intrepid Traveler, copyright 2007.

"Revised update of... Orlando's other theme parks: what to do when you've done Disney" (1999).

PARTIAL CONTENTS: SeaWorld Florida. -Discovery Cove. -Gatorland. -Holy Land Experience. -Kennedy Space Center. -Busch Gardens Tampa. -Water parks. -Dinner attractions. -Who's who of zoos. -Moving Experiences. Balloon rides. Boat rides. -Sports scores. -Spectator sports. Arena football. Auto racing. Jai-alai. Rodeo. -Shop 'til you drop.

1. Orlando region, Florida--Description and travel--Guidebooks. 2. Theme parks--Orlando region, Florida--Guidebooks. 3. Recreation--Orlando region, Florida. 4. Sports--Orlando region, Florida. 5. SeaWorld, Florida--Description and travel--Guidebooks. 6. John F. Kennedy Space Center, Cocoa Beach, Florida--Description and travel--Guidebooks. 7. Busch Gardens, Tampa, Florida--Description and travel--Guidebooks. 8. Shopping--Orlando region, Florida--Guidebooks. 9. Discovery Cove, Florida--Description and travel--Guidebooks. 10. Gatorland, Florida--Description and travel--Guidebooks.

I. Title. II. Title: What to do when you've done Disney & Universal. III. Title: Orlando IV. Intrepid Traveler.

917.5924

Trademarks, Etc.

Photo Credits

Other Books by Kelly Monaghan

Universal Orlando:
The Ultimate Guide To The
Ultimate Theme Park Adventure

Home-Based Travel Agent:
How To Succeed In Your Own
Travel Marketing Business

The Travel Agent's Complete Desk Reference
(co-author)

Air Courier Bargains:
How To Travel World-Wide For Next To Nothing

Fly Cheap!

Air Travel's Bargain Basement

Table of Contents

List of Maps

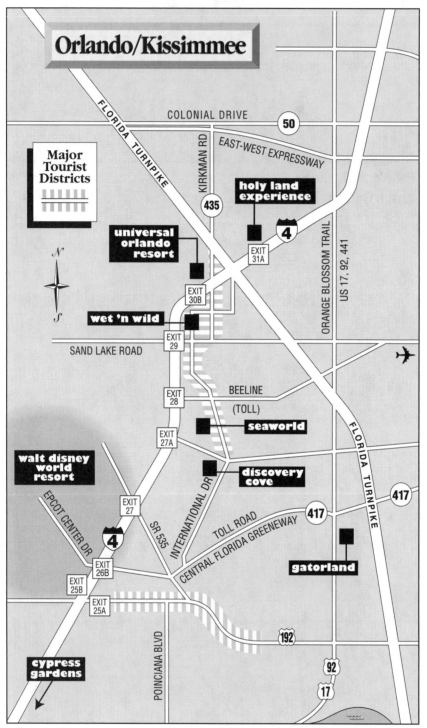

Chapter One:

Introduction & Orientation

DON'T GET ME WRONG. I LOVE DISNEY WORLD AND UNIVERSAL ORLANDO. I visit these splendid theme parks every chance I get. However, as a travel writer, I must cast a canny eye on the marketplace. In doing so, I determined two things. First, my publishing company already has a book on Disney World. I refer, of course, to *The Hassle-Free Walt Disney World® Vacation* by Steven M. Barrett (Intrepid Traveler, $14.95). Second, a terrific guide to Universal Orlando has also been written, this time (fortunately) by me. It's called *Universal Orlando: The Ultimate Guide To The Ultimate Theme Park Adventure* (Intrepid Traveler, $15.95).

Because Disney World and Universal are the 900-pound gorillas of Central Florida tourism, any general guidebook to Central Florida must, of necessity, devote so much space to their multitude of attractions that the area's other attractions receive short shrift, if they are covered at all. This book, then, turns away from Disney World and Universal, not out of disdain, but to lavish on Orlando's other attractions the in-depth treatment that Disney has long enjoyed and that Universal is now beginning to attract. I suspect that readers of this book have already visited Disney World and Universal, perhaps many times, and are ready to explore the other possibilities of a Central Florida vacation. As you will see, they are myriad. In fact, there are so many things to see and do in the Orlando area that at the end of this Introduction I have included a list of "hidden" treasures you might overlook.

When to Come

There are three major questions you must ask yourself when planning a trip to Orlando: How crowded will it be? What will the weather be like? When will my schedule allow me go? For most people, the third question will determine when they go, regardless of the answers to the other two. The dictates of business or the carved-in-stone school calendar will tend to determine when you come to Orlando. For those who can be flexible, however, carefully picking the time of your visit will offer a number of benefits. During slow periods, the crowds at Orlando's major theme parks are noticeably thinner than they are at the height of the summer or during the madness of Christmas week. On top of that, hotel rates are substantially lower and airfare deals abound. Likewise, Orlando in winter can seem positively balmy to those from the North, although it's unlikely you will find the temperature conducive to swimming (except in heated pools). Spring and fall temperatures are close to ideal.

Let's take a look at these two variables: the tourist traffic and the weather.

Orlando's Tourist Traffic

Most major tourist destinations seem to have two seasons — high and low. For most of Florida, the high season stretches from late fall to early spring, the cooler months up North. Low season is the blisteringly hot summer, when Floridians who can afford it head North. Orlando, thanks to its multitude of family-oriented attractions has five or six distinct "seasons," alternating between high and low, reflecting the vacation patterns of its prime customers — kids and their parents.

Orlando hosts over 40 million visitors a year. The heaviest tourist "season" is Christmas vacation, roughly from Christmas eve through January first. Next comes Easter week and Thanksgiving weekend. The entire summer, from Memorial Day in late May to Labor Day in early September, is on a par with Easter and Thanksgiving. There are two other "spikes" in attendance: President's Week in February and College Spring Break. Various colleges have different dates for their Spring Break, which may or may not coincide with Easter; the result is that the period from mid-March through mid-April shows a larger than usual volume of tourist traffic. The slowest period is the lull between Thanksgiving and Christmas. Next slowest (excluding the holidays mentioned earlier) are the months of September, October, November, January, and February. Tourism starts to build again in March, spiking sharply upward for Easter/Spring Break, then dropping off somewhat until Memorial Day.

The best advice is to avoid the absolutely busiest times of the year if possible. If you do come during the summer, as many families must, plan to deal with crowds at the major parks (Disney, Universal, SeaWorld, Busch Gardens) and console yourself with the thought that, by concentrating on the attractions covered in this book, you will avoid the worst crowds.

Orlando's Weather

Orlando's average annual temperature is a lovely 72.4 degrees. But as we've already noted, averages are deceptive. Here are the National Weather Service's generally cited "average" figures for temperature and rainfall throughout the year:

	High (°F)	Low (°F)	Rain (in.)
January	71	49	2.3
February	73	50	2.8
March	78	55	3.2
April	83	59	1.8
May	88	66	3.6

June	91	72	7.3
July	92	73	7.3
August	92	73	6.8
September	90	73	6.0
October	85	66	2.4
November	79	58	2.3
December	73	51	2.2

Use these figures as general guidelines rather than guarantees. While the average monthly rainfall in June might be 7.3 over the course of many years, in June 2005 Orlando International Airport recorded 16.74 inches of rain that month. The same with temperature. January of 2001 saw lows dip into the twenties.

I find Orlando's weather most predictable in the summer when "hot, humid, in the low nineties, with a chance of afternoon thunderstorms" becomes something of a mantra for the TV weather report. Winter weather tends to be more unpredictable with "killer" freezes a possibility. As to those summer thunderstorms, they tend to be localized and mercifully brief (although occasionally quite intense) and needn't disrupt your touring schedule. I was once in Orlando for a summer week when it rained somewhere every day but never on me. Another thing to bear in mind is that June through September is hurricane season, with July and August the most likely months for severe weather.

Getting Oriented in Orlando

Orlando can be confusing. The Orlando metropolitan area comprises three counties and, since you will often hear location indicated by naming the county, it is worth knowing their names and relation to one another. From north to south they are Seminole, Orange, and Osceola. Orlando is in Orange County, Kissimmee is in Osceola. Most of the attractions covered in this book are in Orange and Osceola; only a few are in Seminole or more distant counties.

The area is dotted with lakes, both large and small; so streets stop, start, and take circuitous detours. In European fashion, streets change names as they cross municipal boundaries. On top of that, the area's major highway, Interstate 4, which runs east-west across the state, runs roughly from northeast to southwest through the Orlando metropolitan area and almost directly north-south in the heart of Orlando's tourist district. As a result, streets that are "east" or "south" of I-4 at one point are "west" or "north" of it at another. (See map, page 8.) All of this complicates the process of giving, receiving, and following directions.

Fortunately, most of the Orlando area's attractions are located in two fairly compact tourist districts: International Drive in Orlando and US 192 in Kissimmee, with I-4 forming a direct and easy-to-follow link between them. Attractions that are not located in these two areas are seldom more than a short drive away from an I-4 exit.

International Drive (sometimes abbreviated I Drive and pronounced "Eye Drive," just as I-4 is pronounced "Eye Four") is in Orlando. It is a meandering boulevard that roughly parallels I-4 from Exit 75 on the north to Exit 67 on the south. Many of the major attractions profiled in this book are on it or near it. At the northern end, you will find Universal Orlando (just across I-4) and Wet 'n Wild. At the southern end lies SeaWorld. In between, there are some dinner attractions and a number of smaller attractions, along with dozens of hotels, scores of eateries, several discount outlet malls, and the mammoth Orlando Convention Center. International Drive is glitzy, garish, hyperactive, and a traffic nightmare in the evening and at rush hours.

The second major tourist axis is US 192 (also called Highway 192, and Irlo Bronson Highway), which runs east to west through Kissimmee, crossing I-4 at Exit 64. West of I-4 you will find an entrance to the Disney properties; to the east of I-4 is a gaudy strip of hotels, restaurants, dinner attractions, smaller attractions, miniature golf courses, and discount shopping outlets. This strip is thoughtfully marked with numbered "Mile Markers," which I have used in the text to give directions.

Tip: Chances are you will be staying in or very close to one of the two major tourist areas. When you are traveling from Point A to Point B in the Orlando area, my advice is to travel via US 192 and I-4. This may not always be the most direct or shortest route but it will be the surest route and very often the quickest because there is less chance of getting lost en route. When I give directions in this book I try, wherever possible, to route you via these major arteries.

Keeping Posted

For the very latest information about what's going on in Orlando, your indispensable source of information is the *Orlando Sentinel*, the local daily newspaper. Every Friday, the *Sentinel*'s "Calendar" section offers an entire week's worth of information about films, plays, concerts, nightclubs, art exhibits, and the like, along with capsule reviews of many of the area's restaurants and a guide to area radio stations. Music buffs will appreciate the exhaustive listings of who's playing what where and film fans will find show times for every multiplex from Orlando to the Atlantic coast. There is even a listing of area attractions and a section of personal ads just in case you start feeling lonely. On other days of the week, a one-page "Calendar" section gives details on events for that day, including lesser happenings that don't rate mention in the weekly section. Those who want to get an advance peek at what's going on in Orlando, can visit the *Sentinel*'s "Calendar" section on the Internet at http://www. orlandosentinel.com/entertainment.

Orlando has a free weekly newspaper, the *Orlando Weekly*, that is especially strong on the pop music scene. You will be able to find it in racks near the entrance to book stores, coffee shops, supermarkets, and drugstores.

The Intrepid Traveler, the publisher of this book, maintains a web site containing updated information about all of Orlando's attractions along with other valuable information. Log on at:

http://www.TheOtherOrlando.com

The Orlando FlexTicket

Borrowing a page from the Disney marketing manual, several of Mickey's competitors banded together to offer what has long been a Disney staple — multi-day, multi-park passes at an attractive price. The participating parks are Universal Studios

Florida, Islands of Adventure (IOA), SeaWorld, Wet 'n Wild, and Busch Gardens Africa in Tampa. It's called the Orlando FlexTicket and it works like this:

4-Park, 14-Day Orlando FlexTicket — Universal Studios Florida, IOA, SeaWorld, Wet 'n Wild

Adults	$202.31
Children (3 to 9)	$166.10

5-Park, 14-Day FlexTicket — adds Busch Gardens Africa

Adults	$250.46
Children (3 to 9)	$213.19

Prices include tax. These passes offer unlimited visits to all four or five parks for two weeks and represent an excellent value. On top of that, they offer the come and go as you please convenience of annual passes, albeit for a much shorter time.

FlexTickets may be purchased at any of the participating parks' ticket booths or through your travel agent before coming. They are valid for fourteen consecutive days beginning on the day you first use them. As for parking, you pay at the first park you visit on any given day. Then show your parking ticket and Orlando FlexTicket at the other parks on the same day for complimentary parking.

All About Discounts

Throughout this book, I have listed the standard admission price for every attraction. However, thanks to the cutthroat competition for the attention of tourists in tourist-saturated Orlando, an entire industry of dollars-off coupons and discount ticket outlets has grown up, so you seldom have to pay the posted price.

Coupons

Dollars-off coupons are distributed via attraction web sites and through a variety of free visitors' guides — magazine-sized publications filled with ads for area attractions and restaurants. The coupons you want are either downloadable or found in the freebie publications' ads or separate coupon sections (some booklets are nothing but coupons). There's a good chance you will find several of these throwaway publications in your hotel room or be handed them with your room key or when you pick up your rental car. If not, look around for displays at the airport, car rental agencies, hotel lobbies, and restaurants in the tourist areas. You won't have to look far.

Another source of dollars-off coupons is the brochures for individual attractions. Many of them contain a coupon. You will find them in the same places you find the larger, magazine-format coupon books. Many lobby and restaurant display racks contain dozens of these brochures.

The discounts available from dollars-off coupons are relatively modest, usually a few dollars. Some attractions make their coupons valid for up to four or six people, hence the headlines that shout "up to $16 off!" You are unlikely to find coupons for museums, botanical gardens, and state parks (although anything is possible in this overheated competitive environment).

My suggestion is that you collect as many free visitors' guides as you can get your hands on. Browse the brochure racks and pull out those that appeal. Then, in the comfort of your hotel room, select and cut out offers that appeal to you and keep them in your rental car for ready use.

Yet another option for getting a wide range of modest discounts is the Orlando Magicard. Sponsored by the Orlando Convention and Visitors Bureau, the Magicard looks like a credit card. Flashing it will get you discounts at most area attractions and dinner shows, as well as at some restaurants and area hotels. You can obtain a card prior to your arrival by writing to the Orlando Visitors Center, 8723 International Drive, Orlando, FL 32819. Or call (407) 363-5872. Or order on the Web at www.orland-oinfo.com/magicard. They will send you the card free of charge. You can also pick up the card at the Center once you are in Orlando. Along with the card, you will receive a brochure with the current list of discount offers. The card is good forever; the list of attractions, restaurants, and hotels offering discounts changes periodically.

Tip: If you find yourself near an attraction you'd like to visit but don't have a coupon, stop into nearby restaurants, or even the entrance to a nearby attraction, and look for brochure racks. Chances are you'll find a brochure and coupon for the attraction that caught your eye.

Ticket Brokers

The second major source of discounts is ticket brokers. There are dozens of them scattered around the tourist areas, many of them located in hotel lobbies. Ticket brokers concentrate on the major attractions and the dinner shows. Discounts can be substantial — except for Disney. A 4% discount on Disney tickets is pretty standard. On the other hand, some brokers offer Universal at nearly 15% off and some dinner attractions at 34% off.

Using ticket brokers requires careful comparison shopping since discounts can vary widely from outlet to outlet. As a general rule, the discount ticket booths you find in your hotel lobby or in local restaurants seldom have the best prices. You'll do better at the free-standing ticket outlets. Nonetheless, it's a good idea to shop around. Sometimes even the lowest of the low-price dealers will be undercut by someone else for a particular attraction. Virtually every reputable ticket broker will have a printed price list; collect a goodly supply of these and examine them later in your hotel room to smoke out the best deals. Here are some additional tips:

- Ticket brokers are regulated by both the state of Florida and local authorities. They are required to prominently post the appropriate licenses. If you don't see these certificates displayed, ask to see them.
- Ask about "restocking fees." If you find a lower price elsewhere, you may be able to return your tickets, but many outlets charge a 15% fee when you do so.
- Does the printed price list contain the name, address, and phone number of the broker? The absence of these does not, in and of itself, signal fraud, but there is no reason for a reputable broker to omit them.
- Look for brokers that advertise that they will meet or beat any advertised price. That way, if you find a better deal, you will be protected.

"Free" Tickets

It is actually possible to get "free" (or very cheap) tickets to some major attractions. In return, you must agree to sit through a presentation for a local timeshare resort. You will be assured that there is no obligation, no high-pressure sales pitches. If you insist that you will never, ever buy a timeshare, they will tell you that's no problem, that you'll be able to tell your friends back home about their resort and that's good enough for them. All this may be true. But for me, sitting through a timeshare presentation is about as appealing as a visit to the dentist for root canal work. If you feel different, you can find this kind of offer through ticket brokers or little booths along the tourist strips emblazoned with the words "FREE TICKETS."

How This Book Is Organized

Chapters 2 through *5* cover the major Orlando area attractions, ones that will occupy anywhere from a half a day to several days of your time. I have attempted to cover them in some depth. *Chapters 7* and *8* cover Kennedy Space Center to the east and Busch Gardens Africa to the west. These, too, are major attractions.

The remaining chapters are omnibus chapters; that is, they cover a number of attractions that all have a common theme. The attractions described in these chapters are scattered throughout the Orlando area. At the end of the book, there is an index of rides and attractions, that will be most useful in locating the smaller attractions covered in *Chapters 10* through *18*. It can also be used to locate descriptions of specific attractions at the major parks.

As a general rule, I have tried to restrict the geographic scope of this book to Orlando and its immediate environs while recognizing that there are major attractions farther afield that deserve attention. That means that the farther you drive from Orlando, the more likely you will be to encounter attractions not covered in this book. For example, I have not mentioned the many things to see and do in the Tampa Bay area aside from Busch Gardens and Adventure Island, its next-door water park. Likewise, I have limited my coverage of Daytona Beach and the "Space Coast" to a few major attractions.

Price ranges for hotels (cost of one night's stay in a double room without tax) are indicated as follows:

$	Under $60
$$	$60 - $100
$$$	Over $100
$$$$	Over $150

Finally some highway abbreviations: I stands for Interstate; US for United States (i.e. federal) highways; SR for State Route; CR for County Road.

Hidden Highlights of the Other Orlando

Since there is so much information in this book and since I worry that you might overlook something wonderful, here is a brief and highly opinionated list of lesser-known attractions I think are worth considering:

Dinner shows. Of those listed in *Chapter 10*, my favorite is *Arabian Knights*, but don't overlook Orlando's expanding theater scene (*Chapter 15*), in particular the Or-lando-UCF Shakespeare Festival, a professional troupe offering first-class fare. For dinner, you can select from Orlando's growing list of fine restaurants.

Animal encounters. Discovery Cove (*Chapter 3*) gets all the press, but at Amaz-ing Exotics (*Chapter 13*) you can play with monkeys and apes and pet a tiger. Also worth singling out is the *Serengeti Safari Tour* at Busch Gardens Africa (*Chapter 8*) that lets you hand feed giraffes and other denizens of the Serengeti. During spring, bird watchers will want to flock to the *Alligator Breeding Marsh* at Gatorland (*Chapter 4*), where hundreds of cranes and egrets come to build their nests and rear their young, protected from their natural predators by the gators below.

Natural wonders. Historic Bok Sanctuary (*Chapter 14*) is actually a cunning man-made creation but those who appreciate the art of landscape architecture will find it ravishingly beautiful. For a more down-home experience in the great out-doors, plunge into the natural spring swimming hole at Wekiva Springs State Park (also in *Chapter 14*).

And all the rest. Fantasy of Flight (*Chapter 11*), with its evocative dioramas de-picting the history of flight and its extensive antique plane collection, is worth a side trip for aviation buffs. Fans of Frank Lloyd Wright won't want to miss the largest collection of his buildings to be found in one place (*Chapter 15*). And the ritzy town of Winter Park, with its fabulous art museums and theater (*Chapter 15*) and the boat tour past the homes of the rich but not so famous (*Chapter 16*), is worth a day or two all by itself.

In addition to those mentioned above, *Chapters 2* through *8* contain my personal choices of the must-see or -do attractions at each of the major parks.

Accuracy and Other Impossible Dreams

While I have tried to be as accurate, comprehensive, and up-to-date as possible, these are all unattainable goals. What's most likely to change, alas, are prices. I have quoted the most recent prices. However, some attractions may decide to raise their prices later in the year. Perhaps more disconcerting will be the disappearance of entire attractions, usually smaller and/or newer ones. I sincerely hope that none of the won-derful attractions listed here close down before you get to experience them. Before driving any great distance, however, you may want to call ahead to make sure the at-traction that caught your eye is still open and double check the hours and pricing.

Once again I refer you to my web site for updated information:
http://www.TheOtherOrlando.com

Chapter Two:

SeaWorld Orlando

"I'VE BEEN TO DISNEY," PEOPLE WILL TELL YOU, "BUT Y'KNOW WHAT I THINK is the best thing they've got down there in Orlando? SeaWorld!" I heard it over and over again. In a way this reaction was somewhat surprising. After all, compared to the Magic Kingdom or Universal, SeaWorld is downright modest, with only a smattering of thrill rides.

Of course, this "I-liked-SeaWorld-best" attitude may be one-upmanship — that quirk of human nature that makes us want to look superior. After all, SeaWorld is educational and how much more flattering it is to depict yourself as someone who prefers educational nature shows to mindless carnival rides that merely provide "fun." I'm just enough of a cynic about human nature to give some credence to this theory.

However, I think the real reason lies elsewhere. No matter how well imagined and perfectly realized the attractions at Universal or Disney might be, the wonders on display at SeaWorld were produced by a creative intelligence of an altogether higher order. The animated robotics guys can tinker all they want and the bean-counters in Hollywood can give them ever higher budgets and they still will never produce anything that can match the awe generated by a killer whale soaring 30 feet in the air with his human trainer perched on his snout. No matter how much we are entertained by Universal and Disney, at SeaWorld we cannot help but be reminded, however subliminally, that there are wonders in our world that humankind simply cannot duplicate, let alone surpass.

It's a feeling of which many visitors probably aren't consciously aware. Even if they are, they'd probably feel a little awkward trying to express it. But I am convinced it is there for everyone — believer, agnostic, or atheist. It's the core experience that makes SeaWorld so popular; it's the reason people will tell you they liked SeaWorld best of all. To paraphrase Joyce Kilmer's magnificent cliché about human inadequacy,

I think that Walt will never do
A wonder greater than Shamu.

Before You Come

Gathering Information

You can get up-to-date information on hours and prices by calling (407) 351–3600 and pressing "2." Between 8:00 a.m. and 8:00 p.m. you can speak to a SeaWorld representative at this number.

For the latest on SeaWorld's animals, you can check out the Anheuser-Busch Adventure Parks animal information site on the World Wide Web. The address is www.seaworld.org. For Shamu fans the site to check out is www.shamu.com. Yet another web site provides information for both SeaWorld Orlando and its sister park, Busch Gardens Africa. The address is www.4adventure.com.

Doing Your Homework

There's no real necessity to "bone up" on marine mammals before coming to SeaWorld. The park itself will give you a good introduction to the subject if you half pay attention. However, it is possible that parents might want to generate some interest in their younger children who, perhaps, might not be able to fully appreciate why they should go to SeaWorld instead of spending another day with Mickey and his friends.

There have been a number of excellent videos about SeaWorld that you may be able to find in your local library or video store. Probably easier to come by will be the video of *Free Willy*, the hit movie about a boy's struggle to liberate a killer whale from an amusement park. When your children get the idea that they can meet the star of this movie (one of his cousins actually) at SeaWorld, they should become enthusiastic boosters of the visit.

When's the Best Time to Come?

Even at the height of summer the crowds at SeaWorld are quite manageable compared to those you'll encounter at, say, Disney. Still, it is a good idea to plan on arriving during the off-season, if at all possible. Crowds in January are negligible and the weather cool to moderate, perfect viewing conditions for the outdoor shows. Regardless of the time of year you visit, I would recommend arriving early and planning to stay until the park closes. There are two reasons for this. Early arrivals breeze right in; as the morning wears on, the lines at the ticket booths lengthen. As for staying until the bitter end, some of the best shows (including what is arguably the best show) are only performed in the hour before closing. Compensate for the long day with a leisurely lunch.

Getting There

SeaWorld is located just off I-4 on Central Florida Parkway. If you're coming from the south (i.e. traveling east on I-4) you will use Exit 71 and find yourself pointed directly towards the SeaWorld entrance, about half a mile along on your left. Because there is no exit directly to Central Florida Parkway from Westbound I-4, those coming from the north (i.e. traveling west on I-4) must get off at Exit 72, onto the Bee Line Expressway (Route 528). Don't worry about the sign that says it's a toll road; you won't have to pay one. Take the first exit and loop around to International Drive. Turn left and proceed to Central Florida Parkway and turn right. It's all very clearly marked. This route, by the way, offers a nice backstage peek at *Kraken*, SeaWorld's roller coaster. As you get close to SeaWorld, tune your AM radio to 1540 for a steady stream of information about the park. This will help while away the time spent waiting in line at the parking lot.

Arriving at SeaWorld

Parking fees are $10 for cars and $12 for RVs and trailers and are collected at toll booths at the entrance. If you'd like to park close to the front entrance, you can opt for Shamu's Preferred Parking, available for cars only, for $15. Annual passholders pay nothing for regular parking and get a 50% discount on preferred parking.

Handicapped Parking. Several rows of extra large spaces near the main entrance are provided for the convenience of handicapped visitors. Alert the attendant to your need for handicapped parking and you will be directed accordingly.

The SeaWorld parking lot is divided into sections, and you will be ushered to your space in a very efficiently controlled manner. While the lot is not huge, it's still a very good idea to make a note of which lettered section and numbered row you're parked in. If you are parked any distance from the entrance, you will be directed to a tram that will whisk you to the main entrance. If you arrive after noon, however, you may find yourself on your own. Fortunately, the farthest row is never too far from the park perimeter. You can orient yourself by looking for the centrally located *Sky Tower*; it's the blue spire with the large American flag at the summit.

Once you reach the beautifully designed main entrance, you will find a group of thoughtfully shaded ticket booths where you will purchase your admission. To the left of the ticket windows are the Guest Relations window and the annual pass center. Once inside the park, walk straight ahead to the Information Desk. There you can pick up a large map of the park. On the back you will find a schedule of the day's shows as well as information on any special events happening that day.

Opening and Closing Times

SeaWorld operates seven days a week, 365 days a year. The park opens at 9:00 a.m. and remains open until 6:00, 7:00, 8:00, 9:00, 10:00, or 11:00 p.m. — or even until 1:00 a.m. — depending on the time of year. Unlike Universal and Disney, SeaWorld does not practice soft openings (admitting guests early). During very busy periods, they will start admitting people at 8:30, but these early arrivals are held in the Entrance Plaza (or "mall") just inside the gates, until the park proper opens at 9:00. By the time the last scheduled shows are starting (about 45 minutes to an hour prior to the posted closing time), most of the park's other attractions have either shut down or are in the process of doing so.

The Price of Admission

SeaWorld has several ticket options, including some that offer admission to its sister park, Busch Gardens, in nearby Tampa. Most visitors will be looking at either a one-day admission or the Orlando FlexTicket. At press time, prices (including sales tax) were as follows:

One-Day Admission:

Adults:	$65.97
Children (3 to 9):	$54.20

Children under age 3 are admitted **free**.

Value Ticket:

(One day each at SeaWorld and Busch Gardens Africa.)

Adults:	$106.45
Children & Seniors:	$95.80

Adults pay the same price as children when ordering either one-day or value tickets online seven days in advance. Special deals for Florida residents are announced on the web site. SeaWorld participates in the **Orlando FlexTicket** program described in *Chapter 1: Introduction & Orientation* (page 13).

The Discovery Cove Option

If you are also planning to visit Discovery Cove (described in *Chapter 3*), be aware that your admission fee there includes a seven-day pass to SeaWorld (or Busch Gardens Africa, if you prefer). The pass is valid for seven consecutive days, starting the day of your first visit, and can be activated either before or after your Discovery Cove visit. To get the pass, stop into Guest Relations and show your Discovery Cove confirmation letter. You will be issued a nontransferable credit-card-sized pass. You may be required to produce a photo ID each time you enter the park using this pass.

Adventure Express

For those short on time and long on cash, SeaWorld offers a guided six-hour VIP touring option that guarantees you will hit the highlights and be treated like a celebrity along the way. You'll get to feed stingrays, dolphins, and sea lions and pet a Magellanic penguin. You will also be given reserved seats at the Shamu show, which means very good seats indeed. Similar preferred seating is offered at either the sea lion or dolphin show, depending on scheduling on the day of your visit. Guests on the Adventure Express who meet the minimum height requirements (see ride reviews, below) also get one-time front of the line privileges at the big thrill rides, *Kraken*, *Journey to Atlantis*, and *Wild Arctic*.

None of this comes cheap. The cost is $89 for adults and $79 for children 3 to 9 (younger children tour free) — and that's in addition to the regular price of admission! At least tax and lunch with a choice of sandwich, salad, dessert, and soft drink are included in these prices. There are only 16 spaces available for the Adventure Express, so you may want to reserve a spot by calling (800) 327-2244. Tours leave at varying times in the late morning; there may just be one tour a day during slower periods and as many as four or five during the busier tourist seasons.

If that's not exclusive enough, you can opt for a private version of Adventure Express, dubbed Elite Adventure Express. This private tour offers the same privileges, but is limited exclusively to your party. The tab is $1,100 including tax and lunch for up to 12 guests, plus the regular one-day admission. Book at least two weeks ahead for the Elite Express at (866) 781-1333.

Which Price Is Right?

For most people, a one-day pass will suffice, assuming that you arrive early and stay until closing. Of course, if you've taken my advice and come during one of Orlando's slow periods, there's an excellent chance SeaWorld will offer you a second day free.

The major advantage of taking two days to see SeaWorld is that you can adopt a much more leisurely pace than otherwise, lingering to commune with the sharks or hanging around until something interesting happens at the killer whale observation area. Second day tickets, when available, must be used within seven days. If you'll be visiting Tampa and you are not using the Orlando FlexTicket, the Value Ticket, offering one day each at SeaWorld and Busch Gardens Africa, is a good buy.

Annual Passes & EZ Pay

SeaWorld has several annual pass options that are so reasonable you may want to consider them as an alternative to a one-day admission. For example, the adult annual pass costs less than twice as much as a one-day admission. Some people might consider that worth it for the convenience of coming and going as they please during their Orlando stay. If you plan another Orlando vacation within the next 12 months, the annual pass options become almost irresistible, especially now that SeaWorld offers an EZ Pay option.

Opt for **EZ Pay** and you pay for your annual pass on a monthly basis, interest-free, over the life of the pass. Payments are charged to your credit card; no fees are added.

The passes, called "Passports," take the form of a credit card sized ID. Silver Passports are valid for one year and Gold for two. In the following list of prices, which include tax, the Silver Passport price is given first, followed by the Gold Passport price. Children's prices apply for those 3 to 9, Seniors to those 50 or older.

SeaWorld Passports
Adults:	$101.12 / $154.37
Children & Seniors:	$90.47 / $143.72

SeaWorld - Busch Gardens Passports
(Annual Passes to both SeaWorld and Busch Gardens)
Adults:	$154.37 / $234.25
Children & Seniors:	$143.72 / $223.60

You can add Adventure Island, Busch's water park in Tampa (see *Chapter 9: Water Parks*) to either of the SeaWorld/Busch Gardens passports for an additional fee of about $55, including tax.

Annual passes offer unlimited admission, free parking in the regular lot, and an array of discounts, including a 10% discount at SeaWorld restaurants, 10% or 20% discounts at the shops, plus a 50% discount on preferred parking and all guided tours.

The pass itself is checked carefully at the gate, to make sure it's really you visiting the park, and you may need to show a second, photo ID. At press time, machines that read the "geography" of your hand were being phased in, so all this may change.

I have noticed that annual passes are especially popular with local residents, so much so that during periods when SeaWorld offers its discounts to Florida residents, it can take a good 30 to 45 minutes to have your annual pass processed.

Discounts

In addition to the online, advance-purchase discounts mentioned earlier, look for dollars-off coupons in the usual tourist throwaway publications and at the guest services desk at your hotel. A typical discount is $2.50 off per person for up to six people. Steeper discounts are available from discount ticket brokers (see *Chapter 1: Introduction & Orientation*). Members of AAA receive a 10% discount off regular prices. The deaf, the blind, and those with mental handicaps receive a generous 50% discount. Active military personnel can get a discount by purchasing tickets at their military base. Visiting conventioneers are also eligible for discounts if they show their badges at Guest Services.

Buying Tickets

You can purchase your tickets online (see above) or when you arrive at the park. To save a bit of touring time, you can come by a day or two earlier, in the afternoon when the lines are nonexistent, and buy tickets for use another day. The best way to do this is to park in the lot of the Renaissance Orlando Resort across the street and walk the short distance to the SeaWorld ticket booths. Keep an eye out for the electronic self-serve ticket kiosks as you approach the entrance — lines there may be shorter or non-existent.

Staying Near the Park

If SeaWorld is your primary Orlando destination, you may want to consider staying at one of the handful of hotels that are within walking distance of the front gate. Because of their proximity, few provide shuttle service. They are listed here in order of their distance from the park.

Renaissance Orlando Resort

6677 Sea Harbor Drive
Orlando, FL 32821
(800) 327-6677; (407) 351-5555; fax (407) 351-9991

A luxury resort hotel with a huge central atrium, first-rate restaurants, and many amenities, including 24-hour room service.

Price Range:	$$$ - $$$$
Amenities:	Olympic-size pool, tennis, volleyball, health club, three restaurants, two lounges
Walk to Park:	5 minutes

Hilton Garden Inn

6850 Westwood Boulevard
Orlando, FL 32821
(877) 782-9444; (407) 354-1500; fax (407) 354-1528
> Mid-scale hotel with many amenities.
>
> *Price Range:* $$ - $$$
> *Amenities:*   Heated pool, jacuzzi, kids' play area, restaurant, lounge, evening room service, on-site convenience store, complimentary 24-hour business center
> *Walk to Park:*   5 minutes

International Plaza Resort and Spa

10100 International Drive
Orlando, FL 32821-8095
(800) 327-0363; (407) 352-1100; fax
> Refurbished hotel that caters to conventioneers.
>
> *Price Range:* $$ - $$$$
> *Amenities:*   Three heated pools, two kiddie pools, mini-golf, fitness center, restaurant, lounge, poolside bar
> *Walk to Park:*   5 to 10 minutes

Winfield Inn

6263 Westwood Boulevard
Orlando, FL 32821
(800) 346-1551; (407) 345-8000
> Standard mid-range motel.
>
> *Price Range:* $$-$$$$
> *Amenities:*   Pool and poolside bar, free shuttle
> *Walk to Park:*   5 to 10 minutes

Hawthorn Suites Orlando SeaWorld

6435 Westwood Boulevard
Orlando, FL 32821
(800) 527-1133; (407) 351-6600; fax (407) 351-1977
> All-suite format with kitchenettes in every room.
>
> *Price Range:* $$ - $$$$
> *Amenities:*   Free buffet breakfast, large heated pool, kiddie pool, poolside BBQ grills, children's play area, game room, convenience store, Nintendo and video cassette players in rooms
> *Walk to Park:*   10 to 15 minutes

Extended Stay America & Extended Stay Deluxe

6443 Westwood Boulevard

Orlando, FL 32821
(888) 788-3467 for both; (407) 351-1982, fax (407) 351-1719 for Extended Stay
Deluxe; (407) 352-3454, fax (407) 352-1708 for Extended Stay

Basic all-suite format with kitchenettes; daily and weekly rates.

Price Range: $$-$$$ ExtStay Deluxe; $-$$ ExtStay
Amenities: Seasonal pool and exercise room
Walk to Park: 15 to 20 minutes

Dining at SeaWorld

Dining at SeaWorld is almost entirely of the fast-food variety. There is only one full-service restaurant, **Sharks Underwater Grill**, but it is a winner. Located in the *Shark Encounter* attraction, it is a sleek, modern, atmosphere-drenched eatery with a series of picture windows that look into SeaWorld's enormous shark tank. The good news is that the food is as dramatic as the view, although the prices are on the high end of moderate. The **Dine With Shamu** program, described in detail later in this chapter, offers a chance to enjoy an early evening meal while visiting backstage with Shamu; this option is moderately expensive.

For more casual dining, I recommend **Smoky Creek Grill** for better-than-average slow-smoked barbecue, the **Hospitality Deli** for hefty sandwiches, and **Mango Joe's Cafe**, near *Wild Arctic*, for the fajitas. I find the large, splashy, cafeteria-style restaurants in the Waterfront section a bit of a disappointment.

There is beer to be had, as you might expect at a park owned by Anheuser-Busch, but it seems less omnipresent than it does at some other parks. Indeed, many of the fast-food establishments are alcohol-free. On the other hand, you can get a mixed drink here, at the outdoor **Sand Bar**, at the base of the *Sky Tower*.

You can also get great desserts here. They're made right on the premises and most of the casual eateries offer them. I especially recommend the chocolate cherry and carrot cakes (about $3), but those whose taste runs to fruit for dessert won't be disappointed. Fresh strawberries are readily available. On top of that, the prices at all of SeaWorld's eateries are less than those you'll encounter at other area theme parks.

SeaWorld lets you eat while waiting for or watching the big outdoor stadium shows; there are even snack bars (offering ice cream bars and nachos) conveniently located near the entrances to the stands. Not all eating establishments are open throughout the park's operating hours. A "Dining Guide," listing the various restaurants and their operating hours, is available at the Information Desk in the Entrance Plaza.

Shopping at SeaWorld

Of course, SeaWorld is dotted with strategically located gift and souvenir shops ready to help you lessen the heavy load in your wallet. Inveterate shoppers can soothe their conscience with the thought that a percentage of the money they drop at SeaWorld goes towards helping rescue and care for stranded sea mammals.

Most of the wares on display are of the standard tourist variety but some items deserve special mention. Many of SeaWorld's shops offer some very attractive figurines and small sculptures. They range from quite small objects suitable for a bric-a-brac shelf to fairly large pieces (with fairly large price tags) that are surely displayed with pride by those who buy them. Prices range from under $20 to well over $2,000. If you're in the market for a special gift or are a collector yourself, you will want to give these items more than a cursory look. The shops in the Waterfront section, that flow one into another, offer some very nice clothing items. Most of it is for women, but men might score a good quality Hawaiian-style shirt. Also in these shops is a constantly changing variety of decorative items for the home that might make good gifts for you or someone you love.

A shop that will draw the curious as well as shoppers is **The Oyster's Secret**. Here you can watch through underwater windows as divers plunge downwards in search of pearl-bearing oysters. And if you decide to buy one and want it placed in a custom setting, you will be accommodated.

Good Things to Know About . . .

Access for the Disabled

All parts of SeaWorld are accessible to disabled guests and all the stadium shows have sections set aside for those in wheelchairs. These are some of the best seats in the house. Wheelchairs are available for rent at $10 per day. Electric carts are $35 per day.

Babies

Little ones under three are admitted free and strollers are available for rent if you don't have your own. Single strollers are $10 for the day, double strollers are $18. There are also diaper changing stations in all the major restrooms (men's and women's). In addition, there are "non-gender changing areas" at *Wild Arctic*, the Friends of the Wild shop, and the *Anheuser-Busch Hospitality Center* where you will find diaper vending machines. There are nursing areas near the Friends of the Wild shop and at the Baby Care station near *Shamu's Happy Harbor*, where you can also buy a limited menu of baby food and baby care products.

Drinking

As a reminder, the legal drinking age in Florida is 21 and photo IDs will be requested if there is the slightest doubt. Try to feel flattered rather than annoyed. Taking alcoholic beverages through the turnstiles as you leave the park is not allowed.

Education Staff

It's hard to say too much in praise of the education staff at SeaWorld. There are some 100 employees whose job it is to hang around and answer your questions. They are invariably friendly, enthusiastic, and more than happy to share their considerable knowledge with you. Don't be shy. Taking advantage of this wonderful human resource will immeasurably increase the enjoyment and value of your visit to SeaWorld. Just look for the word "Education" on the employee's name tag. In fact, even employees who are not with the Education Department will likely have the answer to your question.

Emergencies

As a general rule, the moment something goes amiss speak with the nearest Sea-World employee. They will contact security or medical assistance and get the ball rolling towards a solution. There is a first aid station in a tent behind *Stingray Lagoon* in the North End of the park and another near *Shamu's Happy Harbor* in the South End.

Feeding Times

Feeding time is an especially interesting time to visit any of the aquatic habitats. Unfortunately, there is no rigid schedule. By varying feeding times, the trainers more closely approximate the animals' experience in the wild and avoid, to some extent, the repetitive behaviors that characterize many animals in captivity. However, you can simply ask one of the education staff at the exhibit when the animals will next be fed. If your schedule permits, I would recommend returning for this enjoyable spectacle.

Of course, at some exhibits — the dolphins, stingrays, and sea lions — you can feed the animals yourself — for a fee!

Kids' ID System

SeaWorld may be less crowded than Disney World, but it's still remarkably easy to lose track of your little ones here. Stop by Guest Services to pick up wristbands for your young children -- Guest Services will label them with your name and cell phone number so staff members can easily get ahold of you if they encounter your child on the loose. Wristbands are available free of charge, and are uniquely numbered, so that even if the writing on the wristband smears, they can still use this number to look up your information back at Guest Services, should the need arise.

Leaving the Park

You can leave the park at any time and be readmitted free the same day. Just have your hand stamped with a fluorescent symbol on the way out; when you come back, look for the "same day reentry" line and pass your hand under the ultraviolet lamp.

Lockers

Lockers are available just outside the main entrance and in the Entrance Plaza across from Cypress Bakery. The fee is $1 for small lockers, $1.50 for large (quarters only). Once you open your locker, you will have to insert another four or six quarters to lock it again. A change machine is located in the Entrance Plaza locker area. Lockers are also available near the thrill rides *Kraken* and *Journey to Atlantis*.

Money

ATMs are conveniently located throughout the park. The one in the entrance area is just to the left of the ticket booths. All are connected to the Plus, Cirrus, and other networks. A foreign currency exchange window is located just past the ticket windows at Guest Relations; it is open from 10:00 a.m. to 5:00 p.m.

Pets

If you have pets, the toll booth attendant will direct you to the SeaWorld Pet Care facility, very near the main entrance, where Tabby and Bowser can wait for you in air-conditioned comfort. The fee is $6 per pet and you must supply pet food.

Sea Gulls

If you visit from November to February, you will be joined in the park by hordes of sea gulls. These are the New Yorkers of the avian world — loud, boisterous, often rude, but very clever and with the kind of raffish personality that can be endearing. Sea gull season brings with it the increased danger of aerial bombardment, which is unpleasant but not fatal. More amusing (if you're the observer rather than the victim) are the concerted attacks the gulls make on ice cream cones.

Smoking

Thanks to Florida's Clean Indoor Air Act, smoking is prohibited in all restaurants at SeaWorld. Smoking is also prohibited in all show and exhibit areas. Outdoor smoking zones are dotted throughout the park.

Special Diets

Vegetarians can stop at the Information Desk and request the Food Services staff's list of meatless dishes and the restaurants that serve them. Similar lists of seafood and low-fat selections and other dietary notes are available from the same source.

Splash Zones

All of the stadium shows give the adventuresome the opportunity to get wet — in some cases very wet. One advantage of the splash zones is that they are some of the best seats at SeaWorld. But the threat is very, very real.

I am a believer in splash zones for those who come prepared. Those inexpensive rain ponchos that are sold at every major park will hold the damage to a minimum (although there is probably no real way to guard against a direct hit from Shamu!). Kids, especially young boys, will enjoy the exquisite machismo of getting thoroughly soaked.

One word of warning: In the cooler periods of the year, a full soaking will be extremely uncomfortable, and may be courting a cold, or worse. Bring a big towel and a change of clothes, or be prepared to shell out for new duds at the SeaWorld shops.

Sailing the Sea: Your Day at SeaWorld

SeaWorld can be seen quite comfortably in a single day, without rushing madly around or otherwise driving yourself crazy. This is especially true if you've arrived during one of Orlando's slack periods or if you will be forgoing the thrill rides. But even during the most crowded times, SeaWorld is still more manageable than other parks in the area.

SeaWorld is not a large park, but its comfortable layout and the large Bayside Lagoon at its center make it seem larger than it is. Much of the North End of the park is lushly landscaped with large shady trees and bird-filled pools along the walkways. The South End, on the other side of the Lagoon, is open and airy with a gently rolling landscape. In look and feel, it is quite a contrast to the more tightly crammed spaces of the Magic Kingdom and Universal Orlando. Many parts of SeaWorld have the feel of a particularly gracious public park or botanical garden.

One of SeaWorld's key differentiators is the fact that the vast majority of its attractions are either shows that take place in large, sometimes huge, outdoor auditoriums or "continuous viewing" exhibits through which people pass pretty much at their own pace. My observation is that most people pass through pretty quickly so even if there's a line, the wait won't be unbearable. Once inside you can take your own sweet time. Here, briefly, are the different kinds of attractions at SeaWorld:

Rides. There are just three "rides" at SeaWorld but they are doozies.

Outdoor Auditorium Shows. These are SeaWorld's primo attractions — Shamu, the sea lions, the dolphins, and some lesser events. There are plenty of shaded seats for these shows (anywhere from 2,400 to 5,500), but even in slower periods they fill up, which should tell you something about how good the shows are. It is possible to enter these auditoriums after the show has begun if they are not full.

Indoor Theater Shows. Some shows take place indoors, in darkened air-conditioned theaters. None of them involves sea mammals and none of them falls into the must-see category. When these shows begin, the doors close and latecomers must wait for the next performance. Be aware that it is difficult to leave these shows in the middle.

Aquatic Habitats. This is SeaWorld's term for its continuous viewing exhibits of live marine animals. The habitats range from huge tanks like those you may have seen at aquariums to elaborate stage sets the likes of which I can almost guarantee you've never seen before.

Guided Tours. These are small group experiences that operate on a limited schedule and charge a moderate additional fee. They offer unique access to SeaWorld's "backstage" areas and a chance to learn a bit more about some of the park's most interesting inhabitants.

Catch of the Day

If you had very little time to spend at SeaWorld, I would venture to suggest that you could see just a handful of attractions and still feel you got your money's worth — if you picked the right ones. Here, then, is my list of the very best that SeaWorld has to offer:

The three major open-air animal shows — **Believe**, **Clyde & Seamore**, and **Blue Horizons** — are the heart and soul of SeaWorld. Anyone missing these should have his or her head examined.

Close behind are the major "aquatic habitats" — **Wild Arctic** (and the ride that introduces the experience), **Shark Encounter, Key West at SeaWorld**, and **Manatee Rescue.** I have omitted **Pacific Point Preserve** and **Penguin Encounter** (both marvelous) only because you are likely to see their close equivalents elsewhere.

If you have the time, the **Pets Ahoy** and **Odyssea** shows are very entertaining and hold up to repeat viewing. Finally, for thrill seekers, there is the stupendous roller coaster, **Kraken**.

The One-Day Stay

1. Get up early, but not as early as you would if you were heading for Disney or Universal. Remember, when SeaWorld says the park proper opens at 9, it means it. Get there a little earlier perhaps (you can get a bite to eat or browse the shops in the Entrance Plaza starting at 8:30 a.m.), but no need to kill yourself.

2. After purchasing your tickets and entering the park, thrill seekers and ride freaks should head immediately to *Kraken*, followed by *Journey to Atlantis*. (Bear left after the entrance mall and follow the signs and the running kids.) Then plan on doing *Wild Arctic* and its exciting ride later in the day, preferably during a Shamu show when the lines for *Wild Arctic* tend to thin out.

If, for one reason or another you are taking a pass on the thrill rides, proceed immediately to *Wild Arctic*. (Just keep bearing right until you see the Lagoon and circle it in a counterclockwise direction.) If you're not interested in taking the ride, the line for the stationary version is always a good deal shorter, so coming later may be okay. Also, if you'd like to skip the ride portion altogether, it is possible to slip quietly in through the exit in the gift shop and just see the animals.

3. Now's the time to review the schedule printed on the back of the map you got when you entered. First, check the times of the "big three" shows — *Believe*, *Clyde & Seamore*, and *Blue Horizons*. Whatever you do, don't miss these. Don't try to see two shows that start less than an hour apart. Yes, it can be done but you will be making sacrifices.

Instead, schedule your day so you can arrive at the stadium about 20 minutes before show time, perhaps longer during busier seasons. That way you can get a good seat, like dead center for *Believe* or in a splash zone for the kids. There is almost always some sort of pre-show entertainment starting 10 or 15 minutes before the show. It's always fun and, in the case of the warm-up to the sea lion show, often hilarious.

4. Use your time between shows to visit the aquatic habitats. Use the descriptions in the next section and geographical proximity to guide your choices. For example, you can leave the dolphin show and go right into the manatee exhibit. Or you can visit the penguins just before seeing *Clyde & Seamore* and visit *Shark Encounter* immediately after.

5. If you have kids with you, you will miss *Shamu's Happy Harbor* at your peril. Adults, of course, can give it a miss.

6. Fill in the rest of the day with the lesser attractions or return visits to habitats you particularly enjoyed. In my opinion, several of the non-animal shows and attractions can be missed altogether with little sacrifice. If your time is really limited (e.g.

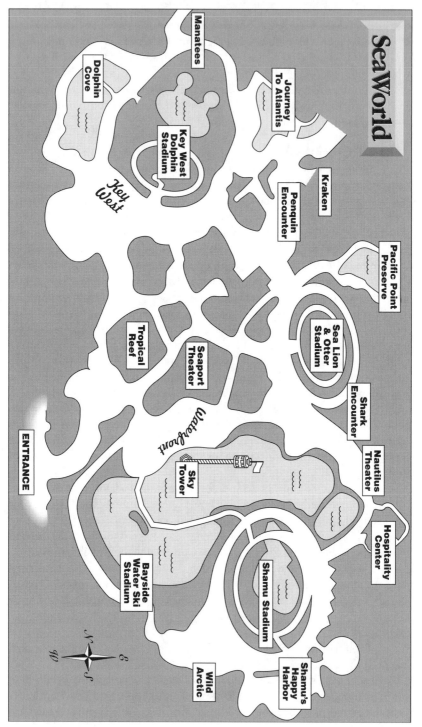

SeaWorld

Manatees

Dolphin
Cove

Journey
To Atlantis

Key West
Dolphin
Stadium

Key
West

Kraken

Penguin
Encounter

Pacific Point
Preserve

Tropical
Reef

Seaport
Theater

Sea Lion
& Otter
Stadium

Shark
Encounter

Waterfront

Nautilus
Theater

ENTRANCE

Sky
Tower

Hospitality
Center

Bayside
Water Ski
Stadium

Shamu Stadium

Wild
Arctic

Shamu's
Happy
Harbor

you got to the park late), I strongly urge you to take my advice. You can always come back another day and prove me wrong.

7. If you stay until the end, as I recommend, you will not want to miss *Sea Lions Tonight* (if it's playing during your visit).

This plan should allow you to see everything you truly want to see in one day and maybe even some attractions you wished you hadn't bothered with.

The Two-Day Stay

If you have the luxury of spending two or more days visiting SeaWorld (Discovery Cove visitors take note), I would recommend relaxing your pace, perhaps leaving the park early on one day to freshen up and catch a dinner show elsewhere. With two days, even a very relaxed pace should allow you to see everything in the park, several of them more than once.

Another strategy to adopt is to use the first day to concentrate on the shows and the second day to concentrate on the rides, the animal habitats and, perhaps, take a guided tour or two.

THE NORTH END

SeaWorld is not neatly divided into "lands" like some other theme parks I might mention (although the Key West area is a step in that direction). The only geographically convenient division of the park is provided by Bayside Lagoon. If you look at the map you collected on arriving at the park, you will notice that the vertical line formed by the *Sky Tower* effectively divides the park in two: the larger northern side ("The North End") is to the left of the Tower; the southern side including most of the Lagoon ("The South End") is to the right. By the way, although Bayside Lagoon is the official name of SeaWorld's artificial lake, many SeaWorld employees have never heard the term used.

For the purposes of describing the attractions at SeaWorld I have adopted this North End/South End division. Please remember that this is my terminology and not SeaWorld's. If you stop a SeaWorld employee and ask, "How do I get to the North?" you may be told to get on a plane and fly to Philadelphia.

The layout and open landscaping of the southern half, combined with the sheer size of the stadiums located there, make getting your bearings relatively easy. In the northern half, however, the layout and lusher landscaping, while pleasing to the eye, can be confusing. When traveling from Point A to Point B in the northern half of the park, use the map to get you started in the right general direction. Then rely on the directional signs, which are posted at nearly every turning, to guide you to your destination.

I begin with the northern half of the park for the simple reason that this is where you enter the park past the Shamu lighthouse in the artificial harbor that graces the airy entrance area. I describe the attractions in geographical, rather than thematic order, starting with *The Waterfront*. From there I proceed in a roughly clockwise direction, returning full-circle to *The Waterfront* and the fabulous *Pets Ahoy* show located there.

The Waterfront

Rating: ★ ★ ★
Type: Themed shopping and dining venue
Time: Continuous viewing
Kelly says: Lovely to look at

Although it is home to two major attractions — Sky Tower and Pets Ahoy, *The Waterfront* is primarily a place to dine, stroll, and shop. Themed beautifully as a fantasy Mediterranean seaside village esplanade, this area is the gateway to the sole walkway across Bayside Lagoon to the southern end of the park.

The Waterfront is home to three large restaurants. All are cafeteria style, all are moderately priced, and none is anything to write home about. I'd give the edge for food to the **Voyagers Wood Fired Pizza** with the pizzas of its name and a pretty decent salmon dish. The **Seafire Grill** serves dry burgers and salads and is home to the nightly Makahiki Luau (reviewed in *Chapter 10: Dinner Attractions*). The smaller **Spice Mill** offers "spicy" dishes and sandwiches and a great view.

Between these lies a series of shops offering some of the nicest merchandise in SeaWorld. Each has its own entrance but they are all linked inside, making for seamless, not to mention cool, shopping. Outside is the esplanade, dotted with coffee stands and snack kiosks and the setting for periodic street shows. On the lower level is a children's water play area and a sea wall where waves crash every few minutes, soaking the delighted kids who gather there precisely for that reason.

Just off shore, on a tiny island at the base of the *Sky Tower*, is the **Sand Bar**, an outdoor bar and one of the nicest places in Orlando to booze it up al fresco.

Sky Tower

Rating: ★ ★ ★
Type: Bird's-eye view of Orlando
Time: Six and half minutes
Kelly says: For those who've seen everything else they want
to see at SeaWorld

Riding the *Sky Tower* will set you back an additional $3.00, unless you have an annual pass, in which case it's free. You'll have to decide whether the six-and-a-half-minute glimpse of Orlando from on high is worth the extra charge. I regularly see people answering that question in the negative.

The *Sky Tower* is a circular viewing platform that rotates slowly while rising from lagoon level to a height of 400 feet. From there you can see the dome of *Spaceship Earth* at Epcot and *Space Mountain* at the Magic Kingdom, as well as some of the Orlando area's other high-rise buildings. Closer by, you will get a superb view of the layout of *Kraken*. If your timing is right you will get to see a load of terrified riders make a complete circuit on the awesome coaster.

There are two levels, each offering a single row of glassed-in seating that circles the capsule. You pick the level of your choice as you enter. The upper level would seem the better choice, and most people head that way, but it only gives you a 10-foot height advantage that doesn't really affect your enjoyment of the experience.

Riding the *Sky Tower* is an enjoyable enough way to kill some time if you aren't eager to see anything else and don't mind paying the extra charge. Seeing SeaWorld from the air can be fascinating. You will also gain an appreciation for the cunning way the park is laid out and see why you've been having difficulty navigating from place to place in the North End.

The *Sky Tower* ride is at the mercy of the elements. Any hint of lightning in the area closes it down, as do high winds, which might buffet the top of the tower even when it's perfectly calm on the ground.

Pets Ahoy (at Seaport Theatre)

Rating: ★ ★ ★ ★
Type: Indoor theater show
Time: 25 minutes
Kelly says: A must for pet lovers

If you saw *Animal Actors* at Universal Studios Florida, you might be tempted to skip this one. However, if you are a pet lover, you'll want to put this charming show on your list. It offers a pleasant break from the hot Florida sun.

The SeaWorld twist here is that almost all the animals in the show were found in Central Florida animal shelters and rescued from an uncertain fate. As a result, the cast list runs heavily to cats and dogs, although there is an amusing pig, a skunk, and even a mouse.

Ace trainer Joel Slaven (of *Ace Ventura: Pet Detective* fame) has done an amazing job here, especially with the cats. Not only do Slaven's pussycats do every doggie trick and do them better but there is a cat who does a tightwire act and one who bounds over the heads of the audience, jumping from one tiny platform to another.

Entertainment at The Waterfront

Rating: ★ ★ ★
Type: Indoor and outdoor acts
Time: Irregular and unpredictable
Kelly says: Pleasant enough

There is a regular and ever-changing menu of entertainment on tap in and around the Waterfront. Some of the entertainment takes the form of street acts that could be animal show and tell, strolling musicians, or cut-up physical comedy. Fairly typical is **Groove Chefs**, an act that has shown some staying power. Three young guys, who are ostensibly chefs at the nearby Seafire Grill, take a break with garbage cans, pots, pans, and drumsticks and rustle up a rhythmic ragout that is sure to get your toes tapping. The rhythms are intricate, the footwork fancy, and the variety of sounds that emerge from their oddball collection of implements quite amusing.

There's indoor entertainment, too, on the stage in the back room of the Seafire Grill. The acts that appear here tend to be in the variety show tradition. They are equally unpredictable and could range from a "dueling pianos" act to magicians. The best part is that you can either enjoy these shows while eating or stroll in just for the show. Sometimes these shows are listed in the show schedule on your map.

Dolphin Nursery

Rating: ★ ★ ★
Type: Small shaded outdoor pool
Time: Continuous viewing
Kelly says: Not much to see but hard to resist

This is where dolphin moms get to enjoy a little maternity leave with their new-borns during the bonding process. A barrier fence prevents you from getting right to the pool's edge, so at best you will just be able to glimpse the little ones as they swim by in close formation with mom.

Still, even a glimpse of a baby dolphin is a hard lure to resist and you will probably want to pause here for a look. Education staffers are on hand to answer your questions. Feedings usually take place in the morning and late afternoon, making those the best times to visit.

Key West at SeaWorld

Key West at SeaWorld is not so much an attraction as a collection of related attractions wrapped in a single theme. Shades of Disney World! The attractions here are aquatic habitats featuring the denizens of warmer waters and the theme, of course, is the casual sophistication and good times atmosphere for which Key West has become famous. On both scores, SeaWorld acquits itself admirably.

Turtle Point

Rating: ★ ★ ★
Type: Aquatic habitat
Time: Continuous viewing
Kelly says: Best when a staffer is present

Turtle Point is small by SeaWorld standards, a shallow sea water pool fringed by white sand beaches. It is home to four species — loggerhead, Kemp's ridley, hawksbill, and green sea turtles, all of them rescued animals.

Turtles, it must be said, are not the most lively creatures SeaWorld has on display. No leaps and twirls here. So, for most folks, this habitat will warrant no more than a quick look. Fortunately, SeaWorld staffers are often hanging out by the pool ready to answer questions. When a group of people gathers and starts exercising its curiosity, a visit to *Turtle Point* can be quite interesting.

Stingray Lagoon

Rating: ★ ★ ★ ★
Type: Aquatic habitat
Time: Continuous viewing
Kelly says: Your best shot at touching a SeaWorld critter

Under a shading roof lies a long, shallow pool with a smaller "nursery pool" in one corner. Its edge is at waist height for easy viewing and interaction. Scores of stingrays lazily circle the main pool, while their "pups" navigate the nursery pool. The mature rays may look scary, but they are remarkably gentle creatures that will tolerate being petted (they feel a bit like slimy felt) and will almost always appreciate a free handout. Small trays of tiny fish called silversides can be purchased for $4 ($3 for annual passholders).

Once again, SeaWorld education staffers make regular appearances here, providing a steady stream of information about these fascinating creatures. The staffers are always ready to answer any questions you might have.

Thanks to the accessibility of the stingrays, this is a very popular attraction. If the pool edge is packed, be patient. Eventually you will be able to make your way forward where your patience is sure to be rewarded.

Dolphin Cove

Rating: ★ ★ ★ ★ +
Type: Aquatic habitat
Time: Continuous viewing
Kelly says: A spectacular SeaWorld habitat

Dolphin Cove lets you get up close to these delightful creatures. This extensive Key West habitat allows petting and feeding on one side and viewing on the other, from both a raised platform and an underwater observation post. Most people start at poolside.

Dolphin feeding here is carried out by paying customers. A small paper tray of smelt-like fish is $5 ($4 for annual passholders) and there is sometimes a two-cup limit per person. Having fish to offer will definitely increase your chances of touching a dolphin, although they will occasionally swim close enough to the edge to allow a foodless hand to sweep along their flanks. But you can't just show up any old time and buy food. It's sold only at specified feeding times and only up to the quantity that SeaWorld's marine dietitians have determined is appropriate to keep the dolphin fit and not fat. If touching a dolphin is a priority for you or your child, I would advise checking out feeding times and arriving a bit early to get on line to purchase food. Otherwise, there is a good chance you will be disappointed.

A number of photographers associated with the Cove's photo concession roam the premises and snap just about everyone who makes it to poolside. The photos are posted on video screens just a few yards away. Two 5x7s or one 8x10 will set you back $20.

Tip: If you're going for a photo, have members of your party stake out a good spot on the edge of the lagoon well in advance of the posted feeding time. Then tip off a photographer as to your location (you'll recognize them by their cameras and headsets).

While touching dolphins seems to be the first order of business for most visitors, don't overlook the underwater viewing area (as many people obviously do). It offers a perspective on these graceful beasts that you just don't get from above and, not incidentally, is a wonderful place to wait out those afternoon summer thunderstorms for which Orlando is famous. It will also give you a deeper appreciation of the skill and craft that went into designing the reef-like pool in which the dolphins live. To get there from the petting and feeding area, walk around the pool to your left.

As at all the habitats, SeaWorld staffers make occasional educational presentations. There is usually a staffer sitting on a life guard's raised chair on the beach across from the petting area. Feel free to hail him or her from the sidelines if you have any questions.

Blue Horizons (at Key West Dolphin Stadium)

Rating: ★ ★ ★ ★ +
Type: Live water show with dolphins, pseudorcas and acrobats
Time: 25 minutes
Kelly says: Cirque du Soleil meets Flipper

This show, which rounds out the Key West experience, is Shamu in miniature, with a large dose of Cirque du Soleil-style pizazz thrown in for good measure. Instead of giant killer whales we have the far slimmer bottle-nosed dolphins and pseudorcas, or "false killer whales." The setting is a swirling, multi-level, multi-platform blue extravaganza of flying manta rays and sea foam over the large dolphin pool.

The show is conceived as the fantasy of Marina, a girl who dreams of "a place where our dreams come true." She dives out her window (don't try this at home) and finds herself in a watery world of wonder where she meets Delphis, a dolphin spirit who transforms into a hunky guy in an anatomically correct wet suit, and Aurora, a bird spirit in gaudy red plumage who soars overhead in an aerial ballet.

Dolphins, pseudorcas, acrobats, high divers, parrots and lorikeets, and even an immense buzzard get in on the act in what is one of SeaWorld's most elaborate spectacles. I counted 18 performers, nine dolphins, and two pseudorcas, as well as a passel of parrots.

The debt to Cirque du Soleil is obvious and they carry it off well. An elaborate aerial harness apparatus enables the performers to soar over the pool in graceful circles and gives the razzle-dazzle divers a quick route back to their high platforms for another spectacular leap.

The marine mammals are no slouches either. At one point, all nine dolphins are in the pool in a three-ring circus of amazing behaviors. At one point, two dolphins propel their trainer in a corkscrew pattern through the water. At another, Delphis and Marina take turns riding a pair of dolphins chariot style around the pool, a foot on the back of each animal.

The show ends with all the performers soaring and diving while the air is alive with multi-colored birds. It's a sure-fire crowd pleaser that marks yet another triumph for the SeaWorld creative team.

Manatee Rescue

Rating: ★ ★ ★ ★ ★
Type: Aquatic habitat
Time: 20 to 30 minutes
Kelly says: For everyone in the family

You don't expect a natural history exhibit to pack an emotional wallop, but this one sure does — and does it very deftly. It is unlikely that anyone in your family will emerge from this experience unaffected.

The manatee is a large, slow-moving marine mammal that favors the shallow brackish waterways along the Florida coast, the very same areas that have become a recreational paradise for boaters and fishermen. As man's presence in their habitat has increased, the manatees' numbers have dwindled. A sign in the entrance to this exhibit informs us that there are only about 2,000 manatees left in Florida and that about 10% of this number die each year. Far fewer are born. It doesn't take a mathematical genius to figure out that at this rate the manatee will be extinct (in the wild, at least) in the very near future.

The message takes on an additional poignancy when we realize that all of the small manatees in the exhibit are orphans and that some of the larger animals have been grievously wounded by their encounters with civilization. One has lost most of its tail, another a front flipper. One of the themes of this exhibit is SeaWorld's ongoing rescue efforts of manatees and other marine mammals. On video, we see a seriously wounded adult nursed back to health and released back into the wild. The news that at least one released manatee has reproduced in the wild cheers us like a major victory.

After viewing the manatees from above — in a pool that re-creates a coastal wetland, with egrets and ibises looking on — we walk down a spiraling walkway into an underground circular theater for a short and highly effective film containing a plea for conservation and protection of the manatee. From there, we pass into the underwater viewing area where the majesty and fragility of this odd beast become even more apparent. Their slow, graceful movements and their rather goofy faces make the manatee instantly appealing. The aquatic setting is lovely too, shared as it is by a variety of native fish. There are glistening tarpon here and a variety of gar, including one large specimen of the alligator gar, a black beast that hovers just under the surface, the reasons for its name instantly apparent. In an interesting bit of verisimilitude, the pool contains tilapia, a fish that is not a native but imported from Africa. It competes with and threatens some native species.

Interactive touch-screen video monitors provide a self-guided wealth of additional information about manatees and the problems they face from habitat destruction and pollution. Staffers from SeaWorld's education department stroll the viewing area on a somewhat irregular schedule. If any are there when you visit, they will be more than happy to answer your questions.

I found this a profoundly moving experience and one to which I returned eagerly. As you leave, you can pick up more information about how to be a responsible boater, diver, and snorkeler in manatee areas. You will also be challenged to make a personal commitment to help the manatee. What will you do?

Photo Op: As you leave the exhibit, look for the sculpture of the manatee cow and her calf floating artfully above the pavement. It makes an excellent backdrop for a family photograph.

Journey to Atlantis

Rating:	★ ★ ★ +
Type:	Combination flume ride and roller coaster
Time:	About 6 minutes
Kelly says:	Wet and wild

It just goes to show you: always heed the warnings of crusty old Greek fishermen, no matter how crazy they seem. Of course, the tourist hordes ignore Stavros' sage advice and set sail on a tour of the ancient city of Atlantis which has mysteriously risen from the Aegean.

Rising some ten stories, Atlantis looks gaudily out of place at SeaWorld, but it sure looks pretty in the golden glow of the setting sun. But it's not the architecture that draws us here. It's the dizzyingly steep water flume emerging from the city walls and the happy screams of those plunging to a watery splashdown. Wend your way through the Greek-village-themed waiting line and be entertained by the news coverage of the eerie reappearance of Atlantis as you wait for your boat.

The voyage gets off to a peaceful start, but after a benign and quite lovely interlude, the boat is seized by the evil Allura, who I gather is a vengeful ancient spirit of some sort. You are winched higher and higher before being sent on a hair-raising journey that combines the scariest elements of a flume ride and a roller coaster. It's a nifty engineering feat but most people probably won't care as they plunge down the 60-foot flume into a tidal wave of water. Another slow ascent gives you a chance to catch your breath before you zip through a fiendishly hidden mini roller coaster to another splashdown, as Allura cackles gleefully. It's all over quickly — too quickly for my taste — but you can always head immediately for the end of the inevitably long line for another go.

It must be said that the storyline for this ride is a bit confusing and hard to follow, which bothers some purists. Most people don;t seem to care.

Tip: This is a very wet ride, especially if you are in the front row of the eight-passenger boat that serves as the ride vehicle. An inexpensive poncho (which you can get at any of the theme parks) provides pretty good protection. Expensive cameras and other items that might not survive a soaking can be checked as you enter the boat, but they are placed in unlocked lockers and no guarantees are provided. Pay lockers are available near the entrance to the waiting line; they cost 50 cents and if you don't have the change you will have to walk over to the nearby lockers for *Kraken*, where a change machine is available.

As you exit the ride, don't miss the lovely **Jewels of the Sea Aquarium**, just off the inevitable gift shop. Hammerhead sharks and stingrays swim above you in a domed aquarium, while angelfish inhabit the aquarium beneath your feet. Around the walls, don't miss the moon jellyfish that glow enchantingly when you press the light button. Just outside the aquarium and gift shop, playful hidden fountains await to soak the unwary.

Photo Op: Just outside the Jewels of the Sea Aquarium is a plaza with a splendid view of the 60-foot flume plunge. If you don't want to take your own pictures, shots of every boatload of happily terrified cruisers are on sale at the ride exit.

Kraken

Rating:	★ ★ ★ ★ ★
Type:	Roller coaster
Time:	2 minutes
Kelly says:	Aieeee!

I must confess I was less than thrilled when *Kraken* was announced. I have always felt that it is the animal shows that make SeaWorld so special and that thrill rides are beside the point here. And truth be told, *Kraken* is something of a distraction if you are watching the *Clyde & Seamore* show or visiting *Pacific Point Preserve* (see below). Of course, SeaWorld doesn't listen to me and coaster enthusiasts will be glad it doesn't. SeaWorld clearly set out to compete head to head with Universal and Disney for coaster bragging rights and, by Neptune, they've succeeded.

Kraken has several claims to fame. For starters, it is higher (at about 150 feet) and faster than any other coaster in Orlando. But the neatest (or scariest) thing about *Kraken* is that the seats are raised slightly so your feet dangle free. So even though the track is beneath your feet at all times, you don't have the same feeling of connected-ness you get on other coasters. Nor do you have the comfort of the overhanging superstructure you get in an inverted coaster. The effect is subtle, yet undeniably ter-rifying.

For a coaster this fast (they claim speeds "in excess of" 65 miles per hour), *Kraken* is also remarkably smooth. Your head may be pressed against the headrest by the G-forces but it won't be buffeted about. Another thing you may notice (if you aren't screaming too loudly) is that *Kraken* is an unusually quiet coaster. Even if you are standing right next to the fence where *Kraken* dips underground at the end of its run, you can barely hear it. Farther away, it is only the shrieks of the riders you hear in the distance. Another item of note is that the ride designers have made a special effort to accommodate those with large upper torso measurements; specially modified seats in rows four and five of each car can handle those with chest measurements of up to 52 inches. There is also a minimum height requirement of 54 inches.

This is an extremely "aggressive" ride, to use the phrase preferred by the design-ers. They even have a sign urging those with prosthetic limbs to make sure they are securely fastened! So you will be well-advised to stow everything that's not firmly attached to your body in the pay lockers at the entrance to the ride. Smaller lockers are available at modest cost. A change machine is provided.

Now you're ready for the experience itself. As you make the excruciatingly slow climb to the 15-story apex of the first hill, show off just how cool you are by taking in the panoramic view of the park you get from the top. It may be the last time on this ride you have your eyes open.

As you enter the first drop, you begin to fully appreciate the exquisite horror afforded by *Kraken's* unique design. The effect is less like riding in a roller coaster than like being shot through the air on a jet-propelled chair, all the while turning and twisting head over heels. There are seven loops — at least I think there are seven loops, because I keep forgetting to count — as the coaster soars over water and dips below ground along over 4,000 feet of torturous turquoise and yellow track.

The 119-foot vertical loop, the 101-foot diving loop, the zero-gravity roll and the cobra roll may all have their equivalents on other coasters, but experiencing them in *Kraken's* raised, exposed seats adds a heightened level of sheer terror that beggars description.

As astonishing as the engineering is, one of the best moments of the ride occurs thanks to the scenic design. It occurs when the coaster dives underground into what is described as the "monster's lair," a tunnel that appears to be on the brink of being totally inundated by a thundering waterfall. But before you have a chance to drown, you are whipped back above the surface and into a flat spin before returning to the starting point. Truly amazing!

On the downside, the experience is short, about two minutes altogether and a full minute of that time is consumed getting you to the top of the first hill and returning you to the starting point after the coaster brakes at the end.

If you'd like to get a preview of *Kraken*, perhaps to decide if you want to subject yourself to its special brand of terror, there are two good vantage points. The first is just to the left of the main entrance, where a viewing area has thoughtfully been provided for the faint of heart. This spot gives you a good view of the first drop and the end of the ride. Over at *Pacific Point Preserve*, you can get a good view of the main section of the ride.

Photo Op: If you have high speed film and a fast shutter speed, you might try for a shot in the viewing area near the large Kraken head where the cars dip underground, just at the ride's end.

And speaking of photos, you can pick up one of you and your terrified fellow riders at the exit to the ride in a variety of mountings, including key chains and snow globes. For a fee, of course, which can run well over $20.

For those who care about such things, *Kraken* takes its name from a mythical sea creature that, in SeaWorld's version at least, looks a lot like a giant dragon eel, a multicolored cousin of the moray. In a cave near the viewing area by the main entrance, you can see actual dragon eels pretending to be embryos in giant Kraken eggs.

Penguin Encounter

Rating:	★ ★ ★ ★
Type:	Aquatic habitat
Time:	Continuous viewing (5 to 10 minutes)
Kelly says:	Kids love this one

This is the only exhibit at SeaWorld that you smell first. It hits you the moment you enter but, for some reason, you get used to it very quickly. Soon you are facing a long glass wall behind which is a charming Antarctic diorama packed with penguins. If you bear to the right as you enter, you are funneled onto a moving conveyor belt that takes you at a steady pace past the viewing area; bearing to the left takes you to a raised, stationary, viewing area. Don't worry if you get on the conveyor belt and discover you want to dawdle; you can get back to the stationary section at the other end.

As you ride the conveyor, the water level is about at your chest, so you get an excellent view of the underwater antics of these remarkable birds as they almost literally "fly" through the water. On land, their movements are considerably less graceful, but their slow waddling has its own kind of grace, especially in the case of the larger king penguins with their yellow-accented faces. Overhead, artificial snow sprinkles down from hatches in the roof. The water temperature, an electronic readout informs us, is 45 degrees Fahrenheit, while the air temperature is maintained at 34 degrees. Chilly for us, perhaps, but these highly adapted creatures are used to a much deeper freeze, as we discover in the Learning Center immediately past the penguins.

Here, interactive teaching aids provide the curious with a wealth of additional information about gentoos, rockhoppers, and chinstraps. Here, too, you can watch informative videos about the hand-rearing of penguins and how they molt, the Antarctic environment and penguin predators, and Isla Noir, a Chilean island that is especially popular with penguins.

Just past the Learning Center is a smaller habitat featuring alcids, a group of birds, including the puffins and murres, that is the northern equivalent of the penguin. Unlike their Antarctic cousins, these birds fly in the air as well as beneath the sea. The alcid viewing area, like the penguin exhibit, is equally divided between land and sea and, if you're in luck, you will see murres "flying" to the bottom to scavenge smelt.

As you leave the exhibit, you will have an opportunity to circle back to the penguin viewing area for another look if you wish.

Pacific Point Preserve

Rating: ★ ★ ★ ★
Type: Outdoor aquatic habitat
Time: Continuous viewing
Kelly says: Don't miss feeding the sea lions

Over 50 sea lions roar and bark with delight in this two-and-a-half-acre, open-air, sunken habitat. SeaWorld's design team traveled to the Pacific Northwest to take molds of the rock outcroppings along the coast to build this remarkable re-creation. Adding to the verisimilitude is a wave machine, similar to those used in the water theme parks, that creates waves of anywhere from a few inches to two feet in height. The viewing area extends entirely around the exhibit, and while the sea lions (and a smaller number of harbor seals) are safely out of reach, it's almost as if you can touch them.

But if you can't pet them, you can feed them. Small trays of fish are available at certain times for $5 a tray ($3 for annual passholders) and their contents will very quickly disappear down a sea lion's gullet. It's all great fun and, if you aren't careful, you can very quickly squander your lunch money. The sea lions, for their part, have learned how to part you from your smelt and will bark furiously and even leap decoratively up onto the edge of the pool until their hunger is satisfied, which it never is. Fortunately, watching other people feed the sea lions is almost as entertaining as doing it yourself. The feeding stations are open regularly and it is only on extremely crowded days that the allotted ration of fish is sold out before closing time.

While their feeding behavior might lead you to believe these animals are tame, they are not. The sea lions you see perform in the *Clyde & Seamore* show just around the corner live separately from their cousins in Pacific Point. They have been trained for years and habituated to interacting with humans. The animals in *Pacific Point Preserve* are wild and like all wild animals unpredictable. In other words, don't dangle little Susie over the edge to get her within smelt-tossing range.

Tip: You might want to ask someone on the education staff when the main feeding will take place that day. While the public certainly helps with the feeding, the staff has to make sure that their charges are adequately fed. They do this by serving up fish by the bucketful at least once a day. This is a highly entertaining ritual so it's worthwhile to check the schedule. Also, the handlers have to hand-feed some of the older sea lions and seals who don't compete well for food with their younger rivals. You and your kids will undoubtedly find this part of the feeding particularly touching.

Clyde & Seamore Take Pirate Island (at Sea Lion & Otter Stadium)

Rating:	★ ★ ★ ★
Type:	Live water show with sea lions, otters, and walruses.
Time:	25 minutes
Kelly says:	The funniest show at SeaWorld

Forget about education. This one's all about high spirits and low humor and it's a sure-fire crowd pleaser. Clyde and Seamore are sea lion versions of Laurel and Hardy, or Ralph Kramden and Ed Norton, or maybe two of the Three Stooges. In any event, they're bumblers.

There's a plot about a search for gold (and fresh fish), a treacherous otter, and (of course) pirates, but it's almost beside the point. The real point of this show is watching Clyde and Seamore cavort up, down, and around the multilevel set and into and out of the pool that rings the lip of the stage. The humor is broad and the little kids love it. One thing that makes the show such a hoot is the slapdash way in which the human performers carry it off, bloopers and all. Some of the gaffes are due to the unpredictability of the animals but other boo-boos seem to be written into the script, although few will suspect as much unless they see the show several times.

If you are lucky, you might get to see a walrus or two make a cameo appearance. Walruses, I am told, are nowhere near as tractable as sea lions and, given their considerable bulk and potential for wreaking havoc, they only appear when they're in the mood. Even then, they may balk at performing, just like a Hollywood star, and the trainers know better than to argue with several tons of balky blubber. As usual, a small child is summoned from the audience to help out (and shake Clyde's flipper). And, of course, there are the usual dire warnings about splash zones, although the wetness quotient is far lower here than at the Shamu show.

Tip: If you arrive more than about 10 minutes early, you will be entertained by **The SeaWorld Mime**. If you arrive fewer than 10 minutes before show time, you may become one of his victims. This is not mime in the cutesy Marcel Marceau tradition — there's no getting trapped inside an invisible box or walking against an imaginary wind. This is mime with an attitude, that mimics, mocks, and plays pranks on the steady stream of people arriving for the show. Those familiar with the work of David Shiner, the clown prince of this genre, will know what to expect. For others, I don't want to give too much away. This is, far and away, the best of SeaWorld's pre-show entertainments. It is an attraction in its own right and not to be missed.

Sea Lions Tonight

Rating:	★ ★ ★ ★ ★
Type:	Live show
Time:	25 minutes
Kelly says:	Hilarious sendup

As the title suggests, this show is performed only at night, only once a day, and only during the summer months when the park is open late. If you are here when this show is being offered, don't miss it!

The goofy guys who brought you Clyde and Seamore let their hair down even farther to bring you this truly funny (and occasionally biting) satire on the *other* shows at SeaWorld. But instead of dolphins and whales, they use sea lions, walruses, and ot-ters. The SeaWorld Mime is dragooned into the show and doesn't seem to be too happy about the dumb things he's called on to do, including standing in for the birds of *Blue Horizons* and donning a whale fluke headpiece for their version of *Believe*.

The show pokes good natured fun at the pretentiousness that lurks just below the surface of shows like *Blue Horizons* and *Believe*. Maybe there's a wee bit of jealousy involved, too. In one of the show's funniest bits, the cast members strut and preen as orca trainers, their wet suits bulging with artificially enhanced muscles, while an enormous lumbering walrus stands in for Shamu. There are jabs taken at *Pets Ahoy*, *Fusion*, and *Kraken* as well. All in all, it adds up to one of the best shows at SeaWorld.

Shark Encounter

Rating:	★ ★ ★ +
Type:	Aquatic habitat
Time:	15 to 20 minutes
Kelly says:	Up close and personal with some scary fish

In *Shark Encounter*, SeaWorld has very cleverly packaged an aquarium-style dis-play of some of the seas' scariest, ugliest, and most dangerous creatures. The tone and lighting of this exhibit is dark and foreboding, with appropriately ominous soundtrack music, but you needn't worry about any unpleasant surprises. When you get right down to it, it's fish in tanks and far too fascinating to be truly scary to any except perhaps the most suggestible kids.

The attraction wraps around **Sharks Underwater Grill** and, in fact, the res-taurant has commandeered what used to be the big attraction — a massive tank brimming with a variety of shark species, with huge picture window viewing areas. You still get a nifty view of the sharks, as we shall see, but something was lost from the attraction when the restaurant was added.

You enter this habitat to the left of the restaurant. A short corridor leads to a clear acrylic tunnel through an artificial tropical reef. This is home to the moray eels — nasty-looking snake-like fish. The moray's coating of yellow slime over its blue flesh gives it a sickly green tint. At first, all you see are the many varieties of reef fish swimming about, but closer inspection reveals the morays poking their heads out of their holes. The more you look, the more you see. There are dozens and dozens of the creatures hidden in the crevices of the reef. From time to time one swims free, undulating its long body right overhead. Looking up you see the surface of the water. The tank has been designed to mimic the natural habitat as closely as possible; the lighting comes from a single overhead source, standing in for the sun.

The tunnel curves around and into a viewing area in which several tanks hold specimens probably best kept separate. First is the delicate and intricately camouflaged lion fish. Looks are deceiving here, because the lion fish's feathery appendages are actually poisoned spines that are highly toxic to swimmers unfortunate enough to come in contact with them.

Tried any fugu at your local sushi bar? You may want to reconsider after viewing the puffer fish on display here. Fugu, as the fish is known in Japan, is one of the world's most poisonous fish. The Japanese consider its edible portions a delicacy, and licensed fugu chefs carefully pare away the poisonous organs. Despite their precautions, several people die each year from fugu poisoning. Swimming unconcernedly with the puffer fish are surgeon fish, a pretty species that carries the marine equivalent of switchblades concealed near the tail. When attacked (or grabbed by unwary fishermen), they lash out with their hidden weapon, inflicting a nasty gash. Across the way are barracuda, looking every bit as terrifying as when I first encountered them while snorkeling in the Caribbean. Had I been to SeaWorld first, I would have known that an attack was unlikely and probably would have made less of a fool of myself.

As you walk down the long tunnel toward the shark encounter that gives the attraction its name, wall displays fill you in on little known shark facts. For example, did you know that a shark's liver takes up nearly 90% of its body cavity and accounts for nearly a quarter of its weight? Scientists theorize that, since the liver contains a great deal of oil and since oil is lighter than water, the shark's huge liver may contribute to its buoyancy.

Look for a series of rectangular windows on your right. Here you can get a glimpse of what the lucky diners in the restaurant are seeing. It's a spectacular sight, even from this somewhat restricted vantage point and it may be enough to make you decide to have lunch there.

At the bottom of the zig-zag tunnel, you reach the attraction's culmination — a slow, stately ride on a conveyer belt through a 124-foot tunnel that takes you right down the middle of the shark tank. About a foot thick, the clear acrylic walls of the tunnel are supporting 450 tons of man-made salt water over your head. Don't worry, you're perfectly safe; the acrylic can withstand a tromping by 372 elephants (as you are informed on exiting).

All around and above you swim small sawtooth sharks, brown sharks, nurse sharks, bull sharks, lemon sharks, and sandpiper sharks. There are no giants here but what the specimens lack in size they more than make up for in number. If you ever encounter sharks in the wild, hopefully there will be nowhere near this many of them.

The next stop is the exit and the blinding Florida sunshine. If you overlooked the pool at the entrance to Sharks Underwater Grill when you entered, take a moment to check it out as you leave. Look for the bridge over a shallow pool in which some of the smaller and less threatening shark specimens are displayed. Here are small hammerheads and nurse sharks along with a variety of rays, including the jet-black bat ray.

Tip: You can satisfy your curiosity and get a great view of the restaurant's shark viewing windows by heading for the bar and having a cool drink. It's seldom crowded at the bar and often you can walk right in, past families waiting for a table. If you're hungry, the full menu is served at the bar and at a number of nearby raised tables.

Odyssea (at Nautilus Theatre)

Rating: ★ ★ ★ ★
Type: Indoor stage show
Time: 25 minutes
Kelly says: A delightful dance and acrobatic fantasy

If you can't afford the astronomical ticket prices of Cirque de Soleil over at Disney, this wordless blend of acrobatics, mime, and dance makes a nice substitute.

The plot, such as it is, involves an amiable innocent with more curiosity than brains who gets sucked into a delightful undersea fantasy world filled with wondrous creatures who form the basis for a series of whimsical routines. A beautiful acrobat on the half-shell performs feats of balance with giant pearls, colorful tropical fish become spinning aerialists, and bizarre multi-colored worm-like critters bounce and wriggle in ways that make you scratch your head and ask, "How'd they do that?" The best is saved for last as a gaggle of zany penguins bounce, tumble, and twist at dizzying speed around their iceberg home.

This show takes a while to hit its stride, but your patience will be rewarded with a fun-filled extravaganza with gorgeous sets, costumes, and lighting that turn the Nautilus Theatre into a watery wonderland.

Paddle Boats

Rating: ★ ★ +
Type: Just what it says
Time: As long as you want, one half hour at a time
Kelly says: Can be skipped

In Bayside Lagoon you can rent large, pink, flamingo-shaped paddle boats for a leisurely outing on the lagoon. The boats seat two adults comfortably and cost $6 a half hour. If you have the time and enjoy this sort of activity, you may want to give them a go.

Life jackets come with your rental and are required wearing. You must be at least 56 inches tall to ride and you must be 16 or older to take a boat out alone. Check the park's daily calendar for opening hours, which vary.

Walk-By Exhibits

In addition to the larger, more formal aquatic habitats and stadium and theater shows, SeaWorld is dotted with a number of smaller, "walk-by" exhibits, typically showcasing the birds who live by the sea. They blend in so well with the landscaping that they seem almost like set decoration, and many people simply breeze by. Most of them are to be found in the northern end of the park.

Certainly some of them, like the sand sculpture exhibits, don't deserve more than a cursory look. Others, like the flamingo exhibit, will reward those who pause for closer inspection and perhaps a photograph. These exhibits are more elaborate and more thoughtfully designed versions of what you might see at the birdhouse of an old-fashioned zoo. In addition to the flamingos, you will find ducks, pelicans, and spoonbills. Signs identify each species and provide interesting tidbits of information about their habitat, range, and habits.

THE SOUTH END

The southern half of SeaWorld lies to the right of the *Sky Tower* on the map, most of it across the wooden walkway that takes you over Bayside Lagoon to Shamu Stadium. The whole feel of this side of the park is quite a bit different, with its large open spaces between huge modern stadiums and buildings.

Once again, I describe the attractions in geographical rather than thematic order, beginning with the *Hospitality Center* and continuing in a clockwise direction around Bayside Lagoon.

Clydesdale Hamlet & Hospitality Center

Rating:	★ ★ +
Type:	Horse stables and free beer
Time:	As long as you want
Kelly says:	For horse lovers and Bud fans

Since Anheuser-Busch, the brewing giant, owns SeaWorld, you probably can't hold it against them for blowing their own horn a bit. And even if you find this sort of blatant self-promotion distasteful, you'll probably have to admit they do a pretty good (and fairly tasteful) job of it.

There are really two attractions here, *Clydesdale Hamlet*, the home of Budweiser's trademark Clydesdale beer wagon team, and the *Anheuser-Busch Hospitality Center*. *Clydesdale Hamlet* is actually a very upscale stable, impeccably clean and not in the least aromatically offensive. This is where the impressive Clydesdales hang out between appearances elsewhere in the park and where you can meet and pet them at times posted in the daily calendar.

These steeds, from Scotland, were originally bred for the heavy work of hauling man's stuff from place to place, and while they may not have the magnificent grace of their racing cousins they are pretty impressive in their own right — all 2,000 pounds of them. They are also pampered, beautifully groomed, and obviously well-cared for. There are stable attendants always close at hand to make sure you don't slip them a sugar cube or a contraband carrot and to regale you with horse lore. Did you know, for example, that if you hold down the jaw of a supine Clydesdale, it will be unable to stand up? Seems they have to be able to raise their heads off the ground first before they begin the process of standing up.

Next door is the *Anheuser-Busch Hospitality Center*, a large, airy pavilion whose architecture reflects that of the stable. It's a lovely building surrounded by immaculate lawns. A comfortable outdoor seating area overlooks a crystal clear lake, fed by a babbling waterfall. It's the nicest place in the park to just sit and take your ease.

Inside you'll find **The Deli** (a fast-food restaurant) and the **Label Stable** (a souvenir shop). The centerpiece of the Center, however, is the free beer dispensing area that faces the main entrance and is backed by huge copper brewing kettles. That's right, free beer. The cups are on the small size (about 10 ounces) and there's a limit (one sample at a time, two per day), but it's still a gracious gesture. Most of Anheuser-Busch's brands are available, including the nonalcoholic O'Doul's.

Here at the Hospitality Center, several times a day, you can attend **Budweiser Beer School**, a pleasant enough way to kill 35 minutes and perhaps get answers to those questions that have been tormenting you for years. Why is it called Budweiser? Who was Anheuser? However, I suspect most people are lured here by the beer tasting that follows some videos about the history of Anheuser-Busch and the art of brewing beer. At the end you get a certificate attesting to your newfound status as a "Beermaster."

Arcade and Midway Games

Rating:	★ +
Type:	Video and "skill" games arcades
Time:	As long as you want
Kelly says:	For video game addicts

My feelings about these money-siphoning operations, located near the Shamu Stadium, can be summed up pretty easily — why bother? The main reason you paid good money to come to SeaWorld is just paces away and everything you can do here, you can do elsewhere for less money. That being said, these venues are clean and attractive and the prizes at Midway Games are better than most.

Believe

Rating:	★ ★ ★ ★ ★
Type:	Live stadium show
Time:	25 minutes
Kelly says:	The acme of the SeaWorld experience

Could there be a better job than being a killer whale trainer and being shot 30 feet into the air off the nose of a 5,000 pound orca? You won't think so after seeing this razzle-dazzle demonstration put on by the dashing young SeaWorld staffers who spend their time teaching the Shamu family some awesome tricks (although the trainers prefer the term "behaviors").

Actually, they aren't "tricks" at all in the common sense of the term. They are

simply extensions of natural behaviors that have been reinforced by the whales' trainers with patient attention and liberal handfuls of smelt. Nor is *Believe* to be confused
with mere entertainment. In keeping with SeaWorld's commitment to conserving
the marine environment and saving endangered marine species, this show teaches
important lessons about the realities of nature and the importance of the marine
mammal husbandry practiced at SeaWorld Orlando and its sister parks around the
country.

The stars of the show are members of the family *orsinus orca*, commonly known
as killer whales and affectionately known by nearly everyone who visits SeaWorld as
Shamu. The first killer whale ever captured was named Namu after a town in British Columbia. Shamu means "mate of Namu" in the language of British Columbia's
native people. Of course, different whales appear in different shows, so the mammoth
performers in this show are, in a sense, playing the role of Shamu.

The "stage" is a huge seven million-gallon pool filled with man-made salt water
kept at a chilly 55 degrees (although the whales are used to much chillier water in
their natural habitats) and completely filtered every 30 minutes. At the back is a small
island platform for the trainers, above which looms a large structure in the shape of
a killer whale's tail fluke and four video screens that move, merge, and spin as the
moment requires. The front of the stage is formed by a six-foot high Lucite wall that
gives those in the first several rows an underwater view. Downstage center is a shallow
lip that allows Shamu to "beach" herself for our enjoyment.

On film, we are told the story of a young lad who carves a wooden pendant
in the shape of a tail fluke and dreams of swimming with the orcas. When the focus
switches from video screen to stage, we discover this kid has grown up to be a Sea-
World trainer. It's a touching story, but the real focus of the show is the awe-inspiring
and absolutely delightful interaction of the whales and their trainers. The whales leap,
glide, dive, and roll with a grace that belies their huge size. The trainers ride on their
charges' bellies, surf the pool on their backs and, in the most breathtaking moments,
soar high aloft, propelled off a whale's snout. Many times, two trainers working with
two whales will perform in perfect synchronization. They make it look easy and natural, but my guess is that it is fiendishly difficult to pull these tandem tricks off.

The video backstory pays off in a segment toward the end of the show in which
a future orca trainer is summoned from the audience to meet Shamu and the tail
fluke pendant is passed to a new generation.

The warnings that precede the show's grand finale are in deadly earnest. If you're
sitting in the first 14 rows, you'll likely get very, very, very wet. Actually, it's possible to
sit in this section and escape a drenching — I've done it. But if you happen to be in
the direct line of one of the salvos of chilly salt water hurled into the audience by the
cupped rear fluke of a five-ton whale, you will be soaked to the skin. It's pretty much
a matter of luck. Some of the biggest laughs come when people who have fled the
"splash zone" for the higher ground of the first promenade get nailed anyway by a
particularly forceful fluke-full of water.

The best seats in the house. Many kids (especially 9- to 13-year-old boys) will
insist on sitting in the splash zone and will feel cheated if they don't get soaked. But

adults should consider sitting here as well. If you wear a rain poncho (which you may already have from a visit to another park) you can protect yourself relatively well, and these seats do offer an excellent view, especially underwater. But the seats higher up, where you are assured of staying dry, offer excellent sight lines and the video coverage of the show assures that you won't miss anything.

Tip: Between shows, follow the pathways that ring Shamu Stadium to locate the ramp to the **Underwater Viewing Area** around back. This is a not-to-be-missed perspective on these magnificent creatures. Especially enchanting is the opportunity to watch Shamu and her much smaller calf, Baby Shamu, swimming gracefully in tandem. The whales are rotated through this viewing pool, so there's no guarantee that a specific whale will be there when you drop by. There are benches in front of the picture windows and if the crowds are thin enough you can watch while you rest.

Dine With Shamu

Rating:	★ ★ ★ ★
Type:	Dinner attraction with additional charge
Time:	About an hour
Kelly says:	For hardcore Shamu fans

After the stadium show, why not join the stars for a nice meal? That's essentially the opportunity afforded by *Dine With Shamu.* The large pool with the underwater viewing area (see above) doubles as an al fresco buffet restaurant for orcas and their guests. It's a pleasant way to get another, more relaxed look at those magnificent orcas. Tables have been set up along one side of the pool, under an awning and a small building behind the tables houses a buffet line.

The meal is scheduled for early evening at a time that varies somewhat with the season. If the park is open late, there may be two shows. It's advisable to check.

The buffet dinner is simple but plentiful. Typically there will be chicken, beef, seafood, and vegetarian main courses, with veggies, rolls and other side dishes. A separate buffet line caters to kids' tastes and both grown-ups and kids share a dessert buffet that includes puddings, brownies, cookies, and the like. Beer and wine, along with iced tea and lemonade are included in the price, which is $37 for adults and $19 for children 3 to 9. (Annual passholders get a $5 discount.) Tax and tip are additional.

The meal I had was adequate, the entrees seeming almost purposely bland, but then the meal is not the main draw here. Shortly after the meal begins, the main business of the evening gets under way — a pleasant encounter with one of the mammoth performers from the Shamu shows.

Typically, two trainers are involved. One works with the animal while the other stands on the opposite side of the pool from the dining area and keeps up a running patter filled with interesting factoids about orcas and how the staff works with them and cares for them. For example, did you know that SeaWorld's killer whales have their teeth brushed every day? Why? Because dental problems are the single biggest cause of orca fatalities in the wild.

There is much less of the flamboyant acrobatics of the main show. There are a few leaps and you are warned that you might get wet, but the trainers seem to keep things fairly subdued. Shamu does emerge onto a shallow slide-out area and seats here are good ones. The trainer encourages questions but you will have to shout them out to be heard.

The whole event from start to finish lasts less than an hour and will seem too short to most folks. I would recommend *Dine with Shamu* only for diehard fans. For others, the price will seem a little steep for what you get.

You can book seats for the show at the front of the park. When you do you will be assigned a table. Reservations can be made by calling 800-327-2424.

Shamu's Happy Harbor

Rating: ★ ★ ★ ★ +
Type: Play area
Time: 30 minutes to an hour
Kelly says: Great for young kids, toddlers, and their long-suffering parents

If *Wild Arctic* (below) represents an attempt to reach out to the thrill-seeking segment of the tourist population, *Shamu's Happy Harbor* seeks to appeal to the youngster too antsy or uninterested to sit still for a fish — no matter how big it is. Here is a way for even very young children to be entertained in that most effective of ways — by doing things for themselves.

Shamu's Happy Harbor is dominated by a four-story, L-shaped, steel framework painted in shades of sea green and pink. At first glance it looks like a construction site gone very wrong. Closer inspection reveals it to be an intricate maze of cargo netting, plastic tubes, and slides that kids can climb up and through to their heart's content. Some chambers in this maze contain tire swings, just like the ones in backyards across America, except that these are two stories above ground level. The cargo netting is completely enclosed in smaller-mesh black netting. While there's no danger of falling, the upper reaches of the structure are quite high and some smaller children may become frightened.

It's not just for kids, either. Adults can join in, too, although some of the parents I watched obviously wished they weren't allowed. While the corridors of netting are big enough to accommodate anyone, the tubes are designed with smaller people in mind. Thus, the average sedentary grown-up will get quite a workout going through them. You're allowed to climb up but stairs are provided for the trip down. Too many middle-aged sprained ankles is my guess.

The larger structure of *Shamu's Happy Harbor* is complemented by any number of lesser activities, called "elements," all of them action-oriented. These will keep kids busy for hours unless you can drag them away to the next show at the Sea Lion and Otter Stadium. There are four-sided, canvas "mountains" that kids can climb with the help of knotted ropes and then slide down, and large inflated rooms in which kids 54 inches and shorter can bounce and tumble.

Standing in front of it all is a kid-sized schooner, the **Wahoo Two**, just waiting to be explored. Nearby, the **Water Works** offers a jumble of tubes and netting that is constantly splashed with jets of water. The far side of the Harbor from the entrance is ringed with a series of smaller kiddie rides including **Jazzy Jellies** (42 in. minimum height), **Swishy Fishies** (36 in. minimum), and, most interestingly, the **Shamu Express** (38 in. minimum), a kiddie roller coaster with cars cleverly themed with Shamu-like tail flukes. At the other end of the Harbor, you'll find **Shamu's Splash Attack**, where you can pay to sling water bombs at a friend. Buckets of seven water-filled balloons are two for $5, and **Op's Beat**, where kids can bang on hanging steel drums to their heart's content.

Shamu's Happy Harbor is an ideal place for parents to take the squirmy baby of the family when he or she gets restless with the more grown-up attractions at SeaWorld.

Photo Op: Just opposite *Shamu's Happy Harbor* is a made-to-order photo backdrop. It's a life-sized model of Shamu and Baby Shamu perfectly posed under a sun awning (to protect your shot from that annoying glare). Place your kid on Shamu's back and click away.

Wild Arctic

Rating: ★ ★ ★ ★ ★
Type: Simulator ride plus a spectacular habitat
Time: 5 minutes for the ride; as long as you want for the habitat
Kelly says: A SeaWorld must-see

That large, techno-modern, warehouse-like building near Shamu Stadium houses one of SeaWorld's most popular attractions — a devilishly clever combination of thrill ride with serene aquatic habitat. All in all, this is one of the most imaginative attractions in Orlando. Mercifully, the waiting line snakes through an area that is shielded from the blazing sun, because the lines can get long.

Tip: To avoid long waits, you will be well advised to see *Wild Arctic* early in the morning. Another option is to visit during performances at nearby Shamu Stadium. But time your visit carefully; the waiting line fills up very quickly when the Shamu show empties out.

During our wait, we are entertained by a fascinating video presentation on the lifestyle of the Inuit peoples who inhabit the frozen realm of the Arctic. And during our slow journey through the line, we are asked to make an important decision: Do we want to take the helicopter ride to the base station or do we want to go by land? It's a choice between "motion" and "non-motion" and it can be important.

The Wild Arctic Ride

If you choose to take the helicopter, be prepared for a whale of a simulator ride (you should pardon the expression). We begin our journey by crossing a metal bridge into the vehicle itself. Once all 59 voyagers are strapped in, the staff exits, the doors close, and the "helicopter" takes off.

The ride, which lasts all of about five minutes, simulates a flight aboard an amphibious (not to mention submersible) helicopter to a research station deep within the Arctic Circle. Despite the gale warnings crackling over the radio, our friendly pilot can't help doing a little sightseeing, including putting the rotors into "whisper mode" so we can drop in on a polar bear family, and dipping below the waves for a glimpse of a narwhal. But his unscheduled detours exact their price and soon we are caught in that gale. At first the pilot prudently puts down on a glacier to await a better reading on the weather but the glacier gives way and we plummet headlong towards the icy waters below.

At the last second, the pilot gets the rotors whirling and we zoom away from certain death. Next, he decides we'll be safer flying through a crevasse, away from the howling winds, but we fly straight into and through an avalanche. Finally, we break through into the clear and the Arctic base station lies dead ahead.

It's a real stomach-churner and remarkably realistic. As I write these words I realize that I'm becoming a little queasy just remembering it all. The action is fast, abrupt, and violent. You'll find yourself being tossed from side to side as you grip the armrests and scream — in excitement or terror, depending on your mood.

Those who choose the "non-motion" alternative for their voyage to the *Wild Arctic*, are escorted past the three simulators to a stationary room where they watch the same video, before entering the Arctic base station.

Tip: The non-motion line moves much, much faster than the line for the simulator ride. If you are pressed for time, you might want to consider making the ultimate sacrifice (or use this as an excuse for missing what can be a very scary ride).

Note: You may want to take an over the counter medication before you head for the park if you are prone to motion sickness but would like to experience the ride.

The Wild Arctic Aquatic Habitat

Once you wobble off the simulator ride, you enter SeaWorld's most elaborately conceived aquatic habitat, one that would have been a five-star attraction even without the exhilarating thrill ride that proceeds it.

The conceit here is that scientists have discovered the wrecked ships from the expedition of John Franklin, a real-life British explorer who disappeared in 1845 while searching for the nonexistent Northwest Passage. The wreck, it seems, has drawn a wide variety of wildlife seeking shelter and prey, so the scientists "stabilized" the wreck and constructed their observation station around it.

The first "room" of the habitat simulates an open-air space, with the domed ceiling standing in for the Arctic sky. A sign informs us that we are 2,967 miles from SeaWorld in Florida. Gray beluga whales (the name is derived from the Russian word for "white") are being fed in a pool directly in front of us. Thankfully, SeaWorld has not attempted to mimic Arctic temperatures.

Next, we enter the winding tunnels of the research station proper. The walls alternate between the ancient wood of the wrecked vessels and the corrugated steel of the modern structure. We view the animals through thick glass walls; on the other side, temperatures are maintained at comfortably frigid levels for their Arctic inhabitants.

Art imitates reality here in the form of the SeaWorld research assistants, clad in their distinctive red parkas. They are here to answer guests' questions but they are also carrying out valuable scientific research by painstakingly recording the behavior patterns of the polar bears and other animals in the exhibits in an attempt to find ways to short-circuit the repetitive motion patterns that befall many animals in captivity. One strategy has been to hide food in nooks and crannies of the habitat, encouraging the animals to use true-to-nature hunting behaviors to find their food. By the way, the fish swimming with the polar bears usually avoid winding up on the dinner table, although the bears sometimes just can't resist taking a swipe at them.

For most people, the highlight of this habitat will be the polar bears, including the famous twins Klondike and Snow, born in the Denver Zoo, abandoned by their mother, nursed through infancy by their zookeepers, and then placed with SeaWorld as the facility best equipped to nurture them to adulthood. Klondike and Snow alternate in the main viewing area with two older bears. Polar bears are solitary animals so the two pairs are kept separate to avoid any unpleasant scenes. As brother and sister, Klondike and Snow enjoy playing together and, thanks to being raised in captivity, they may never have to be separated.

There are also enormous walruses swimming lazily in a separate pool. Harbor seals appear in a video presentation showing the animals in their natural habitat. The narration is cleverly disguised as the radio transmissions of the scientists gathering the footage for research purposes.

After viewing the animals on the surface, we walk down a series of ramps to an underwater viewing area for a completely different and utterly fascinating perspective. Video monitors show what's happening on the surface and simple controls allow visitors to move the cameras remotely to follow the animals when they climb out of the pool. The set decoration below the surface is every bit as imaginative as it is above, simulating the Arctic Sea beneath the ice shelf.

There's much to explore here, including displays that let kids crawl through a simulated polar bear den or poke their heads through the ice, just like a seal. Dotted throughout the exhibit are touch-sensitive video monitors that let us learn more about the animals we are viewing and the environment in which they live. Just before the exit ramp, a small room offers a variety of interactive entertainments.

One lets you plan a six-week expedition to the North Pole, selecting the mode of transportation, date of departure, food supply, and wardrobe. Then you get to find out how wisely you planned. Another computer offers up a printout that tells, among other interesting facts, how many people have been born since the date of your birth.

Tip: The exit is through the Arctic Shop and a prominent sign says "No Re-Entry." However, late in the day, it appears to be easy to sneak back in through the back door if you'd like another peek at this fabulous habitat.

Fusion

Rating:	★ ★ ★ +
Type:	Water-themed show
Time:	20 minutes
Kelly says:	For those who miss *Baywatch*

This boisterous and fun show takes place in that "paradise where the water meets the land," and mixes a little bit of water skiing, a little bit of derring-do, and a lot of bare flesh to very entertaining effect. It takes place in Atlantis Bayside Stadium and uses both the beach and the lagoon as a stage.

Some of the best bits are the simplest, as when two watercraft tow tiered kites that do a little aerial ballet. Then there's a truly impressive high dive off a teensy platform 80 feet up into water just a few feet from the shore; someone must have dug an awfully deep hole.

A highlight of the show is a routine that takes the idea of playing frisbee with your dog to new heights. After watching this young woman put her mutt through its paces, you'll want to schedule some serious training time with your own pet when you get back home.

The real attraction here, I must admit, is the attractive young cast. The guys are all buff, the girls are all gorgeous and they change into a dazzling variety of swimwear that is as colorful as it is sexy. Between water ski stunts they perform energetic dance numbers to an infectious and hyper-amplified pop-rock beat. Get to the show early so your kids can play with the cast members in the sand.

Note: This show is seasonal. Don't look for it in the colder months.

Mistify

Rating:	★ ★ ★ ★
Type:	Light show and fireworks
Time:	20 minutes
Kelly says:	A fitting finale

SeaWorld has tried some of the elements in *Mistify* before, but now they have been all wrapped up in what's billed as the largest and most spectacular finale in the park's history.

Positioned as springing from the imagination of a child, *Mistify* is a phantasmagoria of water- and sea-themed special effects that unfold in the lagoon just offshore from *The Waterfront*. Hundred-foot-tall walls of water spray serve as screens on which laser images of the sea are projected, as flames erupt and fireworks shoot skyward. There are even underwater light effects. It's a joyful mishmash that's sure to delight and send folks off to the parking lots in a jolly mood.

OTHER ADVENTURES

SeaWorld offers a number of "Behind the Scenes" guided tours, as well as animal interactions, and educational activities. The guided tours carry a nominal additional charge, over and above your admission price. The other activities range from moderately pricey to downright expensive but offer some opportunities to interact with or learn about the animals here that you'd be hard-pressed to find elsewhere.

Guided Tours

If you have the time and interest, these one-hour tours can be fascinating. The guides are members of the education staff and are all extremely knowledgeable, personable hosts. At this writing three guided tours are offered on a regular basis. The cost varies seasonally. Adults tickets are $10, $13, or $16 and tickets for kids 3 to 9 are $8,

$10, or $12. Annual passholders get a modest discount. The schedules are somewhat erratic depending on the number of people expected to visit the park that day and other factors.

Since all tours limit the number of participants, signing up early is advisable. To enquire about schedules and availability, head for the tour desk when you arrive. You'll find it almost directly ahead as you pass through the entrance turnstiles. When you purchase your tours, you will be given a ticket with the name and time of your tour. This serves as your "ticket" and lets the guide know who belongs to the tour and who doesn't. Tours begin at different points in the park. The meeting points are marked with signs. You will be given directions to them when you sign up.

Polar Expedition

This tour has three stops. The first two take you "backstage" at *Wild Arctic*. The first stop is the beluga whale holding pool, where you may be lucky enough to see "off-duty" whales relaxing. Also in this area are some of the seals that keep the belugas company in the exhibit. Then it's off past the huge filtration tanks that keep the artificial salt water in the attraction sparkling clean, to the hidden "den" of the polar bears.

Whether you will actually see any bears depends on your luck with timing. Nothing happens on a rigid or even regular schedule with these animals. Their keepers don't want them to become habituated to a set routine and, so, try to keep the daily sequence of events as it is in the wild — fairly random.

Even if you don't get to see bears through the glass in their den, you can see them on the remote video camera that is focused on their public habitat. You will also get a wealth of fascinating information about polar bears in the wild and the behind-the-scenes world of *Wild Arctic*. You might be told, for example, that the water in the exhibit is kept at 45 to 55 degrees Fahrenheit, just warm enough to prevent ice from forming on the bears' fur. When keepers must enter the water, they wear three wet suits and then can only stay in the water ten minutes before hypothermia starts to set in. You'll even get to pet polar bear fur (courtesy of a deceased bear whose pelt remains behind for its educational value).

The next stop, after a short bus ride, is the chilly confines of the Avian Research lab, where you will have a chance to pet a Magellanic penguin (two fingers only, please!). Penguin mothers have a spotty record when it comes to parenting skills. Abandoned or abused chicks are brought here to be reared in a more caring environment. The center even hatches orphaned eggs. Depending on when you visit, you may see young chicks covered in their downy gray baby coats or molting into the more recognizable sleek black and white of their mature feathers. Penguins are gregarious and curious birds and they will take great interest in your visit, waddling over for a closer look and eyeing you with apparent curiosity. Careful of your fingers!

Predators!

Here's a great chance to pet a shark and find out more about these cartilaginous carnivores we all love to hate. For those who don't like to read, taking this tour can serve as an alternative to reading all that informational signage in the *Shark Encounter* exhibit.

You also get to visit the inner workings of the shark tank, where you can gain some appreciation of the water filtration system. Then comes a chance to examine shark jaws, shark skins, and sawfish bones up close. The piece de resistance is a close encounter with a shark — a small, docile critter, but a shark nonetheless. Reach out your hand and enjoy bragging rights back home.

Saving A Species

SeaWorld is far more than "just" a theme park. This engrossing and entertaining tour highlights SeaWorld's role as a major rescuer and rehabilitator of aquatic — and other — animals. What you see on this tour will depend on which animals are currently in the park's care. You will likely get to see manatees and sea turtles that have been injured, typically by the carelessness of Man. You may see some dolphins, but they are usually here for reasons other than injury. Thanks to its reputation, SeaWorld is sometimes given injured animals that are not part of its usual stock in trade — like snakes, rabbits, and exotic birds. These, too, are on display.

The areas you visit also include an aviary where you can hand feed the birds, as well as tanks used to quarantine sea animals that are new to SeaWorld before they are introduced to the exhibits. If you've ever wondered how to rid sea animals of parasites, this is the place to find out. (Answer: Dip them in fresh water for a few seconds.)

Animal Interaction Programs

Yes, you can interact with the animals at SeaWorld — if you have the money and can meet these programs' age and height requirements. SeaWorld offers four interaction programs, ranging in price from $40 to $399 including tax. One lets you swim with Shamu's cousin, the beluga whale, and learn some training commands. Another gives you an up-close look (but no real interaction, thankfully) with a bunch of sharks.

Despite the high prices, the programs are very much in demand and arrangements have to be made well in advance of your visit. Reservations for all these programs can be made by calling (800) 406-2244 or (407) 363-2380. Reservations can also be made at the Tour desk near the front entrance to the park. Most program fees are non-refundable, although you may be able to reschedule.

Marine Mammal Keeper Experience

Think you'd like to rescue injured manatees or care for beluga whales, seals, and other marine mammals? If you've got $399 ($360 for silver and gold passholders, $349 for platinum), are at least 13 years old, 52 inches tall, and can climb a flight of stairs and lift 15 pounds, and can get yourself to the park by 6:30 a.m., here's your chance to find out. Up to four guests per day get to work with SeaWorld's caregivers, helping to prepare the mammals' food (each species has a special diet) and feed and care for them. The experience lasts eight hours (6:30 a.m. to 2:30 p.m.) and the price includes park admission, lunch, a and a souvenir t-shirt.

Sharks Deep Dive

SeaWorld's coolest up-close and personal experience takes daring visitors on a leisurely 30-minute underwater tour of the mammoth shark tank at the *Shark Encounter* attraction. Participants don a wet suit (provided by SeaWorld) and climb into a submerged shark cage that travels, very slowly, along a 125-foot track through the tank. Specially designed helmets allow you to breathe, and talk!, underwater, even if you are not scuba certified. Along the way, guests will be able to ogle (but not touch) the 50 plus sharks in the tank. Also on display, dimly glimpsed through the depths, will be the diners in the Sharks Underwater Grill restaurant.

As you might have guessed, there is an additional charge for this attraction — $150 per person ($140 for silver and gold passholders, $135 for platinum). These prices include tax as well as a souvenir t-shirt and an informative booklet about sharks. Participants must be at least 10 years of age.

Reservations are required — the ride only accommodates two people at a time — and can be made by calling (800) 406-2244 or (407) 363-2380. Reservations can also be made at the tour desk near the front entrance to the park.

Dolphin Nursery Up Close

For die-hard dolphin fans, SeaWorld offers an hour long behind-the-scenes tour of the Dolphin Nursery. Participants must be at least 10 years old. At $40 a person on top of admission to the park, the experience doesn't come cheap, but for dolphin lovers just the opportunity to get a closer look at the babies may be worth the extra dough. Add in a chance to feed the little ones and to pet the mothers and, with the help of animal care staff members, put them through some of their basic "behaviors," or tricks, and to some this may become a very attractive offer. For the more casual visitor, this may look like a bit less of a bargain.

The tour, which runs only once a day, begins with a presentation by an education staffer on dolphin reproductive physiology, gestation, and parenting. After a half-hour or so, the education person turns the group over to the animal care staff, who brief everyone on what they'll be doing with the dolphins, and split the group into two if necessary to ensure that everyone gets a turn at the various interactions.

Then it's off to the dolphin nursery. Baby dolphins, it turns out, are even more fun than puppies: they bounce around, chatter, steal toys and food from each other, and leap straight into the air when they feel they're not the center of attention. Also like puppies, they tend to explore with their mouths and play games that involve lots of nipping, so hands-on time with the babies is limited, though everyone will get to feed them. Time with the adults is more involved, and we're instructed to give the dolphins special cues to perform various behaviors before rewarding them with fish.

Beluga Interaction Program

SeaWorld's latest animal encounter revolves around the snowy white beluga whales that inhabit the *Wild Arctic* exhibit. This innovative two-hour experience allows you to step into the artfully designed Arctic environment and actually slip into the chilly 55-degree water of SeaWorld's simulated Arctic Ocean.

The adventure begins when you and up to three other intrepid souls don a much needed wet suit and take a tour of the behind-the-scenes area of the exhibit. Then you become part of the show for the tourists as you step into the exhibit itself and sit on the simulated icy shore of the whale's tank. Under the watchful eyes of two trainers, you will have a chance to pet and feed Spooky, a 1,700-pound bundle of beluga. You'll even get a cold peck on the cheek. You may have second thoughts about the wisdom of signing up when you slip into the bone-chilling water.

The fee is $179 per person ($169 for silver and gold passholders, $164 for platinum). Participants must be at least 13 years old.

Family Adventures

SeaWorld offers a smorgasbord of special activities, day camps, and sleep-over programs for kids from kindergarten through the eighth grade (roughly ages 5 through 13). A five and a half hour birthday party with a Shamu theme costs $850 (including tax) for groups of up to 20 kids and adults and typically includes invitations, birthday cake, favors, reserved seats at Shamu Stadium, and the chance to feed some animals.

Adventure Camp is the umbrella name for a series of week-long half-day and full-day programs for kids of various ages. A variety of age-appropriate programs are offered during the year. **Day Camps** typically run from 9:00 a.m. to 5:00 p.m. (programs for younger kids end earlier). Prices, including tax, range from $250 for half-day programs to $350 for the full-day sessions. After-camp care, until 6:00 p.m., can be arranged for an additional fee. **Resident Camps**, where the kids stay overnight, can cost over $1,000 per child.

Year round sleep over programs offer bonding experiences for kids and their parents, including such treats as a Halloween outing to *Shark Encounter*. These overnight events cost about $75 to $80 per person (including tax).

For more information on these programs call (866) 479-2267 or (407) 363-2380; passport holders can call (800) 406-2244 for information on discounts. The email address is education@seaworld.org. A brochure spells out the registration process in some detail. A complete health history and medical release form must accompany all registrations.

Chapter Three:

Discovery Cove

As I write these words, the newspaper carries a short piece about a 14-year-old Italian boy saved from drowning in the Gulf of Manfredonia by a dolphin. The lad, a non-swimmer, fell off a sailboat and was sinking under the waves when he felt something pushing him upward. "When I realized it was Filippo, I hung on to him," the boy was quoted as saying. One can only assume that Filippo is Italian for Flipper!

This is only the latest example of a tale that has been told since antiquity. The frescoes of the ancient Minoan civilization of Crete are alive with playful dolphins, and Greek literature is peppered with accounts of dolphins saving wrecked sailors. So humankind's fascination with this playful and occasionally lifesaving creature has a long and honorable pedigree. And as the story about the boy from Manfredonia illustrates, *Flipper*, the hit TV show about a preternaturally precocious dolphin and his towheaded sidekick, clearly has a hold on the world's imagination long after its original primetime run.

The marketing geniuses at SeaWorld were not blind to this intense fascination with the stars of their animal shows and some years ago instituted the Dolphin Interaction Program (now discontinued) that allowed a small number of guests to duck backstage at SeaWorld and actually meet and swim with the stars of the show. Out of this somewhat makeshift idea, SeaWorld has created Discovery Cove, a whole new class of theme park, the first one to be designed specifically for one-to-one human-animal interactions. At Discovery Cove you can not only swim with dolphins but cruise with stingrays, have tropical fish nibble at your fingers, and let exotic birds perch on your head and shoulders while you feed them by hand.

Because of its unique mission, Discovery Cove has been carefully designed to accommodate a limited number of visitors. Only 1,000 people can come to Discovery Cove each day and only 750 of them will be able to swim with the dolphins. Consequently, reservations are mandatory, whether you will be swimming with the dolphins or not. Discovery Cove will admit walk-ups for its "non-swim" program (i.e. you don't get to interact with the dolphins) *if* there is room. That is a very iffy proposition during the warmer months, but your odds of getting in on short notice improve dramatically in the winter.

This limited-capacity policy is, first and foremost, for the protection of the animals, but it has undeniable benefits for the human visitor. The park clearly has room for more than a thousand, so there is plenty of space to spread out on the expansive beaches. No scrambling for lounge chairs, no shoulder-to-shoulder sunbathing and only the very occasional traffic jam at prime snorkeling spots.

Before You Come

Because of its limited capacity and obvious popularity, a visit to Discovery Cove demands advance planning. Reservations are mandatory and making reservations six months or more in advance is not such a silly idea. Somewhat to the surprise of Discovery Cove's marketing people, more visitors (over 50%) want to swim with the dolphins than had been anticipated. So if a dolphin interaction is your goal, the sooner you book, the better your chances.

While it is extremely unlikely that you will be able to book a dolphin swim on short notice, it can happen, especially if you can be flexible on dates. Cancellations do occur. If you want to visit Discovery Cove and not swim with the dolphins, your chances of getting in at the last minute are only slightly better.

The best plan is to phone regularly before your visit and drop by in person once you have reached Orlando. Obviously, the more people in your party who want to swim with the dolphins, the less likely it is you will be successful. It is also possible that there will be openings for just two people when you have a party of four.

There are two ways to make reservations, by phone or on the Internet. The toll-free reservation line is (877) 434-7268. Overseas visitors can call (407) 370-1280. The Internet address is www.discoverycove.com. You can make a reservation for the day you visit but you cannot reserve a specific time to swim with the dolphins until you arrive at the park, which is a good incentive to arrive early on the day of your visit. More on this later.

When's the Best Time To Come?

Although I don't generally recommend coming to Orlando at the height of the summer if you can possibly avoid it, the tropical island beach resort ambiance of Discovery Cove makes it a delightful place to spend a blistering hot summer's day. The salt water pools are kept nice and cool for the animals and make for a bracing dip. Of course, summer brings with it the increased likelihood of stormy weather. Dolphin interactions will be held in the rain, but will be cancelled if there is lightning in the area.

In late spring and early fall, the weather should be closer to ideal. Winter in Orlando can range from the pleasant to the chilly. At this time of the year, the weather may not be ideal for lounging on the beach but the water temperature may be warmer than the air temperature. On the other hand, crowds are generally smaller during the cooler months and the non-swim package is discounted in January and February (see below). Wet suits are available to ease any discomfort of in-the-water activities.

Getting There

Discovery Cove is located just off I-4, near SeaWorld, on Central Florida Parkway so the driving directions are similar. From the south (i.e. traveling east on I-4) use Exit 71 and you will find yourself pointed directly toward Discovery Cove; it's a little more than half a mile along on your right, a short distance past the SeaWorld entrance on the left.

From the north (i.e. traveling west on I-4), get off at Exit 72, onto the Bee Line Expressway (Route 528). Take the first exit and loop around to International Drive. Turn left and proceed to Central Florida Parkway and turn right. The Discovery Cove entrance will be on your left, almost immediately after turning.

Arriving at Discovery Cove

Self-parking is free and just a short walk from the entrance, or you can drive right up to the front door and opt for valet parking for $10 (plus a tip, which will be expected). These options are clearly marked as you drive in.

Opening and Closing Times

The official opening hours are 9:00 a.m. to 5:30 p.m. but since the first dolphin swim begins at 8:50, the doors are open earlier. It is also possible to linger until 6:00 before you are politely pointed to the exit. My personal recommendation is to arrive early, about 8:00 or 8:15, if you are participating in the dolphin swim. I provide some more advice on timing your dolphin swim later. On the other hand, if you are coming in winter, when the first dolphin swim isn't until 10:00 a.m., you can afford to sleep in a bit. If you choose the 'Twilight Discovery' package, you don't have to arrive until three in the afternoon.

The Price of Admission

Prepare yourself for a shock. Discovery Cove is probably the most expensive theme park you will ever visit. But before you flip immediately to the next chapter, read on. On closer examination, Discovery Cove offers extremely good value for your investment. In my opinion, this very special park is worth every penny. At press time, prices (including tax) for everyone over six years of age were as follows:

All-Inclusive Day Package (includes the dolphin swim):

Late March through October:	$297.13
November through late March:	$265.18

Non-Swim Day Package:

Late March through October:	$190.63
November through late March:	$158.68

'Twilight Discovery' Package:

This option is available May 30 to September 1 only and runs from three in the afternoon until 9:00 p.m.

With dolphin swim:	$275.83
Without dolphin swim:	$169.33

Children under 3 are **free**.

Bear in mind that the price of admission includes a continental breakfast, a very nice lunch, and all your beverages (including beer and wine coolers) throughout the day. Admission also includes seven days admission to either SeaWorld or Busch Gardens Tampa. For an additional fee of $30 (plus tax) you get 14 days admission to both parks.

Trainer for a Day

If those prices didn't take your breath away, perhaps you like to upgrade to the "Trainer for a Day" program. For a mere $446.24 (including tax) you will be treated to a "enhanced dolphin interaction and training encounter" as well as a number of other behind-the-scenes activities. Participants must be at least six years of age and those under 13 must be accompanied by a paying adult.

Dolphin Lover's Sleepover

If you really want to get a jump on the crowds, you can arrive the night before for a sleepover under the stars in a cozy tent. You'll get dinner and breakfast in addition to lunch along with a number of other perks. This option costs $446.23 per person ($414.28 for Platinum, Gold and Silver Annual Passholders at SeaWorld or Busch Gardens Tampa) and is available only on a select few dates each year. Call 800-406-2244 or check the web site for details.

Discounts

Discovery Cove has offered occasional discounts, during slower periods, to annual passholders and via radio station promotions. Promotional discounts do not include the seven days of admission to the theme parks.

Cancellation Policy

Because the number of daily visitors is carefully controlled, a visit to Discovery Cove is more like a tour package or a cruise than a visit to a "regular" theme park. The advance reservation and cancellation policies reflect this fact.

All reservations must be prepaid 45 days prior to your visit, or immediately if your planned visit is less than 30 days away. If you have to cancel your reservation you may incur a penalty. Cancellations made more than 30 days before the reserved date get a full refund; between 15 and 29 days, a 50% refund; between 8 and 4 days, 25%. If you cancel fewer than eight days out, you forfeit the entire amount.

Staying Near the Park

The hotels listed in the SeaWorld chapter are also fairly close to Discovery Cove, although the only one that might reasonably be considered within walking distance is the Renaissance Orlando Resort, and it's a fairly long walk. From the other hotels and motels, the most direct route to Discovery Cove is down busy International Drive, which has no sidewalk along this stretch, making for a long, dangerous (and perhaps muddy) walk. Besides, walking to the park doesn't save you any money since parking at Discovery Cove is free.

Good Things to Know About . . .

Access for the Disabled

Discovery Cove has provided ramps with handrails into many of the water areas. Those who can maneuver themselves into the shallows of the Dolphin Lagoon, will be able to experience the dolphin swim. Special wheelchairs that can negotiate Discovery Cove's sandy beaches are available and work is under way to provide a "platform" that will enable guests to get around in their own wheelchairs. Eventually, Discovery Cove plans to introduce special "flotation chairs." Phone ahead to see what will be available when you visit.

Dolphins

Dolphins have such a wonderful public image as cute and cuddly critters that it's easy to forget that they are, in fact, large, powerful, and unpredictable wild animals. The dolphin PR machine likes to play down the fact that, in their natural state, they vie for dominance by biting, scratching, and fighting. Those scrapes and scars and nicks you'll see on your dolphin friend bear mute testimony to this fact of life in the big bad ocean.

I mention this not to frighten or dissuade you — it's not like you'll be diving into a pool of man-eating sharks — but to encourage you to approach these magnificent creatures with the respect they deserve. Follow your trainer-host's directions and you'll do just fine. Do something stupid and you run the slight but very real risk of injury.

Emergencies

The park is dotted with fully certified lifeguards, but any nearby attendant should be your first stop in an emergency. A first-aid station is located near the Tropical Gifts shop not too far from the front entrance.

Getting Oriented

Discovery Cove does not hand you a paper map as other parks do. Since the park is quite compact, there's really no need. The main axis of the park is a paved walkway, with lockers, changing rooms and restaurant to your right (as you walk from the main entrance) and the beach, lagoons, and river to your left. It's hard to get lost but, just in case, mosaic tile maps called "Points of Discovery" are dotted about on low-slung rocks to help you get your bearings.

Leaving the Park

You may leave the park and return during the day. Just make sure to have your hand stamped as you leave.

Lockers & Changing Rooms

Lockers are free and plentiful. There are two locker locations. There is one near the Dolphin Lagoon and another between the dolphin and stingray pools. You will be directed to a locker location depending on the time of your arrival, but if you have a preference it will most likely be honored. Both locker areas are next to spacious and well-appointed changing rooms complete with showers, extra towels, hair blowers, and toiletries.

Money

The best way to handle money at Discovery Cove is not to. The laminated ID card you receive on arrival bears a bar code that can be linked to your credit card. If you prefer the old-fashioned way, all the shops and refreshment stands accept cash and credit cards.

Pets

Discovery Cove does not have its own kennel facilities. If you arrive with a pet, staffers will escort you to SeaWorld's kennels nearby, where the boarding fee is $6 per animal (bring your own food).

Sunscreen

Don't bother lathering yourself with sunscreen prior to your visit. You'll just be asked to shower it off. Discovery Cove provides its guests, free of charge, a special "dolphin-friendly" sunscreen. Take care when applying it, because a little goes a long way. It doesn't seem to disappear as readily as most commercial sunscreens, so if you use too much you'll look a bit like you've dipped your face in flour. If you like it, you can pick up more in the gift shops.

Dive Right In: Your Day at Discovery Cove

At first blush, it may seem there are only a few things to "do" at Discovery Cove, but they somehow manage to add up to a very full, relaxing, and rewarding day. Think of your day at Discovery Cove not as a visit to a mere theme park but as a day spent at a very exclusive tropical resort with some highly unusual amenities and you will not only approach the experience with the right attitude but increase your odds of getting the most from your investment.

Even if you are not planning to swim with the dolphins, I recommend arriving early. And if you *are* swimming with the dolphins I strongly advise being among the first to arrive. That's because your appointment to meet and swim with a dolphin will not be finalized until you arrive (you can request a morning or an afternoon swim when you make your reservation). The earlier you arrive, the more choice you will have.

My personal feeling is that you are better off being in one of the first dolphin swims of the day. The theory is that in the morning the dolphins are more active and curious, because they've had a night to rest and haven't yet spent a day with overexcited tourists. I'm not actually sure how accurate this theory is. After all, the dolphins have been specifically trained for this duty and each dolphin is limited to just six sessions a day. What's more, if a dolphin shows signs of losing interest, the trainers will simply call for a replacement. Still, I find the theory has a certain appeal. Besides, by doing the dolphin swim first thing, you get your day off to a smashing start and you can relax for the rest of the day, without keeping one eye on your watch for fear of missing your appointment with dolphin destiny. And in the summer, a morning swim slot means you will avoid the afternoon thunderstorms that are an Orlando trademark.

So, assuming you are arriving early, here's how your day at Discovery Cove might play out.

My first bit of advice is to arrive dressed for the water. This is Orlando, remember, and no one at your hotel will think it odd that you are strolling through the lobby dressed in a swim suit, t-shirt, and sandals. If you like, you can bring along "regular" clothes to change into at the end of the day.

Arriving at the main entrance is a bit like arriving at a nice hotel, especially if you have opted for valet parking. The large airy lobby, with its exposed wooden beams and a peaked, thatched roof, is what you might expect at a Polynesian resort. Suspended above you, sculpted blue dolphins frolic amid schools of tiny fish. Arriving guests are directed to one of ten check-in counters, so your wait will be minimal.

Your host will find your reservation and check you in. Your photo will be taken with a digital camera and put on a laminated plastic ID card that you can wear around your neck. The card has a bar code that can be linked to your credit card. That way, you can "pay" for anything in the park with your ID card and settle a single bill on leaving the park. It's a terrific convenience and highly recommended.

If you are booked for a dolphin swim, you will also pick a swim time and be assigned to one of three cabanas. The cabanas are not changing rooms, as the term might suggest, but staging areas where you will be briefed prior to your dolphin encounter. It is your responsibility to arrive at your assigned cabana at the appointed time.

Once checked in, you will join a group of eight or so other guests to be escorted into the park itself. Your guide will tell you a bit about what to expect during your stay and direct you to the lockers and cabanas. During this brief introduction, each family group will pose for a picture, which is included in the cost of admission; you can pick it up later in the day or as you leave the park.

You will be issued a mask, snorkel, towel and dolphin-friendly sunscreen. The snorkel is yours to keep, the mask must be returned. You will also be issued a blue and neon-yellow neoprene vest that is a cross between a wet suit and a flotation device. The vest is required wearing in the water. It is actually a clever way to keep you buoyant and visible (and therefore safe) without making you feel dorky. And, like a wet suit, it provides some comfort in the chilly waters of the *Dolphin Lagoon* and *Coral Reef*. If you'd like more wet suit warmth, you can request an actual wet suit, very much like those worn by the trainers. This one comes to mid-thigh and offers more coverage than the vest alone. For non-swimmers and little ones, stiff yellow life-vests are also available. If you mislay your towel during the day, replacements are readily issued.

Your next stop will most likely be the lockers. They are simple wooden affairs located in shaded palapas. The doors of unclaimed lockers will be open and inside you will find the key, which is on a lanyard so you can wear it around your neck. (The ID card and key, by the way, tuck neatly inside your vest, so they don't get in your way during the day.) Near each locker area is a changing room, should you need it.

If your dolphin swim is later in the day, now it is time to take advantage of the continental breakfast buffet, scope out the beach area, and choose a lounge chair or two to accommodate your party. Take your time and pick a spot that offers the ideal combination of sun and shade to suit your tastes.

If you have followed my advice and arranged an early dolphin swim, it will now be time to head to your assigned cabana to begin your experience; you can have breakfast after your dolphin encounter, or you might want to head straight for the *Ray Lagoon*. This is because the rays will be hungriest in the morning. Trying to feed a full stingray in the afternoon can be a daunting challenge.

Otherwise, you can pretty much take things easy for the rest of the day, basking in the sun, swimming in the river or saltwater pools, visiting the *Aviary*, or eavesdropping on the later dolphin swims as the spirit moves you.

The 'Twilight Discovery' Option

If you choose the Twilight Discovery option, which is available only during the summer months, your day begins at three o'clock in the afternoon and ends at about nine. Your experience, though shorter, will be much the same as if you had opted for a full day, but with a few important differences.

Most important to my way of thinking, is that the dolphin interaction is a "wade" rather than a "swim." In the evening, all interactions with the dolphins take place in shallow water. That means you will miss out on the thrill of being towed by the dolphin which is one of the great highlights of the daytime experience. Of course, that dolphin ride takes time, so without it you get a little more one-on-one time with your flippered friend. Although the evening interaction is the same 30 minutes as during the day, many people who have done both report that it seems longer.

Obviously lunch is not included in the evening option, but dinner is and it is a decided step up from the midday fare. Chefs personally prepare delicacies like blackened sea scallops, or grilled steak and shrimp. They'll even help you create your own pasta dish. Desserts are more lavish as well and include flaming bananas Foster.

Live music is part of the experience, too, and you can expect lively limbo dancing on the Laguna Grill patio. The crowds tend to be smaller in the evening and it's possible to slip off somewhere relatively quiet with that special someone and savor the sunset in this very special place.

Attractions at Discovery Cove

Discovery Cove has a limited number of "attractions" but they are some of the best to be found in the Orlando area. They are enjoyable enough that you may be surprised to find a very full day seems all too short.

Swim with the Dolphins

Rating:	★ ★ ★ ★ ★
Type:	Animal interaction
Time:	About 30 minutes
Kelly says:	An unforgettable experience

Your dolphin encounter begins when you arrive at your appointed cabana at the appointed hour for a briefing. This is primarily an exercise in heightening your anticipation with a brief video, but a trainer does put in an appearance to offer some pertinent safety tips, such as keeping your hands away from the dolphin's blow hole. ("It'd be sorta like me sticking my finger in your nose," she points out helpfully.)

Following the briefing you and your "pod" of anywhere from six to nine people will be led to the lagoon. I have heard conflicting reports on the maximum group size for the dolphin encounter. Nine people is said to be the maximum and seven or eight the preferred number. There were six in my group.

At water's edge you meet the two trainers who will guide your encounter. Your first challenge is getting used to the chilly water, which is kept between 72 and 76 degrees Fahrenheit for the comfort of the dolphins.

The dolphins make a splashy entrance, zipping from their holding pen and leaping into the air in greeting before splitting off to head to their respective human pods. Eagerly, you wade to the edge of a sharp drop-off to meet your new dolphin friend. The dolphin you meet may have been specially trained for duty at Discovery Cove or may be an old pro. I swam with Capricorn, an aging movie star of sorts who was 36 and had appeared in *Jaws III*.

Here at the edge of deep water you and the other members of the group will get to rub down your dolphin, a tactile interaction the dolphin obviously enjoys. Then you take the plunge into deep water for the main part of the experience. How many people go out at one time is a function of the size and makeup of your group. Our trainers said they usually take people out as couples, but since there were two singles in our group we went out in threes.

Exactly what you do with your dolphin will depend to some extent on what behaviors the dolphin has been trained to perform, but you will almost certainly be able to give some hand signals to which the dolphin will respond by chattering excitedly or spinning in a circle. The interaction is carefully planned so that every member of your group gets equal access to the dolphin and no one feels cheated of one-on-one time with their frisky friend. You will also have a chance to feed your new friend several times in the course of the interaction. This tends to keep the dolphin interested, but don't be surprised if your dolphin decides to take an unscheduled break to check out something of greater interest elsewhere in the pool. This is normal apparently and if your dolphin shows sufficient lack of interest in the proceedings the trainers will simply call in an understudy.

For most people, the highlight of the interaction comes at the end when they place one arm over the dolphin's back and cup their other hand over a flipper and get towed back to the shallows. There they pose in a sort of hug with their new-found friend for the photographer who has been carefully documenting the entire dolphin interaction for posterity and profit.

Tip: Bring a face mask, minus the snorkel, along for your encounter. The snorkel is not really necessary but the mask will give you an interesting perspective on the dolphin. When not in use, it can be pushed up to your forehead.

Back ashore, you are led to another palapa where a series of iMacs have been set up for you to view the photos of you and your family. The technology is impressive and so are the prices should you decide to purchase a print. It's $30 for a five-by-seven inch print in an inexpensive cardboard frame. and some key chains More practical, but more expensive, are CDs with five photos ($100), ten ($150), or 20 ($200). Most people contented themselves with a single souvenir shot, while I went only moderately crazy. Another option is a 60-minute video of your dolphin encounter. The first half hour is pretty much the same video you saw during your preswim briefing, but the second half stars you. The cost is $60. Of all the elements at Discovery Cove, the pricing of the photos and video was the only thing I heard the slightest complaint about.

Tip: You collect your photos later, at Adventure Photo, next to the main gift shop. Pick them up early and stash them in your locker. A line starts forming at around 3:00 p.m. and it gets longer as the day wears on.

Unfortunately, you are not allowed to take those nifty disposable underwater cameras along with you — the dolphins might pinch them and do themselves an injury, I was told. But if a non-swimming member of your party is an accomplished photographer with a telephoto lens, he or she may be able to get some great shots from the shore.

Tropical River

Rating: ★ ★ +
Type: Circular river
Time: Unlimited
Kelly says: Best for the Aviary

If you've visited a water park, you've probably experienced a variation of this attraction. It's a circular fresh water "river," varying in depth from three to 12 feet, with an artificial current that will bear you lazily along. The river rings the ray pool and the *Coral Reef* and takes about 20 minutes to circumnavigate at an easy pace. This is strictly a one-way river; swimming against the current is discouraged by the lifeguards stationed along the route and it is virtually impossible to be out of sight of a lifeguard. The river is kept several degrees warmer than the saltwater pools. After visiting a saltwater pool like the *Coral Reef*, the river will feel like a warm bath.

Most people bring along their snorkels, although there are no fish in the river and very little to see. An attempt has been made to add visual interest by studding the bottom with chunks of Mayanesque ruins and visitors seem to have created their own decorative touches by arranging stones on the bottom in the form of peace symbols, smiley faces, and hearts.

The edges of the river are attractively landscaped with lush tropical foliage but the banks are high and rocky and there are only four places to enter or exit. The main entrance, between the Dolphin Lagoon and the ray pool, broadens out into a large lagoon-like pool backed by a very pretty waterfall behind which is a cool cave-like area.

The best section of the *Tropical River* is the one that passes through the *Aviary*. Heavy waterfalls at either end prevent the birds from escaping. Inside is a tropical paradise and you may be surprised at how closely you can approach birds perched at the water's edge. You can step out of the river here and visit the birds at even closer range.

Aviary

Rating:	★ ★ ★ ★ +
Type:	Animal interaction
Time:	Continuous viewing
Kelly says:	Discovery Cove's best-kept secret

Imagine a jungle paradise where the birds are so tame they'll eat out of your hand and foot-high deer peek about the blossoms as you pet them. This is what you'll find if you step out of the *Tropical River* into the very special world of Discovery Cove's jungle aviary.

The *Aviary* is populated with some 200 exotic birds representing 100 species from the four corners of the world, many of them so intriguingly colored that they look more like products of the vivid imaginations of folk artists than creatures from the natural world. Since many of the birds found here have been hand-raised by Discovery Cove trainers, they are completely tame and will happily eat out of your hand. Food is readily available from some of those same trainers, who can also answer your questions about which bird is which. Typically there are one or two examples of each species, but in some cases, like the gaudily colored conures, you will see a small flock flying through the trees or perching on the branches. There are actually three aviaries here. There is one on each side of the river and the far aviary has a smaller aviary within it housing tiny birds like hummingbirds.

The type of food you choose — grain pellets, fruit, or meal worms — will determine which birds you attract, and unlike the dolphin encounter, your time here is unlimited. You can also feed the tiny muntjac deer, which have their own special diet. If you'd like to develop your bird-watching skills, ask one of the attendants for a laminated chart that identifies the species in the *Aviary*.

Tip: Most people discover the *Aviary* while cruising down the *Tropical River*, but there are two unmarked land entrances just past the *Ray Lagoon*. They make visiting the *Aviary* several times during the course of the day a very tempting option. Remember, there are three separate areas in the *Aviary*. Don't miss any of them.

Ray Lagoon

Rating: ★ ★ ★
Type: Animal interaction
Time: Continuous viewing
Kelly says: Little kids love it

This shallow saltwater pool seems only slightly larger than the concrete ray pool over at SeaWorld. But instead of hanging over the edge, here you can wade right in and snorkel with these intriguing little critters whose scary look belies their sweet and docile nature. What's more, you don't have to pay a small fortune to feed them here; food is freely available at regular intervals from the attendants, who are extremely knowledgeable sources of information about their charges.

Tip: If you have your heart set on feeding a stingray, come early in the day. Unlike some of us, stingrays are smart enough to stop eating when they are full.

Coral Reef

Rating: ★ ★ ★ +
Type: A swim-through aquatic habitat
Time: Continuous viewing
Kelly says: A great snorkeling experience guaranteed

Having been disappointed on several snorkeling outings in the real tropics, I was impressed by the variety of multicolored tropical fish on display in this clever re-creation of a coral reef. It's not real coral, of course, but a thin film of algae encourages fish to nibble at the simulated coral outcroppings very much as they do on the real thing.

Here you can snorkel to your heart's content without worrying about visibility being lessened by churning surf. Nor do you have to worry about those nasty little things — jellyfish, fire coral, and moray eels — that frequent real reefs. And the sharks and barracudas are thoughtfully kept behind thick (but virtually invisible) sloping glass walls. You get the illusion of swimming above them without the bone-chilling fear that typically arrives with the realization that you are swimming a few feet from something that might eat you.

The fish are fed periodically, and when the water around you is swirling with bits of food, it will also be alive with a kaleidoscope of fish. Put out your hand and the bolder among them will nibble hopefully at your fingertips as large manta rays cruise the depths below.

Dining at Discovery Cove

Your lunch is included in the price of admission and is served cafeteria-style from 11:00 a.m. to 4:00 p.m. at the **Laguna Grill**, another imposing Polynesian-style structure about halfway into the park. Although the service style may bring back memories of your high school lunch room, the food is surprisingly good if somewhat limited in choice.

This is not an all-you-can-eat buffet but a set meal that includes an entree, a side salad, a soft beverage, and a dessert. Your entree can be either a warm dish or a cold salad, with just a few simple choices in each category. The salads are the fairly standard chef's, chicken or seafood, while the hot entrees tend to be simple pasta combinations or stir fry dishes, the sorts of things that can be served up easily from a steam table. Made-to-order burgers are also available. I found the quality to be quite good although not exceptional. All seating is outdoors, most of it well shaded.

Care is taken to assure you get only one "free" meal; an attendant swipes the bar code of your ID card when you pick up your food. If you want seconds or crave another meal later in the day, you will have to pay for it, but the prices are moderate.

There are two **beach bars** located elsewhere in the park, one near the Dolphin Lagoon and the other near the stingray pool and Aviary. Here you can get soft drinks, iced tea, fruit punch, and lemonade as well as beer and wine. More elaborate fruit smoothies and similar concoctions are also available, as are ice cream floats, sundaes and other "fountain treats." Again, the pricing is moderate.

Shopping at Discovery Cove

The relentless merchandising that characterizes virtually all theme parks is mercifully muted at Discovery Cove. The major shopping venue, **Tropical Gifts**, an airy Polynesian-style building, is strategically located near the main entrance, so you can pick up the bathing suit you desperately need as you enter and the high-priced souvenir you almost certainly do not need as you leave.

The merchandise is as airy and high-class as the surroundings. Here you will find the kind of upscale resort wear for men and women that will tempt you even if you didn't forget to pack your bathing suit or outerwear. For those who want a more tangible souvenir, there is a large variety of dolphin figurines and sculptures in all price ranges; the more elaborate sculptures can range up to $20,000. You will also find some very nice jewelry in dolphin, sea turtle, stingray and other deep sea motifs at moderate prices. On a more practical level, you can find things like film and more of that dolphin-friendly sunscreen you got when you arrived. I would recommend picking up one of the inexpensive disposable underwater cameras. You won't be able to take it with you to meet the dolphins, but you'll find plenty of use for it elsewhere in the park.

Near the Tropical Gifts store is the **Dolphin Photo** counter where you come to claim the complimentary family photo that was snapped on your arrival and any dolphin photos you ordered earlier. Nearby are the **Aviary Photo** and **Ray Photo** counters, in case you got snapped at these areas.

Chapter Four:

Gatorland

THOSE BORN DURING WORLD WAR II OR EARLIER, MAY REMEMBER THE ROADSIDE attractions that dotted the tourist landscape. Half carnival side-show, half shanty town, these entrepreneurial "attractions" served as living proof of Mencken's maxim that "no one ever went broke underestimating the taste of the American public." Trading on actual freaks of nature ("See the two-headed calf!") or objects of less certain provenance ("Mummified Indian chief!"), the typical roadside attraction tended to spread incrementally along the highway as the owner figured out new ways to lure the passing parade of cars with stranger wonders or larger souvenir shops featuring the latest in joy buzzers and whoopee cushions. Each year, it seemed, the advertising budget would finance a few more garish billboards, a few more miles away, until tourists knew hundreds of miles in advance that something extraordinary lay ahead. The old roadside attractions were a blight on the landscape. They were tacky, lowbrow, often smelly, and altogether marvelous. They represent one of the most cherished memories of my youth and I wish they were still around.

At Gatorland, they still are - in a way. Gatorland is a modern and evolving nature-themed attraction. It is well-run, clean, and in spite of the 5,000 alligators crammed into its 110 acres, remarkably smell free. But its roots are firmly in the roadside attraction tradition. In fact, that's how it started out back in 1949.

Owen Godwin was a local cattle rancher - Florida was once America's second-biggest cattle producer, after Texas - who decided to turn a liability into an asset. Alligators were the Florida cattleman's nemesis. They would hunker down in water holes and kill unsuspecting calves. This intolerable loss of income prompted a vendetta against the gator, and cattlemen became adept at capturing and killing the scaly predators. Godwin realized not only that there was a market for the hides and meat of the gators he killed but that few of the tourists who whizzed past on highway 441 had ever seen an alligator and might pay for the privilege. So Godwin rounded up some gators and a passel of the snakes that thronged his property and the "Snake & Reptile

Village" was born, beckoning to the southbound tourist traffic. Even today, in spite of Orlando's phenomenal post-Mickey growth, Gatorland's location seems a bit out of the way. In 1949, it really must have seemed in the middle of nowhere.

Gatorland has come a long way since its early days, not so much in its look and feel as in its focus and attitude. For a while Godwin followed the pattern of many roadside attractions. As he prospered, he traveled farther afield, adding "exotic" animals to his collection. Those days are long past and only a few holdovers from that era remain.

For many years, Gatorland was a working alligator "farm," sending over 1,000 gators to market each year. So successful was the Gatorland model that it sparked a renaissance in alligator farming across the American south. So Gatorland phased out its farming operation to concentrate on the zoological side of the operation and the conservation of Florida species. Gatorland is also a partner with the University of Florida in alligator research and is the only place on earth where alligators are bred through artificial insemination.

Compared to the big attractions in town – Disney, Universal, and SeaWorld – Gatorland is downright modest. Many of the exhibits are made of simple cinder block construction painted white and green, and I'm sure the appearance of much of the park hasn't changed a whole lot since the sixties. Rather than a being a drawback, I find this homey quality to be a large part of Gatorland's charm. If you don't come with exaggerated expectations fueled by Hollywood scenic artists and are willing to accept the park on its own low-key terms, you won't be disappointed.

Before You Come

There is no pressing need to do in-depth research prior to a visit, but if you'd like to check prices or hours you can call Gatorland at (800) 393-5297 or (407) 855-5496. The web site is www.gatorland.com. On the web site, you will find a chat Forum where you can ask questions about the park and join in "discussions about crocodilians in general."

When's the Best Time to Come?

Even at the height of the tourist seasons, Gatorland will be far less mobbed than the larger attractions. The best time to visit, then, is dictated more by the patterns of the animals than those of the people who come to see them.

Alligators are cold blooded and derive their warmth from the sun and surrounding atmosphere. Thus, in the winter they tend to be slow moving and sluggish, not that they're particularly lively in the best of circumstances. April and May is breeding time and if you visit then you will be entertained by the bellowing of amorous males attracting their mates. It sounds a bit like a lovesick Harley if you can imagine such a thing. Alligators lay hard-shelled eggs in nests on the ground. So by June you may be able to see nests in the *Alligator Breeding Marsh*. The hatchlings emerge in late August and early September, when visitors will be treated with dozens of joyous events in the **Gator Grunts Nursery**. Birds have their own migratory and mating patterns. Nesting in the *Breeding Marsh* begins in January or February, hits its peak in April and May, and continues through the summer, as various species arrive to hatch and raise their young. Regardless of when you come, don't arrive too late in the day. If you arrive mid-afternoon, you may miss some of the shows.

Getting There

Gatorland is located at 14501 South Orange Blossom Trail, also known as US Routes 441, 17, and 92, in the southern fringes of Orlando. It is seven miles south of the Florida Mall and 3.5 miles north of US 192 in Kissimmee. To reach Gatorland from I-4, take either the Bee Line Expressway (SR 538) or Central Florida Parkway east to Orange Blossom Trail and turn right.

Gatorland will be on your left as you drive south, made prominent by its trademark alligator jaws entrance. There is parking for about 500 cars, which gives you an indication of the size of the crowds they expect. Parking is **free** and all spaces are a short walk from the entrance.

Opening and Closing Times

Gatorland is open from 9:00 a.m. until dusk. In the off season that means until 5:00 p.m., in peak season until 6:00 p.m. Call ahead or check the web site before your visit for exact hours. The park, which is largely out of doors, operates rain or shine, 365 days a year.

The Price of Admission

At press time, admission prices (including tax) were as follows:

Adults:	$19.95
Children (3 to 12):	$12.95

Annual passes are $35.09 and $21.28 (tax included), for adults and kids, respectively. You can upgrade to the annual pass before leaving the park on the day of your visit. If you think you will return within a year, this is a good deal. I suspect it will appeal most to bird watchers and nature photography buffs, who will find plenty to keep them occupied at various times of the year. Gatorland's annual pass is good only for admission to the park. It does not give you a discount on food or at the gift shop, nor does it allow you to bring in guests at a discount.

Discounts

Members of AAA, CAA (Canadian Automobile Association), AARP, and the military receive a 20% discount on admission. Also check the Gatorland web site, where tickets can be purchased online, for additional discount offers. Discounts cannot be combined. Gatorland also offers a series of special discount offers to Florida residents, so locals should inquire about current offerings.

Good Things to Know About . . .

Access for the Disabled

The entire park is accessible to the disabled (with the exception of the third level of the Observation Tower in the *Alligator Breeding Marsh*) and wheelchairs are available on a rental basis for $10.45 (plus tax) per day. There is also an electric scooter available for $21.30 per day. Both rentals require that you leave your driver's license or other photo ID as a deposit.

Babies

Strollers are available from the same location as wheelchairs, also require an ID as deposit, and rent for $7.45 a day. Diaper changing facilities will be found in all restrooms.

Leaving the Park

When you pay your admission, your hand will be stamped with a gator symbol. It allows you to leave (for lunch perhaps?) and return on the same day.

Money

An ATM hooked up to the Cirrus, Plus, PULSE, and STAR systems is located in the gift shop.

Safety

Alligators may look like they never move a muscle but they can move with surprising speed when a meal is in the offing. And to an alligator your toddler looks an awful lot like lunch. The railings over the alligator lake have been fitted with green mesh guards to discourage leaning over the sides. Nonetheless, I have seen people lift their children onto the railings and lean them over for a closer look or to help them feed the gators.

DON'T DO THIS! You will not only give people like me heart failure but if your child wriggles loose and falls he or she could very well be killed.

Special Diets

Gatorland's eateries are not equipped to handle special diets. However, Gatorland welcomes picnickers, so feel free to bring your own meals. In fact, feel free to bring an entire cooler. There are several nice areas to eat your own meals; just ask a park employee. No alcoholic beverages are permitted and Gatorland requests that you do not bring any glass containers into the park.

Eating at Gatorland

Your choice of restaurants at Gatorland is easy; there's really only one. **Pearl's Patio Smokehouse** is a wood-sided, tin-roofed, Florida-style fast-food stand, with paper plates and outdoor seating. A few steps away is a covered seating area, closer to the *Alligator Breeding Marsh*. Here you can sit at a small counter facing a pen holding a pair of emus, who will cruise by looking for a handout.

The featured attraction at Pearl's is alligator served up in two ways: as breaded, deep-fried "nuggets" or (my personal choice) as barbecued ribs, both for about $6 a serving. Or you can get a sampler platter that features both, for $7. It would really be a shame to come to Gatorland and not try this local delicacy. My observation, however, is that many people are not yet ready to take the plunge. If you are one of them, you needn't worry about going hungry. Good old reliable hot dogs, turkey subs, ham and cheese, and smoked chicken breast sandwiches, and French fries are all available at modest prices. Beer is $3.

Tip: Pearl's is right next door to the *Gator Wrestlin'* arena. Consider taking your lunch over there and eating while you grab a good seat and wait for the show to begin.

Other than Pearl's your only choice is the **Ice Cream Churn**, near the *Gator Jumparoo* attraction. The name says it all.

Shopping at Gatorland

What better way to commemorate your visit to Gatorland than with a photo of yourself with a real, live alligator. No, you don't get a chance to pose with any of the 12-foot whoppers you saw in the pool, but you can have your picture taken while holding a small gator whose jaws have thoughtfully been taped shut. If gators aren't your cup of tea, you can also have a boa constrictor draped decoratively over your shoulders. Photo prices start at $10.95 for prints, and $14.95 for T-shirts. The stand can be found right next to the *Gator Jumparoo* area.

In *Alligator Alley,* you may find an outdoor stand that offers a variety of paintings, both complete and completed on-the-spot. The watercolors painted on-demand that feature a child's name done in flowers, bugs, fish and other figures seemed to be popular with shoppers. Listed price for this service was $2 per letter plus $3 for the painting to be rolled and packed in a tube, or $8 for a matte board frame. The stand appears to offer frequent specials, however, so you may get a better deal on the day of your visit.

But the real shopper's paradise is the gift shop through which you stroll on your way out of the park. For such a modest park, Gatorland has a surprisingly upscale gift shop, with an extensive range of alligator skin products. The price tags are truly heart-stopping but if you've done any comparison shopping you will realize there are some real bargains to be had here, from gorgeous boots for men to purses for women to wallets and belts for everyone.

In addition to the pricier items, the gift shop carries a full assortment of standard tourist souvenirs, from mugs and refrigerator magnets to alligator claw backscratchers and games for kids. There's lots to see here and you can always return to shop another day without paying admission to the park.

Swamp Thing: Your (Half) Day at Gatorland

Gatorland has trademarked the phrase "Orlando's best half-day attraction." That seems about right to me. Many people stay for a shorter period and it's doubtful you will stay longer unless you are an ardent bird watcher or a wildlife photographer willing to wait for that perfect shot. In any event, you can take your time here. There is never any need to rush madly from place to place to avoid long lines or crushing crowds.

As I mentioned before, Gatorland is modest in both scale and execution. Unlike the bigger parks, it's not filled with attendants and hosts; you are pretty much on your own, although you can certainly feel free to collar one of the "gator wranglers" with your questions. These guys take turns hand-feeding and wrestling gators and handling deadly snakes. They are knowledgeable, charming, and maybe just a little nuts. They are one of Gatorland's major assets. You will recognize them by their distinctive swamp explorers' outfits that grow wetter and sweatier and dirtier as the day wears on.

The park is an elongated rectangle divided lengthwise into three main parts. The first is a huge alligator-clogged lake that stretches the entire length of the park. When you enter the park from the Gift Shop after paying your admission you step onto a large wooden platform over this lake. The platform is honeycombed with open areas filled with sunbathing and swimming gators. One of these openings is the site of the *Gator Jumparoo* show, Gatorland's signature attraction. Also on this platform is a space set aside for children's birthday parties.

Across the wooden platform, you will find *Alligator Alley*, the second major area of the park. It is a long, narrow, shaded concrete walkway that runs north and south through the middle of the park. It is instantly recognizable by the wavy, blue-green, snake-like line down its middle. Along this walkway you will find a variety of displays, animal pens, and scientific work areas, as well as (at the southern end) the *Gator Wrestlin'* arena and Pearl's Smokehouse.

On the other side of *Alligator Alley* is the third major area, a 10-acre *Alligator Breeding Marsh*, with its wooden walkway and Observation Tower, and behind that the crocodile exhibits. The *Swamp Walk*, reached through a gate at the south end of the park, comprises a separate fourth area.

The Half-Day Stay

When you pay your admission, you will be given a folded Gatorland map with a list of permanent attractions, and a schedule of the day's shows printed on a paper slip and tucked inside. Check to see the starting time of the next show. If you have more than half an hour before show time, spend it gawking at the huge gators in the main pool. This should whet your appetite for what's to come.

Your first order of business should be the live shows. It doesn't much matter in which order you see them. You may want to consider seeing the wrestling show twice. In between shows, you can check out the smaller exhibits dotted along the spine of the park.

Give yourself at least 20 uninterrupted minutes or more to take in the *Alligator Breeding Marsh and Bird Sanctuary*, more if it's nesting season. You'll probably want to spend some time at the highest level of the **Observation Tower** for a great bird's-eye view and then take a leisurely stroll along the water level walkway for a closer look. The *Swamp Walk* is restful but not a must-see unless you're a bird watcher. Remember to bring along your binoculars for a closer look at the wildlife.

Attractions at Gatorland

There are three live shows at Gatorland, each presented several times a day, and they form the heart of the Gatorland experience. The shows let us get close - but not too close - to critters that alternately fascinate and repel us. Since alligators, crocodiles, and other reptiles are a natural source of curiosity for most of us, it's easy for these shows to jump right in and start answering our unasked questions about these scaly creatures. The result is that staple of the modern-day theme park: effortless "edutainment." A group of about five young men and women, all Florida natives, takes turns starring in these exhibitions. They have mastered an easy, laid back, aw-shucks, country boy style that is most ingratiating. The humor - and there's lots of it - is self-deprecating while at the same time letting us city slickers know who's got the really cool job. These guys are the living embodiment of Gatorland and I think you'll find it hard not to like them.

Gator Jumparoo

Rating:	★ ★ ★ ★
Type:	Outdoor show
Time:	15 minutes
Kelly says:	As close as it gets to performing alligators

The scene is a large open square in the wooden platform over the alligator lagoon. The cause for gathering: there's been a mishap in the previous gator wrestlin' show, and now there's an opening for a new gator wrestler. Two enthusiastic backwoods kids, suited up in denim overalls and tagged with goofy country names like Bubba and Lulu Belle, will compete for the slot by feeding the resident gators with increasing daring and dramatic flair. The two are supervised by a slightly more civilized announcer, who warms up the crowd and separates the two wannabes when emotions run high and squabbles break out (such as when Bubba 'flips' his chicken at his opponent – get it? He 'flipped' her the bird…).

After the opening skit, each half of the audience is assigned a key word to encourage the gators to leap for the chicken parts temptingly dangled over the water, the host rings the bell, and the fun begins. Alerted by the commotion, mammoth gators swim lazily into view. Slowly, they zero in on the morsels over their heads. They begin to lunge upwards at the bait, urged on by cheers from the crowd. Alligators jump by curling their tails on the shallow bottom and thrusting upwards. A successful leap is something to see and will make a great snapshot for the photographer with good timing.

Once the gators are suitably excited and the contestants riled up and raring to win the points that will ensure their position as Gatorland's newest wrestler, the host ups the ante. After a brief interlude that involves the use of whole chickens as boxing gloves and an explanation of the difference between crocodiles and alligators ("the spellin'," asserts Bubba, while the other eagerly corrects him: "no, my mama taught me this… crocodile goes best with a merlot, but alligator is nicest with a pinot grigio…"), the competitors retreat to raised platforms on either side of the beach, armed with several whole chicken carcasses, and commence hand-feeding the now-lively gators. The thick leather belts around their waists, attached to thick chains, ensure that while a gator might make off with an arm, the rest of the contestants will be spared.

And despite the clowning and hijinks, they are clearly skilled handlers, expert in the ways of gators and genuinely respectful of the animals. There's no denying that the stars of the show are the imposing carnivores, and the banter is low-key enough to keep the gators at the forefront.

This show appeals to some of our most primordial fascinations with animals and it's an appeal that's hard to deny. Most people find this show very entertaining. Precisely how exciting the show is will depend to some extent on when you visit. During the cooler months, alligators tend to be sluggish. Under optimum conditions, the gators leap lustily, flashing their pale undersides and gaping maws as they snare lunch.

The best seats in the house. First of all, there are no seats, just a railing. If you're not in the first row, your view will be somewhat impaired. The best view is to be found along the side directly facing the small beach and platforms. Arrive about ten minutes early to secure a spot by the rail.

Gator Wrestlin'

Rating:	★ ★ ★ ★ ★
Type:	Outdoor show
Time:	15 minutes
Kelly says:	Best show at Gatorland

Gatorland's best show takes place in an open-air arena next to Pearl's Smokehouse. Covered bleachers face a sunken sandy platform surrounded by a small moat and a raised border that (we hope) keeps the gators from getting out. Twelve gators, about seven or eight feet long, lie on the sand sunning themselves.

This is a two-man show. Ostensibly one is the host and the other the gator wrangler, but I suspect the second man is there in case the wrangler gets in trouble. This show is obviously for real and there's no disguising the fact that it's hard work. ("I never finished school," the wrangler says. "So you kids out there study real hard or you might wind up doin' this.")

Alligator wrestling began, we are told, as a matter of necessity. Alligators would hide in water holes and take the occasional calf. The cattle boss would order the hands to get that gator out. Their courage bolstered by a little moonshine, the ranch hands would oblige. Eventually, the practice became a competitive sport that gave young men a chance to show off their courage and prowess. Which is exactly what happens in this show. The show begins with the wrangler kicking the gators off their sunny perch into the moat. They hiss their annoyance. Then a kid picked from the audience carefully picks out the biggest one for the wrangler to wrestle. Resigned to his fate, the wrangler drags the wriggling, hissing, and none too cooperative beast onto the sandy platform.

Along with an informative patter about alligators, often made breathless by the exertion of keeping a 150-pound gator motionless, the gator wrangler shows off a few of the tricks of the trade - like pulling back the gator's head and placing his chin across its closed jaws. Despite his assurance that it doesn't take much pressure to hold a gator's jaws closed, you respect and admire his gumption. At one point, the wrangler pries the gator's jaws apart to show us his teeth. "If this works, it's gonna make you a pretty nice little snapshot," he says and then adds with perfect backwoods sang froid, "If this don't work, it's gonna make you a pretty nice little snapshot."

Maybe there's less to wrestling gators than meets the eye, but I wouldn't bet on it. The casual machismo and sly good humor with which these fellows put their charges through their paces makes for a thoroughly entertaining 15 minutes. After the show, the stage area is mobbed with audience members eager to ask questions ("Didja ever get bit?") and shake the hand of someone with the guts to wrestle a gator.

Photo op: For $10, you (or your child) can briefly pose sitting on the back of a gator. There is an additional charge for prints of the photo that the park photographer will take of you. The gator's jaws are securely taped shut, and a gator wrangler is close at hand, so there's no real danger. A limited number of opportunities are provided on a first-come-first-served basis before and after selected *Gator Wrestlin'* performances.

Up Close Encounters

Rating:	★ ★ ★ +
Type:	Outdoor show
Time:	15 minutes
Kelly says:	Poisonous snakes and other creepy-crawlies

This show comes by its name honestly, so if getting personal with an assortment of creepy-crawlies isn't your cup of tea, you may want to skip this one in favor of something a bit less heavy on audience participation. Surprise also plays a major role in the unveiling of the various critters, so don't count on your ability to pick and choose which animals you'll want to be friendly with.

That said, this is a fun, irreverent, and highly informative presentation. The hosts explain to us that Gatorland frequently has to deal with surprise drop-offs, as locals unload their unwanted exotic pets here by leaving them in unmarked boxes outside the entrance. Given the indigenous wildlife's propensity to use venom, stingers, and other nasty surprises on unsuspecting box-openers, the staff at Gatorland have tired of risking their lives at this pursuit and so opted to turn the tables and have us, the audience, take over the dirty work – literally. They scamper through the seats, distributing small wooden crates and taking the names of the folks sitting next to them. One by one, they call these audience members onto the stage and introduce them – and the rest of us – to the contents of their crates, which range from scary-looking but mild-mannered tarantulas, to venomous snakes. "Don't step over the Line of Death," the hosts cheerfully warn. Most audience members seemed quite happy to comply.

Gatorland Express Railroad

Rating:	★ ★
Type:	Swamp train ride
Time:	15 minutes
Kelly says:	Easy intro to gator lore

The *Gatorland Express Railroad* leaves about every 20 minutes from a small station behind Lily's Pad. It's a scaled-down steam engine that takes you on a lazy loop circling the *Alligator Breeding Marsh* and crocodile exhibits (see below). While not the most exciting of experiences, it provides a painless introduction to Gatorland and alligator lore. There is, however, an additional $2 charge for this attraction, which is probably not worth it unless your kids insist. On the other hand, the charge lets you ride as often as you wish. In the humid summer months, a chance to sit down in the shade, feel the breeze as the train chugs along, and let someone else show you around shouldn't be underrated.

The engineer/narrator is a gator wrangler taking a break from his more strenuous chores at the live shows. He points out sights of interest along the route and fills you in on Gatorland's purpose and the range of its attractions. The train makes a stop by Pearl's Smokehouse, near the entrance to the *Jungle Crocs*; you can get off here but can't get on.

Alligator Breeding Marsh and Bird Sanctuary

Rating: ★ ★ ★ ★ +
Type: Observation platforms and walkways through a
                 wildlife sanctuary
Time: As long as you wish
Kelly says: Bring your binoculars

This is one of Gatorland's more recent attractions and one of its most successful, in its own low-key way. The concept was ingenious: Build a natural setting in which some 100 female and 30 male alligators would feel free to do what comes naturally and provide a steady stream of new alligators to enthrall visitors and serve the growing market for gator meat and hides. But because birds like to nest over alligator holes for the protection they provide against predators like raccoons, opossum, snakes, and bobcats, Gatorland hoped for a bonus population of wild birds. They built it . . . and they came. So happy with their surroundings are the gators, that some females have taken to setting up their nests underneath the wooden boardwalk, prompting Gatorland staff to build additional barriers at these points to keep protective Mama 'Gator and Foolhardy Tourist safely apart.

Today there are over 1,000 bird nests in active use at Gatorland. Here you will find the magnificent, bright white great egret with its majestic plumage alongside the more dowdy green and blue herons. There are also snowy egrets, cattle egrets, and tricolor egrets. With a bit of luck you might also spot an osprey perched high in a pine tree, surveying the alligator pool below and weighing his chances for a fish dinner.

The *Alligator Breeding Marsh* has three entrances. To the north near *Lilly's Pad* and to the south near Pearl's Smokehouse you can gain access to the wooden walkway that runs the length of the alligator lake. In the middle of the park is a bridge that takes you directly to the Observation Tower. Starting in June you will be able to see alligator nests, some remarkably close to the walkway. Shortly after the eggs have been laid, Gatorland staffers remove them to an incubator to insure hatching. Signs left behind document the date of laying and the number of eggs.

Large, shaded gazebos with wooden benches offer a chance to rest, relax, and contemplate the serenity of the preserve. It's hard to believe some of Florida's scariest critters are basking just feet from where you sit. You'll see plenty of gators from the walkway. They wallow in the mud, float almost submerged in the water, and sun themselves on logs and the opposite shore. But for a really great look, you'll want to climb the Observation Tower.

The **Observation Tower** is a three-story affair located in the center of the walkway. It is accessible from the walkway, of course, but you can also reach the second level via a bridge directly from the park's central spine. An elaborate zigzag ramp next to the bridge makes the tower's middle level accessible to wheelchairs.

If you brought binoculars to Florida, don't forget to bring them to Gatorland. Climb to the top level, where signs point out the direction and distance to major Florida landmarks. Look straight down at the alligator lake and you will see dozens of 10-footers clustered around the base of the platform.

Look across at the opposite shore and you will see more gators amid the foliage; the longer you look, the more you'll see. Look at the trees in spring and you will see dozens of egrets tending their nests. Look closer and you will see the drabber species well camouflaged amid the leaves. A quarter will get you a brief look through a telescope mounted on the railing but when a hawk appears in the high branches, the line gets long.

Tip: For the latest information on who's nesting here, visit the discussion Forum on the Gatorland web site.

Jungle Crocs

Rating:	★ ★ ★ ★
Type:	Walk-by animal exhibit
Time:	Continuous viewing
Kelly says:	Keep an eye out for Blondie, the 'leucistic' croc

It's not quite equal time, but this exhibit gives the alligator's crocodilian cousins a chance to bask in the sun. Down a wooden walkway at the southern end of the *Alligator Breeding Marsh*, Gatorland has assembled one of the largest collections of crocodiles, which can be distinguished from alligators by their pointy snouts and snaggly, protruding teeth. There are saltwater crocs ("salties") from Australia and Southeast Asia, Nile Crocs from (where else?) the Nile, as well as a representative cross section of American and Cuban crocodiles.

Swamp Walk

Rating:	★ ★ ★
Type:	Wooden walkway through a cypress swamp
Time:	Five minutes or as long as you like
Kelly says:	Best for bird watchers

Through an iron gate, across a heavy swinging wooden bridge over an algae-tinged moat with yet more alligators, lies what Gatorland bills as the headwaters of the Everglades. From here, so the sign says, water flows through the Kissimmee lake system to Lake Okeechobee and, thence, to the Everglades.

What we see on this leisurely walk is a wilderness setting with a quiet calm and a very special type of beauty, made all the more enjoyable because, thanks to the raised wooden walkway, we don't have to wade through the muck and the cottonmouth moccasins and the poison ivy to appreciate it. Most folks walk through at a brisk pace, but if you linger you are likely to be rewarded with glimpses of birds and other wildlife that more hurried tourists miss out on.

Much of the Orlando area looked just like this before people started draining the wetlands to farm and, later, build shopping malls. Only the soft whoosh of traffic on nearby highway 441 reminds us that we are in modern, not primordial, Florida.

Giant Gator Lake

Rating: ★ ★ ★ ★
Type: Huge alligators in huge observation area
Time: As long as you wish
Kelly says: Rewards patient viewing

This is the huge lake that lies right next to the Gift Shop and park entrance. The place is home to Gatorland's largest specimens, giant 12-footers who are truly awesome, whether in catatonic repose in the sun or cruising ominously through the murky waters.

Other than feeding them (below), there's not much to do here except watch. At first it will seem that there's nothing much going on. It may even seem that some of these critters are statues. But your patience will be rewarded. As you continue looking you will be able to sort the alligators from the crocodiles and start to notice those nicely camouflaged gators lurking in the shadows or lying submerged and motionless.

Photo Op: If you've got a video camera try for a shot of a white heron hitching a ride on the back of a floating gator. Also, look for a large plaster model of an alligator on the boardwalk; it makes a good prop for a photo of your fearless kids.

Feed the Gators

Rating: ★ ★ +
Type: Audience participation
Time: A few minutes
Kelly says: Fun for the kids

Near the *Gator Jumparoo* platform is a stand selling five turkey hot dogs for $2.50 (with discounts available for those who prefer to buy in bulk) to those who'd like to feed a gator. Don't expect to be able to dangle your hand down like the gator wrangler in the *Jumparoo* show. The trick to feeding gators is to loft your hot dog gently so it lands to either side of the gator's head. They can't see directly in front. Many of the dogs wind up in the beaks of the ugly wood storks that patrol this area. Resist the temptation to hand feed these scavengers; their beaks can draw blood.

Tip: Take your hot dogs over to the *Alligator Breeding Marsh* and feed the gators from the Observation Tower. The gators over here are not as well-fed as those in the *Giant Gator Lake* and will show more interest in your free handouts.

Alligator Alley Animal Exhibits

Rating:	★ ★
Type:	Zoo-like walk-by exhibits
Time:	15 to 30 minutes
Kelly says:	Worth a stroll by; kids will enjoy feeding the lorikeets, goats, and deer

Alligator Alley is lined with a hodge-podge of cages, pens, and glass-walled displays that hearken back to the days when Gatorland was building its collection of "exotic" animals. Today, most of the animals on display are Florida natives like "Judy" the black bear and a small collection of emus, along with a variety of turtles, gators, and crocs.

The **Snakes of Florida** display is one of the more elaborate, housing a representative sample of Florida's 69 snake species behind glass windows and accompanied by helpful bits of written information. The walk-through **Very Merry Aviary** houses a scruffy band of lorikeets whom you can feed ($2 per serving); it is open for hour periods on a regular schedule posted on the door.

Many of the animals, like the macaws and emus (not Florida natives), and the farm animals in **Allie's Barnyard** can be fed. Convenient dispensers at a number of enclosures contain appropriate treats (at 25 cents a modest handful) for the kids to feed to their favorites. Like the aviary, Allie's Barnyard opens up for half-hour to hour-long up close sessions about four times a day, and ice cream cones of critter food sell for $2, or two for $3.

Across the way from Allie's Barnyard, look for **Flamingo Lagoon**, home to a small flock of American flamingos. The graceful pink birds, immortalized by millions of tacky lawn ornaments, are actually a light grey at birth. They get their reddish color from their diet of brine shrimp.

Shell Shack

Rating:	★ ★ ★ +
Type:	Walk-by exhibit with occasional opportunities for interaction
Time:	Continuous viewing, or scheduled times as posted
Kelly says:	Low-key fun for families with small fry

Most of the traffic seems to flow through the right half of *Alligator Alley,* but to the left lie a few treasures worth seeking out. Some of the more impressive inhabitants dwell in an unassuming little enclosure, with a small shed helpfully labeled "Shell Shack." This spot is the home of three Aldabara tortoises, mammoth creatures that range from 500 to 550 pounds apiece. The species comes from an island off the coast of Africa, though these particular tortoises retired here from Busch Gardens. The individuals on display are each over 90 years old, and have a life expectancy of over 150 years. While they're striking enough just to look at from outside the enclosure, an occasional "Meet the Keeper" event, with times helpfully announced on a whiteboard near the shack, affords an opportunity to get closer to these gentle giants.

For a $5 fee, the keeper supplies children with a few quartered carrots skewered on long wands, to permit kiddies to feed the tortoises without getting their fingers too close to their powerful beaks. This seemed an excellent interaction for young children in particular; it was quiet, low-key, and the tortoises, while impressive (and often more than thigh-high to a parent) are slow-moving and so less likely to spook the little ones. Toddlers here looked both more at ease and more excited at the chance to feed and walk around a giant tortoise than the mostly stunned-looking tots getting their photos taken in the gator-wrestling ring. As an added bonus, one parent per child is permitted to enter the enclosure for free, for a better photo opportunity.

Lilly's Pad

Rating: ★ ★ +
Type: Kiddie play area
Time: As long as you wish
Kelly says: For toddlers unimpressed by alligators

Located just a hop, skip, and a jump away from the *Gator Jumparoo* arena and next to the Aldabara tortoises, *Lilly's Pad* offers refuge for squirmy toddlers. This small play area is geared to the wee set with small-scale frog-themed slides and other fun things to do. It's all dry so you don't have to worry about junior getting sopping wet and there is a small shaded area that gives parents some relief from the sun.

Chapter Five:

The Holy Land Experience

When The Holy Land Experience, Orlando's newest theme park, opened in February of 2001, it garnered worldwide publicity, much of it tinged with controversy. It received hoots and sniggers from secularists for whom religion is, at best, a quaint anachronism. It also took flak from some religious leaders who took exception to the very idea of the new park.

Aside from referring one and all to the First Amendment of the U.S. Constitution, I do not wish to get involved in whatever controversy there may be about The Holy Land Experience. I would, however, like to report that, taken on its own terms, it is a remarkably successful endeavor.

Using popular media for religious messages has a long and honorable tradition, from the mystery plays of medieval Europe, that sought to teach Bible stories to the illiterate, to the Mitzvah-Mobiles of modern day New York that reach out to lapsed Jews. So why not a theme park that seeks to bring to life the Jerusalem of the time of Jesus Christ and teach, nay preach, a religious message to those who come to gawk? It may not be for everyone but the medium just might get the message across to people unlikely to pull out and dust off that Gideons Bible in their motel room.

Reflecting the Jewish heritage of its founder, Marvin Rosenthal, The Holy Land Experience places considerable emphasis on the Jewishness of Jesus and his milieu. He was a rabbi, as the park's explicators point out. Much is made of the historical and archaeological accuracy of the exhibits and biblical text is often linked with historical fact. Some of the park's "cast members" (to use a Disney turn of phrase) are dressed as priests of the Herodic Temple, and everyone on the park staff greets you with a hearty "Shalom!" Ancient Hebrew hymns highlight some of the live performances, several of the exhibits pay homage to the Judaic traditions of the Old Testament, and Jewish prayer shawls and menorahs are sold in the gift shops. Indeed, reflecting the ongoing Christian connection with the Holy Land, 80% of the merchandise sold in the shops is imported from Israel.

The Holy Land Experience is not a large park, just 15 acres, about the size of a small "land" at one of the major Orlando parks. It is also worth noting that, scenically, The Holy Land Experience is extremely well executed. The lead design firm was ITEC Entertainment Corp., the same outfit responsible for much of the theme-ing of Islands of Adventure over at Universal Orlando. They've also done work for Disney and their experience shows, although they were obviously working with a more limited budget here. Still, the results are impressive and The Holy Land Experience compares favorably with other "minor" parks in the Orlando area.

Those drawn to the evangelical Christian message will find a visit to The Holy Land Experience to be enlightening and moving. But religious belief or religious yearning are not prerequisites for admission, and non-believers should not dismiss The Holy Land Experience out of hand. Lovers of history, theology, or archeology will find much of interest, and the park is as scenic and well-maintained as any in town.

Before You Come

If you would like current information about operating hours and schedules, you can call, toll-free, (866) USA-HOLYLAND (872-4659). The local number is (407) 872-2272. The web site for the park, www.holylandexperience.com, contains basic information and is a good place to check for late-breaking developments.

If you haven't already read the Bible, it's unlikely you'll do so just to prepare for a theme park visit, but here's a fairly painless assignment anyway. Pull out the Bible in your hotel room and glance through the closing chapters of Exodus, starting at Chapter 36, to learn a bit about the construction of the wilderness tabernacle. If you like, continue on into the first several chapters of Leviticus to learn about the practice of blood sacrifice. One of the more interesting presentations at The Holy Land Experience is based on these sections of the Good Book.

Getting There

The Holy Land Experience is located at 4655 Vineland Road at the corner of Conroy Road. It is just off Exit 72 on I-4 and can be clearly seen from the highway. Coming from the south (that is, traveling east on I-4), turn left at the top of the exit ramp, cross the bridge, and take the first right. Coming from the north (west on I-4), keep turning right from the top of the exit ramp. This will take you into the parking lot of The Holy Land Experience. Parking is $5 for all vehicles.

Opening and Closing Times

The Holy Land Experience is open year-round every day except Sundays, Thanksgiving, and Christmas. Normal operating hours are:

Monday to Saturday, 10:00 a.m. to 5:00 p.m.

During holiday periods, hours may be changed or extended. Call for more information.

The Price of Admission

The Holy Land Experience has several ticket options. Because it is a not-for-profit ministry, no taxes are levied on the admission charges.

One-Day Plus Seven Pass

Adult:	$35
Child (6-12):	$23
Seniors (55+)	$30

Children under 6 are admitted free. The next seven days are free, so this is really an eight-day pass.

Jerusalem Gold Annual Pass

All ages	$70

Which Price Is Right?

For most people, a one-day plus seven pass is the only option. The price will no doubt seem very fair to committed believers, but I suspect it will discourage the merely curious. The annual pass will appeal most to those who live in the Orlando area or who visit regularly and who would like to take maximum advantage of the daily Bible presentation. Annual passholders get free parking, merchandise discounts, and discounted admission for friends.

Good Things To Know About . . .

Access for the Disabled

All of The Holy Land Experience is wheelchair accessible. Wheelchairs may be rented in the Old Scroll Shop, which is directly in front of you as you enter. Wheelchair rental is $7. Motorized scooters are $20. American sign language interpretation is available free by advance reservation; call (866) 872-4659

Babies

Strollers are available for rent in the Old Scroll Shop. Single strollers are $5, doubles are $7. Diaper changing areas are available in all the restrooms in the park.

Dress Code

The Holy Land Experience expects its guests to dress appropriately. While recognizing that most people are here on vacation, the management draws the line at halter tops, short-shorts, and other forms of dress deemed (in their opinion) to be immodest. They also refuse entry to those who arrive "in costume."

Bible Study and Church Services

The Holy Land Experience offers **free** Thursday night bible study sessions at 7:30 p.m. and Sunday church services at 10:30 a.m. Parking is also **free** for these events.

First Aid

First aid facilities are available in the Guest Services office near the front.

Group Rates

If you have a group of 15 or more adults, you can qualify for reduced rates. You must reserve ahead and put down a deposit within a month of making the reservation. The remainder of the total cost must be paid in full three weeks prior to your visit. Your tickets will be held at Guest Services pending your arrival. Call the park for current group rates.

Leaving the Park

If you wish to leave the park during the day, make sure to retain your ticket. You can use it to regain admittance later in the day. Leaving for lunch is an option, and there are numerous restaurants a short drive away at the Millennia Mall complex.

Lost and Found

If you lose something during your visit, chances are excellent it will turn up at Lost and Found in Guest Services. This is a religious theme park after all.

Money

ATMs are located in Guest Services and the Shofar Shop.

Pets

The Holy Land Experience has no pet boarding facilities, and no animals (other than seeing-eye dogs) are allowed in the park. Plan accordingly.

Prayer & Religious Activity

The management of The Holy Land Experience expects some exhibits to move visitors to prayer. However, they reserve the right to eject those whose religious activity (in their sole opinion) is creating a disturbance.

Sun

Much of The Holy Land Experience takes place outdoors under the broiling Florida sun. The Plaza of the Nations, an uncovered marble square, can get brutal on the warmest days. Although some events are moved indoors during the height of summer, head coverings and sunscreen are highly recommended.

Rain

In the event of rain, outdoor presentations may be moved inside to the Shofar auditorium. However, the actors are game for performing outdoors in a drizzle, since "the rain falls on the just and unjust alike."

Smoking and Alcohol

The Holy Land Experience is a non-smoking, alcohol-free facility.

Weddings

Using the Temple and the Plaza of Nations can make for a spectacular wedding.

Call (866) 872-4659 for more information.

Dining at The Holy Land Experience

You have three dining choices, a cafe and two outdoor stands. The **Oasis Palms Cafe** is a small cafeteria seating just 120 people, half of them outside at tables overlooking the Oasis Lagoon and its towering jet-like fountain. The food is billed as American and Middle Eastern, and in true theme park style they even serve "Goliath Burgers," which are traditional American fare, as are the fries you can get to accompany them. Other entrees include David's Grilled Chicken Sandwich and the vegetarian Mediterranean Sampler platter. The Bedouin Beef gyros are particularly tasty. **Simeon's Corner** is an outdoor snack stand serving hot dogs, pretzels, and cold drinks. The **Royal Portico Eatery** serves hot turkey legs, ice cream, and smoothies.

Shopping at The Holy Land Experience

There are no money changers in the Temple, but there is shopping nearby, much of it near the front entrance. A lot of the merchandise is from Israel, including some lovely Havdalah candles, cups and plates, and Nativity scenes carved from olive wood. There is original religious art at prices (up to $5,000) that might make you say a quick prayer. You can also find Bibles and a variety of devotional books, audiotapes, and videos, although not as many as you might expect. Indeed, the proselytizing seems decidedly muted. A section of The Old Scroll shop near the entrance has a children's area featuring a big-screen TV and Biblical videos.

The Pilgrim's Way: Your Day at The Holy Land Experience

The Holy Land Experience is recommended as a full-day experience, although to fully absorb all the park has to offer will require coming back for at least a second visit. When you arrive, you will be given a fold-out map that contains information about the park's amenities and services. You will also get a separate schedule of live shows and other events that you can use to plan your day.

There are two types of attractions: "Featured Venues," indoor, theater-style shows, about 20 to 30 minutes in length, that operate on a more or less continuous schedule, and "Live Shows and Presentations," a mixture of musical shows and dramatic presentations, both indoors and outdoors, most of which have just one performance each day. In addition, a 20-minute guided tour of the park is offered each morning.

I found the most workable strategy was to arrive early and see a few of the live performances first. The schedule is such that you have a comfortable amount of time to move from one show to the next and get a good seat. During the hottest part of the day (for you summer visitors), you can see the indoor presentations.

This touring strategy will take you into the late afternoon. If you wish, you can linger and see some of the shows again while waiting for nightfall. You can also have dinner at the Oasis Palms. But even if you leave early, you might want to return after dark (remember to save your ticket) when the park is open late for the holidays. The Plaza of Nations, with its torches lit, is especially nice at night.

Attractions at The Holy Land Experience

As I mentioned, there are two types of attractions. I will begin with a description of a sampling of the Live Performances and then move on to the Featured Venues. It is unlikely that you will be able to see all of the live shows. For one thing, not all shows are presented every day, and if you try to catch every live show offered, you will not only have to skip lunch but probably won't have time for the Featured Venues, all of which are very much worth seeing. My best advice is to scan the schedule, pick out the live shows that appeal the most and plan your day accordingly.

Behold the Lamb

Rating: ★ ★ ★ +
Type: Musical Passion drama
Time: 20 minutes
Kelly says: Moving and dramatic

This musical dramatization of the crucifixion is the centerpiece of the live performances at the park. Roman soldiers announce that they are executing Jesus for treason against the Rome, and lead him through the crowd to the cross on Calvary Hill above the Garden Tomb. The entire event is presented in graphic, even gory detail, and parents with young children may want to beware. The cast, Holy Land's "CENTURY" ensemble, performs with obvious emotion and commitment befitting the subject.

The show features a number of songs, including "Alive" and "Via Dolorosa," delivered by talented singers in an inoffensive Andrew Lloyd Webber-ish pop-Broadway style. A film of the production is available for purchase on video and DVD in the Shofar Shop near the Jerusalem model.

Qumran Cave Presentation

Rating: ★ ★ ★
Type: Historical and archeological talk
Time: 15 minutes
Kelly says: Great for the scholarly

The Qumran caves, which are still announced as a "coming attraction," are the backdrop for this scholarly chat about the significance of the discovery in 1947 of a trove of ancient biblical texts belonging to the Essenes, an ascetic sect of Jews who had a monastery of sorts in the desert. There are some fascinating tidbits about the historical context of the scrolls, but the main point made here is the amazing integrity of the Scriptures. Scholars have found just 17 minor differences between the Qumran version of the Book of Isaiah and texts dating from hundreds of years later.

KidVenture

Rating: ★ ★ ★+
Type: Outdoor show and play area
Time: 15 minutes for the show
Kelly says: Interactive biblical fun

The performance may leave something to be desired but this is a great idea — actors from The Holy Land ensemble get volunteers from the audience for some good-natured acting out of favorite tales from the Bible. The show I caught featured David (played by a grown-up) and Goliath (played by a kid in a big helmet). The moral being "life is full of giants. But when we place our trust in God, He'll slay our giants for us."

The KidVenture area doubles as a play area where kids can burn off some excess energy when they aren't feeling particularly devotional. There's a small-scale climbing wall and a misting area to help overheated kids cool off.

Praise

Rating: ★ ★ ★ +
Type: Indoor musical show
Time: 35 minutes
Kelly says: Nice voices, interesting survey

Praise begins with a lovely rendition of an ancient Hebrew hymn and continues through the ages to present a survey of devotional music from various cultures and periods. By and large, and as might be expected, the more modern pieces tended to be the best. The Gregorian chant left, shall we say, something to be desired and a comment that seemed to dismiss modern abstract art as ungodly struck me as just plain odd.

Moses

Rating: ★ ★ ★ +
Type: Musical show and preaching
Time: 30 minutes
Kelly says: An odd but effective mix

A video introduction sets the scene: It's ancient Egypt, not a great time to be an infant Jewish boy, because the Pharaoh wants you dead. Segue to live action and a musical dramatization of the rescue of Moses, his discovery by a princess, and the fateful decisions that saved his life. It's nicely done.

Almost as entertaining is the show's second segment when an accomplished preacher takes over to narrate the continued story of how Moses became God's chosen vessel to free the Israelites from bondage. The best part is the preacher's rendition of the various ways in which Moses tried to talk his way out of what must have seemed a hopeless mission.

Seasonal Pageants

Rating:	★ ★ ★
Type:	Multi-location musical dramas
Time:	40 minutes
Kelly says:	Large-scale expressions of faith

During the Christmas and Easter seasons additional live performances with an appropriate holiday theme will almost certainly be added, oftentimes displacing one or more of the shows already mentioned. Some, but by no means all, special holiday shows may require an additional charge.

During the Christmas season, you might see *Come To The Manger*, while at Easter you might see *Follow Me: The Road To Resurrection*. These shows are more elaborate versions of the shows described above. The Christmas show I saw, for example, involved five separate locations around the park and featured a dramatic entrance by the three wise men. The music is in the quasi-operatic Andrew Lloyd Webber mode and many of the vocal performances are quite accomplished.

Typically, there will be two shows a day, one in the early afternoon and one just before the park closes in the evening. However, I am told there are changes in the works, so if you are planning on visiting during a holiday period, it's a good idea to call ahead or visit the Holy Land web site to find out what will be playing when you arrive.

The Wilderness Tabernacle

Rating:	★ ★ ★ ★
Type:	Stage show with special effects
Time:	25 minutes
Kelly says:	Interesting evocation

Of all the attractions at The Holy Land Experience, this is the most theme-park-like. In a darkened theater, we see a dramatized recreation of the tabernacle God commanded Moses to build in the wilderness after the exodus from Egypt. As a voice-over narrator tells the history of the tabernacle, an actor representing Aaron, the very first High Priest, mimes the rituals and sacrifices being described. Because the Bible (Exodus, Chapter 36ff) gives fairly complete instructions for building the tabernacle, the recreation is remarkably evocative.

The presentation progresses from the sacrificial altar and bronze laver (or purification bath) outside into the tabernacle itself. There we see the Holy Place, an antechamber with three ritual objects, and the Holy of Holies itself where the Arc of the Covenant resided and into which the High Priest entered just once a year. The presentation ends with a "Shekinah Glory" special effect that is straight out of "Raiders of the Lost Ark."

All in all, I found this show a fascinating use of theme park show biz to teach a religious and archaeological lesson.

A video version with a good deal of additional material and detail on the Tabernacle is available at the gift shop.

Calvary's Garden Tomb

Rating: ★ ★ ★
Type: Re-creation of Christ's tomb
Time: Continuous viewing
Kelly says: Best as a stage set

In a sunken garden setting, the approach lined with white lilies at Easter time, lies this imaginative reconstruction of Christ's tomb. The huge circular stone door is rolled aside as it was on the third day when the women who came to anoint Christ's body discovered He was risen. If you step inside you see a typical tomb of the period, the winding cloths in disarray, and a small sign that says. "He is not here for He is risen."

Benches in front of the tomb allow a place for quiet contemplation. Above the tomb rise the three crosses of the crucifixion. The tomb makes a compelling backdrop for occasional live performances dramatizing Biblical themes.

Note: Many of the plants in the park have signage explaining their biblical connections. Here at the tomb, for example, a sign in front of an aloe plant tells us that the plant was often used for embalming and offers a Bible verse (John 19:39) in which the plant is mentioned.

Temple of the Great King and Plaza of the Nations

Rating: ★ ★ ★
Type: Historical recreation
Time: Continuous viewing
Kelly says: A fitting setting for the shows

The *Temple of the Great King* is a one-third scale re-creation of Herod's Temple, which stood on Jerusalem's Mount Moriah in the first century A.D. What we see is actually just the Temple's facade and a courtyard in front of it surrounded by 30 Corinthian columns with golden capitals. Supposedly, this is all archaeologically accurate. Be that as it may, the *Plaza of Nations*, as this space is called, is a dazzling centerpiece for The Holy Land Experience. Add a high priest in white robes and bulbous turban, blowing a shofar to summon the faithful, and a uniformed Roman solider striding purposefully about and you have a nice, if pared down, evocation of ancient Jerusalem.

Some of the live performances take place here, using the semicircular steps to the Temple as a stage. Seating is provided by folding chairs arranged in a semicircle facing the Temple.

Tip: When watching shows in the Plaza of the Nations, take a seat on the far right (as you face the Temple). From here it is a straight shot to the line for the film *Seed of Promise* in the *Theater of Life* (see below).

The Seed of Promise (in the Theater of Life)

Rating: ★ ★ ★
Type: Religious film
Time: 30 minutes
Kelly says: Well-done

A 150-seat theater hidden away behind the facade of the *Temple of the Great*

King is used for the screening of a devotional film that speaks directly to believers. This handsomely produced film, shot on location in Israel in high-definition video, encapsulates the religious message of The Holy Land Experience. Beginning with a depiction of the Roman sack of Jerusalem in 70 A.D., the film travels back in time to the Creation, where we see Adam and Eve in the Garden of Eden, and forward again to the almost sacrifice of Abraham atop Mount Moriah. The film ends with Jesus, arisen from the dead, visiting the lands around Jerusalem and making Himself known to His followers. The official stance of The Holy Land Experience is strictly non-denominational, but if there is an underlying theological point of view to the place it is no doubt encapsulated in this brief and compelling presentation.

I can't help commenting on the way Hollywood cliché has of trumping historical accuracy in films of this sort. Eve is shown as a blonde (with tan lines, yet!) and Jesus, always shot from the back, appears to have used blonde highlighter in His tawny hair. At least Abraham and Isaac appear to be of their time and place.

The film is shown every 30 minutes on the quarter-hour.

Jerusalem Model A.D. 66

Rating:	★ ★ ★ ★
Type:	Large city model
Time:	Continuous viewing
Kelly says:	Come for the informative talks

A large room in a building past the *Plaza of the Nations* houses a fascinating scale model of Jerusalem as it existed in 66 A.D. Why 66 A.D.? Because, with the completion of the northern wall, this was the largest the ancient city ever grew. Four years later, it was obliterated by the Romans in retaliation for Jewish uppityness.

The model, which measures 45 feet by 25 feet, is historically accurate with one exception. The houses have been enlarged to show detail. The housing was actually six times as dense and the streets 15 times as narrow as depicted. In fact, the houses were packed so closely together that in Jesus's time you could leap from roof to roof and traverse the entire length of the city without ever touching the ground.

That last tidbit, was gleaned from the fascinating half-hour talks that are given here. I strongly urge you not to miss these entertaining mini-lectures. Without them, the display is merely interesting, but the talks make this the best attraction at The Holy Land Experience.

Several times a day, a knowledgeable biblical scholar (most if not all of them are preachers) steps onto a small open space next to the Temple Mount and, with the aid of a laser pointer, conducts a guided tour of the Jerusalem that Jesus knew. In a fascinating blend of Bible stories with historical records and archaeological excavation, he brings oft-told stories of the work and especially the Passion of Jesus to life. I was fascinated to learn, for example, that Jesus' description of Gehenna (Hell) was a direct reference to the trash heap that burned ceaselessly outside Jerusalem's walls. His contemporary listeners would have known immediately what He was talking about. A DVD version of this talk is available for purchase and may make an excellent souvenir of your visit.

Bible Lecture (in the Shofar Auditorium)

Rating: Decide for yourself
Type: Classroom-style lecture
Time: 30 minutes
Kelly says: For the serious student of the Bible

Behind the model of Jerusalem lies the 510-seat Shofar Auditorium. Here, half-hour lectures on a variety of Bible-related topics are given by recognized experts in the field. The schedule has been somewhat erratic in the past, but recently these talks have been presented daily. From what I observed, the presentations follow the tradition of close Bible reading and explication that is the hallmark of contemporary evangelical Christianity.

The Scriptorium

Rating: ★ ★ ★ +
Type: Guided, themed museum
Time: 55 minutes
Kelly says: Well done, but for the serious-minded

Themed after a fourth century Byzantine monastery, the Scriptorium houses the Robert and Judith Van Kampen collection of biblical manuscripts, codices, incunabula, and other rare books that document the history of how the Bible has been preserved, published, and disseminated through the ages.

This is not your typical museum, however, with its treasures arrayed in well-lit rooms and accompanied by explanatory text. The Scriptorium's designers, seemingly inspired by nearby theme parks, have created a richly themed, walking tour that uses set elements, decoration, smoke effects, dramatic lighting, and speaking mechanical figures to tell, not the Bible story but the story of the Bible, which is touted in media-savvy terms as "the best-selling book of all time."

This is a guided tour in the sense that a voice-over narration (some tours are in Spanish) offers tidbits of information about the articles on exhibit as changes in lighting signal guests to move on to the next chamber. Along the way, the narrator offers a distinctly evangelical interpretation of the propagation of the Christian faith, the Protestant Reformation, and the subsequent spread of various Christian sects to the New World. Highlights include 4,000-year-old cuneiform tablets, a "Tyndale Bible" reputedly stained with the blood of a martyr who died for possessing it, a recreation of Gutenberg's printing press, and a narrow escape through Wycliffe's fireplace to elude persecutors. There are also many beautiful Christian and Jewish scrolls, manuscripts, codices, incunabula, and rare first editions of printed Bibles and devotional literature.

The tour culminates with a soul-stirring evocation of major Biblical figures from the Old and New Testaments and, just as a reminder, a recitation of the Ten Commandments, complete with Charlton Heston-worthy lighting effects. Guests are then led into a well-appointed modern living room with television blaring for a final exhortation to take the time to reconnect with the word of God.

Serious Bible students and lovers of rare books will find much of interest here. Committed Christians will doubtless be moved by some moments in the tour. Others might be less impressed, I'm afraid. The tour's length and stately pace could well prove a problem for younger visitors and the easily bored. There is no exit once the tour commences.

Near the exit, in a small room, the Ex Libris Book Shoppe features a video presentation called **A Day In The Life Of A Monk**, which chronicles the daily routine of the pre-Reformation monastics who played such a pivotal role in preserving ancient scriptures (and along with them a great deal of the wisdom of ancient Rome and Greece, although this isn't mentioned). It's in black and white and runs on a continuous loop. The more historically minded should find it interesting.

Chapter Six:

Cypress Gardens

THIS IS WHERE IT ALL BEGAN. YES, IT'S TRUE, SILVER SPRINGS WAS RUNNING GLASS bottom boats before the turn of the century, but that was simply a matter of capitalizing on a ready-made attraction. In the opinion of many, the Central Florida theme park phenomenon actually began when Dick Pope carved a man-made paradise out of a patch of swampy cypress forest along the east shore of Lake Eloise to create Cypress Gardens in 1936. Most people thought he was nuts. One newspaper called him "the Swami of the Swamp."

But Cypress Gardens soon became world-renowned for its spectacular botanical gardens and its innovative water ski spectaculars. As theme parks boomed in the 1970s, Cypress Gardens retained much of the easygoing, leisurely air that characterized its early days, relegating it to perennial also-ran status and gaining a reputation, partially deserved, as a park for senior citizens.

The story almost came to an end in 2003, when Cypress Gardens closed, seemingly forever, a victim to changing tastes, declining attendance, and mounting financial losses. It looked like the park's prized lakeside real estate would be turned into luxury home sites. But the park had its fierce partisans and the idea of Cypress Gardens refused to die.

Then an amusement park owner from Georgia decided to rescue Cypress Gardens. The results have been mixed. Purists note that many of the park's best features have suffered due to a variety of cost-cutting measures. There is less horticulture than before, the dining isn't what it used to be, and a somewhat cheesy amusement park has been tacked on. On the other hand, the new management has retained the robust line up of musical concerts featuring oldie-but-goodie stars and old timers can easily avoid the newer elements and enjoy the somewhat diminished pleasures of the park's older areas. Whatever the carping of the purists, there's still plenty here to engage visitors of all ages, just so long as they don't come expecting another Universal Orlando or SeaWorld. Or the Cypress Gardens of yesteryear.

Before You Come

If you'd like to get advance information on what will be going on at Cypress Gardens during the time of your visit, give them a call at (863) 324-2111. They'll be happy to fill you in on the events calendar or send information. Cypress Gardens also maintains a colorful web site at

www.cypressgardens.com

When's the Best Time to Come?

Crowds are never a factor in picking the date of your visit; Cypress Gardens is rarely mobbed. And thanks to the wizardry of the horticultural staff, there's always something to see. I recommend spring and fall, since the weather is close to ideal; the summer can be stifling and winter is unpredictable, with temperatures ranging from pleasant to quite chilly. On the other hand, the night ski show is presented only in the summer and that's pretty nifty. Whenever you visit, plan to stay late enough to enjoy the spectacular sunsets over Lake Eloise.

Getting There

Cypress Gardens is a leisurely one-hour drive from Orlando (less, if you drive like the locals who take the 65 miles per hour speed limit as a suggested minimum). The easiest way to get there is to follow I-4 West to Route 27 South. Turn right at State Route 540. Cypress Gardens is a bit less than four miles along on your left.

Parking at Cypress Gardens

Cypress Gardens' parking is $9 for cars and $11 for RVs and trailers in a long narrow lot at one end of the park property. When crowds warrant, a tram pulled by a large pick up truck ferries arriving guests from the far reaches of the lot to the entrance. A $25 annual parking pass, which is discussed below, is also available.

Opening and Closing Times

Unlike many area theme parks, Cypress Gardens does not open early but it often boogies late. The park opens every day of the year at 10:00 a.m. Closing time varies from 6:00 p.m. during slower periods to 7:00, 8:00, 9:00 or 10:00 p.m. The schedule is somewhat erratic; a color-coded calendar on the web site will be invaluable in planning your visit. The park is closed on Christmas and Easter.

The Price of Admission

Cypress Gardens sells admission by the day and by the year. At press time, prices (not including tax) were as follows:

One-Day Pass:

Regular:	$39.95
Juniors (3 to 9):	$34.95
Seniors (55+):	$34.95

A second-day-free option seems pretty standard, so this is actually a two-day admission.

Annual Passport:

    All ages: $64.95

This option is good for the calendar year only; it will be discounted to $59.95 as the year wears on.

Gold Passport:

    All ages: $99.95

Platinum Passport:

    All ages: $129.95

Annual Parking Pass:

    All ages: $25.00

The regular annual pass, called a Passport, is only valid until the end of the current calendar year. So if you purchase it in June, it still expires at the end of December. About halfway through the year, the price of the pass is discounted. It offers admission to Wild Adventures in Valdosta, Georgia, Cypress Garden's sister park. It also offers admission to all concerts at the park. The major drawback of the annual pass is that it does not offer free parking. You can purchase a $25 Annual Parking Pass, which pays for itself in three visits, but if you are visiting on three or more days, you might just as well get the Gold Passport. Not even the friendly people in Guest Services could explain the logic of the Annual Passport to me.

Since the Gold Passport is valid for a full calendar year, includes free parking, a variety of discounts, and costs about what three separate admissions would cost, it is clearly the way to go. The Platinum Passport adds more discounts. The annual passes make the most sense for Florida residents or others who find themselves in the Winter Haven area on a regular basis. If you decide you want one, step into Guest Services in Jubilee Junction; they will create your photo ID Passport while you wait.

Staying Near the Park

If Cypress Gardens is your primary destination, or if you just want to spare yourself the drive back to Orlando, you may want to stay near the main gate. Although the hotel below is practically adjacent to the park walls, it is a long walk to the entrance. So you may want to consider the motels found three to four miles west along Route 540 (Cypress Gardens Boulevard) in the town of Winter Haven. None is within walking distance.

Best Western Admiral's Inn

5665 Cypress Gardens Boulevard
Winter Haven, FL 33884
(800) 247-2799; (863) 324-5950; fax (863) 324-2376

    Standard mid-range motel.

    Price Range: $$ - $$$

    Amenities: Pool, restaurant, lounge

    Walk to Park: 25 minutes

Special Events

Cypress Gardens offers a robust schedule of musical events — 100 or more a year. Most of the headliners are stars who shone much more brightly several decades ago. The acts range from easy-listening bands like Les Brown, to country stars like Loretta Lynn and Glen Campbell, to aging rockers like Chubby Checker, with the occasional comedy act thrown in for good measure. The events take place in the expansive, open-air **Star Haven Amphitheater,** which can hold several thousand fans. It often fills up.

If the musical selection is to your taste and you live within hailing distance of Cypress Gardens, this is one of the best arguments for an annual pass and an indisputable entertainment bargain.

The entertainment menu often offers special treats geared to holidays such as Christmas and the Fourth of July. Expect special musical shows, indoors and out, with an accent on good old-fashioned American themes.

Dining and Shopping at Cypress Gardens

Your dining choices at Cypress Gardens are mostly of the fast-food variety and very little of it justifies the prices being charged. The only reason to endure the buffet at Aunt Julie's Country Kitchen is the delightful view from the open-air terrace.

Like the dining, the shopping is not a reason in itself to visit the park. There are some nice things to be found at several of the shops and if you need to stock up on decorations for your Christmas tree, Kringle's Christmas Shop offers a wide selection of tasteful tree ornaments along with decorative accessories for the rest of the house.

Good Things to Know About . . .

Access for the Disabled

Almost all of the park is wheelchair accessible, although some of the inclines are best negotiated with the help of a companion. The exceptions are the boat rides which may not be able to accommodate all disabled guests. Both wheelchairs and electric scooters can be rented just inside the entrance at the Jubilee Mercantile shop. Wheelchairs are $7.50 per day. Electric scooters are $32.10 a day, including tax.

Babies

Strollers can be rented near the entrance, on your left as you enter. Single strollers are $7.49 per day, doubles are $9.63 (including tax). Diaper changing stations can be found in most restrooms, men's and women's.

Emergencies

There is a first aid station in the Adventure Grove section. If you or someone in your party has a problem, contact the nearest park employee.

Junior Belles

One of the best things in the park is this program that lets your little girl get all dolled up, just like the grown-up Southern Belles, and stroll about the park for two hours in her finery. There is a $25 charge. Photos are extra, but reasonably priced.

Leaving the Park

You may leave the park and return during the day. Just make sure to have your hand stamped as you leave. This is true even if you have an annual pass!

Lockers

Coin-operated lockers ($1 for each use) are conveniently located throughout the park.

Money

There are ATMs scattered about the park, too, their locations marked on the park map. A fee of about $2 is charged for their use.

Pets

There is a small kennel for cats and dogs, but space is limited.

Safety

Cypress Gardens is open to all the birds and animals who take it into their minds to pay a visit. The park warns people not to feed the birds or other little critters because they are wild and unpredictable and may become aggressive. That's good advice, but the squirrels are hard to resist. It's unlikely that you'll see an alligator during your visit but, if you do, remember that feeding wild alligators is not only stupid but illegal.

Special Diets

If you have special dietary needs, your best bet is Aunt Julie's Country Kitchen, which offers a number of special meals on request.

Smelling the Flowers: Your Day at Cypress Gardens

Cypress Gardens can easily be seen and appreciated in a day. You may not see everything, but as you read through the descriptions that follow, you will probably find there are some things you won't mind missing.

Cypress Gardens' fame rests primarily on its spectacular gardens and the water skiing, but the park has developed other attractions as well.

Variety Entertainment. Cypress Gardens presents a regular schedule of family-style entertainment, from singers, to comedy, to an ice show.

Animals. Cypress Gardens has a small zoo with a mix of Florida and exotic species. There are show-and-tell presentations starring reptiles and such.

Rides. Thanks to the addition of a small amusement park, Cypress Gardens is now a "ride" park, albeit on a rather small scale.

This is good sized park, and when you take into account the meandering paths through the many garden areas, you can walk a fair distance during your visit. The park comprises 200 acres and runs north to south along the shore of Lake Eloise; the sole entrance is at the south end and it is a long walk to the far northern reaches of the park. The park is divided (at least in my mind) into three main areas. **Jubilee Junction**, modeled on a quaint country village, is your introduction to the park. It is primarily a dining and shopping venue, although the ice show is located here. Off Jubilee Junction is *Nature's Way*, housing the park's animal attractions. The northern end of the park, what I call **"The Gardens,"** encompasses the original botanical gardens, the ski show arena, and *Topiary Trail*. **Adventure Grove**, housing the amusement park rides, and **Splash Island**, a vest-pocket water park, form the third area, which lies roughly alongside Jubilee Junction and the Gardens.

The One-Day Stay

As you enter the park, pick up a copy of the large one-sheet flyer with a map of the park and a schedule of shows and events. Scan this for the show times of the entertainments you most want to see and plan accordingly. In my opinion, the only must-sees are the water ski show and the ice skating show.

If you arrive at opening time, the Jubilee Junction area may not be open yet and the first water ski show will be at least an hour away. So a visit to the botanical gardens at the far end of the park is a logical first step. This is also a good time to see them, before the heat of the day. Depending on how long it takes you to see the gardens, you may finish up just in time to catch the first performance of the water ski show. After the show, stroll through *Topiary Trail* en route back to Jubilee Junction. If a show of *Living Gardens* in underway, you may want to pause,

Now you have the afternoon to tour the attractions in Jubilee Junction, Nature's Way, Adventure Grove, and Splash Island and enjoy a leisurely lunch. Lines are an issue in the amusement park only on the busiest days. In addition to the shows recommended above, don't miss *Wings of Wonder*. *Sunshine Sky Adventure* is a fun diversion that can be squeezed in just about anytime you like; it only takes five minutes.

Another option is to save your visit to the botanical gardens for late in the day, towards sunset. Photographers, especially, may find the afternoon sun and the lengthening shadows a plus.

"The Gardens"

At the north end of the park is what I call "The Gardens," which comprises what the management refers to as "the original gardens" and the water ski arena. Proceeding south, you enter *Topiary Trail*, a gentle valley that extends from the water ski arena to the entrance to Jubilee Junction. Here you will find the lovely Italian Fountain and the Mediterranean Waterfall. The waterfall is artificial and fed by thousands of gallons of recycled lake water; the stream that flows from its base to the lake marks the approximate center line of the park.

For this survey of Cypress Gardens attractions, I will start at the north end of the park, describing the "original" botanical gardens and their surrounding attractions, and then move directly to Jubilee Junction at the opposite end. Finally, I will describe Adventure Grove and Splash Island.

For those with sufficient time, starting at the north end of the park and slowly wending your way southward is a highly efficient way in which to see the entire park. Assuming that there will be a few attractions you will pass up, the entire tour can be done in a day. Those who want to be absolutely thorough will probably have to return a second day to complete their survey.

The Gardens area contains relatively few attractions but they are the ones for which Cypress Gardens is justly famous. The water ski show area with its twin stadiums is the most prominent landmark in this section, so we'll start there.

Ski Show Spectacular

Rating: ★ ★ ★ ★
Type: Water ski spectacular
Time: 30 minutes
Kelly says: A pared-down classic

Water skiing has been a Cypress Gardens trademark since the early 1940s. The current incarnation of the show is simplicity itself, showcasing talented athletes who, by dint of hard work, have become the best in the world at what they do. The result is a display of water skiing artistry that moves deftly from the pretty nifty to the truly amazing.

Three lovely "Aqua Maids" appear throughout the show, performing a variety of graceful maneuvers in a variety of pretty costumes that display their ample grace, but the heart of the show is the stunt skiing, and that is the province of the men. Barefoot water skiing seems amazing enough to me but these guys do it in more ways than you'd imagine possible, from starting out face down and backwards in the water to jumping off regular water skis at 45 miles an hour. On a variety of skis and ski boards, they twist and flip and dismount spectacularly at the foot of the stands.

There is also an interlude of "adagio" skiing, a male-female team on a single pair of skis who engage in a series of graceful lifts as they speed along at 40 miles an hour. The form was borrowed from ice skating and adapted to water skis in the early seventies; I can't help feeling it's a lot harder on water.

In the guise of "The Rampmasters," the guys put on a display of gutsy ramp jumping that involves aerial spins over the heads of their colleagues, back and front flips in unison, and something called a "gainer," a sideways flip at nearly 50 miles an hour. In every show there is an amiable goof-off who provides an opportunity for some hijinks and derring-do that may not be pretty but is still pretty amazing.

As a sort of bonus, they throw in something that has little to do with water skiing, except perhaps that the hang glider involved gets his initial lift by being towed behind a boat. The announcer points him out off in the distance and then the crowd gapes skyward as the high flying daredevil circles downward to a pinpoint landing on the beach. Pretty neat if you've never seen it done before.

The show ends with a three-level human pyramid — three Aqua Maids held aloft by the guys. It makes for a rousing finish.

Historical note: Those who remember Cypress Gardens from the "old days" will notice that the current show is much smaller. The cast has been cut from twelve to seven and the more spectacular stunts, including a twelve-person, four-level pyramid, have been eliminated.

Night Magic

Rating:	★ ★ ★ ★ +
Type:	Nighttime ski show with fireworks
Time:	20 minutes
Kelly says:	Better than the daytime show

On summer weekends, when the park is open late, Cypress Gardens adds an additional ski show just after dark. It contains many of the same elements as the daytime show, minus the comedy, but this time the tow boats are outlined in tiny lights and the skiers are picked out by giant spotlights as they zip across the lake's surface, their flips and stunts punctuated by bursts of fireworks shot from a platform in the lake. Stunts that looked pretty nifty in the bright sunlight seem almost magical at night, with the skiers' colorful costumes glowing in the bright spotlights. The hang glider is there, too, this time with fireworks streamers marking his descent to a perfect lakeside touchdown.

The show ends with a razzle-dazzle fireworks display to the accompaniment of rousing music. Sometimes Nature decides to become part of the show, with spectacular thunderstorms lighting up the far horizon. On such a night, this is the best show in Florida.

Botanical Gardens

Rating:	★ ★ ★ ★ ★
Type:	Beautifully landscaped gardens
Time:	40 to 45 minutes or as long as you wish
Kelly says:	Among the best of its kind in the world and a photographer's paradise

By definition, botanical gardens are a sort of museum. Most botanical gardens seem to strive for order. Succulents here, pines there, palms over there. Tropical plants in this area, temperate plants in that area. That way people can study them better. Completeness is also a goal, trying to have more epiphytes than the next botanical garden, for example. The aesthetics of display, while important, often seem to be a secondary concern, except in the more formal gardens.

The designers of Cypress Gardens, however, seem to have started by asking a simple yet powerful question — "How can we produce the most stunning visual spectacle possible?" — and letting everything else follow from there. The result is a remarkable blend of over-the-top landscaping hyperbole and serene beauty.

These 16 acres contain over 8,000 different kinds of plants, trees, and flowers collected from 90 different countries. There are over 60 varieties of azaleas alone. I have no idea whether that means the collection is unusually complete (I mention azaleas only because it's a flower I recognize). Nor do I know if the designers have carefully segregated tropical plants from the temperate varieties (I suspect they have not). But I can't imagine anyone will care.

Here the purely aesthetic experience is paramount. A leisurely stroll, with open eyes and a receptive soul, will yield abundant treasures. And if you're a typical vacation photographer, bring along a few more rolls of film (or memory cards) than usual. You'll find ample use for them. As large as it is, the garden is not a maze and there's little likelihood of getting lost.

Tip: The garden is dotted with wooden benches. Bring a handkerchief or paper towel, as many of them are wet in the morning hours, before the sun has had a chance to dry them off.

As you enter the gardens, you cross a bridge onto a chain of man-made islands. To your left is Lake Eloise, its shore guarded by stately cypress trees emerging from the shallow water. To the right is a man-made canal. Must-see sights along this archipelago are the **Big Lagoon**, across which you might see a pretty Southern Belle gracing one of Cypress Garden's loveliest vistas. At the end of the island is a typical Dick Pope inspiration, the **Florida Pool.** This is a swimming pool in the shape of the state of Florida, nestled right against the lake shore. It's fenced off now and used primarily for publicity shots. Its main claim to immortality is its appearance in the 1953 Esther Williams film, *Easy To Love.*

The **Oriental Gardens** are an oasis of cool serenity presided over by a towering Buddha. A wooden "Japanese tea house" offers a place to sit in the shade and survey the scene. Even those seemingly immune to Nature's wonders will be startled by the massive **banyan tree**. This behemoth began its tenure at Cypress Gardens as a 50-pound sapling in a bucket. Today it's larger than your average castle, with its aerial root system creating a charming maze of paths through its very heart.

Perhaps the most beautiful spot in the entire gardens is the **Gazebo**. This is no rustic wooden affair but a resplendent white-domed structure, inspired by Greek architecture, supported by eight fluted columns, and flanked by gently bubbling fountains. Also known as the "Love Chapel," it was the site of the over 300 weddings that took place at Cypress Gardens each year. The Gazebo stands at the top of a rise that looks down across the Big Lagoon and out to Lake Eloise; the view from here is as fine as the reverse view from below. An ingenious **photo op** has been provided here. You stand facing a large mirror with your back to the Gazebo. Place your camera on the small platform (also facing the mirror), set the timer, and smile. You'll get a lovely shot of yourself with the Gazebo in the background and the words "Cypress Gardens" floating on the mirror.

Twice a day, there are **Garden Tours with the Experts** that give you a chance to get those burning horticultural questions answered. The schedule is printed on the back of the park map; tours are not available every day.

The Southern Belles

The Southern Belles deserve a special note. Although the botanical gardens seem to be their "natural habitat," they will be seen in all areas of the park. The story of their origins is another example of the wonderfully ingenious and utterly benign hucksterism that characterizes the history of Cypress Gardens.

It seems that in 1940 a devastating winter freeze killed the colorful but delicate flame vines that framed the entrance at that time. The interior of the park had been saved by the heat of many oil heaters and looked just fine. Visitors didn't know this, however, and when they saw the wilted entrance they assumed the worst and kept on driving.

Noticing this, Julie Pope, Dick's wife, rounded up a bevy of local high school girls and outfitted them in colorful antebellum hoop-skirted gowns. She then placed them strategically in front of the damaged flame vines to wave at approaching cars. Not only did attendance pick up, but the visitors were so enchanted by the girls that another Cypress Gardens tradition was born. Today, the Southern Belles take turns sitting decorously in the hot Florida sun to serve as beautiful props in tourists' photos. Their bright and fanciful gowns are another Cypress Gardens trademark. All of them are made by hand at the park. Each one takes some 13 yards of fabric, 5 yards of lining, over 63 yards of lace, and more than 45 hours to complete. Since that moment of inspiration in 1940, over 800 of them have been created.

Cypress Belle

Rating: ★ ★ ★
Type: Lake cruise
Time: 45 minutes
Kelly says: Great for house hunting

Several times a day, a re-creation of a nineteenth century paddle wheel steamer sets out for a slow turn around Lake Eloise. The narrated tour will point out the Lake's bird life and, if you're lucky, you may see an alligator sunning itself on a dock. But the best part of the trip is a chance to survey the lakeside homes, some of which are quite grand. If any are on the market, chances are your guide will let you know.

There is a $6 charge for this cruise. In the evenings, at 6:00 p.m. (5:00 p.m. on Sundays), the *Cypress Belle* sets sail on a ninety-minute prime rib dinner cruise. The charge is $27 for adults, $22 for children 5 to 12.

Cypress Cove Ferry Line

Rating: ★ ★ ★
Type: Boat ride
Time: 5 - 10 minutes
Kelly says: Shortcut with a view

Save a little time and get another perspective on the park on this lazy pontoon boat ride that links the Gardens with the *Nature's Way* area of Jubilee Junction. There are 18 comfortable seats and room for wheelchairs aboard and your pilot doubles as tour guide.

The Living Gardens

Rating: ★ ★ ★
Type: Slo-mo "living statue"
Time: 20 minutes
Kelly says: Ingenious but makes its point quickly

This show couldn't be simpler. An attractive young woman, elaborately made up to resemble an ornate Victorian statue stands on a platform along *Topiary Trail*, the garden that links the Botanical Gardens to Jubilee Junction. To the accompaniment of saccharine pop music and operatic arias, she goes through a series of slow-motion poses as water spouts from her finger tips and the top of her elaborate hairdo.

I must say, she brings a remarkable degree of romantic intensity to this little exercise, but after five minutes or so you get the idea and the act become repetitious. For me the best part was the end, when a burly workman unplugs the hoses that create the living fountain, assists the performer during her equally slow-motion dismount, and then carts her off to her dressing room on (I'm not making this up) a hand truck.

And All The Rest...

Topiary Trail is a spacious area given over to displays of giant bugs, bears, and bunnies, all carefully crafted out of flowering greenery by Cypress Gardens' topiary magicians. An elaborate fountain and artificial waterfall offer attractive backdrops for photos and a stroll down to the lake gives you a different, if distant, view of the water ski show. **Adventure Arcade** is an air-conditioned corridor near the ski stadium that links the Gardens with Adventure Grove and Splash Island. Here you can waste some money playing carnival-style skill games.

Jubilee Junction

At the South end of the park, Jubilee Junction greets you on your arrival, evoking a make-believe antebellum Southland that probably never existed in quite this quaint a form. The long promenade is accented by flowers and shaded by oaks dripping theatrically in Spanish moss. Along this central corridor is artfully arranged a collection of shops, restaurants, and entertainments in gracious pastel-painted clapboard buildings. The area is actually quite compact, yet it seems wonderfully spacious and contains a multiplicity of things to see and do.

The following attractions are described in roughly the order in which you will encounter them as you walk through Jubilee Junction from *Topiary Trail*:

The Royal Palm Theater: "Cypress Gardens on Ice"

Rating: ★ ★ ★ +
Type: Ice show
Time: 25 minutes
Kelly says: Glitzy and fun

The Royal Palm evokes an old Southern playhouse, complete with faux marble columns at the entrance. Inside is an 800-seat auditorium with a standard proscenium stage. The stage area has been converted into an ice rink but, given the shallowness of the performing area, some compromises have been made. Don't expect the electrifying leaps you may have seen in other ice shows where the skaters have the advantage of larger arenas.

That being said, the small cast of performers who grace this show do the most with the space available as they present an entertaining show that changes theme from time to time. A chorus of pretty girls backs a trio of principal skaters who perform a variety of adagio numbers, in which a boy-girl pair perform a series of acrobatic dance moves involving graceful lifts, and solo routines, in which individual skaters show off their specialties. All of this is leavened with light-hearted humorous numbers that are virtually guaranteed to raise a chuckle.

To top it all off, the designers have contributed some lovely costumes and exciting visual effects. There are about four shows a day. If this sort of thing appeals, check the schedule to make sure you don't miss it. However, if you remember the larger shows that used to be mounted in this space, be prepared for a bit of a let down.

Between ice shows, the Royal Palm will sometimes feature **Song and Dance** shows that tend to be more earnest than artful. They feature young performers and songs that appeal to the American heart.

Wings of Wonder

Rating:	★ ★ ★ ★ +
Type:	Butterfly-filled conservatory
Time:	Continuous viewing
Kelly says:	One of Cypress Gardens' best

What an inspired idea this is! Build a 5,500 square foot Victorian style glass conservatory and run a stream through it. Keep the glass walls and roof sparkling clean. Plant the conservatory with the kinds of trees, plants, and flowers that butterflies love. Then fill the space with over 1,000 free-flying butterflies, exotic waterfowl, and a few iguanas.

The result is pure enchantment and an experience that will reward patient viewing. The more you look, the more butterflies you will see. Some of them are so ingeniously camouflaged, it may be many minutes before you realize they are there at all. A looping path takes you through this wonderland, past babbling waterfalls and quiet ponds as butterflies flutter all about you. At the back, you can see butterflies in the pupal stage, just before they emerge in all their splendor; with a bit of luck, you may see one break through to the light. Somewhere between 700 and 1,000 butterflies are hatched each week in this fashion to keep the conservatory well stocked.

Sunshine Sky Adventure

Rating:	★ ★ ★ ★
Type:	Aerial platform ride
Time:	5 minutes
Kelly says:	A too-short bird's eye view

Tucked away behind the shops of Jubilee Junction is a 370-ton counterbalance that is used to loft a circular platform 153 feet in the air (roughly 16 stories high), where it rotates to give its passengers a panoramic view of Cypress Gardens and Lake Eloise. Off in the distance, you can see the silhouette of stately Bok Tower, 11 miles away. Seating is single-file around the edge of the platform and once the platform is airborne, you can stand and move to the rail for a better look.

This is a fun way to get another perspective on the park, and the lofty vantage point offers photographers many wonderful **photo ops**. At five minutes from start to finish, this ride is a bit too short for my taste, but it's free and you can ride as often as you wish (or until your film runs out). The location of this attraction and the mobile platform itself have been cleverly hidden behind trees and buildings. You can see the raised platform from elsewhere in the park, but you could spend all day in Jubilee Junction and never suspect it was there.

Tip: Ride this one at sunset, several times, if you wish.

Nature's Way

Rating:	★ ★ +
Type:	Small zoo
Time:	Continuous viewing
Kelly says:	Worth a stroll-through en route to the shows in *Nature's Theatre*

This vest-pocket zoo is tucked away in a corner of the park under an attractively shaded canopy of moss-draped oaks. Most animals are held in roughly circular sunken pits, eliminating the need for bars.

Most of the animals are Florida natives (although there is a handsome black leopard in the collection). Along the shores of Lake Eloise you will find **Nature's Boardwalk**, a charming area offering a chance to feed the emus and such and delightful views across the lake. Then you can gawk at Mighty Mike, a stunning 13-foot specimen in **Gator Gulch**. Also in this area is the **Birdwalk Aviary**, a walk-in exhibit of birds and a few tiny muntjac, or barking, deer. The big draw here are the chattering, multi-hued lorys and lorikeets that you can feed.

With the possible exception of the python, you can see more, larger, and better displayed specimens elsewhere in the Orlando area. Still, this makes a pleasant time-killer as you wait for the nature shows to begin.

Several times each day, the keepers host **Animal Encounters and Talk**s. The schedule is printed on the back of the park map.

Nature's Theatre: "Swamp Critters"

Rating:	★ ★ ★
Type:	Nature show
Time:	15 minutes
Kelly says:	Too short

Nature's Theatre is a simple tarp-covered amphitheater that serves as the venue for a series of educational nature shows hosted by Cypress Gardens' staff members, who show off some of their more intriguing charges. Check the schedule for show times.

Exactly what you will see is hard to predict, but generally the show includes at least one raptor, such as a horned owl or red-tailed hawk. The raptors are Cypress Gardens' lineup of injured birds of prey that can never be released back to the wild and are living out their lives in the comfort and security of the Gardens. They earn their room and board by posing for your photos during this informative presentation. You may also see macaws, baby alligators, and a snake or two. For each animal, the handlers present a fascinating sampler of natural history tidbits. Some critters are paraded in front of the audience for those who wish to touch or take close-up photos.

Nature's Theatre: "Tricks of the Trade"

Rating: ★ ★ ★
Type: More animal show and tell
Time: 20 minutes
Kelly says: Animal training 101

Cypress Gardens is planning new animal shows and their future stars need to be trained. Since a big part of that training involves getting the little critters used to an audience, their trainers have cleverly decided to turn the training process into a simple but entertaining show.

While a trainer keeps up a steady patter of fun facts about positive reinforcement, animal behaviors, and nature trivia, a series of animals are brought out to greet the crowd. Some go through simple "A to B behaviors," in which they run along a predetermined route in order to get a rewarding treat. Others are there simply to see and be seen.

"Treasure of Cypress Cove"

Rating: ★ ★ +
Type: Slapstick comedy show
Time: 20 minutes
Kelly says: Aimed squarely at the kiddie set

"How much does it cost to get a pirate's ears pierced?"

"A buck an ear."

If this is your idea of rollicking humor, you'll love this show.

Three young guys play an assortment of dim-witted pirates in search of a cursed treasure. With broad humor, excruciating puns, and the occasional spray of water sent into the first several rows of the audience, they keep little kids (and more than a few adults) giggling happily.

And All The Rest...

Jubilee Junction has a number of minor attractions, some of which are well worth a look. **When Radios Were Radios** is a simple display of old-time radios that date back to the dawn of the electronic age. Visitors "of a certain age" are sure to spot some models they listened to when they were kids. **Planes, Trains and Automobiles** houses a super model train set that depicts a coast to coast trainscape, complete with purple mountains majesty and fruited plains. Past *Wings of Wonder* lies **Plantation Gardens**, a series of small, formal, themed gardens. Past the gardens, you can stroll down to the lake. It's one of the park's least visited areas and one of the loveliest.

Adventure Grove & Splash Island

The third and newest major area of Cypress Gardens houses a collection of amusement park rides and a water park and is intended to attract a demographic of younger kids and teens that shunned the old Cypress Gardens. It seems to be working. The good news for those who are not interested in this sort of thing is that this section is well separated from the rest of the park and can be avoided with ease.

There are three entrances. At the southern end, you can enter from Jubilee Junction, past Guest Services and Star Haven Amphitheatre. In the middle, you will find **Adventure Arcade**, a video and carnival game area that links it with the ski stadium. At the north end, past the water park, you can enter from the Botanical Gardens.

Adventure Grove

Rating: ★ ★ ★
Type: Amusement park rides
Time: As long as you (and junior) can stand
Kelly says: Head here with squirmy kids and teens

This large area, about as large as the rest of Jubilee Junction, houses some three dozen amusement park rides, only a handful of them rising above the level you'd expect to find at a well-appointed county fair or traveling carnival. Among the more interesting rides are the three roller coasters. None will rival the mega-coasters at the major theme parks but they provide modest thrills for the younger set. **Triple Hurricane**, named for the three storms that slammed Cypress Gardens during its refurbishment, is an attractive 20-seater wooden coaster, while **Swamp Thing** is an inverted steel coaster, also a 20-seater, as is **Okeechobee Rampage**, a small steel coaster.

There are two water-park style rides. **Storm Surge** takes 8-person round rafts up a steep hill and sends them spinning down a corkscrew chute. **Wave Runner** is a twin, enclosed water slide that uses 2-person rafts. Some people say it's the best ride in Adventure Grove.

Also of note is **Paradise Sky Wheel**, a Ferris wheel that sits over the old sinkhole that graced Cypress Gardens former entrance. There are also plenty of rides set aside just for the littlest visitors.

"Farmyard Frolics"

Rating: ★ ★ +
Type: Comedy magic show
Time: 15 minutes
Kelly says: Mildly entertaining for young kids

This open-air show in Adventure Grove, with seating on low-slung benches, features two none-too-bright hillbilly types serving up a number of magic tricks, interspersed with country songs and high-stepping clog dancing.

Kids will get a kick out of the way these guys make a variety of barnyard critters appear out of thin air. At one point they turn two white doves in a small box into one large white rabbit.

In the show's best bit, the smaller of the two gets squished paper thin in a crazy farm implement, only to be reconstituted with an artfully employed air pump.

Splash Island

Rating: ★ ★ ★
Type: Mini water park
Time: As much as you want
Kelly says: A nice addition

With just two "rides" Splash Island hardly qualifies as a full-fledged water park, but it is a thoughtful addition to the park for those looking for a break from the summer heat.

Circling the area is **Paradise River,** where you can grab an inner tube ($4) and take a lazy float. Another great way to relax is to sun yourself on the shores of **Kowabunga Bay,** a medium-sized wave pool. For active kids, there is **Polynesian Adventure**, a colorful, multi-level, water-soaked play area that is the best thing at *Splash Island*. At its apex, a huge bucket in the shape of a tiki god fills with water and periodically tips over, much to the delight of the kids below.

Voodoo Plunge consists of three speed slides. Two are fairly straightforward, but the third is a completely enclosed tube with a zippy corkscrew near the top. Next door is **Tonga Tubes**, where you grab your own inner tube and climb to the top to descend through one of two twisting flumes, with both open and enclosed sections, to a splashdown in a small pool.

Chapter Seven:

Kennedy Space Center

ABOUT AN HOUR FROM ORLANDO (AND DISNEY'S TOMORROWLAND) IS A PLACE where the fantasy drops away, replaced by awe-inspiring reality. It is here, at the John F. Kennedy Space Center, smack in the middle of a wildlife refuge, that real people, riding real live spaceships, are blasted into outer space on a variety of scientific missions. Nearby Cape Canaveral handles military and commercial launches. On the fringes of this very serious enterprise, the Kennedy Space Center Visitor Complex (a separate entity) lets us earthbound types get a peek at this very special world and imagine — just for a moment — what it must be like to be on the cutting edge of tomorrow. If you time your visit just right, you can even see the actual space shuttle roaring into the heavens towards another rendezvous with the future.

The Kennedy Space Center (or "KSC" for short) is immense, one-fifth the size of the state of Rhode Island. Only 6,000 of its 140,000 acres are used for operations; the rest is a wildlife refuge. Most people are amazed to learn that this monument to high-tech is home to more endangered species (15) than any other place in the United States except the Everglades. There are also 310 types of birds flitting between the launch pads. Yet over the years, the complex has logged some 3,000 launches. As you might expect, you will only get to see a small sliver of Kennedy Space Center's vastness but the access you are granted is remarkable.

For those who care about such things, I should note that no taxpayer money is used to support the visitor facilities, tours, or other tourist activities at Kennedy Space Center. All of these are run by a private company, Delaware North Parks Services, and are entirely self-supporting.

Before You Come

Doing homework for your visit to Kennedy Space Center is not absolutely necessary, but it helps if you have at least some background knowledge of the space program. A painless way to get that background is to head down to the video store and rent *The Right Stuff* and *Apollo 13*. Both films are a lot of fun to watch and offer great insight into the human as well as the technical dimensions of the space program. Somewhat harder to find but worth looking for is the Discovery Channel special, *The Space Shuttle*.

For information about the Kennedy Space Center Visitor Complex itself, call (321) 449-4444. Ask for brochures and they will patch you into a voice mail system where you can record your name and address. The brochures are free and take about one week to arrive.

The Visitor Complex brochure, with its schedule of tours and films, can help you plan out your day in advance. Readers with an Internet connection can log on at www.kennedyspacecenter.com and follow the prompts.

Another way to get an advance look at the Center is to call either the (321) number above or (800) 621-9826 and order the *Kennedy Space Center Visitor Complex* tour book. It is $5.99, plus $4 shipping and takes about a week to arrive. It doesn't provide tour and film times but it will certainly whet your appetite and help you decide how to focus your time during your visit.

When's the Best Time to Come?

To a great extent, attendance at KSC reflects the seasonal ebb and flow of tourists described in *Chapter 1*. However, attendance is also greatly affected by the launch schedule at the Kennedy Space Center.

The days before and after a launch tend to be busier than usual as excitement builds in anticipation of the big event. The day of a launch, the Visitor Complex closes for the six hours preceding the blast-off. If the shuttle launches before 9:00 a.m., the center is open all day. Given the fact that launches are frequently delayed, however, the six-hour pre-launch closing can mean that the Visitor Complex will be open for just a few hours or not at all on a launch day.

So even though seeing a launch is one of the neatest things to do while you're in Florida, a visit to Kennedy Space Center at that time may not be an ideal choice — unless you don't mind missing some things or will be able to spend more than a day on the Space Coast.

For a recorded message giving dates and other information about upcoming shuttle launches dial (321) 867-4636. If you are interested in seeing a shuttle launch, see the discussion on getting tickets and the best view at the end of this chapter.

Getting There

The easiest way to reach KSC from Orlando is to get on the Bee Line Expressway (SR 528) headed east. The tolls will set you back $2.75 each way but it's the fastest route (about an hour or so). Turn off onto SR 407 North, and then onto SR 405 East, which will lead you directly to the Visitor Complex. You can also take SR 50 (Orlando's East Colonial Drive) to route 405. It takes a bit longer but it's free.

Once you get on SR 405, don't be misled by the *Astronaut Hall of Fame*, which you will pass on the right. The main entrance to Kennedy Space Center is farther along, also on the right, and also graced with a life-size replica of the space shuttle.

The *Astronaut Hall of Fame* is owned by KSC, but is a semi-separate attraction and is described in *Chapter 11: Another Roadside Attraction*.

Once you get to the KSC Visitor Complex, parking is provided **free** in lots with sections named after shuttle craft.

Opening and Closing Times

Hours for the Visitor Complex vary throughout the year. Opening time is invariably 9:00 a.m. but the closing time changes to keep pace with sunset. The earliest closing time is 5:30 p.m. and the latest is usually 7:00 p.m. However, you should call for exact times.

Tours and IMAX films begin at 10:00 a.m. Tours stop departing about three hours prior to the closing time of the Visitor Complex. The last showing of the IMAX films is usually about one or two hours prior to closing. Some attractions at the Visitor Complex also close early.

The Price of Admission

You enter the Kennedy Space Center Visitor Complex through a Ticket Plaza that is themed to evoke the International Space Station. The ticket booths take the form of space station modules, while the overhead shading is provided by large solar panels. A few space-walking astronauts float above, adding to the effect. There are about 20 ticket windows, with the Will Call windows located to your far left as you approach the Ticket Plaza.

Kennedy Space Center offers a number of admission options, which can be moderately confusing. I'll try to sort through them. Prices, before tax, are as follows:

Standard Admission:

Adults:	$31
Children (3 to 11):	$21

This is a one-day admission ticket that includes access to all the exhibits at the Visitor Complex, the main Kennedy Space Center bus tour, and admission to the IMAX films.

Maximum Access Admission:

Adults:	$38
Children (3 to 11):	$28

This option adds admission to the *U.S. Astronaut Hall of Fame* and its simulator rides (described in *Chapter 11: Another Roadside Attraction*). It also adds a second day of admission to the Visitors Complex and the IMAX films.

Combo Pass:

Adults:	$55.99
Children (3 to 11):	$39.99

This package includes the Maximum Access option and one of the special interest tours, *Cape Canaveral Then & Now* or *NASA Up Close*, both described later.

Specialty Tour Tickets:

Adults:	$22
Children (3 to 11):	$16

These prices are per tour. In other words, if you are an adult and want to take both tours, it will set you back $44 (unless you opted for the Combo Pass, in which case one tour is already paid for). These prices are in addition to the cost of regular admission. In other words, you can't show up just to take one of these tours.

Annual Pass

The Kennedy Space Center Visitor Complex offers an annual pass option as follows (prices do not include tax):

Adults:	$50
Children (3 to 11):	$35

The annual pass allows unlimited access to the Visitor Complex, the KSC bus tour, and the IMAX films, plus priority purchase of tickets to view shuttle launches. Annual passholders also get a discount of $3.50 on tickets for each of up to six guests as well as a subscription to the quarterly Visitor Complex newsletter. Passholders must show the pass and a photo ID each time they enter.

Which Price Is Right?

This is a tough call and the answer will depend on your level of interest in the space program and how much time you can devote to visiting KSC. If you have just one day, many people will be perfectly satisfied with the Standard one-day admission. Choose the Maximum Access option only if you *must* do the simulator rides at the *Astronaut Hall of Fame*.

If you have two days to spend, then by all means try the Combo Pass. The special interest tours are well worth taking and the two day option lets you do at least one. Just be sure to check the departure schedules, as departures are limited. If you want to do *both* special interest tours you will have to purchase both the Combo Pass and one separate tour ticket. If you feel you can take a pass on the special interest tours, then the Maximum Access pass gives you plenty to do in two days and, for adults, is only $7 more than the Standard one-day admission. The annual pass will appeal primarily to space junkies who live nearby or who visit the area several times a year.

Good Things to Know About . . .

Access for the Disabled

All of KSC Visitor Complex is wheelchair accessible. **Free** wheelchairs may be obtained at the Information counter in Information Central, the first building you enter after paying your admission. The IMAX films are equipped with devices for the hearing impaired.

Audio Tours

Audio tours of the Visitor Complex are available at the Information counter in Information Central. The cost is $6.36, tax included. In addition to English, audio tours are available in Spanish, French, German, Italian, Portuguese, and Japanese. In fact, these tours seem to be most popular with non-English speakers.

Babies

Stroller rentals are **free** at KSC (at the Information counter in Information Central). Diaper changing tables are located in some restrooms, including the men's room at the Orbit Restaurant.

First Aid

There is a well-equipped first aid station with a nurse on duty from 9:00 a.m. to 5:00 p.m. It is located near the bus boarding area.

Leaving the Park

Since the Kennedy Space Center is far from any population center, it is unlikely you will want to leave during your visit but if you decide to do so, just get your hand stamped at the exit and you will be able to reenter.

Money

You will find ATMs to the right of the Ticket Plaza, on the wall of the Space Shop across from the *Astronaut Encounter*, and at the Apollo/Saturn V Center. They are connected to all the major bank systems and credit cards.

Pets

Pets will be boarded **free** of charge during your visit. The pet kennel is to your right as you approach Information Central.

Security

Security is exceptionally tight. All visitors must pass through metal detectors and a battery of additional security personnel stands ready to conduct more detailed searches. Coolers and backpacks are banned and no lockers are available, so plan on leaving your excess stuff in the car and traveling light.

Blast Off:
Your Day at Kennedy Space Center

I have found that it is impossible to see everything at Kennedy Space Center in one day. It is, however, possible to see most of it if you get there early and step lively for the next 8 to 10 hours. Even a delay of a few hours will decrease your chances of seeing as much as possible. It will help to understand that there are three main components to the KSC experience: the Visitor Complex houses most of the exhibits and the wonderful IMAX films; the bus tours leave from the Visitor Complex and let you explore the working end of the Space Center; the *Astronaut Hall of Fame* is a separate (and optional) attraction about a mile from the Visitor Center that houses a museum and a number of space-program-themed simulators.

When you arrive at the Visitor Complex, your first stop is the Ticket Plaza where you collect your access badge. Once you have your badge, you proceed through a building called Information Central. This is really just a spacious antechamber containing the Information counter, which doubles as Lost and Found. Pass through this building and you are in the Visitor Complex itself. Kennedy Space Center and the adjacent Cape Canaveral Air Force Station cover a great deal of territory. The Visitor Complex, by contrast, is quite small; you can walk from one end to the other in about five minutes. Your visit to Kennedy Space Center will be centered here — except when you leave on the bus tour.

The One-Day Stay

Getting the most out of a one-day visit to Kennedy Space Center requires early arrival and careful planning.

When you purchase tickets, you will be handed a map of the Complex and a schedule of tours, IMAX film showings, and other events. Pause a moment in the coolness of Information Central to orient yourself with the map and plan your day with the schedule. Note that the bus tour of Kennedy Space Center, called simply *KSC Tour*, has continuous departures (ending between about 2:15 p.m. and 2:45 p.m., depending on closing time), while the *Cape Canaveral Then & Now Tour* has just one departure and the *NASA Up Close Tour* has only a few. So if you have paid the premium to take either of the latter tours (you can realistically take only one), plan your day around it. (Since both special interest tours drop you off at the Saturn V Center, you have the option of skipping the main KSC Tour; if you do, your time constraints are lessened considerably.) Seeing both IMAX films in one day may prove tricky. Most people choose *Space Station 3D*, largely I suspect because of the 3D, but it is an excellent choice.

If you have chosen the Maximum Access option, plan on retrieving your car and heading to the *U.S. Astronaut Hall of Fame* as soon as you have wrapped up at the Visitors Complex. The *Hall of Fame* stays open a little later than KSC proper; just be prepared for crowds.

If you plan on doing all or most of the major, scheduled attractions, you will discover that once you have mapped out your schedule, you will have a half hour or an hour here and there during the day to see what's left and eat. I suggest grabbing your food on the run if you want to maximize your touring time. There are plenty of freestanding kiosks scattered about, making this a viable strategy.

You can use the descriptions below and your own taste to determine which of the "what's left" will most appeal to you. I strongly recommend the *Launch Status Center* and the *Astronaut Encounter*.

The Two-Day Stay

If you have more than one day to allocate to visiting the Kennedy Space Center Visitor Complex your task becomes much easier, and only slightly more expensive. Purchase the Maximum Access pass or the Combo Pass, if you want to take one of the special interest tours. Then on the first day, take the main KSC Bus Tour and one of the special tours. On the second day, take the other special interest tour if you wish (remember, it will cost extra!) and see any exhibits or films you didn't have time for the first day. Budget a more leisurely visit to the *Hall of Fame*, perhaps on the morning of the second day when the crowds won't be as intimidating.

Special Note: During times of launches or heightened security, the two special bus tours, *NASA Up Close* and *Cape Canaveral Then & Now*, both described below, may be cancelled. In that case, it will be very easy to see KSC in a single day.

Attractions at the Visitor Complex

Most of the attractions at the Visitor Complex are available for continuous viewing, except the IMAX films and the *Astronaut Encounter* which have frequently scheduled showings throughout the day. The exhibits range from the compelling to the easy to miss. They are described here starting from Information Central and proceeding in a roughly clockwise path to the back of the Complex. Since distances are short, see the ones that appeal most first, then visit the others as time permits.

Robot Scouts

Rating:	★ ★ ★
Type:	Walk-through presentation, with animated displays
Time:	20 minutes
Kelly says:	A well-done introduction to unmanned space exploration

Our host for this clever overview of current unmanned space exploration missions is Starquester 2000, a robot himself who has been temporarily grounded by a faulty navigational system. As we walk along a twisting, darkened corridor, we pause at six windows where we get a quick and painless overview of the Voyager, Viking, Cassini, and other missions, as well as the Hubble Space Telescope. These robot scouts attempt to determine if life exists elsewhere in the solar system, whether humans can survive on the various planets and moons they have visited, and in general just how the universe works.

It's a reminder of how many stunning discoveries have been made in the last few decades by these remote controlled "trailblazers for human exploration," as Starquester never tires of calling them. And even though this attraction looks forward to a human presence on Mars, it is also a reminder that unmanned space exploration will be standard operating procedure for the foreseeable future.

Universe Theater: "Quest for Life"

Rating:	★ ★ +
Type:	Film
Time:	About 20 minutes
Kelly says:	An okay time-killer

On the other side of the Information Central building, a comfortable theater specializes in showing short films on various aspects of space and the space program.

These films run continuously, with a short break between showings. The current offering is *Quest for Life,* an earnest but not terribly compelling film that surveys the latest scientific theories about the origins of life on earth and then speculates on the likelihood of life existing elsewhere in the universe. The filmmakers use extremely optimistic odds in making their calculations, odds that have been challenged by some scientists, although the controversy on this point is not noted in the film.

Nature & Technology

Rating:	★ ★
Type:	Diorama
Time:	Continuous viewing
Kelly says:	Can be skipped

Tucked around the corner from the Universe Theater is this small display about the Merritt Island National Wildlife Refuge (see *Chapter 14: Gardens & Edens*). It consists of an "immersive" diorama depicting the wildlife and natural scenery that surround the Space Center.

Children's Play Dome

Rating:	★ ★ ★
Type:	Playground and jungle gym
Time:	Unlimited
Kelly says:	A great place for the little ones to let off steam

Beneath this geodesic dome, kids and their parents will find a small jungle gym, riddled with climbing tunnels and thoughtfully equipped with cubby holes for sneakers and other valuables, as well as a kid-sized space shuttle, where you can enthusiastically reenact the historic moments you've just witnessed. Parents will appreciate the picnic tables tucked under the dome, perfect for resting one's feet while the small fry tear around, and a nice spot for a snack break away from the Florida sun.

Early Space Exploration

Rating:	★ ★ ★ +
Type:	Space program museum
Time:	Continuous viewing
Kelly says:	An eye-popping encounter with history

A portion of the original control room from the Mission Control building used during the Mercury and early Gemini missions has been transported here from its original home on Cape Canaveral. I found this small room, which looks a bit like a set from a low-budget 1950s television series, absolutely entrancing. It bears mute testimony to the speed at which our technology is exploding. The view you get is the same President Kennedy once enjoyed when he came to the Cape to witness a launch.

Otherwise, this is a once-over-lightly history of the early space program. Sometimes, the Beatles seem to get equal billing with the Mercury astronauts, but if you take the time to read the signage, you'll learn quite a bit. And the few artifacts on display, actual Mercury and Gemini capsules prominent among them, are fascinating.

Rocket Garden

Rating: ★ ★ ★
Type: Outdoor display of rockets
Time: Continuous viewing
Kelly says: Great photo backdrops

This may remind you of a sculpture garden at a museum of modern art. Indeed, some of the rocket engines on display look just as arty and a lot prettier than some modern art. The stars of the show, however, are the big rockets. A plaque gives the vital statistics for each object for the technically inclined, but most people will be content to gawk and have their pictures taken in front of these amazing machines.

The *Rocket Garden* can be appreciated from a distance, but the Apollo-Saturn service arm, once part of the gantry that served the giant Saturn rockets, is worth a visit. Armstrong, Aldrin, and Collins strode down this metal walkway en route to the moon. Also worth a closer look is the mammoth Saturn 1B rocket lying on its side on the far side of the garden; this behemoth generated a thrust of 1.3 million pounds as it lofted Skylab astronauts into orbit back in the seventies.

Guided tours of the area are available twice daily, with the schedule posted on a sign. This is a great chance to hear some stories that illuminate the human dimension of the space program.

Mad Mission to Mars 2025

Rating: ★ ★ ★
Type: Live show
Time: About 30 minutes
Kelly says: Aimed squarely at the kids

Just opposite the Universe Theater is another show venue, this one showcasing a half-hour of up-tempo silliness hosted by two twenty-something rocket scientists, one of whom is just a little madder than the other.

Using a variety of props, gimmicks, audience volunteers, and an animated 3-D floating robot named WD-4D (get it?), the two provide an overview of the serious science behind a hoped-for mission to explore the Red Planet. There's even a hip-hop rendition of Newton's Laws of Motion. It's virtually incomprehensible, of course, but it is mildly diverting which, I suppose, is the point. The kids love it.

Exploration in the New Millennium

Rating: ★ ★ +
Type: Displays on Mars and beyond
Time: Continuous viewing
Kelly says: On and off fun, if you have the time

This walk-through grab bag of displays and short films links the explorers of old with those yet unborn, with the vastness of space substituting for the oceans crossed by the Vikings and Columbus. To keep younger kids interested, you may want to pick up an Exploration Passport that can be stamped at various stations throughout the exhibit.

You'll find a nifty mock-up of the Viking Mars lander in a simulated Martian landscape. Nearby, a three-screen video presentation on the **Exploration of the Solar System** is perhaps the most informative display here. Farther along you will find a small display on Mars featuring an opportunity, so we are told, to touch an actual piece of Mars. But this is not a sample brought back from Mars by one of those robot scouts. It's a slice of a meteorite that scientists say originally came from Mars, which to my way of thinking is not quite the same thing. A better idea here is a place where you can leave your signature electronically so it can be transported to Mars on a future mission. Another simple, but fascinating, touch is a curving wall on which the sun, planets, and moons of our solar system are painted to scale to illustrate their relative size.

At the end of the exhibit is a small theater showing **Space Race 3000**, a fanciful TV broadcast from the far-distant future about a race to Proxima Centauri to test three very different forms of interstellar propulsion — an antimatter engine, a light sail, and a ram scoop.

Astronaut Encounter

Rating: ★ ★ ★ ★
Type: Meet a real live astronaut
Time: About 20 minutes
Kelly says: Best for the astronaut Q&A

This is one of the Visitor Complex's more inspired attractions, despite some unnecessary padding. A perky host warms up the audience with some space program trivia and then clowns around with two young volunteers from the audience. That's the unnecessary part. But about ten minutes into the show, a real live veteran of the space program shows up and things get considerably more interesting.

All the astronauts who appear in this show are the real McCoy, with at least one space flight to their credit, and some of the big names of the space program have appeared on this stage. The astronaut chats for a bit and then segues effortlessly into a question and answer period that can be great fun. The host circulates through the audience with the mike so everyone can be heard. For some reason, the show always seems to end with a kid asking how the astronauts go to the bathroom in space. Just like a space mission, this show is planned to the last detail. After the Q&A, the astronaut hangs around for **photo ops**.

IMAX Theater Exhibits

Rating: ★ ★ +
Type: Various displays
Time: Continuous viewing
Kelly says: If you have the time

A number of exhibits and displays are scattered about the large building that houses the IMAX film theaters (see below). If you have a few moments to spare before or after the show — or have ducked inside to escape a rain shower — you might want to take a quick look around.

At one end of the building is an art gallery featuring works commissioned by NASA to commemorate the space program. They range from hyperrealism to the surreal to the completely abstract and are worth at least a quick look. At the other end is a space used for temporary or traveling displays; these can range from the excellent to the merely interesting. In a passage between the two theaters you will find a small display explaining the process whereby shuttles are prepared, launched, retrieved, and prepped yet again for flight.

Astronaut Memorial (Space Mirror)

Rating: ★ ★ ★
Type: Memorial to fallen astronauts
Time: Continuous viewing
Kelly says: Intricate, intriguing, and moving

At first this monument to those who have lost their lives in the space program struck me as a bit of overkill. But as I examined the intricate mechanism that uses the sun's beams to illuminate the 16 names on this massive memorial, I came to realize how fitting it is to blend the high-tech and the heavenly to honor these special people. The entire memorial tilts and swivels to follow the sun across the sky as mirrors collect and focus the sun's rays onto clear glass names in a huge black marble slab. From the opposite side the effect is startling. The memorial is handsomely sited at the end of a large pool at the back of the IMAX Theater; a small kiosk on the side of that building houses computers that offer background information on the astronauts honored on the memorial.

Shuttle Plaza/Explorer

Rating: ★ ★ +
Type: Full-scale shuttle model
Time: Continuous viewing with the possibility of long waits
Kelly says: If you have time

The full-scale model of the space shuttle is certainly impressive. But don't be surprised if you find a visit a bit of a let down, especially if you've had to wait 40 minutes or an hour for a glimpse inside. The line spirals up an elaborate exterior superstructure (which also contains an elevator for the disabled). You can step in on two levels — the cockpit and, immediately below it, the crew compartment. To your left is the huge empty cargo bay. What stuck me most was how cramped the space allotted to the crew is. Not even a New York landlord would have the gall to call this a studio apartment. This attraction closes down when lightning is spotted within 30 miles of the Visitor Complex. Guided tours of the Shuttle Plaza area, which also contains two booster rockets, are offered from time to time.

Launch Status Center

Rating: ★ ★ ★ ★ +
Type: Live briefings and educational displays

Time:	Briefings last about 20 minutes
Kelly says:	The best thing at the Visitor Complex

The modest looking, almost anonymous, white geodesic dome near the Explorer mock-up in Shuttle Plaza houses what is, in my opinion, the best thing at the Visitor Complex. There are models and displays here of the retrievable solid rocket boosters and their motors, a manned maneuvering unit, even an outer-space soft drink dispenser. Perhaps the most fascinating artifact is an actual solid rocket booster nose cone from the 66th shuttle mission; usually these sink to the bottom of the ocean and are replaced, but this one remained afloat long enough to be retrieved.

The main attractions here, however, are the live briefings that occur every hour on the hour from 11:00 a.m. to 5:00 p.m. Held in front of a set of simulated mission control panels like those used in astronaut training, they feature a live "communicator" and live shots from remote video cameras strategically stationed around the working heart of the Space Center, including the Vehicle Assembly Building and the launch pad itself.

No matter when you visit, there will always be something going on at the Space Center and this is your opportunity to get the inside scoop. Obviously, the most interesting time to come here is in the days and hours before a launch and during an actual mission, when you'll get to see the live video feed from the shuttle itself. However, a visit is worthwhile no matter where they are in the launch cycle. The communicators are veritable encyclopedias of information about the space program, and I would urge you not to be shy about asking questions once the formal briefing is over.

Center for Space Education

Rating:	★ ★ ★
Type:	Hands-on science displays open to public
Time:	Continuous viewing
Kelly says:	For teachers and budding astronauts

On the opposite side of the Visitor Complex grounds from Shuttle Plaza, set well away from the other attractions, this large building houses the educational outreach component of the Kennedy Space Center. Inside, teachers will find a library and resource center just for them. Special programs for visiting school groups are also held in this building. The **Exploration Station** is open to the general public. It is a largish room filled with hands-on, interactive exhibits that demonstrate basic principles of science. This will probably most appeal to younger kids.

The Bus Tours

The only way to see the working end of the Space Center is by taking a guided bus tour. Three tours are offered, representing the past, present, and future of the space program. All tours leave from an efficient bus terminal at one end of the Visitor Complex. The buses are much like regular city buses except they have much larger windows. No food is allowed aboard the buses and the only beverage allowed is bottled water, which is available for purchase at the Visitors Complex and each stop of the

KSC Tour. It's not a bad idea to bring some, especially in the warmer months.

The *KSC Tour,* included in the price of admission, visits the Kennedy Space Center on Merritt Island. This tour is quite clearly the star of the show, with continuous departures starting at 10:00 a.m. and continuing until about three hours prior to closing. There are two stops on this tour and you can stay as long at each of them as you wish because the buses run continuously. This system has obvious advantages but the downside is that crowds can build up, making the bus loading process slow and chaotic. So it's best to take this tour early in the day.

There are also two "special interest tours" that cost an additional $22 for adults or $16 for children. The *Cape Canaveral Then & Now* has one departure daily and the *NASA Up Close* tour has about five or six; each of these tours is limited to a single busload, about 50 people. Realistically speaking, on a one-day visit you will be able to take only one special interest tour in addition to the *KSC Tour,* not both.

The ticketing procedure is also somewhat cumbersome. You must first purchase your tickets at the Ticket Plaza, then proceed to the Information counter in Information Central to make your reservations for a specific departure time. In the case of the Cape Canaveral tour, there are additional security procedures that require signing in and showing photo ID such as a drivers license. Foreign visitors should bring their passport. Failure to follow these procedures can result in confusion at tour time; you may even be denied boarding.

There is one thing that all tours have in common: they all finish up with visits to the Apollo/Saturn V Center and the International Space Station Center (ISSC). For that reason alone, I have given all tours the same five-star rating.

Special Note: Because of the steady stream of commercial launch activity at Cape Canaveral, the Cape tour is sometimes curtailed or unavailable. And during times of heightened security, both of the special interest tours may be cancelled.

Another unpredictable element, in terms of what you will see, is the wildlife at the Center. Alligators, sometimes jokingly referred to as part of the security system, are sighted frequently and there are bald eagle nests along the tour routes.

The standard narration on the tours will be supplemented — or interrupted — whenever the driver feels it's time to add his or her own commentary or release a late-breaking news bulletin ("Wild hogs on the left!"). Foreign language narration, in French, German, Spanish, and Portuguese, is available on tape on a first-come, first-served basis.

Kennedy Space Center Tour

Rating: ★ ★ ★ ★ ★
Time: 2 to 3 hours
Kelly says: The next best thing to becoming an astronaut

The bus tour of Kennedy Space Center, with the Apollo/Saturn V Center, is yet another "must-see" stop on the Central Florida tourist circuit. And no wonder. This tour takes you to the sites where the space shuttle is prepared and launched. It also gives you an opportunity to gape and gawk at an actual Saturn V rocket. It's as close as you'll come to being launched into space without joining the astronaut corps.

There are two stops on this tour — the LC-39 Observation Gantry and the Apollo/Saturn V Center. You will also get to drive by the Vehicle Assembly Building, where the space shuttle is mated with its immense fuel tanks prior to each launch.

The **LC-39 Observation Gantry** ("LC" stands for "launch complex") is a four-story tower that offers a bird's-eye view of launch pads 39A and B, from which all shuttle flights depart. If you visit close to a launch, you'll see the support structure that completely surrounds the shuttle. It is only removed a few hours prior to launch. You may also get a chance for an up-close photo of the massive crawler transporters that carry the shuttle from the **Vehicle Assembly Building** (VAB) to the launch pad. These six-million-pound vehicles roar along at one-half mile per hour when fully loaded and get an incredible 35 feet per gallon.

You'll also get close to the VAB itself. One of the largest buildings in the world, its roof covers five acres. It encloses so much space that it has its own atmosphere and it has actually rained inside. It was here that the gigantic Saturn V rockets used in the Apollo program were assembled. The shuttles seem tiny by comparison.

The undisputed highlight of this tour is a visit to the **Apollo/Saturn V Center**. The building is massive — and it has to be to house a refurbished, 363-foot-tall Saturn V moon rocket, one of only three in existence. Before you get to see the star of this show, you enter the **Firing Room** where the actual mission control consoles used during the Apollo missions form a backdrop for a video and audio re-creation of the launch of Apollo VIII, the first manned lunar mission.

Then you step into the massive building that houses the Saturn V, suspended horizontally in one long open space. No description can prepare you for just how immense this thing actually is. The word "awesome" moves from hyperbole to understatement. Arrayed around, alongside, and under the rocket are interpretive displays filled with astounding facts about this magnificent achievement.

Before you leave, be sure to visit the **Lunar Theater**, where you will see a re-creation of the first landing on the moon and be reminded of just how touch-and-go this mission was up to the very last second. After the show, you step into the **New Frontiers Gallery** for a preview of space missions yet to come.

The final stop on your tour is a visit to the **International Space Station Center** (ISSC). Here, after a brief introductory film on the space station program, you will have the opportunity to actually observe construction of the station's modular capsules from a second-story observation deck over the assembly room floor. This is the closest you can come to the day-to-day activities that make Kennedy Space Center such an incredible place. You'll also get to explore life-sized models of the various capsules already in space; you can walk through mock-up laboratories, kitchens, sleeping areas, and bathrooms, all built to scale. The spartan living quarters and clever use of every last inch of space convey what it's like to be an astronaut today better than any film.

If you don't linger at the various stops, you can complete this tour in about two hours, but rushing through is a mistake. Take your time, invest three or four hours and enjoy yourself. There are places to eat at each stop and the Apollo/Saturn V Center even boasts the **Moon Rock Cafe,** the "only place on earth where you can dine next to a piece of the moon." Between stops a taped commentary plays on ceiling-mounted video monitors; it provides some interesting background information on the Center and its operations. This tour is an exciting experience for anyone. For Americans, it should be a source of deep patriotic pride.

Tip: Try for a seat on the right side of the bus as you shuttle from stop to stop.

NASA Up Close Tour

Rating: ★ ★ ★ ★ ★
Time: 90 minutes
Kelly says: In the footsteps of the astronauts

In a sense *NASA Up Close* begins where the *KSC Tour* leaves off, offering you extra special access to places you glimpsed from afar on the main tour. With the expert guidance of a space program expert who is a gold mine of little known facts, you get to visit the **Space Station Processing Facility** (SSPF). From a long, glass-walled observation platform you can watch elements of the space station being readied in ultra-clean conditions for eventual transfer into space. It can take six months or more to get these massive building blocks prepped for their journey into orbit.

There is another stop near **Launch Pads 39A and B** at a special seaside view-ing platform that offers one of the best **photo ops** to be had at KSC. With the tower-ing pads to one side and the Atlantic Ocean to the other, you'll get a terrific view of the rotating service structure that swings away for the actual launch, the flame trench that harnesses and channels the inferno created by the shuttle's rockets, and the mas-sive lightning rods that protect the shuttle from Florida's stormy weather.

You also get closer to the **Vehicle Assembly Building**. It looks immense from the vantage point offered on the *KSC Tour*, but now it is positively awe-inspiring. Every mission begins with an inch-by-inch journey on the **Crawler Transporter**, which you'll revisit on this tour. And since all space missions must come to an end, the **Shuttle Landing Facility** looks after the longest and widest landing strip in the world, giving returning astronauts plenty of margin for error because the glid-ing space shuttle gets only one shot at landing. The tour ends at the Apollo/Saturn V Center, described above. From there, you can take a bus straight back to the Visitor Complex, or proceed to the International Space Station Center.

Note: If you take this tour, you may want to skip the main *KSC Tour*. Yes, you will miss the LC-39 Observation Gantry, but you will get a closer look at pads 39A and B on this tour.

Cape Canaveral Then & Now Tour

Rating: ★ ★ ★ ★ ★
Time: Approximately 3 hours
Kelly says: Stirring history for true space buffs

This tour is sometimes changed or modified to accommodate launch activity, making it difficult to predict what you will actually see on the day of your visit. It also requires a much greater exercise of the imagination than does the *KSC Tour* (although that's probably a good thing). Still, I suspect there will be those who will slightly prefer this tour to the other. The main reason is that on this one you actually get to enter the places where space history was made, even if those places are now mere empty concrete spaces where towering launch gantries once stood.

It was from Cape Canaveral that the first Americans were launched into space. You can walk through a blockhouse that housed mission control for the early Mercury missions and stroll out to the pad from which puny looking Redstone rockets launched the first Americans into space using a gantry jury-rigged from an old oil drilling rig. The room-sized computer used for these launches could be replaced by a modern laptop, with plenty of room left over on the hard drive for games. Next door is a small museum with a collection of artifacts relating to the early days of the space program.

Much of the launch pad area has been turned into a sort of outdoor sculpture garden displaying two dozen or so rockets and missiles, including my personal favorite, the sleekly magnificent and rather sexy Snark.

Another powerful moment comes on a visit to the actual launch pad on which Apollo astronauts Gus Grissom, Ed White, and Roger Chaffee lost their lives in a tragic fire during a dress rehearsal of the first Apollo flight. The site is now a monument to their memory. Another monument of sorts that is glimpsed on this tour is the Minuteman missile silo in which the remains of the Space Shuttle Challenger were placed after the investigation of that accident.

Cape Canaveral entered the space age in 1950 with tests of captured German V-2 rockets. But it is far from being a dusty museum or a monument to the past. It is a bustling modern spaceport from which a wide variety of unmanned military, scientific, and commercial satellites are launched into orbit, including many of the satellites that provide our telephone communications and weather forecasting. As you drive around, you may catch glimpses of preparations for upcoming launches.

The narration for this tour is handled by both the driver and a guide, who banter back and forth much in the style of co-hosts on a morning news program. Their knowledge is considerable and their devotion to their jobs and the history entrusted to them apparent. Either side of the bus is okay since you get to walk up to and into the most interesting sights. As with *NASA Up Close*, you will be dropped off at the Apollo/Saturn Center at the end of your tour, where you may take a bus straight back to the Visitor Complex, or proceed to the International Space Station Center.

The IMAX Films

If you've never seen an IMAX film, this is an excellent place to remedy that situation. IMAX is an ultra-large film format, ten times larger than standard 35mm film and three times the size of the 70mm films you see at your local movie theater. It is projected on a screen some five and a half stories high and 70 feet wide. The sound system is equally impressive, producing bass tones you will feel in your bones.

The IMAX Theater at the Visitor Complex contains two back-to-back IMAX theaters, the only such IMAX "multiplex" in the world. The auditoriums are small relative to the size of the screen, so I would recommend showing up early so you can grab a seat towards the back of the house. There are doors on five levels and I find the seats in the middle of the third level to be just about ideal.

Magnificent Desolation: Walking on the Moon 3D

Rating: ★ ★ ★ ★
Time: 40 minutes

This 3D film shows us what things were like for the 12 men lucky enough to walk on the moon, everything from first impressions, to first words, to dealing with locomotion in a low-gravity environment (it seems more than a few took face-first tumbles while getting their space legs), to what they came away with, and what they left behind. Using historic footage, computer-generated images, and live-action recreations, as well as voice-overs from the men who made it to the moon, the film shows us what an extraordinary thing it is to walk on the moon, and celebrates the people who made it there, and the people who made it possible. Tom Hanks makes an enthusiastic and down-to-earth narrator for this spectacle, and the film concludes with a look to the future, including a survey of current plans to return to the moon.

Space Station 3D

Rating: ★ ★ ★ ★ +
Time: 45 minutes

If shots of the astronauts and the Space Shuttle in orbit look nifty in IMAX, wait until you see them in IMAX 3-D. The 3-D is far more than a mere gimmick in this enthralling film about the International Space Station. The sequences featuring the launches of the Russian Soyuz and the U.S. Shuttle, with debris and smoke rushing toward you at dizzying speed as the powerful sound system makes your seat vibrate, are incredible, but they are just a warm up for the shots in space. There are some jaw-dropping, vertigo-inducing shots of astronauts working outside the space station while earth drifts serenely by 250 miles below. And there are plenty of shots of the astronauts taking care of business and just horsing around in the zero-G interior of their orbiting home. Watch out for those free-floating oranges! *Magnificent Desolaton* is a wonderful film, but if you have time to see only one of the IMAX movies make it this one.

Eating at Kennedy Space Center

While you won't have to subsist on the powdered drinks and squeeze-tube dinners that were once standard fare for astronauts, neither can you expect a gourmet dining experience at KSC Visitor Complex. The eateries here are geared to processing hundreds of generally young diners in a quick and efficient manner, and the food quality seldom rises above fast-food or cafeteria level. One of the management's best inspirations has been to dispatch dozens of freestanding food carts to various points in the Visitor Complex. They offer everything from ice cream snacks to fruit to more substantial fare like hot dogs. Given the difficulty of squeezing everything into a one-day visit to the Center, it makes a lot of sense to eat on the run from these carts and save the big sit-down meal for later in the evening.

If you have the time, I recommend the only full-service restaurant at the Visitor Complex, **Mila's Roadhouse**, overlooking the *Space Mirror*. The decor is vaguely fifties or sixties in feel (there are a few outdoor tables) and the menu runs to home-cooked meat-and-veg meals, burgers, and beef and chicken sandwiches at moderate prices. Those craving something a bit less heavy will enjoy the Sunshine Salad ($9), a meal-sized concoction of mixed greens, cranberries, walnuts, and feta cheese, topped with a raspberry vinaigrette. Next door is **The Orbit**, a large, noisy fast-food emporium with a modern metallic high-tech decor. Service is cafeteria style, with a large central carousel dispensing beverages, salads, sandwiches, and desserts. On one side of the carousel you can get pizzas and pasta dishes, on the other side, a steam table offers roast beef, turkey, chicken, and fried fish dinners with a choice of vegetables. Beer and wine are served at both locations. There is fast food at the Apollo/Saturn V Center's **Moon Rock Cafe**. If you are trying to pack as much as possible into a one-day visit, grabbing a hot dog on this tour and eating it while waiting for the bus is a good strategy.

Shopping at Kennedy Space Center

The largest selection of KSC souvenirs and outer-space themed merchandise to be found anywhere is yours to browse through in the mammoth, two-level **Space Shop** that lies between Information Central and the bus depot. Here you will find everything from t-shirts priced well under $20 to leather bomber jackets with the NASA logo for over $200. There are smaller shops with much the same merchandise, including one at the Saturn V facility that is visited on all of the bus tours.

Tip: For a nifty (and cheap!) souvenir or gift, buy a postcard and stamp and mail it here. It will arrive with a special Kennedy Space Center cancellation. Philatelists take note.

Seeing a Shuttle Launch

You've probably seen film clips of shuttle launches on TV. You've probably seen them dozens of times. But, to quote Al Jolson, you ain't seen nothin' yet! Seeing a shuttle launch live and in person is one of the truly great experiences a Florida vacation has to offer. Catching at least a glimpse of a launch is surprisingly easy. On a clear day, the rising shuttle is visible from the Orlando area. Getting a closer look, however, requires a bit of planning.

First, you must understand that you don't have to be close to the launching pad to get ringside seats. In fact, no one can be close to the launching pad. The greatest danger a launch poses to bystanders is, surprisingly, the noise generated by the awesome engines. It is, I am told, the loudest man-made sound next to the explosion of a thermonuclear device. An elaborate sound suppression system clicks in at launch time, spewing 300,000 gallons of water on the escaping gases from the rocket engines. Were it not for this system, the observers in the press and VIP section, some three and a half miles away, would permanently lose their hearing.

Unless you're a credentialed reporter, a relative of an astronaut, a federal official, or have some inside pull at NASA, you will be a good bit farther way. But you can still have an excellent view and an experience you will remember for the rest of your life.

On days when a shuttle launch is scheduled, the Kennedy Space Center allows visitors who have pre-purchased Maximum Access tickets for that day to view the proceedings from the Visitor Complex. Maximum Access tickets for shuttle launch days arrive in the mail with a special automobile decal, and a roadblock is set up several miles down State Road 405, near the *Astronaut Hall of Fame*. The guards check incoming cars for decals, and visitors without a decal will be turned away.

At the Center, tour buses may run on a limited schedule on launch day, depending on the time of launch, or they may not run at all. But the entire Visitor Complex plays a live broadcast over the PA system of the events unfolding, including updates from mission control, and a jumbo TV screen in the *Rocket Garden* plays a live NASA TV feed.

The best viewing venue for the general public, however, is along the NASA Causeway that runs from Merritt Island to Cape Canaveral Air Force base across the Banana River. This puts you approximately six miles from the launch pad. There's nothing fancy about the viewing area; KSC buses you to the Causeway and lets you sit or stand on the grassy area between the road and the river. No seating is provided, but you can remain aboard the air conditioned bus if you prefer. The shuttle will be visible to the naked eye across the water to the north; a pair of binoculars will allow you to see the vapor pouring off the fuel tanks.

Viewing a launch from this vantage point requires a modest investment and some advance planning. The Kennedy Space Center Visitor Complex sells approximately 5,000 tickets for its buses to the viewing area. The cost is $15 for all ages, in addition to regular Maximum Access admission. Tickets may be purchased by calling (321) 449-4400 or on the Internet at www.kennedyspacecenter.com. (See below for a free alternative.)

The demand for these tickets is unpredictable. On at least one occasion, they sold out within an hour of first being offered. For other launches, typically those scheduled during the wee hours of the morning, the demand has been considerably less intense. If you find that the launch is sold out, there is still a slim chance you may be able to get tickets. Very occasionally a few tickets go back on sale on launch day. So if you arrive bright and early that morning, you just may be able to buy a ticket. No guarantees, of course, but for a sold-out launch it's your best bet. Given the uncertainty of the actual launch date, you will have to check back regularly to plan your visit. A recorded message at (321) 867-4636 provides the latest information.

On Launch Day

Plan on pulling on to SR 405 (from the west) or SR 3 (from the south) several hours before the scheduled launch time. Park your car in the Visitors Complex parking lots and head for the buses that will shuttle you to the viewing area. Once there, remember you are on government property and in a wildlife refuge to boot, so there are a few simple rules. Cooking and fires are prohibited, as are alcoholic beverages.

You are not allowed to fish, wade, swim, or feed the wildlife (there are some manatee holding pens along the causeway viewing area). If you have a pet, you'll have to make arrangements to leave it behind.

The atmosphere at the viewing area is infectiously cheerful and friendly. People seem to instantly become one happy family. At the launch I attended, a professor of astronomy from a nearby university was letting passersby take a peek at the shuttle through his eight-inch telescope. Dotted along the viewing area are NASA Exchange trailers selling snacks and souvenirs. The prices for food and drink are surprisingly cheap, especially considering you are a captive audience.

A public address system mounted on poles carries live announcements from NASA mission control. As launch time approaches, you will hear the actual conversations between mission control and the shuttle crew. A few minutes before the launch, several local radio stations begin live coverage. Among them are 580AM, 90.7FM, and 107.1FM.

At the actual launch, you will see a flash of light a second or two before blast-off. Then the shuttle disappears in a towering cloud of white exhaust only to emerge a moment later, its engines spewing a blinding flame. The shuttle will be well up into the air before you hear the sound, but when it arrives at your viewing point you will feel the land tremble beneath your feet as well as hear the throaty rumble of the booster rockets. As it continues its eight minute journey to orbit, arcing gracefully to the east, the shuttle looks like a tiny toy atop a massive column of white clouds.

About two and half minutes into the flight, the booster rockets drop away. (If you have binoculars, you may be able to spot the parachutes that lower them to the sea for recovery by NASA ships.) At this point, the shuttle becomes a star-like point of light hurtling into the history books. I was lucky. The launch I observed went up on the dot. But you should be aware that, more often than not, the shuttle doesn't go up on schedule. If there are delays for weather or technical glitches, you will be kept posted. If the launch is scrubbed (that is, canceled) you can still enjoy the Visitor Complex.

Seeing a Launch for Free

If you'd rather not pay the KSC admission fee and the $15 extra charge to be bussed out to the NASA Causeway, you can still get an excellent view of the launch from Space View Park in nearby Titusville. Take Exit 80 from I-95 (SR 406, Garden Street). The park is two blocks south of SR 406. Nearby Veterans Memorial Park often has a loudspeaker broadcasting the audio feed from NASA. Get there early.

Seeing a Rocket Launch

While they don't have quite the same cachet as a Shuttle launch, the more regular launches of commercial and military satellites that take place on Cape Canaveral are pretty fun to watch. When they are in the offing, visitors are given advance notice and will be advised as to the best places along the *KSC Tour* from which to get a view of the big event.

Chapter Eight:

Busch Gardens
Africa

BUSCH GARDENS IS A SOMEWHAT SCHIZOPHRENIC MIXTURE OF ZOOLOGICAL PARK and amusement park, with a dash of variety show thrown in. Given the seemingly disparate demands of these elements, the designers have done an admirable job of creating an attractive whole. Aesthetically, a stroll through Busch Gardens is one of the most pleasing in Central Florida.

Like any good theme park, Busch Gardens has one. In this case it's Africa, the mysterious continent so linked in the popular imagination with wild animals and adventure. Borrowing a page from the Disney manual, the park is divided into nine "lands," or as Busch calls them, "themed areas." With few exceptions, they take their names from countries or regions in Africa. The metaphor works wonderfully for the zoo side of things, although it results in the occasional oddity (Bengal tigers in the Congo?). It is largely extraneous to the park's other elements. A roller coaster is a roller coaster, whether it's named after an Egyptian god (*Montu*) or in a Congolese dialect (*Kumba*). Switch the locations of these giant coasters and no one would know the difference. On the other hand, who cares?

Since this book focuses on Orlando, the question naturally arises: Why schlep to Tampa for another theme park? There are two main answers: the animals and the roller coasters. Disney's Animal Kingdom has created some competition to Busch's great apes and white Bengal tigers, but it has just one roller coaster. There are other reasons, as well. For early risers at least, Busch Gardens is a very doable day trip from Orlando. The participation of Busch Gardens in the Orlando FlexTicket program (see *Chapter 1: Introduction & Orientation*) adds another incentive to make the trip.

Finally, Busch Gardens has a personality and an allure all its own. The innovative animal habitats temper the frenzy of the rides, and the rides give you something to do when just sitting and watching begins to pale. The park is beautifully designed with some absolutely enchanting nooks and crannies. While it's a great place to do things, Busch Gardens is also a delightful place simply to be.

My only caution would be that the amusement park side of the equation can tend to overshadow the zoo. Many of the animal exhibits reward quiet, patient observation, but the excitement generated by the smorgasbord of giant roller coasters and splashy water rides will make it hard to cultivate a contemplative state of mind, especially for the younger members of your party. Perhaps the best strategy is to use exhibits like the *Myombe Reserve* (great apes), *Edge of Africa* (lions and hippos), and the walk-through aviary to cool out and cool down between bouts of manic activity. Another strategy is to devote one visit to the amusement park rides, another to the zoo exhibits.

Gathering Information

You can hear some recorded information and, if you're lucky, reach a real live person by calling (888) 800-5447. In Tampa, you can call the Guest Relations number, (813) 987-5888, during park hours.

For the latest on Busch Gardens' zoo animals, you can check out the park's animal information site at www.buschgardens.org.

Another web site provides information for the amusement park side of Busch Gardens Africa. The address is www.buschgardens.com. An unofficial fan web site, www.bgtguide.com, is a good source of late-breaking news.

When's the Best Time to Come?

Plotting the best time of year at which to visit is less of a consideration than with the other major theme parks of Central Florida. According to the trade paper *Amusement Business*, Busch Gardens gets half the visitors Universal hosts each year and less than a third of those who show up at the Magic Kingdom. On the other hand, attendance continues to grow and on several recent visits large groups of foreign tourists and American high school kids were much in evidence.

Getting There

Busch Gardens is roughly 75 miles from Universal Orlando, about 65 miles from the intersection of I-4 and US 192 in Kissimmee. You can drive there in about one and a quarter to one and a half hours depending on where you start and how closely you observe the posted speed limit. Drive west on I-4 to Exit 7 (US 92 West, Hillsborough Avenue). Go about 1.5 miles and turn right on 56th Street (SR 583); go another two miles and turn right on Busch Boulevard. Busch Gardens is about two miles ahead on your right.

Shuttle Bus Service

If you'd rather not drive from Orlando, you can take advantage of the shuttle bus service that Busch operates from the Orlando area. The fare is $10 per person, but if you have a five-park FlexTicket the service is free. There are seven pick-up points conveniently located along Orlando's I-4 corridor, including Universal Orlando, SeaWorld, and Old Town in Kissimmee. Buses depart between roughly 8:30 a.m. and 10:00 a.m. with return journeys timed to the current closing hours at Busch Gardens

Africa, which vary seasonally (see below). Reservations are required check the latest schedule and pick-up points, call (800) 221-1339.

Parking at Busch Gardens Africa

You know you're almost at Busch Gardens when you see the giant roller coaster *Montu* looming overhead. You'll probably also hear the screams as you pull into the parking lot. Actually, there are a series of parking lots with room for 5,000 vehicles. Lots A and B are near the park entrance and are reserved for handicapped and pre-ferred parking, respectively. There is much more parking across the street, which is where you will most likely be stowing your car. Trams snake their way back and forth to the entrance, but if you're in A or B it's just as easy to walk.

Motorcycles and cars park for $8, campers and trailers for $9, tax included. If you have any Busch Gardens annual pass, parking is free. Preferred Parking, in Lot B, costs $12 ($5 for annual passholders).

Opening and Closing Times

The park is usually open from 10:00 a.m. to 6:00 p.m. every day of the year. However, during the summer months and at holiday times the hours are extended, with opening at 9:00 a.m. and closing pushed back until 7:00, 8:00, or 9:00 p.m. The Morocco section stays open a half-hour or so later than the rest of the park to accommodate last-minute shoppers. Call Guest Relations at (813) 987-5888 for the exact current operating hours.

The Price of Admission

Busch Gardens sells only one-day admissions, but adults can get a discount if they purchase their tickets seven days in advance on the Internet. The following prices include tax (which is slightly higher than in Orlando). The discounted price is given in parentheses.

One Day Admission:

Adults:	$62 ($51.30)
Children (3 to 9):	$51.30

Children under age 3 are admitted **free**.

Two-Park Ticket:

(One day each at Busch Gardens and SeaWorld)

Adults:	$106.95 ($96.25)
Children:	$96.25

Two-Day Two-Park Ticket:

(One day each at Busch Gardens and Adventure Island)

Adults:	$78.05
Children:	$67.35

Visa, MasterCard, and Discover credit cards are accepted.

Busch Gardens participates in the **Orlando FlexTicket** program described in *Chapter 1: Introduction & Orientation* (page 13).

Annual Passes

Busch Gardens Africa offers a variety of annual pass options, called "Passports." Silver Passports are valid for one year and Gold Passports for two. If you are at the park, you will find the Pass Center located to your right as you approach the main ticket windows. In the following list of prices, which include tax, the Silver Passport price is given first, followed by the Gold Passport price. Seniors are those 50 years or older.

Busch Gardens Passports
Unlimited access to Busch Gardens Africa.

Adults:	$101.59 / $155.09
Children & Seniors:	$90.89 / $144.39

Busch Gardens – Adventure Island Passports
Annual pass to both Busch Gardens and Adventure Island, the nearby Busch water park (see *Chapter 9: Water Parks*).

Adults:	$144.39 / $208.59
Children & Seniors:	$133.69 / $197.89

Busch Gardens – SeaWorld Passports
Annual Pass to both Busch Gardens and SeaWorld Orlando.

Adults:	$155.09 / $235.34
Children & Seniors:	$144.39 / $224.64

Busch Gardens – SeaWorld – Adventure Island Passports
Annual Pass to Busch Gardens, Adventure Island, and SeaWorld.

Adults:	$197.87 / $288.84
Children & Seniors:	$187.19 / $278.14

Platinum Passports
Two-year Pass to all Busch parks, in Florida and around the country (except Discovery Cove), plus a dazzling array of special perks.

Adults:	$320.94
Children & Seniors:	$310.24

The amount of a one-day admission can be applied to these passes, but only if you upgrade on the day you buy it.

EZ Pay

Busch offers the option of paying for your Passport in equal monthly installments over the 12- or 24-month term of the Passport. Payments are charged to your credit card and no finance charges or fees are added. This option makes an annual pass almost irresistible.

Discounts

I have already mentioned the discount given on tickets purchased seven days in advance on the Busch Gardens web site. Once you're in Tampa, you may find dollars-off coupons for Busch Gardens in all the usual places (see *Chapter 1: Introduction & Orientation*). Discounted tickets are also available from hotel Guest Services desks and ticket brokers in the Orlando area. In addition to the discounts accorded to senior citizens purchasing annual passes, AAA cardholders can get a $5 discount on one-day admissions at the ticket booths, while handicapped guests receive a 50% discount. Special deals are offered to Florida residents during the off-season (fall to spring); call for details. Annual passholders receive a 10% discount on merchandise in park shops and at the larger eateries as well as a $30 discount on admission to Discovery Cove in Orlando.

Buying Tickets

If you have not taken advantage of the savings offered by the online, advance purchase option described above, tickets can be purchased as you arrive, at ticket booths immediately in front of the park entrance. However, you can save yourself a bit of time by purchasing your tickets the day before, in the afternoon, when there are no lines. If you are based in Orlando, you can purchase a discounted combination ticket when you visit SeaWorld. You can also purchase Busch Gardens tickets at SeaWorld even if you are not visiting SeaWorld.

Busch Gardens tickets are available through several local Tampa hotels, so you might want to check with the concierge or the front desk if you are staying nearby. Other options are to purchase tickets through your travel agent before you leave home or at a discount on the Busch Gardens web site (see above).

Staying Near the Park

If you'd like to spend a few days at Busch Gardens or just want to avoid doing the roundtrip from Orlando in one day, you may want to consider staying at one of the motels within walking distance of the park, none of which is particularly fancy. Other, more upscale hotel choices are available just a short drive away.

Howard Johnson

4139 East Busch Boulevard
Tampa, FL 33612
(813) 988-9191; fax (813) 988-9195
A standard mid-range motel.
Price Range: $$ – $$$
Amenities: Pool
Walk to Park: 10 minutes

Days Inn

2901 East Busch Boulevard
Tampa, FL 33612
(813) 933-6471
A standard mid-range motel.
Price Range: $$ – $$$
Amenities: Pool, restaurant
Walk to Park: 20 minutes

Baymont Inn & Suites
9202 North 30th Street
Tampa, FL 33612
(813) 930-6900; fax (813) 930-0563
> Another mid-range hotel.
> *Price Range:* $$ – $$$
> *Amenities:* Pool
> *Walk to Park:* 20 minutes

Red Roof Inn
2307 East Busch Boulevard
Tampa, FL 33612
(813) 932-0073; fax (813) 933-5689
> A nice, clean budget motel.
> *Price Range:* $$
> *Amenities:* Small pool
> *Walk to Park:* 30 minutes

Special Events
Busch Gardens Africa hosts a growing number of razzle-dazzle themed events timed to the calendar. The oldest of these is an alcohol-free New Year's Eve celebration for young people and families. Halloween shenanigans are in evidence during October. These are typically after-hours affairs that require a hefty separate admission (a recent Howl-O-Scream event was $58). However, if you purchase your tickets in advance or have an annual pass, discounts are substantial.

During the Christmas season there are nightly tree lighting ceremonies and in the fall the park hosts a series of big band concerts. A patriotic July Fourth celebration was in the planning stages at press time. To learn more about what events may be planned during your visit and to get the latest on ticket prices, call toll-free (888) 800-5447.

Dining at Busch Gardens Africa
On the whole, the dining experience at Busch Gardens is a step down from that at its sister park, SeaWorld, in Orlando. However, **Crown Colony House**, the single full-service restaurant (in the Crown Colony section, 'natch), has a limited menu but some very tasty dishes. In addition to the luxury of being waited on, the main draw here is the great view of the *Serengeti Plain*. No reservations are accepted so you can't call ahead and reserve a table by the great semicircular sweep of window overlooking the Plain, but you can request one and wait until it becomes available.

For more casual dining, I recommend the **Desert Grill** in Timbuktu, where you can be entertained in air-conditioned comfort while you dine, the **Zambia Smokehouse** for decent barbecue amid the roars and screams of *SheiKra* in Stanleyville, and the outdoor **Zagora Cafe** in Morocco. And speaking of Morocco, I find it disappointing that Busch Gardens has not chosen to extend its African theme to its restaurant menus. I found myself wishing for something akin to the first-rate Moroccan restaurant at Epcot in Walt Disney World Resort.

(An interesting note: No straws are served at any of the park's restaurants or fast-food outlets in deference to the safety of the animals.)

Shopping at Busch Gardens Africa

The souvenir hunter will not leave disappointed. There are plenty of logo-bearing gadgets, gizmos, and wearables from which to choose. The t-shirts with tigers and gorillas are especially attractive. Tiger fanciers will also be drawn to the beach towels with the large white Bengal tiger portrait.

Best of all are the genuine African crafts to be found here and there around the park. Look for them in Morocco, Crown Colony, and Timbuktu. The prices can be steep for some of the nicer pieces, but there are some very attractive (and attractively priced) smaller items to be found. Clothing is another good buy at Busch, with some of the better shops located in Morocco and Crown Colony.

Most of the shops offer a free package pick-up service that lets you collect your purchases near the front entrance on your way out, so you needn't worry about lugging things about for half the day. You can avail yourself of Busch Gardens' mail order services by dialing (800) 410-9453 or (813) 987-5060.

Good Things to Know About ...

Access for the Disabled

Handicapped parking spaces are provided directly in front of the park's main entrance for those with a valid permit. Otherwise, physically challenged guests may be dropped off at the main entrance. The entire park is wheelchair accessible and companion bathrooms are dotted about the park. Some physically challenged guests may not be able to experience certain rides due to safety considerations. An "Access Guide" is available at Guest Relations near the main entrance.

Wheelchair and motorized cart rentals are handled out of a concession next to the Jeepers and Creepers shop in Morocco. Wheelchairs are $10 a day. Motorized carts are $35. Motorized carts are popular, so plan to get there early to be sure you get one.

Animal Observation

Busch Gardens does an excellent job of displaying its animals in natural settings. One consequence of that is that they can sometimes be hard to see. So if spying out elands or catching a glimpse of a rare rhino baby is important to you, consider bringing along a pair of binoculars. They will come in handy on the *Skyride*, the *Trans-Veldt Railroad*, and even at lunch in the Crown Colony House restaurant.

Babies

Diaper changing tables are located in restrooms throughout the park. A nursing area is located in Land of the Dragons.

If you don't have your own, you can rent strollers at the concession next to Jeepers and Creepers in Morocco. Nifty looking Jeep Strollers are $10 for the full day, double strollers are $15.

Drinking

As a reminder, the legal drinking age in Florida is 21 and photo IDs will be requested if there is the slightest doubt.

First Aid

First aid stations are located in Timbuktu behind the Desert Grill restaurant and in Crown Colony in the *Skyride* building. If emergency aid is needed, contact the nearest employee.

Getting Wet

The signs say, "This is a water attraction. Riders will get wet and possibly soaked." This is not marketing hyperbole but a simple statement of fact. The water rides at Busch Gardens are one of its best kept secrets (the mammoth roller coasters get most of the publicity), but they pose some problems for the unprepared. Kids probably won't care, but adults can get positively cranky when wandering around sopping wet.

The three major water rides, in increasing order of wetness, are *Stanley Falls Log Flume, Congo River Rapids*, and the absolutely soaking *Tanganyika Tidal Wave*. (The *Mizzly Marsh* section of Land of the Dragons can also get tykes very wet.) Fortunately, these three rides are within a short distance of each other, in the Congo and Stanleyville, allowing you to implement the following strategy:

First, dress appropriately. Wear a bathing suit and t-shirt under a dressier outer layer. Wear shoes you don't mind getting wet; sports sandals are ideal. Bring a tote bag in which you can put things, like cameras, that shouldn't get wet. You can also pack a towel and it's probably a good idea to bring along the plastic laundry bag from your motel room.

Plan to do the water rides in sequence. When you're ready to start, strip off your outer layer, put it in the tote bag along with your other belongings, and stash everything in a convenient locker. There are lockers dotted throughout the Congo and Stanleyville. A helpful locker symbol on the map of the park will help you locate the nearest one. Now you're ready to enjoy the rides without worry.

Once you've completed the circuit, and especially if you rode the *Tidal Wave*, you will be soaked to the skin. You now have a choice. If it's a hot summer day, you may want to let your clothes dry as you see the rest of the park. Don't worry about feeling foolish; you'll see of plenty of other folks in the same boat, and your damp clothes will feel just great in the Florida heat. In cooler weather, however, it's a good idea to return to the locker, grab your stuff, head to a nearby restroom, and change into dry clothes. Use the plastic laundry bag for the wet stuff.

The alternative is to buy a Busch Gardens poncho (they make nice souvenirs and are readily available at shops near the water rides) and hope for the best. This is far less fun and you'll probably get pretty wet anyway.

Lost Children

If you become separated from your child, contact the nearest employee. Found children are returned to the Security Office next door to the Marrakesh Theater in Morocco.

Leaving the Park

Just have your hand stamped at the exit for readmittance on the same day. Your parking stub will get you back into the lot free.

Money

Busch Gardens has thoughtfully dotted ATMs around the park, just in case you run out of cash. You will find them just outside the main entrance, as well as in Morocco, Stanleyville, and Timbuktu, conveniently located near the shops. They are connected to the Plus, MoneyStation, and Cirrus systems. In addition, you can get cash advances on your American Express, Visa, MasterCard, or Discover card.

Pets

There is a Pet Care Center located near the main tram stop in Parking Lot C. The simple facility charges $6 per pet ($5 for annual passholders). They provide water; the owner provides food. If your pet needs walking during the day, that is your responsibility.

Rain Checks

Busch Gardens Africa offers a "rain guarantee." If you feel your visit has been ruined by the rain, they will issue a complimentary ticket valid for another day's admission within the next seven days.

Smoking

To comply with Florida's strict anti-smoking legislation, smoking is banned in all restaurants, rides, shows, exhibits, and most public areas. For the still-addicted, Busch provides "Designated Smoking Areas," outdoor ghettos that are called out on the park map by little red circles containing a smoking cigarette.

On Safari:
Your Day at Busch Gardens

The bad news is that it's difficult — probably impossible — to see all of Busch Gardens in a day. The good news is that most people will be happy to forego some of the attractions. The more sedate will happily pass up the roller coasters to spend time observing the great apes, while the speed demons will be far happier being flung about on *Montu* or challenging their fear limit on *SheiKra* than sitting still for a show in The Desert Grill.

In many respects, Busch Gardens is a "typical" theme park. Each area of the park is decorated and landscaped to reflect its particular "theme," which is also reflected in the decor of the shops and restaurants (although not necessarily in the merchandise and food being offered). The attendants wear appropriate uniforms and a variety of rides, exhibits, attractions, and "streetmosphere" compete for your attention. If you've been to any of the other big theme parks in Central Florida, it's unlikely you'll find anything radically different about Busch Gardens.

As I noted earlier, Busch Gardens combines a number of seemingly disparate elements into an eclectic whole. Here, then, are some of the elements in the Busch Gardens mix:

The Zoo. Home to 2,700 animals, representing hundreds of species (the numbers will probably have risen by the time you visit), Busch Gardens is one of the major zoological parks in the nation. It is also a highly enlightened zoo, embodying the latest thinking about how animals should be housed and displayed to the public. You will receive an understated but persistent message about the importance of conserving and protecting the planet's animal heritage. Like its sister park, SeaWorld in Orlando, Busch Gardens boasts a zoological staff that is friendly, visible, approachable, and more than happy to answer questions.

Meet The Keeper. One way in which the staff helps spread the conservation message is through regular "Meet The Keepers" shows built around feeding and caring for the animals. The presence of food means that the animals are usually at their most active during these shows; the attendants also attempt to coax their charges into appropriate poses for those with cameras. Meet The Keeper sessions are listed on the back of the large Busch Gardens map you pick up just inside the main entrance.

Roller Coasters. Busch Gardens boasts one of the largest concentrations of roller coasters in the nation. They range from the relatively modest *Scorpion* to the truly awesome *SheiKra*. Even the smallest of these rides features elements, like loops, that are not to be found on just any roller coaster. You will be well advised to take advantage of the coin-operated lockers located near every roller coaster to store your loose gear. Anyone who is serious about their roller coasters will definitely want to put Busch Gardens on their must-see list for their Central Florida vacation.

Water Rides. Busch Gardens is also home to a group of water rides that are designed to get you very, very, very wet. They are great fun, but require some planning and strategizing. Unless, of course, you're a young boy, in which case you simply won't mind walking through the park sopping wet from the top of your head to the toes of your $100 sneakers. See *Good Things to Know About ... Getting Wet*, above.

Live Shows. There is a regular schedule of entertainment throughout the day in open-air amphitheaters and indoor, air-conditioned theaters. A few are animal-oriented, but most are pure variety entertainment shows that change periodically. Most shows don't gear up until 11:00 a.m. or noon. Thereafter, they run pretty regularly until closing time. The show schedule is printed on the back of the large Busch Gardens map you pick up at the main entrance.

Orientation to Busch Gardens

Your very first step on any visit to Busch Gardens Africa is to pick up a copy of the park map at the main entrance. One side contains a full-color map of the park; the other side is packed with helpful information, such as an "Entertainment Guide" that lists performance times for the park's stage shows and the Meet The Keeper "animal enrichment" programs scheduled at various animal exhibits for the day of your visit. You will also find information about any special or seasonal events that may be happening that day.

As you will see by perusing the map, Busch Gardens is divided into eight "themed areas" (nine if, like me, you count Land of the Dragons as a separate area), most of them named after a country or region of Africa. Each area is relatively compact but the entire park is quite large (335 acres), making covering the entire place a bit of a challenge, especially on foot.

In describing the nine areas, I will start with Morocco, the first area you encounter as you enter the park, and then proceed clockwise around the park, ending with the newest themed area, Egypt. I am not suggesting that you tour Busch Gardens in this order (although it would be the most direct route if you were to walk the entire park). Use the descriptions that follow, along with the suggestions given above, to pick and choose the attractions that best suit your tastes and that you can comfortably fit into the time available. Remember that you can use the *Skyride* between the Congo and Crown Colony to cut down on the walking.

In addition to the attractions listed below, Busch Gardens features a number of strolling musical groups playing peppy music designed to put a bit of bounce back in your step as you stroll the grounds. The **Mystic Sheiks of Morocco** are a brass marching band outfitted in snappy red and black uniforms that make them look like a military band from a very hip African nation. They are most frequently sighted in Morocco and Crown Colony. The **Men of Note** offer up the kind of close harmony, a capella doo-wop music more associated with the streets of Philadelphia than the souks of Morocco. Still, they can often be found entertaining departing guests there.

Big Game

For those with limited time or who want to skim the cream of this multifaceted park, here are my selections for the trophy-winning attractions at Busch Gardens:

For coaster fans, **SheiKra**, **Montu** and **Kumba** are musts and you'll want to ride **Gwazi** just to be complete. Of the water rides, **Congo River Rapids** is my favorite and the **Tanganyika Tidal Wave** is highly recommended for those who want to get totally drenched. The best theater show by far is **KaTonga**.

Animal lovers will not want to miss the chimps and gorillas in **Myombe Reserve** or the tigers on **Claw Island**. **Edge of Africa** is another must-see animal habitat, but the **Serengeti Safari Tour** (for an extra charge) is the best way to get close to the animals. **Rhino Rally** is a fun way to get an all-too brief glimpse of some other veldt dwellers combined with a mild thrill ride on a raging river. And finally, if you have preschoolers in tow, you will not want to miss the spectacular **Land of the Dragons**.

The One-Day Stay for Ride Fans

1. Plan to arrive at the opening bell. As soon as the park opens, grab a map just inside the turnstiles and proceed directly to *SheiKra* in Stanleyville (bear left), bypassing *Gwazi* for now. If crowds are sparse, and if you dare, ride *SheiKra* more than once. (If *Rhino Rally* is on your list, try to get there first thing in the morning, before you ride anything else; lines form quickly and the ride handles many fewer riders per hour than the coasters.)

2. After *SheiKra*, continue to the Congo and ride *Kumba*. If the *Skyride* is operating, you can use it to head to *Montu* in Egypt; otherwise just walk. Then, walk back through Egypt, Crown Colony and Morroco to *Gwazi*.

3. Once you've done the coasters, head back to Stanleyville and ride *Stanley Falls* and the *Tanganyika Tidal Wave*, finishing up with a ride on *Congo River Rapids*. Now head south, pausing to admire the tigers on *Claw Island* as you check the map and Entertainment Guide. If the timing's right, catch the *Skyride* again and head back to the Moroccan Palace Theater to catch *KaTonga*.

4. After lunch, you have several choices. You can hit your favorite rides again, try the lesser rides, or (my personal suggestion) visit the various zoo attractions, perhaps catching another show at some point in the afternoon. Don't forget to check the schedule of Meet The Keeper shows.

The One-Day Stay for the More Sedate

1. If you are not a ride fanatic you don't have to kill yourself to get there at the minute the park opens, although a full day at Busch Gardens, taken at a moderate pace, is a full day well-spent. For now, I'll assume you are arriving early. Grab a park map and the Entertainment Guide and bear to the right as you stroll towards Crown Colony. En route, peruse the times for the variety shows and the Meet The Keeper sessions.

2. If you plan to take the *Serengeti Safari Tour*, sign up now. Take a leisurely tour of *Edge of Africa*, and if you're interested and the lines aren't too long, you might want to walk to Egypt and pop into *King Tut's Tomb*. Otherwise, stroll to Nairobi for a visit to *Myombe Reserve* and the *Nairobi Field Station*. Don't dismiss *Rhino Rally* out of hand. Although it is touted as a "thrill ride," the thrills are very muted and the wildlife worth a look.

3. Now board the *Trans-Veldt Railroad* at the Nairobi Station for the journey around the Serengeti.

4. Now you're ready to see some shows. You can walk to Timbuktu for the musical variety show at the Desert Grill (and have lunch if you haven't grabbed a bite yet) or you can stroll the other way to catch *KaTonga* at the Moroccan Palace.

5. Round out your day with a visit to Bird Gardens and the *Wild Wings of Africa* show. If you have little ones in tow, don't forget to let them have their own special time in Land of the Dragons.

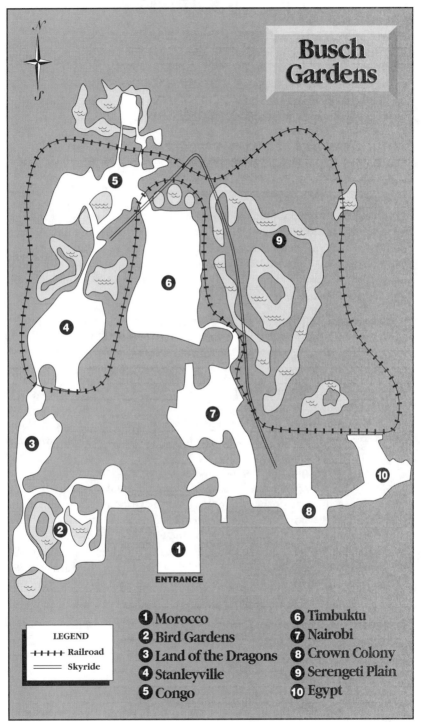

Busch Gardens

LEGEND
+++++ Railroad
===== Skyride

1 Morocco
2 Bird Gardens
3 Land of the Dragons
4 Stanleyville
5 Congo
6 Timbuktu
7 Nairobi
8 Crown Colony
9 Serengeti Plain
10 Egypt

ENTRANCE

Morocco

For most folks, Morocco is the first stop in the park, so some of the available space is given over to housekeeping. Here you'll find Guest Relations and the Adventure Tour Center, where you can make arrangements for the special tours described at the end of this chapter. Just around the corner to your right is the stroller and wheelchair rental concession. Since Morocco is also the exit to the park, a fair amount of space is given to souvenir and other shops, the better to lure those on the way out.

Note: On especially busy days, they open the Nairobi Gate, which is directly to the right of where the parking lot tram drops off new arrivals. This entrance lets visitors into the park at a point about equidistant from Nairobi, Crown Colony, and Morocco.

Otherwise, the main business of Morocco is stage shows of one sort or another. There are two theaters (reviewed below) and an outdoor stage, the **Sultan's Tent**, where a snake charmer appears from time to time. There is also an **alligator pond**, where several times a day a Meet The Keeper show takes place. It's a zoologically correct version of the more popularized shows you get at Gatorland and other gator-themed attractions.

Moroccan Roll (Marrakesh Theater)

Rating: ★ ★ ★ +
Type: Live stage show
Time: 25 minutes
Kelly says: Rock with a North African roll

On a thrust stage with Moorish arches and purple curtains, this peppy revue pays homage to the Morocco theme using a succession of rock standards with North African overtones. If tunes like "Rock the Casbah" and "Walk Like an Egyptian" ring a bell then you get the idea.

A Jim Carrey-esque master of ceremonies in peddler's robes and a fez cracks jokes as ancient as any pyramid and coaxes "volunteers" from the audience between numbers. The performers are attractive young singers and dancers, along with a trumpeter and electric guitarist. Sometimes the theme gets a little lost as "Midnight at the Oasis" segues into "Living La Vida Loca." By show's end all pretense disappears in rousing renditions of "Old Time Rock and Roll" and "The Heart of Rock 'n Roll." There are some very competent pop voices in the ensemble and the dancing makes up in showbiz pizzazz what it lacks in precision. After the show, some of the performers mingle with the audience for **photo ops**.

KaTonga (Moroccan Palace Theater)

Rating: ★ ★ ★ ★ ★
Type: Indoor theater show
Time: About 40 minutes
Kelly says: Simply marvelous and not to be missed

The 1,200-seat Moroccan Palace Theater is an extremely well-appointed performance space capable of Broadway-quality spectacle. Busch Gardens has risen to the challenge with *KaTonga*, a dazzling musical extravaganza that sets a new (and very high) standard for theme park entertainment. "KaTonga" is apparently an African word for "a special place where tales are told," or something along those lines. A quartet of master storytellers from across Africa are gathered for a sort of competition and the tales they tell are brought magically to life by a troupe of multi-talented dancers, puppeteers, and acrobats from around the world. The morals to these stories teach timeless truths: strive to be the best, know yourself, seek out love, and above all, celebrate life.

Too often, in shows of this type, everything's a mishmash of clashing motifs and styles. But here, the music, singing, costumes, lighting, puppets, choreography, and special effects come together beautifully to create a unified artistic vision. All in all, this is the best theatrical theme park show in all of Central Florida and I include the shows at Walt Disney World in that reckoning. Don't miss it.

Bird Gardens

As the name suggests, Bird Gardens houses most of the birds in the Busch Gardens zoo collection. In addition to the few larger bird displays mentioned below, the area is dotted with flamingos and other exotic water fowl, their wings obviously clipped, in beautifully landscaped open settings with ponds and streams. They are joined by a rotating group of visiting Florida species. Some of the walkways are lined with gaudy parrots in free-hanging cages. Over all, the effect is enchanting, rather like the private gardens of a rich and tasteful eccentric.

Bird Gardens is also home to *Gwazi*, a mammoth twin-track wooden roller coaster that greets you as you enter. Near *Gwazi*, you will find **River Rumble**, a water game, and **Xtreme Zone**, where you can climb a simulated cliff or bounce on a trampoline. There is an additional charge for these activities. A short stroll away and often overlooked is **Eagle Canyon**, a quiet corner devoted to these magnificent raptors.

Gwazi

Rating:	★ ★ ★ ★ +
Type:	Dueling wooden coasters
Time:	About two and a half minutes
Kelly says:	Up-to-date nostalgia

For those who remember the days when all roller coasters were made of wood, *Gwazi* will be like a stroll down memory lane — until the first drop reminds you that this isn't your father's coaster.

The "gimmick" here, of course, is that there are two separate coasters, each holding 24 passengers, one representing a tiger, the other a lion. As you snake your way to the departure platforms, you get to choose which one you'll take on and each route has its own theming — the lion territory evokes an African desert environment, while the tiger territory is reminiscent of the jungles and streams of Asia. The dueling trains depart simultaneously and "race" to the finish with six "fly-bys" along the way. The close encounters may not be quite as scary as on some of the dueling steel coasters — the realities of wooden coasters mandate a decent amount of space between the rail and the edge of the superstructure — but they are pretty scary nonetheless. Likewise, the ride itself may seem tamer. After all, it's hard to do an inversion on a wooden coaster. But the rumble and rattle of wood makes *Gwazi* seem faster than its 50 miles per hour and on some of the turns the cars seem to be at right angles to the ground. Wooden coasters also have a liveliness that steel coasters don't. Coaster enthusiasts would say, "it's alive!" which is another way of saying that the give in the wood makes each ride seem different from the last.

Tip: Any serious coaster buff will want to ride at least twice, once on each track. After many rides, coaster mavens seem to agree: the lion coaster has the steeper first drop, but the tiger coaster is, over all, the more intense experience.

There are some other good things to be said about *Gwazi*. It lasts longer than some of its zippier competitors and because the height restriction here is only 48 inches, more members of the family will get a chance to ride. *Gwazi* is also quite beautiful, in a way in which the more modern steel coasters aren't. The wood is weathered rather than the more traditional white and blends in nicely with the African conical thatched roof motif of the entrance. And from the top you get a fascinating (but brief) glimpse of one of the park's "backstage" areas, as well as the surrounding terrain.

Even if you don't choose to ride, *Gwazi* is worth checking out if only to marvel at the way a million board feet of lumber have been put together to create this behemoth. It has a delightfully scary way of looking rather flimsy in spite of its massive size. One good vantage point is to be had just inside the exit, where riders can purchase pictures to commemorate the experience. Another place to get a fairly good look is further into Bird Gardens, near the eagle display and the Clydesdale statue.

Wild Wings of Africa (in Bird Theater)

Rating:	★ ★ ★ ★
Type:	Live amphitheater show
Time:	About 20 minutes
Kelly says:	Fascinating birds and lore

This show is perfect theme park edutainment. A parrot talks and even sings on cue. A variety of multicolored parrots and raptors fly through hoops, swoop low over the seats, and land on volunteers brought up from the audience. Enormous storks, vultures, and even an Andean condor fly in for guest appearances. All of this is accompanied by a steady flow of fascinating facts and lore about the birds on display. The show's indisputable star is Lolita, an Amazonian parrot, who does a deft comedy routine with her handler.

An engaging team of bird handlers carries the show along with good humor and cool professionalism, but it's the birds that count here. They are so fascinating that this is perhaps the best animal show in the park.

Note: This show seems to change more than most. Sometimes they try different things to make the show more interesting, not always with great success. Other times accommodations have to be made due to the availability of avian performers, so the show you see on your visit may be slightly different from the one described here. Although I have liked some versions of this show better than others, it has always been worth seeing.

Hospitality House Stage

Rating: ★ ★ +
Type: Live music
Time: About 20 minutes
Kelly says: Diverting with lunch

On a small outdoor stage near the Hospitality House (see below), a cheerful ragtime band holds forth on a regular schedule. The selections are all likely to be familiar and they are all certified toe-tappers put over with a great deal of good-humored élan. If you find yourself near here at show time, why not grab a free beer and a pizza slice inside and give a listen?

Budweiser Beer School

Rating: ★ ★
Type: An edutainment commercial
Time: 45 minutes
Kelly says: Best for the air conditioning

This is a pleasant enough way to kill some time and perhaps get answers to those questions that have been tormenting you for years. Why is it called Budweiser? Who was Anheuser? However, I suspect most people are lured here by the beer tasting that follows some videos about the history of Anheuser-Busch and the art of brewing beer. At the end you get a certificate attesting to your newfound status as a "Beermaster."

Aviary

Rating: ★ ★ ★ +
Type: Walk-through animal exhibit
Time: Continuous viewing
Kelly says: A lovely place to pause

This is a smallish habitat compared to others in the park, but its size belies its enchantment. Essentially a large tent made of a dark mesh fabric, the aviary lets you visit a wide variety of tropical birds in a remarkably realistic setting, instead of peering at them through the bars of a cage. Benches allow for long and leisurely viewing and a large illustrated guidebook lets you tell one species from another. Some, like the roseate spoonbill, may look familiar but others, like the odd Abdim's Stork and a beautiful blue Victoria Crowned Pigeon that thinks it's a peacock, will probably be new to you.

I have discovered that the longer you sit and relax here, the more the mesh tent fades from your consciousness. What remains is a charming encounter with some very lovely birds.

Land of the Dragons

Sandwiched between Bird Gardens to the south and Stanleyville to the north is a play area just for the preschool set. Other theme parks in Central Florida have similar kiddie areas but nowhere will you find the concept pulled off with as much wit and verve as the Land of the Dragons. Here, the clever design of *Fievel's Playland* at Universal and the size of *Shamu's Happy Harbor* at SeaWorld come together to create the only five-star kiddie attraction in this book.

There are animals to be seen here, too, of course. At one end are the iguanas, monitor lizards, and komodo dragon that give the area its name. At the other, in a separate circular area, is *Lory Landing,* described below. But the emphasis is on fun in the Land of the Dragons and the little ones will not be disappointed.

Interactive Play Areas

Rating: ★ ★ ★ ★ ★
Type: Hands-on activity
Time: As long as you want
Kelly says: The best of its kind in Central Florida

Most of the Land of the Dragons is given over to a series of loosely connected climb-up, crawl-through, slide-down play areas that can keep little ones occupied for hours. I have given them the rather cumbersome name of "interactive play areas," but each has its own identity and special attractions, as we shall see.

Dominating the north end of the area is the **Dragon's Nest**, an elaborate two-story structure colorfully painted and shaded by a large tarp covering and towering live oak trees. On the lower level, it features a net climb, an "air bounce" (a large inflated floor on which kids can jump to their hearts' content), and a "ball crawl" (a pit filled with colored plastic balls into which kids can literally dive). The upper level is reached either via the net climb or, for less agile adults, a stairway. There you will find a two-level, kid-sized, climb-through, maze-like environment forming a delightful obstacle course. No one higher than 56 inches is allowed in this one, so Mom and Dad are excused.

From this upper level extend two rope bridges. Both go to the **Tree House**, one directly and the other via an intermediate tower, from which kids can zip down a corkscrew slide to ground level. The Tree House itself is a kid's fantasy of a humongous old tree girdled by a spiral wooden staircase leading to a "secret" room at the top. Along the way, climbers can detour into jungle gym-like environments that snake off through the Land of the Dragons. Kids will love it; nervous parents may find it hard to keep track of their little ones.

At the foot of the Tree House lies **Mizzly Marsh**, a watery play area where kids can really get soaked. The marsh leads through and around the old tree and comes complete with a friendly dragon whose snake-like body appears and disappears beneath the water.

Set apart and surrounded by a fence is the **Dragon Diggery**, a large and ingeniously designed sandbox with adorable playhouses, one in the shape of a giant mushroom.

The overall effect of these interlocking entertainments is pure delight. Not only is virtually every activity conceived by the preschool mind represented here, but the design and attention to detail are wonderfully imaginative. Even the trash cans are part of the theme. They're called Gobblety Goop, and let you shove your candy wrappers and soda cups down a dragon's throat.

Tip: If your kids are old enough to be turned loose in the Land of the Dragons, you can draw some comfort in the knowledge that there is only one way out, at the southern end. There is no exit at the north end, near *Lory Landing*.

Kiddie Rides

Rating:	★ ★ ★
Type:	Mechanical rides for toddlers
Time:	A few minutes each
Kelly says:	Variations on a single theme

Sprinkled around Land of the Dragons are small kiddie rides. You know the kind of thing: tiny vehicles that go round and round in a tiny circle with tiny little people sitting in them. The ones here are better designed and executed than most, with cutesy names like *Eggery Deggery*, *Chug-A-Tug*, and *Dapper Flappers*. If your kids are the right age (under three) they should have a ball here.

Friends Forever

Rating:	★ ★ ★ +
Type:	Live outdoor show
Time:	About 15 minutes
Kelly says:	Entertainment for tots

This is a delightful little singalong and audience participation show for the kids. Adults should check their sophistication at the door. Dumphrey, the Fire-Breathing Dragon who is sort of the mascot for Land of the Dragons, and a beautiful princess help a dashing knight search for his lost dog, Percy, and the kids in the audience get to help. Along the way they learn lessons about diversity and tolerance. Dumphrey is a costumed character, of course, but Percy is played by a real live dog and he just may be the best actor of the bunch. It's all good fun and the little tots at whom this show is aimed seem to love every minute of it.

Lory Landing

Rating:	★ ★ ★ +
Type:	Walk-through animal exhibit
Time:	As long as you like
Kelly says:	Close encounters with inquisitive charmers

Lorys and lorikeets are the main attraction in this aviary within an aviary. About halfway between parakeets and parrots in size, lorys are as curious as they are colorful. As you walk through their jungle-themed aviary, they are likely to land on your head, shoulder, or arm to check out your shiny jewelry or angle for a handout. Busch

Gardens encourages this by selling "lory nectar" ($3) just in case you forgot to bring your own.

This is great fun for kids (grown-ups, too!) and well worth a visit. In the antechamber to the lorys' digs are large cages displaying their larger cousins — cockatoos, macaws, and the like.

Stanleyville

Stanleyville is a compact, cleverly designed area that quite literally has something for everyone. At the southern end is what is arguably the best roller coaster in all of central Florida, the first stop we encounter on the park-circling *Trans-Veldt Railroad,* as well as a quite nice barbecue restaurant. At the other end are two delightful water rides and in the middle is a spacious theater that serves up some first-rate live entertainment on a somewhat erratic schedule. The only downside is that there are very few animals to be seen here, but I seriously doubt you'll care.

SheiKra

Rating:	★ ★ ★ ★ ★
Type:	Vertical dive coaster
Time:	3 minutes
Kelly says:	Gulp!

SheiKra (pronounced SHEEK-rah) is America's first "vertical dive roller coaster" and its debut cements Busch Gardens' reputation as *the* central Florida destination for coaster freaks. If pushing yourself to the limit is your idea of having a good time, then you will not want to miss this fall-filled fear-fest.

Although *SheiKra* officially lasts a full three minutes, the first 70 seconds or so are taken up by the slow crawl to a height of 200 feet where, after a tight U-turn, you reach the first drop. There you pause just over the lip for several hours (okay, three or four seconds) as you contemplate your fate. Then you drop straight down at a 90 degree angle before swooping upwards to do it all again.

The second drop takes you straight through the mist-filled center of a ruined tower, underground, up again for another tight turn, and down for a watery splashdown that slows you for a quick return to safety.

The best seats in the house. The ride vehicles are broad and compact, with three eight-seat rows. On top of that, they feature "stadium-style seating," meaning that each row is a little higher than the one in front of it. The result is that virtually every seat gives you a great view of the terrors that face you. Still, the true believers will want to ride until they get into the first row for the unobstructed view of the first drop during that eternal pause.

One of the best touches in this ride is a simple engineering trick used in that final splashdown. Twin tubes mounted on the outside rear edges of the ride vehicle dip into the water on either side of the track, sending up two towering plumes that crash down on the kids who have eagerly gathered at pool's edge. And thanks to the clever siting of the ride, you will have plenty of time to figure out exactly how it's done.

In fact, *SheiKra* offers the best views for non-riders of any Busch Gardens coaster, so you can walk under and around it and get an excellent idea of exactly what you are missing. That is almost as much fun as riding. Almost.

Trans-Veldt Railroad

Rating:	★ ★ ★
Type:	Steam railroad journey
Time:	30 – 35 minutes for a complete circuit
Kelly says:	Shuttle with a view

Right under *SheiKra*, you can board a reconstruction of the type of steam railroad that served as mass transit in turn-of-the-century Africa, rest your weary feet, and get some great views of the animals of the *Serengeti Plain*. This is one of two vehicular viewing venues for the Serengeti (the *Skyride*, described in the Crown Colony section below, is the other).

It makes a leisurely circuit of the park in a generally counterclockwise direction with stops in Nairobi (the closest stop to the main entrance) and the Congo (near Timbuktu). Since you can board or exit at any of the three stops, the *Trans-Veldt* is a great way to cut down on your walking time, and it provides glimpses of animals you probably wouldn't see otherwise.

As you travel from Stanleyville to Nairobi you will get a tantalizing preview glimpse of *Rhino Rally* (described below), which might help you decide if you want to brave its long lines. Continuing through Egypt on your way to the Congo, you will pass right through the superstructure of *Montu* and enter the Serengeti where you will see giraffes and a variety of veldt antelopes. Too bad you can't stop for a longer look. A narrator on the train helps make sure you don't miss any of the animals and offers interesting facts about the ones you do see.

After the Congo stop, the train loops around the Congo and back to Stanleyville. This portion is the least scenic, although it does provide some fun, "backstage" glimpses of the park, including a close-up look at some portions of *Kumba*. In fact, the route of the *Trans-Veldt* takes you past every roller coaster in the park.

Tip: The left-hand side of the train offers the most interesting views of the Serengeti.

Stanleyville Theater

Rating:	★ ★ ★ to ★ ★ ★ ★ ★
Type:	Live entertainment
Time:	Varies
Kelly says:	Keep your fingers crossed

It's hard to predict what, if anything, you'll be able to see here when you visit. The schedule is erratic and anything but predictable. But if you're lucky, you may be able to catch your favorites star of yesteryear in live performance, making this the hottest show in town.

Past acts that have played here include Gary Lewis and the Playboys, Herman's Hermits, and Juice Newton. There have been Big Bands, too, like the Tommy Dorsey,

Glenn Miller, and Les Brown Orchestras. Performances tend to be from Thursday through Sunday only, so plan accordingly if this sort of thing interests you.

Usually, there are three shows a day and tickets, which are free, are required. You can get them near the theater.

Stanley Falls Log Flume

Rating:	★ ★ ★ +
Type:	Water ride
Time:	About 2 minutes
Kelly says:	The last drop is a doozy

This is a fairly ordinary log flume ride, especially when compared to more recent variations on the theme. On the other hand, it is one of the longest in the nation, they say. The car in which you ride is a log-shaped contraption with two seating areas scooped out of it. Each car holds four people, adults or children. However, when the lines aren't too long you can ride two to a car.

Your log rumbles along at a moderate pace in a water-filled flume, takes a few turns, and then climbs slowly to a modest height. The first small drop is merely preparation for the finale, a slow ride up yet another steep grade and an exhilarating drop to the bottom in full view of the passing crowds. Like all water rides, this one has a warning about getting wet, but the cars, with their scooped out fronts, seem designed to direct the wave generated by the final splashdown away from the passengers. It's unlikely that you'll get seriously soaked on this one.

As you exit, pause for a moment to commune with the black and white ruffed lemurs with their beautiful coats and long, bushy tails.

Tanganyika Tidal Wave

Rating:	★ ★ ★ ★
Type:	Water ride
Time:	About 2 minutes
Kelly says:	A first-class soaking

If the nearby *Stanley Falls Log Flume* lulled you into a false sense of security about staying dry, this one will dispel any such notions. Like the log flume ride, this is all about the final drop. In fact, until then, this ride is far tamer. It snakes lazily through a narrow waterway past stilt houses, whose porches are piled high with Central African trade goods, before taking a slow climb to the top.

Then, all bets are off as the 25-passenger car on which you're riding plunges wildly down a sharp incline into a shallow pool of water, sending a drenching wave over not just the passengers but the spectators who have eagerly gathered on a bridge overhead. No two ways about it. This one really soaks you. Even with a poncho you'll still be pretty darned damp. Since you're probably soaked to the skin anyway, why not top the ride off by standing on the bridge and waiting for the next car to come by? For those who don't want to take the ride or get soaked on the bridge, there is a glassed in viewing section that offers the thrill of a wall of water rushing at you, without the soaking effects.

See *Good Things to Know About … Getting Wet*, earlier in this chapter, for some tips on negotiating Busch Gardens' water rides.

The Congo

The Congo is another compact, cleverly designed area with twisting tree-shaded walks and a number of spectator bridges over rides and animal habitats. Most of the space is given over to some of Busch Gardens' premiere thrill rides, so expect lots of excited kids and teenagers jostling for space. The Congo is also home to the park's ravishing and much-ballyhooed white Bengal tigers. The predominant architectural motif is round buildings with conical wooden stick roofs.

In addition to the major attractions profiled below, the Congo contains a bumper car ride (**Ubanga-Banga Bumper Cars**), a trio of kiddie rides (**Pygmy Village**), and remote control trucks and boats. The *Skyride* (described in the Crown Colony section, below) offers a shortcut to Crown Colony and Egypt. There is also a stop for the *Trans-Veldt Railroad* (described in the Stanleyville section, above).

Kumba
Rating: ★ ★ ★ ★ ★
Type: Steel roller coaster
Time: Just under 3 minutes
Kelly says: Yet another superb roller coaster

Before *Montu* opened (see Egypt, below), *Kumba* was Busch Gardens' block-buster ride. It's still pretty amazing and is the largest of its kind in the southeastern United States. *Kumba* means "roar" in a Congolese dialect, the P.R. people say, and it's well named. Riders are braced with shoulder restraints into 32-seat vehicles (eight rows, four abreast) that roar along almost 4,000 feet of blue steel track that winds up, around, over, and through the surrounding scenery. There are loops, camelbacks, and corkscrews to terrify or thrill you, as the case may be. One of the more disorienting maneuvers takes you on a "cobra roll" around a spectator bridge, which is a great place for the faint of heart to get an idea of what they're missing. Remember to wave to Aunt Martha as you whiz by.

Claw Island
Rating: ★ ★ ★ ★
Type: Animal habitat
Time: Continuous viewing
Kelly says: A treat for tiger fanciers

Claw Island is the Hollywood-ish name for an intriguing habitat housing some of Busch Gardens' most beautiful residents. Here, in a deep pit, on a small, green, palm-dotted island, you'll find five magnificent Bengal tigers. One bears the tawny coat we are all familiar with, three have dark stripes on white coats, and the fifth is completely white. These rare white tigers were prized by Indian royalty, and no wonder. They are truly awe-inspiring.

Claw Island's pit is surrounded by gazebo viewing areas and a wooden spectator bridge, all of which have heavy rope netting to make doubly sure that no one climbs or falls in. By walking around the perimeter you should be able to get good views of the tigers.

Most of the time, they are just lounging around (these are cats, after all). If you're lucky enough to chance by at feeding time things can get a bit livelier. Unfortunately, feedings are haphazard, to prevent the animals from becoming habituated. You can ask at the nearby gift shop when feeding time will be, but the information provided is not always accurate.

Congo River Rapids

Rating:	★ ★ ★ ★ ★
Type:	Water ride
Time:	About 3 minutes
Kelly says:	The best of the water rides

It doesn't have the steep drops of the flume rides in Stanleyville, but for me *Congo River Rapids* provides the most enjoyable overall water ride experience in Busch Gardens. Here you climb aboard 12-seater circular rafts that are then set adrift to float freely along a rapids-filled stretch of river. The raft twists, turns, and spins as it bumps off the sides and various cunningly placed obstacles in the stream. In addition to the raging waters, which periodically slosh into the raft, the course is punctuated with waterfalls and waterspouts, all of which have the potential to drench you to the skin. The most insidious threat of all comes from your fellow park visitors, who are encouraged to spray you with water cannon (at 25 cents a shot) from the pedestrian walkway that skirts the ride.

Despite all the white water, the raft proceeds at a relatively stately pace and the "river" drops only several feet over its quarter-mile course. The real excitement is generated by the ever-present threat of a soaking. How wet you get is only somewhat a matter of chance. It seems that the wetness quotient has been increased since the ride first opened. Time was that some people emerged virtually unscathed, while others got soaked. Now it seems that almost everyone get thoroughly doused. On a hot Florida afternoon, that seems to be just the ticket, which makes this my favorite water ride and explains the five-star rating.

Timbuktu

Timbuktu is, of course, the legendary sub-Saharan trade crossroads that figures prominently in the popular imagination of adventure and exploration. Here at Busch Gardens, Timbuktu is an open, sun-drenched plaza dotted with palm trees and featuring architecture that mimics the mud towers of its namesake. There is precious little shade here unless you venture indoors. The attractions in Timbuktu are a mismatched assortment, having little to do with either Timbuktu or even Africa. But then, Timbuktu is emblematic of far-flung trade, so perhaps it's not so farfetched that it contains an eclectic grab bag of themed attractions from around the world.

There are no zoo animals here. In their place are a variety of typical **amusement park rides**, including Busch Gardens' only **carousel** and several other **kiddie rides**. Also at hand are a collection of **midway games**, cleverly disguised as a sub-Saharan marketplace, and a **video arcade**.

The Scorpion

Rating: ★ ★ ★ +
Type: A beginner's roller coaster
Time: About a minute
Kelly says: Roller coasters 101

This is the place to come to decide if you have what it takes to tackle the bigger coasters in the park. *The Scorpion* is far and away the tamest of the lot, although it does have one up-and-over loop. So if you've never been "inverted," this is as good a place to start as any. Otherwise, it's no more terrifying than, say, Disney's *Thunder Mountain*.

Cheetah Chase

Rating: ★ ★ ★
Type: A "baby" roller coaster
Time: About a minute and a half
Kelly says: Take the kiddies

If the *Scorpion* is too much for you, head here. It's what's known in the amusement park trade as a "wild mouse" ride. Little four-seater cars zip along a sinuous elevated track with sharp turns and a few mild drops. Kids love it but adults sit high in the little cars and may feel exposed, which can be fun (or not) depending on your taste. The ride does give you a nicely elevated view of the surrounding Timbuktu area.

One downside to the ride is that only two widely-spaced cars are on the track at any given time. This is for safety reasons, but it does lead to slow loading times, which can translate into long waits in line.

Pirates 4-D (Timbuktu Theater)

Rating: ★ ★ ★
Type: 3-D film
Time: About 25 minutes
Kelly says: A 3-D show that makes a splash

With this show, Busch Gardens takes on Disney and Universal in the 3-D movie sweepstakes and comes in a solid third. Starring Leslie Nielsen as Captain Lucky and Eric Idle as his sidekick Pierre, *Pirates 4-D* tells the tale of an evil pirate — that would be Captain Lucky — who returns to Dead Man's Cave to reclaim his buried treasure. What the crew doesn't know is that Captain Lucky buried his former crew along with the treasure and plans to do likewise with his current collection of scalawags.

What Captain Lucky doesn't know is that one member of his old crew — the cabin boy — survived and has rigged the entire island with devilishly clever booby traps.

Much of the fun of the film comes from setting off those traps, which involve crabs and spiders and bats and bees, along with an array of seat-side special effects that place the creepy crawlies in our midst. It's all great fun and not really very scary, although very young tots don't seem to know that.

An additional attraction is the air-conditioned Timbuktu Theater, making this a great show to catch during the hottest part of the afternoon. The flick unspools regularly throughout the day.

Best seats in the house. The seats in the front half of the house get the best of the water effects.

The Phoenix

Rating:	★ ★ ★
Type:	Amusement park ride
Time:	5 minutes
Kelly says:	Only if you haven't done it before

This is a very familiar amusement park ride. A curved boat-like car seating 50 people swings back and forth, gaining height. At the apex of its swing, it pauses and the passengers hang briefly upside down, screaming merrily. Then on the next swing it goes completely up and over.

Chances are, there's a ride like this at an amusement park somewhere near your home, which leads to the question: Ride this one or spend the time doing things you can't do near home? I'd recommend the latter.

Musical Variety Show at the Desert Grill Restaurant

Rating:	★ ★ ★ ★
Type:	Musical variety show
Time:	About 20 minutes
Kelly says:	Best with a meal

What you see here during your visit to Busch Gardens is hard to predict. That's because the stage at the spacious and blessedly cool Desert Grill plays host to a constantly changing roster of musical and dance variety troupes. What's easy to predict is the quality of the shows, which in my experience have been uniformly excellent.

Typically, you will be entertained by a young, energetic, and talented cast. Some shows I've seen have involved intricate percussion and acrobatics. Others have featured championship ballroom dancers, strutting their stuff in a variety of dancing styles. Many times the show will spill out into the audience and they always seem to be looking for a way to get the kids involved. It's all bright and cheerful and makes for a pleasant way to end a meal.

The meal comes courtesy of the Desert Grill restaurant, a cafeteria-style eatery to the side of the main auditorium. All seating in the theater is at long trestle tables, set perpendicular to the stage. It's best to arrive a half an hour or so before the posted show time. That should give you time to get your meal and eat most of it before the show starts, so you can enjoy the music over dessert.

Nairobi

This is Busch Gardens' most zoo-like themed area. To the east, the plains of the Serengeti stretch as far as the eye can see. On the other side are a string of animal exhibits ranging from the merely interesting to the truly wondrous. In addition to those described below, there are displays of **Aldabra tortoises**, **Asian elephants** and **dromedary camels**, with occasional Meet The Keeper and Animal Encounter sessions. The *Trans-Veldt Railroad* (described in the Stanleyville section, above) stops right in the middle. The showpiece of Nairobi, however, is the *Rhino Rally* attraction, which is part African animal encounter and part thrill ride.

Rhino Rally

Rating: ★ ★ ★ +
Type: Drive-through animal tour and water ride
Time: 7 minutes
Kelly says: Nifty idea that's more clever than thrilling

Rhino Rally artfully blends safari-style animal encounters with a tame water ride. The ride is carved out of a 22-acre patch of the *Serengeti Plain* near the border between Nairobi and Timbuktu. But, unlike rides at other parks that use animated robotic figures, *Rhino Rally* calls on its cast of exotic African water buffalo, zebras, antelope, elephants, and rhinos to play themselves in a real-life action adventure.

The adventure begins as you board a 17-passenger converted Land Rover with your guide and driver to take part in the 34th annual running of Rhino Rally, an off-road race along the Zambezi River across the rugged and dangerous terrain of the African veldt. One adult in the group is chosen to ride next to the driver (a great seat, by the way) and serve as the navigator who, in off-road rally tradition, will be blamed if anything goes wrong. Along the way, your sturdy vehicle splashes through crocodile-infested waters and comes almost face to face with elephants, rhinos, and other wild critters. The course has been cleverly designed to allow the Land Rovers to nosedive into streams and water holes and cross narrow bridges over deep ravines.

The trip provides close-up, although brief, encounters with elephants, Grant's zebras, cape buffalo and scimitar-horned oryx. The ancient Egyptians, we learn, domesticated these beasts and forced their long curving horns to grow together into a single horn, creating the myth of the unicorn. After driving past two rare white rhinos (they are actually gray), the vehicle fords a stream filled with real crocodiles cruising just a few feet away.

Then, as often happens in theme park thrill rides, things go awry and, of course, it's all the navigator's fault. A fateful wrong turn takes your vehicle into a tree-shaded gulch just as a cloudburst hits, obscuring the view out the front window. As your driver nervously tries to cross a rickety pontoon bridge, a freak flash flood comes roaring over a cliff on the left. Before you can say "Dr. Livingstone, I presume," the bridge breaks apart, carrying you and your vehicle on an unscheduled ride down a meandering river.

After drifting through a narrow canyon and under a drenching waterfall, the bridge fragment on which your vehicle is riding crashes against yet another washed out bridge and comes to a bumpy halt. Fortunately, your intrepid guide is able to drive out of this predicament and up the side of the river, bringing everyone safely to the finish line.

A great deal of the fun of this ride is supplied by the driver/guide. The best ones really get into the spirit of things, teaching you a few handy Swahili phrases and getting everyone involved in the action. So you'll probably want to ride more than once. The problem with that is the line quickly grows to daunting lengths. Figure on an hour's wait unless you arrive at opening time.

Tip: If you are alone or if there are just two of you, you may be able to get in a vehicle a bit sooner by following the sign for the single riders line. If you are waiting in the main line, you can accomplish much the same thing by holding one or two fingers aloft during the boarding process. Ride attendants sometimes look for singles or couples to fill in empty spots on the Land Rover that's about to depart.

The best seats in the house. The seats on the left hand side of the vehicle offer not only the best views of the wildlife but a front row seat to the spectacular flash flood. You will, however, get wet.

Myombe Reserve: The Great Ape Domain

Rating: ★ ★ ★ ★ ★
Type: Ape habitat
Time: Continuous viewing
Kelly says: The zoo's crown jewel

Of all the animal habitats at Busch Gardens, this is the hands-down winner. The beautifully imagined setting here would be almost worth the visit without the chimps and gorillas. But it is these fascinating primates that we come to see, and the scenic designers and landscape architects have given them a home that provides plenty of variety for the animals while making it easy for us to spy on them. The achievement is remarkable and ranks right up there with the spectacular habitats at SeaWorld.

The habitat is divided in two, with the first area given over to a band of nine chimpanzees in a rocky, multi-leveled environment complete with spectacular waterfalls, calm pools, and a grassy forest clearing with plenty of climbing space. Best of all is a glassed-in viewing area that allows us to spy on the chimps' private behavior.

Passing through a tunnel, we reach the lowland gorilla habitat. There's a wonderful theatricality to this entrance as we pass through a simulated jungle fog to "discover" the gorillas grazing on our left. Talk about gorillas in the mist! In addition to a glassed viewing area, this habitat features a small amphitheater for extended observation and video cameras that allow us to observe individuals in the far reaches of the habitat.

There's plenty of explanatory information provided on blackboards (the conceit here is that we are visiting a jungle outpost of a scientific expedition), drawings in large, plastic-covered notebooks that we can leaf through, and voice-over narration in the hidden viewing area. If you only have time for one zoo exhibit between roller coaster rides, make it this one. The entrance to Myombe Reserve is opposite the Moroccan Palace Theater; the exit leads you into the rest of the Nairobi section.

Nairobi Field Station

Rating:	★ ★ ★ ★
Type:	Newborn animal exhibit
Time:	Continuous viewing
Kelly says:	Lifestyles of the cutest and cuddliest

One of the main missions of today's enlightened zoological parks is the propagation of species, especially threatened and endangered ones. Busch Gardens takes this responsibility very seriously and, rather than leave things to chance, they scoop up newborns, bring them here, and give them the kind of tender loving care that will best ensure their survival. What you see here will, naturally, depend on who's been giving birth in the days and weeks prior to your visit. If you're lucky you'll see something cute and cuddly. What you're most likely to see, however, are fledgling birds that can look downright ugly.

Question and answer sessions with the keepers of the nursery are held several times a day. Times are posted on a sign at the entrance.

Curiosity Caverns

Rating:	★ ★ +
Type:	Walk-through exhibit
Time:	Continuous viewing
Kelly says:	A real "Bat Cave"

Decorated to evoke a prehistoric cave, complete with wall paintings, this darkened walk-through tunnel displays, behind plate glass windows, a variety of critters that most people think of as "creepy," although the nocturnal marmoset is positively cuddly. Aside from the snakes and reptiles, the main attractions here are the bats. Fruit bats cavort in a large enclosure decorated with bare trees artfully draped with bananas, apples, and other yummy treats. Nearby, in a smaller display, are the vampire bats (yes, they really exist!), the animal blood on which they thrive served up on dainty trays hanging in their cages.

Crown Colony and the Serengeti Plain

This area takes its theme from the great British colonial enclaves of East Africa, where the well-heeled lived the good life and played cricket and polo while being waited on by the unshod. A real British Colonial would probably not recognize the place, but for the rest of us it'll do just fine. The overall impression is one of casual elegance and good taste. Crown Colony serves as a comfortable home to several attractions (like the Clydesdale stables, and the **Show Jumping Hall of Fame**) that stretch the African metaphor a bit. It is also the home of the Crown Colony House, a very nice full-service sit-down restaurant.

Edge of Africa

Rating: ★ ★ ★ ★ ★
Type: Brilliant animal habitat
Time: Continuous viewing
Kelly says: Up close and personal with lions and hippos

With *Edge of Africa*, Busch Gardens has created an animal habitat to rival *Myombe*. Here, on a looping trail that evokes a number of African themes, are displayed a compact colony of adorable meerkats, a pride of lions, a pack of hyenas, a few hippos, and a troop of ring-tailed lemurs. The genius of the design is in the glass walls that allow you, literally, to come nose to nose with some of these animals.

The best display is built around the metaphor of a scientific encampment on the Serengeti that has been invaded by lions or hyenas (the zoo operation alternates these species in the exhibit). Two Land Rovers are built into the glass wall that separates you from the beasts, allowing you to climb into the vehicles and re-create an actual safari experience. At feeding time, the handlers drop meat morsels into the enclosure from above the Land Rovers, encouraging the animals to climb into the backs and onto the hoods of the vehicles. The effect is breathtaking as you sit a hand's breadth away from these snarling carnivores.

The hippo exhibit evokes an African river village with the huts raised over the water on stilts. The viewing area is nicely shaded by the huts and the extensive glass wall allows a terrific underwater perspective on these beasts. While they may seem lumbering on land, under water they are surprisingly graceful as they lope past swarms of freshwater tropical fish. One visitor compared them to flying pigs.

The key to really enjoying *Edge of Africa* is to come at feeding time when the animals will be at their most active and most visible. At other times they will most likely be off relaxing in the shade somewhere. The attendants doing the feeding are all experienced animal handlers who are more than happy to share their extensive knowledge with you, so don't be shy about asking questions. Unfortunately, there is no regular feeding schedule. Feeding times are varied to mimic, to some small extent, life in the wild, where animals can never predict when (or even if) their next meal is coming.

The solution is to ask the attendants at the attraction when feeding time will be. You may have to be persistent and you must also be willing to drop whatever you're doing elsewhere in the park to return at the appointed time. Take it from me, it's worth it.

Note: The main entrance to *Edge of Africa* is in Crown Colony but you can also reach the attraction from Egypt.

Serengeti Safari Tour

Rating: ★ ★ ★ ★ ★
Type: Guided tour
Time: 30 minutes
Kelly says: A safari for those who can't get to Africa

First the bad news: There is a hefty extra charge for this attraction of $34 for

everyone five and older (annual passholders get a $2 discount). That wi
a budget-buster for many families; but if the cost doesn't scare you of
provide experiences you'll remember for a good long time. If it's any consoiau
a heck of a lot cheaper than going to Africa.

The tour begins when about 20 people are loaded on to the standing-room-
only back of a flatbed truck. A small awning provides some shade at the front, but
since it is lowered for the animal feedings much of the time you will be in the searing
sun; a hat, not to mention water, is not a bad idea. Your friendly tour guide, a Busch
Gardens' education staffer, lays down a few simple safety instructions and then it's off
to the interior of the Plain for the real highlight of the tour — a chance to hand feed
the giraffes and elands. Along the way, you will see ostriches and maribou storks, but
the giraffes are the stars of the show.

The adult giraffes tower over you, while the youngsters just get their heads over
the edge of the truck. They are remarkably tame and will let you pet their stiff, tawny
necks and soft muzzles. You may also get a demonstration of how they use their long
black tongues to pluck the dainty leaves off thorny acacia bushes. For most people,
this is the highlight of the tour. To have two or three of these gentle giants leaning
into the back of the truck as you feed them and stroke their powerful necks is a very
special experience indeed.

The best seats in the house. The back of the truck where you stand has a padded
rail around the rim. I suggest positioning yourself at one of the back corners since
giraffes will often trail after the slow-moving vehicle looking for another handout.

Tip: The trucks have a maximum capacity of 20 people and on a typical day
there are just five tours. While the high price keeps the crowds down, tours do fill
up quickly. You can reserve ahead for the first tour of each day only, which departs at
11:15 a.m. and is the only morning tour. The morning tour also offers the advantage
of beating the heat of midday. Call (813) 984-4043 to make your reservation. When
you arrive at the park, look for the Adventure Tour Center in Morocco (on your left),
where you can pay for your tour with cash or credit card. If you don't reserve ahead,
you must sign up in advance for one of the afternoon tours when you get to the park;
it is wise to do so early.

Serengeti Plain

Rating:	★ ★ ★
Type:	Extensive animal habitat
Time:	Continuous viewing but access is limited
Kelly says:	Takes persistence to see it all

This is one of Busch Gardens' major zoological achievements, a 50-acre preserve
that evokes the vast grasslands of Eastern Africa. (Serengeti is a Masai word meaning
"plain without end.") Here, Busch displays a representative cross-section of African
plains dwellers, from charming curiosities like giraffes and the endangered black rhi-
noceros, to the herd animals — lithe gazelles and lumbering wildebeest (or gnus).
There are some African birds here, too, like the maribou stork, but most of the birds
you will see are what Busch Gardens calls "fly-ins," Florida species that recognize a

good deal when they see one. The rule of thumb is that if it's a bird and white, it's a Tampa Bay local.

It's a brilliant idea and, by and large, well executed, although it still looks far more like Florida scrub land than the real Serengeti. The concept and the design involve a number of tradeoffs. By mimicking nature, the designers have made the animals hard to see — just like in the wild. Although you can see into the Serengeti from Nairobi or the terrace of the Crown Colony House, the only way to get a good look is to go inside. Unless you are willing to pay the stiff extra fee for the *Serengeti Safari Tour*, that can be accomplished only by the *Skyride* (see below) and by the *Trans-Veldt Railroad* (see the Stanleyville section, above) that circles the perimeter. So your routes through the Serengeti are predetermined as are the lengths of your visits. This creates a number of minor problems. There's no guarantee that the animals will be in prime viewing position (or even visible) when you pass by, although it's unlikely that you will miss much. And, if an animal catches your fancy or is doing something particularly interesting, your vehicle simply keeps on going; you don't have the luxury of stopping. You also have no control over how close you can get to the animals (with the notable exception of the *Serengeti Safari Tour*).

That being said, the *Serengeti Plain* remains a major feather in Busch Gardens' zoological cap. The animals enjoy a much more spacious and natural environment than they would have in a more "traditional" zoo and we probably shouldn't complain too much about the compromises we must make for their comfort.

Those who want to make the investment of time and money can visit the Serengeti many times — on the *Skyride* over the plain, the train ride around it, the truck tour, and from vantage points in *Edge of Africa* and around the perimeter. The nature of the park experience, however, suggests that most people will glimpse the animals briefly on the short rides. And that's too bad.

The Skyride

Rating:	★ ★ ★
Type:	Suspended gondola ride
Time:	5 minutes
Kelly says:	Shortcut with a view

If you've been on the sky ride at Disney World, you know what this one's all about. This isn't intended as a tour of the *Serengeti Plain*, although it does pass over *Edge of Africa* and *Rhino Rally* and offers a glimpse of the plains animals in the distance. Rather, this is a one-way shortcut from Crown Colony to the Congo, or vice versa. Your vehicle is a small four-seat gondola suspended from an overhead cable. You can board at either end, but you cannot stay aboard for a roundtrip. The ride dips down for a dog-leg left turn at a checkpoint on the northern end of the *Serengeti*. This is not a disembarkation point but is used primarily to adjust the spacing between gondolas to assure a smooth arrival.

You can get good views of the Serengeti on this ride, although most people will take the opportunity to check out the action on *Montu* and *Kumba* or perhaps to spot the towers of Adventure Island, Busch Gardens' water park, down the road.

Clydesdale Hamlet

Rating: ★ ★ +
Type: Horse stables
Time: Continuous viewing
Kelly says: For horse lovers and Bud fans

This is a smaller version of the Clydesdale Hamlet at SeaWorld. The horses are magnificent; there may be a foal on view during your visit. Even if you aren't a horse lover, the stroll through the stables makes a pleasant detour en route to Egypt. The Clydesdales also pose for **photo ops** several times a day. Check the Meet The Keepers schedule on the back of the large map you picked up at the main entrance when you arrived.

Egypt

This is Busch Gardens' newest "land" and one of its smallest, at least in terms of strolling space and amenities. Its primary purpose is to give the mega–coaster *Montu* a home. The King Tut attraction seems a bit of an afterthought, and the only eatery here is a kiosk dispensing snacks. The shopping is a bit more elaborate but not much.

The design evokes upper Egypt as it might have looked about the time Howard Carter was unearthing King Tut's treasure. The scale is appropriately grandiose but the statuary and wall carvings fall well short of the originals. Still, it's pleasant enough. There's a clever "archaeological dig, " called **Sifting Sands**, that is, in fact, a shaded sand box in which little ones can uncover the past. A small selection of **midway games** is also offered.

For most people, however, Egypt will be glimpsed briefly en route to the massive temple gates at the end, beyond which lurks the terrifying *Montu*.

Montu

Rating: ★ ★ ★ ★ ★
Type: Inverted roller coaster
Time: About 3 minutes
Kelly says: The next best (i.e. scariest) thing to *SheiKra*

This one is truly terrifying. It is also, for those who care about such things, the tallest and longest inverted steel roller coaster in the southeastern United States.

Montu (named for a hawk-headed Egyptian god of war) takes the formula of *Kumba* and quite literally turns it on its head. Instead of sitting in a car with the track under your feet, you sit (or should I say "hang") in a car with the track overhead. Once you leave the station, your feet hang free as you pass over a pit filled with live crocodiles and climb to a dizzying 150 feet above the ground before being dropped 13 stories, shot through a 360 degree "camelback loop" that produces an eternity of weightlessness (actually a mere three seconds), and zipped, zoomed, and zapped along nearly 4,000 feet of track that twists over, above, and even into the ground. Fortunately, when you dip below ground level you do so in archaeological "excavation trenches," in keeping with the Egyptian theme. There's not much to see in these trenches, but then you don't spend much time in them and you'll probably have your eyes jammed shut anyway.

Each car holds 32 passengers. At maximum capacity, 1,700 guests can be pumped through this attraction each hour. Nonetheless, lines can be formidable. If this is your kind of ride, plan on arriving early during busy seasons.

The best seats in the house. The best (and scariest) seats are in the front row. Otherwise, the outside seats are the ones to hope for. Given the overhead design of this ride, the interior seats offer a very obstructed view, which may not be a problem if you tend to ride with your eyes shut most of the time. Getting the front seats is pretty much the luck of the draw, although every once in a while you may be able to step in when the faint of heart opt out of the front row.

Even if you can't or don't ride roller coasters, *Montu* is worth a visit for a close-up view of the crazy people who are riding. Position yourself at the black iron fence that you see as you pass through the massive temple gates that lead to the ride. Here you'll get an exhilarating close-up look of 32 pairs of feet as they come zipping out of the first trench. If you do ride, don't forget to look for your terrified or giddy face on the instant photos they sell.

King Tut's Tomb

Rating: ★ ★ +
Type: Walk-through attraction
Time: About 10 minutes
Kelly says: A "spirited" guide to an ancient tomb

Here's your chance to walk in the footsteps of Howard Carter, the legendary archaeologist who discovered King Tut's tomb in the 1920s. As you wait in the darkened entrance to the tomb, old newspaper headlines and period newsreels re-create the excitement and wonder of the discovery. Then, the projector jams, the film melts and, as you enter the tomb proper, the spirit of Tut himself takes over as tour guide.

What you see is a re-creation of the tomb as it looked at the time of discovery, the many treasures and priceless artifacts piled in jumbled disarray. As lights illuminate specific artifacts, Tut tells us about his gilded throne, his golden chariot, and his teenage bride. Moving to the burial chamber, we see his solid gold sarcophagus and the golden goddesses who guarded the cabinet containing alabaster urns filled with his internal organs.

For newcomers to Egyptology, this attraction will serve as an intriguing introduction. The marvelously air-conditioned tomb also makes for a pleasant break from the burning Florida sun. Those who are familiar with Tut may want to skip this one.

Guided Tours

Busch Gardens Africa offers a number of special tours in addition to the *Serengeti Safari Tour* (see Crown Colony, above). These offer special perks, behind-the-scenes access, and up-close encounters with some of its animal charges. There is a hefty extra charge for these special experiences, but if you have the budget I think you'll find it money well spent. The fees given below (which do not include tax) are in addition to regular park admission and no annual passholder or other discounts are offered. Prices were accurate at press time but are subject to change, so it's best to call prior to your visit to double check prices and availability. You can call toll-free at (888) 800-5447 and ask to be connected to the tour department. The direct line is (813) 984-4043. Children under five are not permitted on any animal interactions, although they can participate in other elements of some tours; bilingual guides can be arranged with prior notice.

Saving a Species Tour

This $45 tour adds a visit to the endangered white rhinos to the giraffe feeding of the *Serengeti Safari Tour*, described above. Participants also learn a bit about conservation efforts and the good work of the World Wildlife Fund, which gets a donation of $2 from the cost of the tour.

Sunset on the Serengeti

This is an adults-only version of the *Serengeti Safari Tour*. It begins in the Crown Colony Brew Master's Club with a tall frosty lager. Then it's off to feed the giraffes while knocking back a few more Anheuser-Busch brews. Presumably, they make sure no one is FUI (feeding under the influence). This one is $40 per over-21 head.

Animal Adventure Tour

This two-hour tour focuses on the animals of the park, with an emphasis on the newest additions to the Busch Gardens family. Consequently, the menu may change depending on who's given birth most recently. At each stop, you get a personal briefing from the keepers. The tour visits the Clydesdale stables and *Edge of Africa*. Then you climb aboard a truck for your own *Serengeti Safari Tour* (see above). From there, you visit the rhinos and the elephants. A stop at the *Nairobi Field Station* might also be included. At most stops you will get to hand feed the animals and the tour guide will provide you with free ice-cold water during the tour.

There is just one *Animal Adventure Tour* each day, at 1:30 p.m. The tour, which is accessible to handicapped guests, costs $120 for all ages and is limited to seven people, so prior reservations are recommended. Otherwise, you can stop by the Expedition Africa shop to see if any slots are available. This tour is a sure-fire hit for animal lovers. If you are planning on taking the $34 *Serengeti Safari Tour* anyway, you may want to consider upgrading to this very special experience.

Guided Adventure Tour

This four-hour guided tour combines the animal encounters of the *Serengeti Safari Tour* with visits to *Edge of Africa* and the park's major rides and shows. Guests on this tour get front of the line access to *Kumba*, *Gwazi*, and *Montu* and the best seats in the house for the shows, as well as lunch at Crown Colony House. You also receive a 20% discount on all park merchandise and free stroller and wheelchair rental.

The tour costs $95 for adults and $85 for kids and is limited to 15 people. Make a reservation before arriving or look for the "Guided Tour Adventure Center" in the entrance plaza to the park. Tours depart once a day at 10:20 a.m.

Adventure Thrill Tour

This four-hour tour is for those who want to concentrate on the rides. For $75 (or $65 for kids 3 to 9), you get front of the line access to most of the major thrill rides and water rides as well as preferred seating for at least two shows, including *Ka Tonga*. Lunch at Crown Colony House is also included. Some people will no doubt find the front of the line privileges worth the extra cost.

Elite Adventure Tour

This $200 all-day extravaganza is Busch Gardens' VIP tour and it can last as long as you wish, although at this price you'll probably want to arrive early and stay until the park closes. The Elite Adventure Tour offers the front of the line access, priority seating, and discounts of the *Guided Adventure Tour*, plus a free continental breakfast, lunch, and a free Fuji camera. This one must be booked at least 24 hours in advance, but large groups should book at least a week in advance.

Ultimate Adventure Tour

This one adds the *Animal Adventure Tour* to the *Elite Adventure Tour* and costs $250 for everyone five and up.

Adventure Camps

If you really want to be nice to your kids, you won't just take them to Busch Gardens, you'll leave them there. Busch Gardens operates a number of sleepover camps for kids from grade six through high school. There's even a program that takes college kids. With nifty names like Zooventures and Young Explorers, these camps last from three to nine days and cost from $800 to over $2,000. Housing is dorm style on Busch Gardens property.

And if you think it's unfair that kids have all the fun, ask about the Family Sleepovers that let adults tag along. For more information and to request a catalog of camp programs at all of the Busch parks (the SeaWorlds in Orlando, San Antonio, and San Diego also offer programs), call (877) 248-2267 or (813) 987-5252.

Chapter Nine:

Water Parks

ORLANDO IS THE HOME OF THE WATER PARK AS WE KNOW IT TODAY. GEORGE D. Millay, a former SeaWorld official, started it all in 1977 with the opening of Wet 'n Wild. Since then, the concept has been copied, most noticeably by Disney, whose nearby complex has two water-themed parks — Typhoon Lagoon and Blizzard Beach — both beautifully designed in the Disney tradition. Despite its deep pockets and design talent, Disney hasn't buried the competition. Wet 'n Wild is still going strong and, to the west, the folks at Busch have built Adventure Island, right next to Busch Gardens Africa in Tampa. Both of these water parks offer plenty of thrills at a competitive price. And SeaWorld is planning its own water park for 2008.

An often overlooked selling point of these non-Disney water parks is that they all have numerous hotels and motels just a short drive away. Wet 'n Wild has many hotels within walking distance. This makes them especially easy to visit. If you are staying near one of these parks, there is little need, in my opinion, to trek all the way to Disney for a water park experience.

Like any self-respecting theme park, a water park has rides. But the rides here don't rely on mechanical wonders or ingenious special effects. Indeed they are the essence of simplicity: You walk up and then, with a little help from gravity and a stream of water, you come down. The fun comes from the many variations the designers work on this simple theme.

Slides

These are the most basic rides. After climbing a high tower, you slide down a flume on a cushion of running water, either on your back, on a rubber mat, in a one- or two-person inner tube, or in a raft that can carry anywhere from two to five people. Virtually every slide will have a series of swooping turns and sudden drops. Some are open to the sky, others are completely enclosed tubes. All slides dump you in a pool at the bottom of the run.

Speed Slides

Speed slides appeal to the daredevil. They are simple, narrow, flat-bottomed slides; some are pitched at an angle that approaches the vertical, others descend in a series of stair steps. Most culminate in a long, flat stretch that allows you to decelerate; a few end in splash pools. They offer a short, intense experience.

Wave Pools

These large, fan-shaped swimming pools have a beach-like entrance at the wide end and slope to a depth of about eight feet at the other. A clever hydraulic system sets waves running from the wall to the beach, mimicking the action of the ocean. Most wave pools have several modes, producing a steady flow of varying wave heights or a sort of random choppiness. Sometimes rented inner tubes are available for use in the wave pool.

Good Things to Know About . . .

Dress Codes

Simply put: wear a swimsuit. Most parks prohibit shorts, cut-off jeans, or anything with zippers, buckles, or metal rivets, as these things can scratch and damage the slides. Those with fair skin can wear t-shirts if they wish. Some rides may require that you remove your shirt, which you can usually clutch to your chest as you zoom down. Most people go barefoot, as the parks are designed with your feet's comfort in mind. If you prefer to wear waterproof sandals or other footwear designed for water sports, they are permitted.

Leaving the Park

All the parks reviewed here let you leave the park and return the same day. Just make sure to have your hand stamped before leaving.

Lockers

All water parks provide rental lockers and changing areas. Most people wear their swimsuits under their street clothes and disrobe by their locker. At day's end, they take their street clothes to a changing area, towel down, and get dressed, popping their wet suits into a plastic bag. The plastic laundry bag from your hotel room is ideal for this purpose.

Safety

Water park rides are safe, just as long as you follow the common sense rules posted at the rides and obey the instructions of the ride attendants. You are more likely to run into problems with the sun (see below) or with physical exertion if you are out of shape. You will climb more stairs at a visit to a water park than most people climb in a month. If you're not in peak condition, take it slow; pause from time to time and take in the sights.

The Sun

The Central Florida sun can be brutal. If you don't have a good base tan, a day at a water park can result in a painful sunburn, even on a cloudy day. Don't let it happen to you. Use sun block and use it liberally. Most overlooked place to protect: your feet. The sun also saps your body of moisture. Be sure to drink plenty of liquids throughout the day.

Towels

At Wet 'n Wild you can rent towels for a modest fee. Adventure Island, at my last visit, was not renting towels but said they were considering doing so, "because we get so many requests." It's easy (not to mention cheaper) to bring your own, even if it's one borrowed from your hotel.

Eating at the Water Parks

Water parks are like a day at the beach. Consequently, dining (if that's the right word) is a pretty basic experience. Most park eateries offer walk-up window service, paper plates, plastic utensils, and outdoor seating, some of it shaded. The bill of fare seldom ventures out of the hot dog, hamburger, pizza, barbecue, and ice cream categories. The prices are modest. You really have to work hard to spend more than $10 per person for a meal. In short, food at the water parks has been designed with kids and teenagers in mind, so I have not covered the restaurants in the reviews that follow. Suffice it to say you won't go hungry.

However, in my opinion, the best way to eat at the water parks is to bypass the fast-food eateries altogether and bring your own. If you are the picnicking type, I don't have to tell you what to do. Others should be aware that Florida supermarkets are cornucopias of picnic supplies. The folks at the deli counter will be more than happy to fix you up with a sumptuous repast. You can even pick up an inexpensive cooler while you're there along with ice to keep things cool. All the parks prohibit alcoholic beverages and glass containers.

Most people simply find a suitable picnic bench when they arrive and stake it out with a beach towel and their cooler, returning at lunch time. If you feel uncomfortable doing this, you can leave your cooler in the car and retrieve it at lunch time. (Don't forget to get your hand stamped!) Another option would be to use one of the rental lockers.

Shopping at the Water Parks

The casual attitude of these parks toward eating is echoed in the shopping. Don't worry, you'll be able to get that nifty t-shirt or the key chain with the park's logo if you must. But the shops are fairly basic even at their most spacious. The best thing about them is the canny selection of merchandise. If you get to the park and find yourself saying, "Oh no, I forgot my . . ." chances are you'll be able to find it in the shop.

In addition to the usual gamut of souvenirs and t-shirts are swim suits (some of them quite snazzy), sandals, sun block and tanning lotions, film, combs, brushes and other toiletries, towels, sunglasses, trashy novels — in short, everything you need for a day at the beach. Forgetful picnickers will also be pleased to know that they can find soft drinks, snack foods, and candy bars at most of the shops.

Wet 'n Wild

6200 International Drive
Orlando, FL 32819
(800) 992-WILD; (407) 351-1800
www.wetnwild.com

The original Orlando water park is still the best. Add to that its location in the heart of Orlando's tourist country and its partnership in the Orlando FlexTicket program (see *Chapter 1*) and you have a real winner.

The park layout is compact and efficient with little wasted space. The style is sleekly modern and the maintenance is first rate — even though Wet 'n Wild is the oldest water park in the area, it looks as if it opened just last week.

Getting There

Wet 'n Wild is located in the heart of Orlando's prime tourist area on International Drive at the corner of Universal Boulevard, right off I-4 Exit 75A.

Opening and Closing Times

Thanks to heated water on its slides and in its pools, Wet 'n Wild is the only non-Disney water park that is open year-round, although it can get plenty chilly in the winter months. The hours of operation vary from 10:00 a.m. to 5:00 p.m. from late October to around the end of March to 9:00 a.m. to 10:00 p.m. at the height of the summer. Call the information lines above for specific park hours during your visit.

The Price of Admission

The following prices include tax:

Adults:	$38.29
Children (3 to 9):	$31.90
Children under 3 **free**.	
Seniors (55+):	$17.55
Annual Pass (all ages):	$79.88
Florida resident annual pass:	$30.83
Weekday Annual Pass (all ages):	$50.06

Parking is $7 for cars, $8 for RVs and vans.

For the best prices on annual passes, check Wet 'n Wild's Internet site. Prices may be higher at the gate.

Wet 'n Wild participates in the **Orlando FlexTicket** program described in *Chapter 1: Introduction & Orientation* (page 13). In addition, the park offers discounts for entry in the afternoon year round. Call for details.

Rentals

The following are available for rent or loan at the round kiosk located to your right as you enter the park:

Lockers are $5, or $9 for the family (large) lockers, plus a $2 deposit.

Inner tubes are $4, plus a $2 deposit.

Towels are $2, plus a $2 deposit.

Life vests are **free**.

A Combo of towel, tube, and a locker is $9, plus a $4 deposit.

A "Wild One" Combo of towel, locker, tube, and a ride on *Wild One* is $13 plus a $4 deposit.

Rides and Attractions at Wet 'n Wild

Wet 'n Wild is a compact and tightly packed park that somehow avoids feeling cramped. For the purposes of describing its attractions I have divided the park into three slices. I will start on the left-hand side of the park (as you enter the front gate), then proceed to the center section, and finally describe the slides and such on the right-hand side.

Kid's Park

This delightful, multi-level water play area is a sort of Wet 'n Wild in miniature for the kiddie set, those 48 inches and shorter. At the top, there are some twisting water slides that can be negotiated with or without tiny inner tubes. On the other side is a mini-version of the *Surf Lagoon* wave pool surrounded by a Lilliputian *Lazy River*. In between are shallow pools with fountains, showers, water cannons, and a variety of other interactive play areas, all watched over by vigilant lifeguards. Looming overhead is a gigantic bucket that slowly fills with water and periodically tips over, sending a cascade of water onto the squealing kids below. Surrounding the *Kid's Park* is a seating area filled with shaded tables and chairs where Mom and Dad can take their ease while junior wears himself out nearby.

Mach 5

The massive tower that houses *Mach 5* and two other rides looks like a giant pasta factory after a nasty explosion; flumes twist every which way. At the entrance, you grab a blue toboggan-like mat; the front end curves up and over two hand holds. Then there is a very long climb to the top where you will find three flumes labeled A, B, and C. They all seem to offer pretty much the same experience, but you'll probably want to try all three anyway. I sure did. You ride belly down on your mat and take a few gently corkscrewing turns. But then there is a quick drop followed by a sharp turn followed by another drop and so on until you zip into and across the splashdown pool. Keeping your feet raised will decrease the coefficient of drag and give you a slightly zippier ride.

The Blast

This two-passenger tube ride is one of Wet 'n Wild's two "themed" rides. It whisks you through a multi-colored and fanciful landscape that is part psychedelic daydream and part factory floor. As you whish past funny looking machines, pipes and chutes blast you with water at unexpected moments, usually when you've just been disoriented by another twist or turn in the chute. The real fun, however, is saved for last, with an exhilarating waterfall plunge into the pool that marks the ride's end.

The Flyer

This newer ride also shares the *Mach 5* tower and, while it starts at about the same height as *Raging Rapids*, it's a much faster, scarier ride. This time there's nothing to drag to the top with you; your vehicle awaits at the launching area. It's a bright green two-, three-, or four-person raft (no single riders), with built-in hand grips. Hang on tight because the turns are sharp and the raft gets thrown high up the curved side walls as you zoom quickly to the bottom. This is a justifiably popular ride with a lot of repeat riders.

The Surge

The Surge shares a tower with *Disco H²O*, Wet 'n Wild's newest ride. The lines for both attractions are parallel, and can get quite lengthy, so be sure to get in the correct line at the beginning, lest you end up at the wrong attraction when you get to the top! For *The Surge,* riders board rafts, large four-person circular affairs. You sit in the bottom of the raft, facing toward the center, and grab hand holds on the floor. Then the attendant gives the raft a good spin as he sends you on your way down the first fall. The flumes are larger versions of those at *Mach 5* and the descent seems somewhat slower. The turns, however, are deceptive. Depending on where you're sitting as the raft enters a turn, you can find yourself sliding high on the curved walls, and when you hit one of the frequents drops backwards you'll feel your tummy do a little flip.

Disco H²O

Missed the disco era? Well, hustle on over to this ride and climb aboard one of the four-person rafts for a plunge down a time warp that takes you back to the groovy seventies. There, in a darkened circular chamber, you'll spin round and round a watery disco dance hall filled with funky music and fun light effects as you are drawn ever closer to a hole that sucks you back to the well-lit present. It's almost enough to make me like disco. Almost.

The Black Hole

The last slide ride on this side of the park, *The Black Hole* works an interesting variation on the theme. Here you ride a two-person, Siamese inner tube down completely enclosed black tubes. It's not totally dark, however; a thin line of light at the top gives some illumination and lets you know which way the tube will twist next. Although the darkness adds a special thrill, *The Black Hole* is not especially scary or fast, especially compared to, say, *Mach 5*. If you choose the tube to your right as you enter the launch area, you'll get a few extra bumps. A single person can ride alone, occupying the front hole in the inner tube.

Knee Ski/Wakeboarding

Rounding things off on the left side of the park is something completely different — a modified water-skiing experience. You kneel on a small surfboard specially designed for this sort of thing; molded rubber impressions make it easy to stay on and a mandatory life-jacket protects you if you fall off. And instead of a speedboat, your tow line hangs from a sort of cable-car arrangement that tows you in a long circle around a lake. The entire course is surrounded by a wooden dock and, should you fall, you are never more than a few strokes from the edge. Ladders like those in swimming pools are provided at regular intervals, making this a very safe ride.

Dunkings are rare, however. Given the special design of the board, the low center of gravity, and the moderate speed of the tow line, most people complete the circuit easily. So don't let a lack of experience with water skiing keep you from enjoying this ride.

Note: This attraction is only open May through September.

Surf Lagoon

Moving to the center section of the park we find, appropriately enough, the centerpiece of Wet 'n Wild. This is an artificial ocean. Well, actually, it's a fan shaped swimming pool with a hydraulic system that sends out pulsing waves in which you can jump and frolic. You can also bounce around on top of them in an inner tube. At the "ocean" end of the pool, a waterfall splashes off the back wall and onto swimmers bobbing in the waves below. At the "beach" end of the pool, you'll find plenty of lounge chairs for soaking up the sun.

Volleyball Courts

Squeezed between the back of the wave pool and the arcade are two side-by-side volleyball courts. The surface is soft beach sand. Balls can be obtained free of charge at the Courtesy Counter at the front of the park. If there are people waiting, you are asked to limit games to 15 minutes or 11 points, whichever comes first. The courts are occasionally reserved for the use of private groups visiting the park.

Wild One

Head past the volleyball courts on to the dock and hang a right. Down at the end is *Wild One*, the only ride at Wet 'n Wild that requires an additional charge over and above the admission to the park, $5 including tax. The ride is worth the extra expense. You are towed in a large inner tube behind a jet ski as it races around the Wet 'n Wild lake. The fun here is in the turns as the two inner tubes being towed accelerate sharply in wide arcs to keep up with the jet ski's tight turns. The ride lasts about two minutes.

Note: This attraction is only open May through September.

Bubble Up

As you move to the right side of the park, you encounter *Bubble Up*. This attraction is just for kids. Too bad, because it looks fun. In the center of a pool stands a large blue and white rubber mountain; at the top is a circular fountain producing a steady downpour. The object is to grab the knotted rope hanging down from the summit and pull yourself to the top up the slippery sides. Once there you can slide back down into the pool.

Bubba Tub

This is a deceptively simple ride that packs a wallop. Five-person circular rafts zip down a broad, straight slide that features three sharp drops on the speedy trip to the bottom. The ever-helpful attendant gives the raft a spin at takeoff so it's hard to predict whether you'll go down backwards or not. It's a short ride, almost guaranteed to raise a scream or two, and a lot of fun.

Lazy River

Circling *Bubble Up* and the *Bubba Tub* is a swift-moving stream, about 10 feet wide and three feet deep, cleverly themed to evoke old Florida, complete with boat docks and rustic billboards. There are a number of entrances and you can enter or exit at any of them. Grab one of the floating tubes or, to assure you'll have one, bring your rented tube and float along with the current; it takes about five minutes to make one complete circuit. It is also possible to swim or float down *Lazy River* unaided, and many people choose this option.

The Storm

Riders of *The Storm* zip down a towering chute into an open air bowl, where they spin wildly around at speeds of up to 45 miles per hour as spectators cheer them on. Then they drop through a hole in the middle of the bowl into a waiting splash pool.

Der Stuka

Behind the *Bubba Tub*, you will find a high tower housing three speed slides — *Der Stuka*, *Bomb Bay*, and *Blue Niagara* — billed as the tallest and fastest in the world. Like all speed slides, *Der Stuka* is simplicity itself. You lie down on your back, cross your ankles, fold your arms over your chest, and an attendant nudges you over the edge of a precipitously angled free fall. You'll reach speeds approaching 50 mph before a long trough of shallow water brings you to a halt.

Bomb Bay

Bomb Bay is right next to *Der Stuka*. Its slide is precisely the same height, length, and angle of its neighbor. So what's the difference? Here you step into a bomb-shaped capsule that is then precisely positioned over the slide. The floor drops away and you are off to a literally flying start down the slide. Thanks to the gravity assisted head start, this slide is even faster than *Der Stuka*, or at least it seems that way.

Blue Niagara

After *Der Stuka* and *Bomb Bay*, *Blue Niagara*, which shares the same tower with the two speed slides, seems tame by comparison. But looks are deceiving. *Blue Niagara*, which takes off from a point slightly below the top of the tower, consists of a pair of blue-green translucent tubes that corkscrew around each other at a seemingly modest angle.

You enter feet first, riding on your back. If you're wearing a t-shirt, you'll be asked to remove it. The reason quickly becomes clear. The speed you pick up as you hurtle down the ride could wrap a t-shirt around your face very quickly. As it is, you may get a nose-full of water as you splash down at the end of this exhilarating twist-a-rama.

Hydra Fighter

This clever little bit of fun is billed as the "first interactive water ride." Essentially, it is a series of tandem swings in which the riders sit back to back with a high power water cannon between their legs. With a bit of teamwork, riders can use their water cannons to swing themselves higher and higher. Or they can just squirt anyone in range while they bounce around aimlessly. Before hopping on yourself, take some time to observe the proper technique.

There are two towers with three arms, at the end of which dangle the two-seat gondolas; so the three-minute ride can accommodate 12 people at a time.

Adventure Island

10001 McKinley Drive
Tampa, FL 33674
(888) 800-5447; (813) 987-5660
www.adventureisland.com

Busch's entry into the Central Florida water park market is a winner, and if your only shot at a water park is during a visit to Tampa, it's the obvious choice. While I give a slight edge to Wet 'n Wild, Adventure Island, with its artful design and pleasing layout, runs a close second.

Getting There

Adventure Island is right across the street from Busch Gardens Tampa, two miles west of I-75 and two miles east of I-275. Drive past the Busch Gardens parking lots (heading north) and keep a sharp lookout for the entrance on your right. The main gate is easy to miss if you're not careful.

Opening and Closing Times

The park is open daily from mid March to early September and then weekends only to late October. It is closed the rest of the year. Park hours range from 10:00 a.m. to 5:00 p.m. in slower periods to 9:00 a.m. to 8:00 p.m. on summer weekends. Call for the exact schedule, or request a brochure that has a calendar chart with operating hours.

The Price of Admission

Like its sister park, Busch Gardens Africa, Adventure Island offers online discounts for tickets purchased seven days in advance. Those prices are listed in parentheses. The following prices include tax:

One Day Admission:

Adults:	$37.40 ($34.19)
Children (3 to 9):	$35.26 ($32.05)

Children under 3 are **free**.

Two-Day Two-Park Ticket:
(One day each at Busch Gardens and Adventure Island)

Adults:	$78.05
Children:	$67.35

In addition, Adventure Island offers discounts for entry in the afternoon. Call for details.

Adventure Island does not offer a separate annual pass option. See *Chapter 8: Busch Gardens Africa* for pricing information on various annual pass options that include Adventure Island.

Parking is $5 per vehicle, motorcycles park **free**. If you hold any Busch Gardens annual pass, parking is **free**.

Rentals

Lockers are $8. You receive a $3 gift card when you return the key.

Beach umbrellas are $10, including the $3 gift card.

Strollers and wheelchairs are $10.

Volleyballs are **free** with a photo ID or annual pass.

The admission price includes **free** use of inner tubes in designated areas of the park and life vests for all guests.

Rides and Attractions at Adventure Island

Adventure Island is laid out in a sort of figure eight. I have described its attractions in the approximate order you would encounter them on a counterclockwise circumnavigation of the park.

Beach Areas

As you move from the entrance plaza and walk down the steps into the park proper, you see a delightful sandy expanse in front of you. It's ideal for sunning and relaxing (although not for picnicking) with its many lounge chairs. Many people prefer to spread a beach towel on the pristine white sands. The entire area is ringed by an ankle-deep stream so as you exit you can rinse the sand off your feet. Similar areas are dotted around the park.

Runaway Rapids

This series of five water slides is so ingeniously snaked through a simulated rocky canyon that you are hard-pressed to spot the flumes as you wend your way to the top. To the left are two child-sized slides on which parents and tots can descend together. To the right and higher up are the three adult flumes. Here, as at other slides in the park, red and green traffic lights regulate the flow of visitors down the slides.

You ride these slides on your back or sitting up; there are no mats or tubes used. As a result, they can get off to a slow start but they pick up speed as you hit the dips and turns about a third of the way down. Of the three adult slides, the one on the left seems the zippiest, while the one in the middle is the tamest. None of them are super scary, however, and most people should thoroughly enjoy the brief ride to the shallow pool below.

Wahoo Run

Adventure Island's newest ride is a twisty, turny mega slide designed for large rafts holding up to five riders. As you zip down 600 feet of corkscrewing blue tunnels at up to 15 feet per second, you pass under four waterfall curtains that guarantee a thorough drenching before you are deposited in a splash pool at the bottom. This is a great family ride.

Paradise Lagoon

This is a swimming pool with pizzazz. At one end, two short tubes (one slightly curved) let you slide down about 15 feet before dropping you from a height of about

3 feet into 10-foot-deep water. A short distance away, you can leap from an 8-foot-high rocky cliff, just like at the old swimmin' hole. Although the pool seems deep enough (10 feet), head-first dives are not allowed. At the pool's narrowest point, you can test your balance and coordination by trying to cross a series of inflated stepping stones while holding on to an overhead rope net.

Endless Surf

Adventure Island's 17,000-square-foot wave pool generates five-foot-high waves for body surfing as well as random choppiness for what is billed as a "storm-splashing environment." This is the smallest of the wave pools at the two parks reviewed here, with a correspondingly small lounging area at the beach end. Waves are set off in 10-minute cycles, with a digital clock at the deep end counting down the minutes until the next wave of waves.

Fabian's Funport

Adventure Island's kiddie pool follows the formula to a "T." The ankle- to calf-deep pool is abuzz with spritzing and spraying water fountains, some of which let kids determine when they get doused. A raised play area features mini water slides and water cannons with just enough range to spray unwary adults at the pool's edge. A unique touch here is an adjacent mini version of the wave pool, scaled down to toddler size. A raised seating area lets grown-ups relax while keeping an eagle eye on their busy charges.

Rambling Bayou

Adventure Island's version of the continuous looping river is delightful, with a few unique touches — a dousing waterfall that is marvelously refreshing on a steamy day, followed by a gentle misting rain provided by overhead sprinklers.

Spike Zone

This is by far the nicest volleyball venue at the water parks reviewed in this book. In fact, these 11 "groomed" courts have hosted professional tournaments. Most of the play, however, is by amateurs. Even if you're not into competing, the layout makes it easy to watch.

Water Moccasin

Three translucent green tubes descend from this moderately high tower. The center one drops sharply to the splashdown pool, while the two other tubes curve right and left respectively for a corkscrew descent. This is a body slide (you ride lying down on your back) that offers the thrill of a speed slide in the middle tube and a rapidly accelerating descent through the others.

Key West Rapids

The tallest ride at Adventure Island attracts long lines due in part to slow loading times. Fortunately the wait is made easier to take by the spectacular view of next-door

Busch Gardens. In the distance, past the loops and sworls of Montu, you can see the downtown Tampa skyline.

Here you pick up a single or two-rider tube at the bottom and climb up for a looping and swooping descent on a broad open-air flume. The ride is punctuated twice by rapids-like terraces where attendants (I call them the Rapids Rangers), regulate the flow of riders. Thanks to the two pauses, this ride never attains the speed of similar rides at the other parks, but it offers an enjoyable descent nonetheless.

Splash Attack

This is a more elaborate version of *Fabian's Funport* and draws an older crowd — kids from 8 to about 15. The multi-level play area (much like that found in Land of the Dragons at nearby Busch Gardens) is alive with spritzes, sprays, spouts, and hidden geysers that erupt to catch the unwary. A variety of ingenious hand-operated devices lets kids determine to some extent who gets doused and when. A huge bucket at the summit tips over every now and then, soaking everyone below.

Caribbean Corkscrew

This ride is almost identical to *Blue Niagara* at Wet 'n Wild, although to my untutored eye the angle of descent seems slightly narrower. You probably won't care as you spiral down and around one of these two tubes, which are twisted around each other like braided hair, picking up speed until you are deposited in the long deceleration pool. Holding your nose is highly recommended for this one.

Riptide

Riptide adds the thrill of competition to the speed slide concept. A pair of twin enclosed speed slides, one red, one blue, take off from a single high platform. One pair of tubes swerves left, the other right, before rejoining for parallel splashdowns. No one knows who's winning until the final moments of the ride.

Gulf Scream

Right next to *Riptide*, these two slides offer a toned down speed slide experience and, by comparison, the ride down is leisurely. If you're uncertain about tackling *Riptide*, test your mettle here.

Aruba Tuba

Aruba Tuba shares a tower with the *Calypso Coaster*. As with *Key West Rapids*, you pick up your single or double tube at the entrance and climb to the top. This ride, as the name implies, descends through a tube that is mostly enclosed with a few brief openings to the sky. Periodically, you are plunged into total darkness, adding to the excitement generated by the speed, sudden turns, and sharp dips of the ride. All in all, one of Adventure Island's zippiest experiences. You emerge into a pool with a convenient exit into *Ramblin' Bayou*, just in case you feel a need for a marked change of pace.

Calypso Coaster

Unlike its sister ride, *Aruba Tuba, Calypso Coaster* is an open flume. It is also wider, allowing for more side-to-side motion at the expense of speed. But there's no drop-off in excitement as you are swooped high on the sides of the flume in the sharp turns you encounter on the way down. Of the two, I give *Aruba Tuba* slightly higher marks in the thrills department, but it's a very close call.

Everglides

This ride is unique among the parks reviewed in this book. It is a slide — a speed slide in fact — but instead of descending on your back or in a tube, you sit upright on a heavy yellow, molded plastic gizmo that's a cross between a boogie board and a sled. As you sit in the ready position, held back from the steep precipice by a metal gate, you might start to have second thoughts. But then the gate drops, the platform tilts, and you are sent zipping down the slide. The best part of the ride is when you hit the water. Instead of slowing down quickly, you go skimming across the surface for about 20 yards before slowing to a stop. If you're doing it right, you'll hardly get wet. The major error to be made on this ride is placing your center of gravity too far back. If you do, you're liable to be flipped over backwards for a very unceremonious dunking.

Chapter Ten:

Dinner Attractions

THE CONCEPT OF THE "DINNER ATTRACTION" IS NOT UNIQUE TO ORLANDO, BUT surely there can be few places on earth where there are so many and such elaborate examples. At a typical dinner attraction (there are exceptions) the dinner is not a separate component; instead, the meal and the theme of the show are closely intertwined and usually something will be going on as you eat. Beer and wine (along with soft drinks) are poured freely from pitchers throughout the evening. The shows have been created specifically for the attraction; everything from the decorations on the wall to the plates you eat off reflect the theme. By and large, the shows at a dinner attraction are permanent, whereas a dinner theater changes shows regularly.

Dinner attractions are unabashedly "touristy." You'll have plenty of opportunity to buy souvenir mugs, a photo souvenir (often in the form of a key ring), and other tourist paraphernalia. There is plenty of audience participation; in fact, sometimes it's the best part of the show. Many (but by no means all) dinner attractions have an element of competition built in, with various sections of the audience being assigned to cheer on various contestants. And finally there is the matter of scale. With the exception of the murder mystery shows, Orlando's dinner attractions are huge productions put on in large arenas and halls, some of which seat over 1,000 people. There are exceptions to these rules, but they describe the dinner attraction experience.

In this chapter, I have reviewed all the non-Disney dinner attractions (and one true dinner theater) in the Orlando area. For pageantry and large-scale spectacle there are *Arabian Nights*, *Dixie Stampede*, *Medieval Times*, and *Pirates Dinner Adventure*. For musical entertainment there are *Makahiki Luau*, *Capone's*, and the *Starlight Theater*. For magic fans there are the WonderWorks and Skull Kingdom magic shows, both on International Drive. Finally, for comedy/mystery fans there are *Capone's* (again), *Dottie's Comedy Theater*, *MurderWatch Mystery Theater*, and *Sleuths*. I have tried to give you a good idea of the nature of each experience, bearing in mind that not everyone shares the same taste.

In my opinion a trip to Orlando is not complete without a visit to one of these attractions. If you have the time (and the stamina), catch two or more shows representing different genres. I don't think you'll regret it.

Tip: Discounts to most dinner attractions are readily available. Look for online specials on their web sites, dollars-off deals in coupon booklets, and reduced-price tickets at ticket brokers (see *Chapter 1: Introduction & Orientation*).

Arabian Nights

6225 West Irlo Bronson Highway (Route 192), Kissimmee 34746
(800) 553-6116; (407) 239-9223; from Canada: (800) 533-3615
www.arabian-nights.com

Prices:	Adults $56.60, children (3 to 11) $31.03, seniors (55+) $37. Additional discounts for online booking. Prices do not include tax or tip.
Times:	Daily. Show times vary and there are frequently two shows a night, so check. Matinees sometimes available.
Directions:	I-4 to Exit 64, then east on Route 192 for less than a quarter of a mile. The entrance road is on your left, with the theater itself set well back from the highway.

Orlando residents have voted *Arabian Nights* their favorite dinner attraction year after year, and it's easy to see why. Beautiful horses, impeccably trained and put through their intricate paces by a young and vivacious team of riders, are hard to beat. The show may appeal most to horse lovers and riders, but the old clichés "something for everyone" and "fun for the whole family" are not out of place here.

Arabian Nights is huge; it has to be to accommodate the 20,000 square foot arena the horses need to strut their stuff. Each side of the arena is flanked by seven steeply banked rows of seats; all told, the house can hold 1,200 spectators and every seat provides a good view of the action.

The "seats" are actually a series of benches, each seating 12 people at a small counter on which you will be served your dinner. The fare is simple but satisfying — salad, a choice of prime rib, chopped steak with gravy, grilled chicken, or chicken tenders, with garlic mashed potatoes and a medley of vegetables, plus dessert. Vegetarian lasagna is also available. Unlimited beer, wine, and soft drinks are included in the price. Carafes of fancier wine can be ordered separately (for $18 and up), as can mixed drinks.

The doors open about an hour and a half prior to show time if you'd like to come for pre-show drinks and non-equestrian live entertainment that sets the mood for the entire evening: exotic, but family-friendly. There's a belly dancer who pulls kids from the audience on stage for impromptu dancing lessons (and some great photo ops for proud parents), and a talented acrobat who will later make an appearance in the show proper. For the show itself, we are guests at a feast celebrating the marriage of the Sultan's daughter, Scheherazade, to Prince Khalid. But the real emcees are a pair of genies; one wise and experienced, the other just getting started in magic and whose spells tend to have unpredictable consequences. It's just enough of a "plot" on which to string a series of scenes that show off the beauty and skills of *Arabian Nights'* $4 million stable of horses. More than 60 appear in each show.

While there are plenty of stunts involved in this show, the main emphasis is on the horses themselves, with their trainers and riders playing important supporting roles. Much of the evening involves intricate dressage and group riding in which the training of the horses and the precision of the riders are essential. Horses dance, prance, and strut to the music. An old cowboy and his horse perform a hilarious alcoholic routine, and the audience roars as the horse sneaks sips of the cowboy's whiskey. In one sequence, horses and riders do a square dance. One of the evening's most stunning moments comes when a magnificent, riderless black stallion performs an intricate series of movements in response to the subtle signals of his trainer.

Action fans won't be disappointed here. A circus sequence offers a chance for daring bareback riders to show their stuff and contains a hilarious comedy bit. There are cowboys and Indians with stunts straight out of the movies. Riders race around the arena standing up on the backs of two horses. There is even a Roman chariot race, complete with a spectacular "accident." All of this is performed by a remarkably small cadre of talented performers who change costumes and wigs with amazing rapidity to reappear over and over in new guises. Still, it is the horses that command our admiration. At show's end, many of the equine performers romp about spiritedly in the arena; many people linger just to watch them play.

Before, during, and after the show, flash photography is permitted and performers offer lots of photo opportunities to those quick with the shutter, but video recording during the show is prohibited.

Note: A VIP ticket ($15 additional for adults, $13 for kids) adds preferred seating, a souvenir poster, a free drink at the pre-show bar, and the opportunity to meet several of the show's equine and human stars, including the aforementioned black stallion, down on the floor of the arena before the rest of the audience takes its seats.

Capone's Dinner & Show
4740 West Highway 192, Kissimmee 34746
(800) 220-8428; (407) 397-2378
www.alcapones.com

Prices:	Adults $45.99, children (4 to 12) $27.99. Plus tax and tip. 50% discounts frequently available.
Times:	8:00 p.m. nightly during spring and summer, 7:30 during fall and winter.
Directions:	On the south side of 192, a short distance east of the junction with SR 535, between Mile Markers 12 and 13.

Somewhere along the tawdry, commercial strip of Route 192 in Kissimmee you'll find an innocent ice cream parlor. But as with so much in the Orlando area, there's more here than meets the eye. For you see, the ice cream parlor is just a front for a speakeasy, Prohibition style. Yes, we've gone back in time again to 1930s Chicago, where the action owes a lot to Damon Runyon via *Guys and Dolls* and the Chicago accents sound straight outta Brooklyn.

Capone's Dinner & Show is a cheerful mishmash of Broadway show, nightclub cabaret, sketch comedy revue, and all-you-can-eat Eye-talian buffet — that's buffet, as in Warren or Jimmy. Dinner includes the usual soft drinks, plus beer, sangria, and rum runners. In addition, there's a cash bar for serious drinkers.

The fun begins when you arrive and pick up your tickets at the box office. You're instructed to knock three times at the secret door and give a password. Then you get in line outside, where black-vested waiters warm up the crowd with the wisecracking rudeness that is to become the evening's hallmark. So be forewarned: Don't wear garish tourist garb unless you can take some good-natured ribbing.

Once the show's ready to begin, each party is led to the secret door, knocks three times, and gives the password — and they don't let you in until you get it right. Once inside, you're in a spacious nightclub with a large stage. The waiters — with names like Babyface — take drink orders and keep up a cheerful patter laced with film noir gangster patois. Much of the seating is in long rows of tables, so you'll have a chance to chat with the folks on either side of you; it's a fun way to get an idea of the wide cross section of types and nationalities drawn to Orlando.

The show, which revolves around two pairs of star-crossed lovers, freely borrows plot elements from *Guys and Dolls*, *Some Like It Hot*, and any number of old gangster movies. Best of all is the kewpie doll leading lady, dumb and delicious, with a voice that would shatter fine crystal. The cast relies heavily on intentionally bad jokes and audience interaction to generate laughs. More often than not they succeed. Throw in some leggy chorines, a bit of torch singing, and a better than average buffet dinner and you have a winning combo that has stood Orlando's test of time. It's hard not to like this bunch, even if they don't always shoot straight.

Chamber of Magic at Skull Kingdom

5933 American Way, Orlando 32819
(407) 354-1564
www.skullkingdom.com

Prices:	Adults $19.75, seniors (65+) & children (7 and under) $15.97, plus tax and tip
Times:	Daily 6:00 p.m. and 8:00 p.m.
Directions:	Take I-4 Exit 75A to the corner of I-Drive and Universal Boulevard

You don't have to brave the ghouls and goblins of *Skull Kingdom* (described in *Chapter 11: Another Roadside Attraction*) to enjoy this show, which has its own entrance at the back of the foreboding castle on I-Drive. And you don't have to be afraid the kids will be freaked out by anything grisly; this show is all about fun.

This show specializes in what's known in the trade as "comedy magic." That means you won't see the elaborate apparatus used at the WonderWorks Magic Show (reviewed below); there are no beautiful assistants sawn in half; in fact, you may have to do without the beautiful assistant altogether, although the occasional magician who performs here has a lovely sidekick. What you will see can best be described as a magic show with some stand-up comedy thrown in. The blend varies from performer to performer, but more often than not it adds up to a funny and enjoyable show indeed. The magic is fun, too, consisting of small scale tricks that often seem to be going awry before they wind up amazing you.

The space is intimate and just a wee bit spooky, but never mind, your sleight of hand host will soon put you at ease. All-you-can-eat pizza, half plain, half pepperoni is included in the admission, as is all-you-can-drink beer or soda. It's far from gourmet, but it will do.

Dixie Stampede

8251 Vineland Avenue, Orlando
(866) 443-4943; (407) 238-4455
www.dixiestampede.com

Prices:	Adults $49.99, children (4–11) $21.99. AARP & AAA discount of $4. Plus tax and tip.
Times:	Wed–Sun 6:30 (arr 5:15); some Friday and Saturday 8:30 shows added during high season
Directions:	Take I-4 Exit 68; then north on Vineland.

Dixie Stampede is Orlando's third horse-themed dinner attraction and it seems to have borrowed elements of the other two. But since this one is presented by Dolly Parton the expectation is that it will be, well, bigger.

Like *Arabian Nights*, there is an emphasis on beautiful horses and riding skills, although Dolly's show has fewer horses and less horsemanship (but just as much horsing around). Like *Medieval Times*, described later, there is a competition and you get to cheer for your side while you eat your dinner with your fingers. There are a number of Parton-owned *Dixie Stampedes* in the South, but this one is unique in that it serves beer and wine.

The show begins as you walk from the parking lot past outdoor horse stalls where the show's true stars take their ease while waiting for the action to begin. Inside, you are ushered past photographers waiting to snap an optional souvenir photo and through the gift shop to the "carriage house" where a short pre-show entertainment gets the crowd warmed up. Recently, the featured act was Lucas, a comic juggler who does some amazing things with a variety of props, including golf equipment, while keeping up a family-friendly patter that has the audience chuckling along with him.

Fancy frozen drinks are served here, along with peanuts and popcorn, but while the drinks contain no alcohol, the prices pack a $4 wallop. At least you get to keep the boot-shaped souvenir mug they're served in.

After the preshow, the audience is ushered into the main arena, a cavernous U-shaped arena with tiered bench seating much like that at Arabian Nights. Here *Dixie Stampede* seeks to settle "once and for all," by friendly competition, that "legendary rivalry" between the North and the South — represented by opposite sides of the arena — while you eat a quite tasty meal.

A brief survey of American history takes us from free ranging buffalo to the Civil War, which to judge from this show seems to have been a good-natured dust up between fun-loving youths. Song and dance routines salute Southern romance on the one hand and Yankee ingenuity on the other. All this is interspersed with a few horse tricks, some comedy routines, and dinner.

The meal, by the way, is simple but quite good, with the main attractions being a small, but juicy chicken and slices of barbecued pork. Dessert is a flaky apple turnover. It's all washed down with unlimited iced tea and soda; the beer and wine is limited to two servings. The eat-with-your-fingers aspect is cute and no one seemed to complain, but it seems a bit out of sync with the rest of the theme.

The main order of business, however, is that promised competition, which gets under way just about time you're finishing off the main course. The audience is shamelessly egged on to root for their side while booing and hissing the other and folks seem to get into the spirit of the whole thing with alacrity. A series of games follows, most of them equine versions of the sort of silly games played at country picnics, pitting North against South. Not all games involve horses, though. In fact, some of the most enjoyable feature little kids from the audience chasing chickens, piglets decked out in the Blue and the Grey, and racing ostriches.

The finale, introduced by Dolly herself on film, is a rousing patriotic salute to America. Not only are all the riders carrying flags and dressed in red, white and blue, they're decked out in red and white lights as well. For an American audience it's a stirring, if somewhat hokey, way to end the show, but I couldn't help wondering what the foreign tourists were making of it all.

Dottie's Comedy Theater

7052 International Drive, Orlando 32819
(407) 226-3680
www.dottiesorlando.com

Prices:	Adults $23.95, children (4-12) $16.95, includes two free drinks
Times:	Kids' shows Tuesday to Sunday 6:00 p.m.; PG-13 shows Tuesday to Sunday 8:00 p.m.; adult shows (18 and up) Thursday to Saturday 10:15 p.m.
Directions:	From I-4 Exit 74, go east (Sand Lake Road), left on International Drive, theater is on your left

This probably doesn't really count as a "dinner" show, unless you count beer and popcorn as dinner. But, hey, you're on vacation so why not? What you lose in nutritional value you'll more than make up in belly laughs.

Dottie's bills itself as the only "three headliner comedy show outside Las Vegas," by which they mean that the three comics who each do about a half hour of stand up in this ninety-minute show have decades of television, cruise ship, and lounge experience under their belts and have earned their "headliner" status fair and square.

Taking note of its family-friendly setting, Dottie's appeals to all ages. There is an early show just for the kiddies, while the main show is strictly PG-13. Even the late-night "adult" show, advertised as "18 and up," is not too raunchy.

The three pros who make up the evening's entertainment work the 160-seat room with consummate ease, trading quips with the audience and reliably delivering a steady stream of laughs. Remote controlled overhead lights add a nice touch of razzle dazzle to the proceedings.

The concession stand outside the main lounge sells snacks and, for an extra charge, premium beers and such. After the show, you'll have a chance to meet the stars who have CDs, DVDs, and funny t-shirts to sell.

Makahiki Luau

In the SeaWorld park
(800) 327-2424; (407) 351-3600

Prices:	Adults $45.95, children (3 to 9) $29.95. Plus tax and tip. Park admission not required.
Times:	Daily at 6:30 p.m.
Directions:	In the SeaWorld park, in the Seafire Grill restaurant.

At dusk, a ceremonial procession makes its way through the Waterfront in the SeaWorld park, heralding the approach of a Polynesian tribal chieftain. A warrior blows a conch shell to announce the arrival of the Grand Kahuna. A welcoming ceremony complete with dancing briefly enlivens the wharfside while the park's visitors look on. Then, those who have ponied up for the luau are ushered into a spacious theater in the back of the nearby Seafire Grill restaurant where they are transported to the lush South Seas. Giant tikis flank the raised semicircular stage and family-style tables radiate outwards to give everyone a good view.

The show, which begins as the crowd settles in, is hosted by the Grand Kahuna himself, a sumo-sized mountain of a man, with the assistance of a guitar and ukulele trio singing songs of the island from the authentic to the hokey commercial variety.

Most of the show is given over to the dancers, four bare-chested men and four lissome young women who constantly reappear in new and ever more colorful costumes to evoke a variety of styles and moods. The sets change along with the costumes and the wide variety of colorful backdrops makes this one of the most scenically lavish luaus I've seen. The dancing is never less than enchanting and in the war chant numbers rather exciting. What's more, the dancing never veers towards the offensive, making this a perfectly G-rated show.

The Grand Kahuna proves a charming host and the evening's highlight comes when he recounts the Hawaiian foundation myth about how Sky Father and Earth Mother peopled the islands with their children, providing them with beautiful plants and animals to keep them happy. The story reaches its climax with a Fire Dance finale that is literally incendiary, as a dancer wearing nothing but a loincloth twirls a flaming baton and rests the burning ends on his tongue and the soles of his feet.

All of this, our host explains, to illustrate "the light of life that shines in the sky and in every one of us." The sentiment is typical of the gentle spirit of this show, which is apparently a family affair. At one point, the Grand Kahuna introduces his son and daughter, charming youngsters who seem to be having just as much fun as the audience. The show ends with a hip hop updating of "Aloha Oi" that is cheerfully infectious.

The food may not be quite as good as the show, but there is plenty of it, all served family style. First comes a selection of fresh fruit. Among the three entrees, the mahi-mahi in piña colada sauce is a standout. The sweet and sour chicken and BBQ spareribs are okay, as are the mixed steamed vegetables. Dessert is a "lava cake with peanut butter drizzle" accompanied by coffee. The admission price includes the meal, one complimentary cocktail, and complimentary soft drinks, coffee, or unlimited iced tea. For the drinkers in the crowd, a cash bar is available.

Medieval Times

4510 Highway 192, Kissimmee 34746
(888) 935-6878; (407) 396-1518
www.medievaltimes.com

Prices:	Adults $50.95, children (3 to 12) $34.95. Plus tax and tip. 10% discount for seniors (55+).
Times:	Nightly. Show times vary from month to month. Call for current schedule.
Directions:	On the south side of 192, between Mile Markers 14 & 15.

Back in time to the year 1093 we go as we cross a drawbridge over a murky moat and enter a "climate-controlled castle," guided by wenches and squires with a decidedly contemporary look about them. *Medieval Times*, in Kissimmee, is a cheerfully gaudy evocation of a time most of us know so little about that we'll never know if they've got it right — although I strongly suspect that Ethelred the Unready wouldn't recognize the joint.

Actually, *Medieval Times* tells us more about American tourism than it does about eleventh century Europe. The emphasis here is more on showing visitors an old-fashioned good time than on chivalry and historical accuracy. The medieval theme is merely a convenient excuse on which to hang a display of horse-riding skills.

Medieval Times is a bit like a large ride at one of the nearby theme parks. As you enter, you are issued a color-coded cardboard crown and have your picture taken for the inevitable (and optional) souvenir photo of yourself in chivalric garb. The large, banner-bedecked anteroom in which you wait for the show to begin does a brisk trade in tourist items and souvenirs, including some lovely goblets and very authentic looking swords.

A burly bearded knight is your host. His booming voice, with its idiosyncratic mock-formal cadences, will become familiar over the course of the evening as he explains the seating process, exhorts you to be of good cheer, introduces you to the players, narrates the ongoing pomp and pageantry, and chides one and all for not having enough fun.

The dinner show itself takes place in a long, cavernous room in which guests are arrayed on six tiers of seats flanking a 70-yard-long, sand-covered arena. Each row consists of a long bench and counter arrangement so that everyone can eat and have a good view of the show. Each side of the arena has three color-coded sections that correspond to the color of the crown you have been given. Where you sit determines which of the color-coded knights you cheer for during the festivities.

The meal and the show unfold simultaneously. The meal is simple — soup, a small, whole roasted chicken, a pork rib, a roasted potato — but the herbed chicken is roasted to perfection and the ribs melt off the bone. In addition, you get to eat with your fingers: It's 1093, remember. I can't explain the psychology, but it helps put you in a suitably barbaric mood to cheer on your knight. (Vegetarians will be accommodated on request.)

The show begins slowly and builds to a climax of clashing battle-axes and broad-swords that throw off showers of sparks into the night. Demonstrations of equestrian skills and the royal sport of falconry give way to our six mounted knights, young men who race back and forth on their charging steeds, plucking rings from the air and throwing spears at targets.

Before long the crowd is pounding the tables and cheering lustily for their armor-clad champions. Successful knights are awarded flowers that, in the spirit of chivalry, they share with young women in the crowd who have caught their eye. These guys are good at what they do and you may find yourself wondering if there's a career in this and, if not, what their day job is.

The show plays out to a specially composed score with stirring classical overtones (it was recorded by the City of Prague Philharmonic) that sets just the right martial tone. The main event is the joust in which the knights compete against each other, charging full tilt down the lists, shattering their lances on their opponents' shields, and taking theatrical falls to the soft earth beneath. The battle continues on foot with mace and sword and at least as much verisimilitude as you get in professional wrestling.

There is actually a plot cleverly woven into the show. It involves betrayal, prophecy, treason, and the love of a feisty princess; it leads to a surprise ending that brings the crowd to its feet.

This ain't art but it's a lot of fun. And the folks putting on the show not only know their business but keep getting better at it. I've seen three versions of this show and the current one is the best yet. Even if you've been to *Medieval Times* before, a return visit is worth considering.

MurderWatch Mystery Theater

1850 Hotel Plaza Boulevard, Lake Buena Vista 32830
(in Baskerville's Restaurant in the Grosvenor Resort Hotel)
(407) 827-6534
www.murderwatch.com

Prices:	Adults $39.95, children (9 and under) $10.95. Prices include tax and gratuity.
Times:	Saturdays only at 6:00 p.m. and 8:00 p.m.
Directions:	I-4 to Exit 68, west on SR 535 (Apopka-Vine-

land Road), then left on Hotel Plaza Boulevard
(opposite the Crossroads Shopping Center). The
Grosvenor Resort is on the right.

In the elegant confines of Baskerville's Restaurant, decorated with etchings of scenes from the works of Sir Arthur Conan Doyle, a sumptuous buffet is being served. A cabaret act has been laid on for the entertainment of the guests but, as is so typical of the underbelly of show biz, jealousies and intrigue are waiting just off stage. Before long, murder most foul has reared its ugly head and the game is afoot.

This entertaining dinner party cum murder mystery features a female hostess-detective — "My name is Holmes, Shirley Holmes" — who clues us in on the rules of the game, keeps track of the body count, and catalogues the growing number of clues.

There are several different shows in the repertory of this talented local outfit, but I'm told the one I saw offers pretty typical mixture of merriment and mayhem. The action, which cleverly involves the professional and personal jealousies of the lounge-singing act that is the evening's nominal entertainment, takes place throughout the large dining area. While it is always possible to see what is happening, it's not always possible to hear, given the distance of your seat from the action of the moment. Audience members are encouraged to get up, move around the room, eavesdrop, and ask pointed questions, but good manners seem to keep most people in their seats. Nonetheless, by the time the evening winds to its conclusion, you will know all the dramatis personae and their relationships with each other and have your own suspicions about who dunnit.

As amateur detectives, the audience's task is to solve the crime by listening to four widely divergent versions of "what really happened" and then voting with their feet by gathering in different corners of the room with the cast member they believe to be telling the truth.

In this show, the action is virtually continuous throughout the meal and wraps up shortly after everyone has had dessert — about two and a half hours. The cast is smoothly professional, good singers, and expert kibitzers with the audience (some of whom wind up becoming suspects in the final line-up). Virtually every table in the restaurant is visited by one or more cast members during the course of the evening, giving you a chance to size up the suspects at close range. The humor, while sometimes on the racy side, is strictly PG and the kids seem to love it. In fact, there is a special kids' version of the show that is used when the number of children in the audience reaches critical mass. After the show, you can have your picture taken with cast members in a nearby room decorated to re-create Sherlock Holmes' study at 221B Baker Street.

One of the drawbacks of the show is that it only takes place on Saturdays. On the plus side is that it takes place in Baskerville's, a lovely restaurant at the Grosvenor Resort Hotel, on Disney property, which probably explains why the food here is the best of any Orlando area dinner attraction. It's an all-you-can-eat affair, with at least three entree choices in addition to carved-to-order roast beef au jus and Yorkshire pudding. The dessert array is especially bountiful and of the highest quality. Unlimited beer and wine and full bar service are available for an additional fee.

Finding the show can be a bit tricky if you're not familiar with the hotel's layout. Depending on which elevator you get on, push either "5" or "M" (for Mezzanine); they both take you to the fifth floor where the restaurant is located. Perhaps the simplest way is to avail yourself of the valet parking at the hotel entrance ($6) and have the doorman direct you to the staircase in the lobby that leads upstairs to the restaurant. Dreamland Productions, which puts on *MurderWatch Mystery Theater*, may have other shows taking place at other venues in the area during your visit.

Pirates Dinner Adventure

6400 Carrier Drive, Orlando 32819
(800) 866-2469; (407) 248-0590
www.orlandopirates.com

Prices:	Adults $55.33, children (3 to 11) $34.03. Prices include tax but not gratuity.
Times:	Show times vary from 6:00 to 8:30 p.m. Call to check. Doors open an hour prior.
Directions:	From I-4 Exit 74, go east (Sand Lake Road), left on International Drive, then right on Carrier.

If there were Academy Awards for Orlando dinner shows, *Pirates Dinner Adventure* would have to get the best set award. This cheerful mélange of old-time Technicolor pirate movie, Broadway musical, and big top circus unfolds in a fog-shrouded domed arena dominated by a towering and ghostly pirate vessel a-sail on the watery deep. They're pretty generous with the special effects, as well, and pyrotechnic wizardry is very much in evidence. Parents with very young children, who may be alarmed by all the crashing and booming, may want to consider a more low-key dinner show. Older kids, however, should have a blast with this rollicking performance.

The fun starts in a large antechamber where a Festival, celebrating the arrival of Princess Anita, welcomes arriving guests with Gypsy fortune tellers, face painting for kids, a mini-maritime museum, and a very funny comic host who pulls audience members on-stage for various routines (after all, this is the affair that bills itself as "the world's most interactive dinner show"). There are hors d'oeuvres, and a cash bar, and even a tiny arcade for die-hard video game freaks. The show proper gets under way with the explosive entrance of a band of oddly friendly pirates who are, funnily enough, color-coded to correspond with your seating tickets. They kidnap the princess and a comely gypsy wench, and then, for good measure, shanghai the entire audience, shepherding us to their outlaw realm.

We know these pirates can't be all bad when they announce that they will serve us a sumptuous meal, just to prepare us for the torture, maiming, and certain death that will follow shortly. They even take the time to bond with their captives, as each pirate works his color-coded section into a frenzy, to ensure that they'll cheer him on and boo his opponents in any contests of wit, skill or luck that might come up.

The meal served is a hearty one: yellow rice with roasted pork or chicken. Considerate pirates that they are, vegetarian lasagna is also available upon request, although guests are advised to alert the staff ahead of time to be sure they'll have some ready to go. Then we settle back for a celebration of swashbuckling derring do on the high seas.

In a plot that defies rational explication, we find ourselves caught up in a story that involves the love of a young pirate lad for a princess, family ties, trampolines, crew rivalries that require will require the audience's participation to be settled, jumping rope, and – would you believe? – a circus aerial act. There is also a delightfully droll and smarmy pirate captain, accompanied by his wife, a feisty redhead with a voice like cannon fire. They make a highly entertaining couple.

Punctuated by song, the fast and furious action moves left and right, up and down, comes from behind us, and soars high over our heads. The "Golden Gypsy" dances high above, the pirates compete in wacky games of skill, and kids from the audience are taken aboard to be sworn in as swashbuckling buccaneers. All too soon it seems, the King's army arrives to save the day, though things are cleverly rigged such that the audience can't help but cheer them on. There will probably be times during all this when you don't know what the heck is going on, but you'll probably enjoying yourself too much to care.

All this cheerfully chaotic mayhem is carried forward by a game and talented young cast. The male pirate chorus is especially fine. Don't be surprised if you find yourself singing along to the refrain of "Drink, Drink, Drink." And speaking of drinking, beer, wine, and soda flow freely during the meal and afterwards.

For those who care to linger after the show, there is a "Pirates' Buccaneer Bash" where cast members are available for photos, the cash bar re-opens, and guests are invited to stick around for dancing, sing-alongs and socializing.

Sleuths Mystery Show & Dinner

8267 International Drive, Orlando 32819
(800) 393-1985; (407) 363-1985
www.sleuths.com

Prices:	Adults $47.95, children (3 to 11) $23.95. Prices do not include tax or gratuity.
Times:	Varies. Call for current schedule.
Directions:	From I-4 Exit 74 go east on Sand Lake, then left on I-Drive; the theaters are on the left just north of the Mercado.

Nestled incongruously in a suburban-style strip mall in the middle of the gaudy International Drive tourist strip is one of Orlando's most enjoyable attractions. Sleuths presents a rotating menu of a dozen hilarious whodunits served up with relish before, during, and after dinner.

You may find yourself invited to Lord Mansfield's Fox Hunt Banquet or discover yourself one of the alumni attending a reunion at genteel Luray Academy. Whatever the premise, the hilarity is virtually guaranteed, thanks to an ensemble of accomplished (and wonderfully hammy) local actors with a gift for improvisation and the quick comeback. Most of the fun and the biggest laughs come from the unscripted interactions with the "guests" who are made to feel very much part of the action. There are over ten different shows served up by Sleuths, so if you find this sort of thing to your liking you'll be able to return many times before you start to get bored or run out of new material.

As you arrive for dinner, you will meet some of the cast members ushering guests to their tables and passing hors d'oeuvres. After the salad course, the murder mystery proper unfolds on a minuscule set at the front of the house. Don't be surprised if you're called from your seat to participate in some bit of lunacy. At one show I saw, four people found themselves galloping through the house on make-believe horses while the rest of the audience bayed like hounds. But, if you're shy, don't fret; cast members seem to have an uncanny knack for not disturbing those who'd rather not be chosen for "stardom."

The humor is broad, with a healthy dose of double entendre. The cast members throw themselves into their parts but occasionally drop out of character in gales of suppressed laughter. And the audience never hesitates to pitch in, gleefully pointing out telltale clues that those on stage have missed. Before long, someone turns up dead and everyone in the cast seems to have a motive.

Now it's your turn to play detective. Each table of eight is asked to name a spokesperson. During dinner, each table mulls over the clues and tries to come up with one telling question that will uncover some yet-unknown fact that will point to the murderer. Each audience member is asked to write down their solution to the crime — who dunnit, with what, and why.

Another bit of good news is that the food, while simple, is quite tasty. The choices are limited — Cornish hen, prime rib (for an extra charge), and vegetarian or meatball lasagna. I'd recommend the Cornish hen. Beer, wine, and soft drinks are poured freely.

After dinner, the cast reappears and submits itself to the interrogation of the audience. This is no dry exercise in forensic logic. Thanks to the expert ad-libbing of the cast, the laughter continues virtually nonstop. Ultimately, the wrongdoer is identified and audience members who guessed right win a prize.

Sleuths has become so popular that it now supports three separate theaters in its strip mall home. One of them regularly features a **Merry Mystery Dinner Adventure** especially for kids aged 3 to 12. The two show in this series are *Faire of the Shire* and *Juniper Junior*. They offer cameo roles for the kiddies in a mystery that includes magic but no mayhem. Prices are cheaper for this show ($28 for adults, $16 for children 3 to 12) and the kids' meal is a marvelous creation called Worms Underground — a toadstool formed by a pizza atop a ramekin of buttered noodles sits on green pea grass studded with chicken nugget rocks. I'm told it's what the actors in the show always order.

One indicator of the success of the *Sleuths* experience is that, by show's end, the audience feels part of the family. The cast members graciously thank you for your attendance and point out the valuable service you perform in helping a local business survive and thrive without being owned by Disney or ABC. Hear! Hear!

Starlight Theater

3376 Edgewater Drive, Orlando 32804

(407) 843-6275

www.starlightorlando.com

Prices: Matinees are $45, evening shows $49. Price includes three-course dinner.

Times: Performances Wednesday through Sunday; matinees Wednesday, Thursday, and Saturday. Matinees: Dining 11:00 a.m., Curtain 1:00 p.m. Evenings: Dining 6:00 p.m., Curtain 8:00 p.m. Sundays: Dining 4:30 p.m., Curtain 6:30 p.m.

Directions: I-4 to Exit 86, then west on Par Street, which dead ends into Edgewater. The theater is at the back of the mall in front of you.

Of all the dinner attractions in Orlando, this is the only one that is a "dinner theater" in the classic sense of the term — you have dinner and then watch a Broadway musical. The Starlight is somewhat off the beaten tourist track, tucked away in the College Park neighborhood of Orlando's northeast. It is open year round and presents about nine shows a year, each running about six weeks. Every show is a musical with the repertory drawn from familiar recent hits and old favorites, everything from *Cabaret* and *Pirates of Penzance* to *Grease* and *Fiddler on the Roof.* Every December, the theater mounts a "Holiday Spectacular." The shows I've seen here have been very good indeed.

The theater is at the back of a former retail mall. While the space was obviously intended for other uses, it has been cleverly converted to a 300-seat theater with tables arrayed on tiers around three sides of the stage floor; ramps slope gently down to the stage. Thanks to the use of ramps, every part of the theater is wheelchair accessible. The entire space is decorated in subdued black and red, with large Broadway posters ringing the walls. The tiny lamps on each table add a touch of elegance and intimacy. The lobby is equally attractive, with a cascading sheet of water serving as a curtain on the wide front windows. Small tables and chic seating give it the air of a smart cocktail lounge, which is what the lobby becomes on Friday and Saturday after the show.

Most dinner theaters offer a none too fancy buffet dinner. Starlight ups the ante with a three-course meal served at your table by a team of attentive servers. The good news is that the food is excellent, easily the best dinner theater fare I've ever had. The menu changes every few shows and might include entrees like fennel-crusted pork tenderloin served over "Dixie polenta" with an apple and Vidalia onion compote. The desserts are first rate, too.

Dinner is served for about two hours prior to showtime. Dessert is brought to your table during the intermission. There is a bar in the lobby and drinks are also served at your table. Wine is available by the glass and by the bottle.

The Starlight draws its talent from Orlando's broad pool of Disney, Universal, and cruise line performers, as well as from local college drama departments. The performers are non-Equity (that is, they are not members of the actors' union), but the standards are obviously high and you just might get a chance to see a star in the making. So save that program!

Tip: Tables have two or four seats. If you are a couple, request a two-seat table. If none is available, you will be seated at a four-seat table and may be joined by another couple (unless you purchase every seat at the table).

WonderWorks Magic Show

9067 International Drive, Orlando 32819

(407) 351-8800

www.wonderworksonline.com/magic.html

Prices:	Adults $37.95, children (4 to 12) and seniors (55+) $27.95, includes admission to WonderWorks; for show and food only, adults $21.95, children and seniors $14.95; prices do not include tax
Times:	Nightly at 6:00 and 8:00 p.m.
Directions:	From I-4 Exit 74, drive east on Sand Lake Road, turn right on International Drive; the show takes place in WonderWorks, next door to the Pointe★Orlando shopping center.

As I watched this enthralling show, I was reminded of what a terrific disappearing act top-notch magic has done over the last few decades. Thanks to the demise of the great television variety shows of the fifties and sixties, there's a good possibility that your kids (or maybe even you!) have never seen a really good magician perform up close. You can remedy that sorry circumstance by heading for WonderWorks, the interactive attraction in the upside down house (see *Chapter 11: Another Roadside Attraction*).

Every night, in a small 130-seat nightclub-like room at the back of Mazzarella's Pizzeria, you can catch a one-hour show featuring some truly first-rate prestidigitation. The show changes from time to time (I have seen shows called *Shazam, Night of Wonder,* and *The Outta Control Magic Comedy Dinner Show*) but the basic formula remains pretty much the same, whether the accent is on Vegas-style razzle dazzle or broad comedy. Most shows progress from standard playing card and ball tricks to some truly amazing stunts. Often you will see some personal object borrowed from an audience member get smashed or burned beyond recognition only to reappear in perfect condition elsewhere. Some tricks involve elaborate contraptions in which the stars are locked and sometimes chopped, sliced, and diced (or so it would seem).

There is great emphasis placed on audience involvement, with pride of place given to the youngsters, whose sense of awe and wonder is evident in their fresh faces. Adults get their chance to shine as well in routines that are as light-hearted and humorous as they are mystifying. The result is a thoroughly entertaining interlude.

What makes this a dinner attraction is the all-you-can eat pizza and all-you-can drink beer, wine, and soda. The pizzas, which are quite good and don't skimp on the cheese, are half plain and half pepperoni, and as one disappears another arrives to take its place. The doors open and food service begins about 30 minutes prior to show time and service continues throughout the show.

The "Magic Combo" package includes admission to both the show and the WonderWorks attraction and touring the attraction after seeing the show makes for an enjoyable and entertainment-packed evening. You can also opt just to eat and see the show, in which case the show becomes one of Orlando's best entertainment bargains. Reservations are recommended, especially during busier periods, because seating is limited. The only nearby parking is in the lot of the next door Pointe★Orlando shopping mall. Unfortunately, WonderWorks does not validate parking tickets, so expect to pay about $3 or $4 for it, depending on how long you linger at the attraction.

Chapter Eleven:

Another Roadside Attraction

EARLIER, I MENTIONED THE GREAT AMERICAN TRADITION OF THE ROADSIDE ATTRACTION — those weird, often wacky, always wonderful come-ons that beckoned from the highway's edge, all designed to amuse or entertain or mystify, all designed to part the tourist from his money and keep him happy while they did it.

Fortunately for us, the tradition is alive and well and flourishing in the fertile tourist environment of Central Florida. Of course, a lot has changed; the attractions listed here are clean and modern, there's nothing suspect or fraudulent going on, and no one is trying to con you out of anything. But a lot remains the same. Gathered together in this chapter then is a cornucopia of museums, monuments, mysteries, and amusements that, in my opinion, partake of this noble legacy of American showmanship. Enjoy!

American Police Hall of Fame and Museum

6350 Horizon Drive, Titusville 32780

(321) 264-0911

www.aphf.org

Admission:	Adults $12, children (4 to 12) and seniors (60+) $8
Hours:	Daily 10:00 a.m. to 6:00 p.m.
Location:	On SR 450, just east of US 1, on the way to Kennedy Space Center.

This attraction honors the more than 7,000 peace officers who have died in the line of duty, each of their names carved in marble. More names are added each year. Surrounding the memorial hall are exhibits of police memorabilia. There are badges from across the country and police hats from around the world. One section highlights forensic methods, another features execution paraphernalia, while others display classic firearms and improvised weapons taken off bad guys. On a more whimsical note, there are movie props from *Robocop* and a police car used in *Blade Runner*. Helicopter rides ($25 to $153) take off just outside the front entrance and an attached gun range allows visitors to test their skills.

Nearby: Enchanted Forest, Kennedy Space Center, Warbirds Museum.

Astronaut Hall of Fame

6225 Vectorspace Boulevard, Titusville 32780
(321) 269-6100
www.astronauthalloffame.com

Admission:	Adults $17, children (3 to 11) $13, plus tax
Hours:	Daily 10:00 a.m. to 7:00 p.m.
Location:	On SR 405, just off US 1, on the way to Kennedy Space Center

Just before you reach Kennedy Space Center you pass a beautifully designed museum/simulator attraction called the *Astronaut Hall of Fame.* Admission here is included in some of the ticket options offered by the Space Center Visitors Complex, but it can be visited separately. For more information on admission packages, see *Chapter 7: Kennedy Space Center.*

The museum portion of the experience pays homage to the seven Mercury and 13 Gemini astronauts who worked in the days when space travel was new enough that we could all keep track of who was who. More recently, 22 Apollo and Skylab astronauts were added to the *Hall of Fame.* Also on display are actual Mercury, Gemini, and Apollo capsules. There is even a Mercury model into which you can squeeze yourself — or try to. If you ever wondered why the early astronauts referred to the Mercury program as "man in a can," this experience will explain it all.

Probably of more interest to most visitors, especially the younger ones, will be the variety of simulated experiences this attraction has to offer. The **G Force Trainer** puts you in a centrifuge that simulates 4-Gs of acceleration. A video screen in front of you shows what a jet pilot might see while zooming through the wild blue yonder. Amazingly, there is no sensation of spinning, just eight minutes of the rather uncomfortable pull of rapid acceleration. The **Mission To Mars** simulation takes you on a bumpy ride across the surface of the Red Planet. And the **Moonwalk**, a harness-like contraption, allows those over 40 inches tall and weighing between 60 and 150 pounds (which means kids, mostly, although a few skinny adults qualify) experience what one-sixth gravity feels like.

The adjoining education center is the site of **Camp Kennedy Space Center**, a week-long summer camp for kids 8 to 14, and the **Astronaut Training Experience**, a one-day program designed for adults who are jealous of all that fun the kids are having.

Allow about two to three hours to fully experience this attraction. If you just want to hit the highlights, it will take far less time. Since many Kennedy Space Center visitors who include the *Hall of Fame* in their admission package stop here late in the day, it can get very crowded after 4:00 p.m.

Nearby: Enchanted Forest, Kennedy Space Center, Police Hall of Fame, Warbirds Museum.

Citrus Tower

141 North US 27, Clermont 34711

(352) 394-4061

www.citrustower.com

Admission: (Elevator to top of tower) Adults $3.50,
children (3 to 15) $1

Hours: Monday to Thursday 9:00 a.m. to 6:00 p.m., Friday and Saturday 9:00 a.m. to 9:00 p.m.

Location: Half a mile north of SR 50

The Florida Citrus Tower is a monument to a vanished industry. While I was visiting, another tourist told of coming here as a child in the fifties. "All you could see was miles and miles of orange trees," he remembered. "There's not much to see now." A series of devastating freezes over the past two decades has forced Florida's citrus industry farther south. Today, the fields around the Tower are more likely to hold a new subdivision.

From the observation platform at the tower's top you can see 35 miles in all directions. You can even make out downtown Orlando and the taller buildings at Disney World in the hazy distance. Later, you'll be able to argue that you were as high as it is possible to get in the state of Florida. (Historic Bok Sanctuary in Lake Wales, see *Chapter 14*, also claims this distinction.)

Nearby: Lakeridge Winery, Presidents Hall of Fame.

Daytona USA

1801 West International Speedway, Daytona 32114

(386) 947-6800

www.daytonausa.com

Admission: For attraction and tour, adults $22.90, children (6 to 12) $16.50, seniors (60+) $19.70. Tour only $9.05 for all.

Hours: Daily 9:00 a.m. to 7:00 p.m. (tours end at 5:30)

Location: From I-95, take Exit 261 and drive east on US 92 for 1.4 miles

Hard-core fans driving to or from Orlando will want to make the pilgrimage to this shrine to the NASCAR experience. Others should seize on the opportunity to find out what makes the uniquely American sport of stock car racing so special to millions. Nestled in the shadow of the Daytona Speedway, *DaytonaUSA* gives visitors a chance to taste, ever so briefly, ever so slightly, what it must be like to roar around this legendary track and stand, triumphant, in the winner's circle.

For my money, the star of the show is the tram tour of the 480-acre track complex. It puts those NASCAR clips you've seen on TV in awesome perspective. Inside, you can relive the highlights of auto racing in Daytona, a tradition that dates back to 1903, when rich vacationers took to racing their newfangled automobiles on the hard-packed sand of Daytona's beaches. You can also put yourself in the action with a number of simulations. Perhaps the most accessible is the 45-minute 3-D IMAX film celebrating NASCAR, with some breathtaking front-seat shots, For those who really want to feel part of the action, **Acceleration Alley** ($5 extra) is a full-scale simulator ride that puts you in a NASCAR race car tearing around a computer-generated version of the Speedway.

Fantasy of Flight

1400 Broadway, Polk City 33868
(863) 984-3500
www.fantasyofflight.com

Admission:	Adults $26.95, seniors (55+) $24.95, children (6 to 15) $13.95. Annual pass $59.95
Hours:	Daily 10:00 a.m. to 5:00 p.m. Closed Christmas and Thanksgiving
	Restaurant open 11:00 a.m. to 3:00 p.m.
Location:	Exit 44 off I-4, about 50 miles west of Orlando

Vintage aircraft collector Kermit Weeks has turned his avocation into an irresistible roadside attraction that is definitely worth a visit if you are traveling between Orlando and Tampa. Just off I-4, *Fantasy of Flight*, with its Compass Rose restaurant, makes a great place to take a breakfast or lunch break. You can tour the exhibits and have a meal in less than two hours. Come for lunch and the afternoon if you want to take the free tours.

There are three major sections to *Fantasy of Flight*. The first is a **walk-through history of manned flight**, with an accent on its wartime uses. Using dioramas, sound, film, and life-sized figures, it's the equivalent of a Disney World "dark ride" without the vehicles. You start your journey in the hold of an old war transport. Suddenly, the jump master is ushering you out the open door of the plane. The engines roar, the cold wind whistles through your hair, you step out into the pitch blackness of the nighttime sky; all you can see is stars. Soon you find yourself at the dawn of flight, as a nineteenth century hot-air balloon is preparing to take off. Then you are in the trenches of World War I, a tri-plane about to crash into your position. Next you are at a remote World War II airstrip. As a new replacement in the 95th Bomber Group, you receive a briefing and then step aboard a restored B-17 Flying Fortress. As you walk through the aircraft you hear the voices of the crew during a mission over Europe, antiaircraft fire bursting all around you. Stepping across the bomb bay catwalk, you see the doors open beneath you as 500-pound bombs rain down on the fields and cities below. All of this is beautifully realized. The sets are terrific, the lighting dramatic, the soundtrack ingenious, the planes authentic in every detail. I found the B-17 mission to be truly moving.

The second section is a large, spotless, sun-filled **hangar** displaying Weeks' collection. There are reproductions of the Wright brothers' 1903 flyer and Lindbergh's "Spirit of St. Louis." There are a few oddities, like the 1959 Roadair, an attempt to build a flying automobile. But most of the planes are the real thing. The oil leaks, captured in sand filled pans, tell you that many of these planes still fly. You'll see the actual 1929 Ford Tri-Motor used in the film *Indiana Jones and the Temple of Doom*.

There are World War II immortals as well, the B-24J Liberator, a heavy bomber, and the Grumman FM2 Wildcat, the U.S. Navy fighter that shone in the early days of the war. There's even a Nazi short-take off and landing plane, the Storch, that once saved Mussolini's neck by plucking him from a remote mountain resort.

There are several **guided tours** given in the afternoon; arrive by 11:30 if you want to take them all. The **Tram Tour** provides a good overall look at the hangar and some otherwise restricted areas. Other tours focus on various aspects of vintage aircraft restoration and will be especially interesting to aficionados. The **aerial demonstration of the day**, however, which takes place in the late afternoon (weather permitting), will appeal to just about everyone.

By this time, you may wish you were able to get behind the controls of one of these great machines. Fortunately the price of admission includes unlimited flight time aboard the eight simulators in **Fighter Town**, *Fantasy of Flight's* third main section. Aboard the Yorktown aircraft carrier, you can strap yourself into a virtual Corsair and go gunning for Zeroes over tropical islands in "Battle over the Pacific." Each sortie lasts seven minutes.

The experience is surprisingly realistic. A flight instructor monitors your progress and provides helpful hints — like don't fly upside down. You can fly against the computer or against another pilot in a different simulator. It's also possible for teams to fly against each other. After your own flight, you'll probably want to go to the control tower to see how things look from the flight instructor's point of view.

When you leave the hangar area, you find yourself back where you began. If you'd like to walk through the dioramas again (and you might), help yourself. Otherwise you can visit the gift shop (leather bomber jackets just $300!) or stop into the **Compass Rose restaurant**, a beautifully designed re-creation of the kind of Art Deco restaurant you might have found at a fancy airport in the 1930s. The Compass Rose opens at 11:00 a.m. and makes a good choice for lunch. If a visit puts you in the mood to take to the air, check into the hot air balloon and plane rides available here (see *Chapter 16: Moving Experiences*).

Nearby: Frank Lloyd Wright buildings, Polk Museum of Art, Water Ski Experience.

Florida Air Museum
4175 Medulla Road, Lakeland Linder Regional Airport, Lakeland 33807
(863) 644-0741
www.sun-n-fun.org

Admission:	Adults $8, seniors (55+) $6, children (8 to 12) $4, children 7 and under **free**
Hours:	Monday to Friday 9:00 a.m. to 5:00 p.m.; Saturday 10:00 a.m. to 4:00 p.m.; Sunday noon to 4:00 p.m.
Location:	In the middle of nowhere. From I-4 Exit 25, drive south on County Line Road, turn left on Medulla Road.

Small even tiny personal aircraft, hand-built from scratch, from plans, or from kit, are the focus of this small spic and span museum. In addition to more familiar types of craft are gliders, ultralights, and gyrocopters. My favorite was a replica of the 1913 wood, wire, and cloth Laird Baby Biplane, built by aviation pioneer Matty Laird when he was just 16. One wall is given over to a chronological history of Florida aviation from 1900 to 1941 and other displays remember National Airlines, Howard Hughes' 1938 flight around the world, and his fabled "Spruce Goose" megaplane. A hangar a short drive away houses larger World War II military planes.

Reaching the Florida Air Museum takes some stick-to-itiveness. It's truly off the beaten path, but if you're really into this type of aircraft the trip will be worthwhile. Every April there is a fly-in for personal plane enthusiasts.

Fun Spot

5551 Del Verde Way, Orlando 32819
(407) 363-3867
www.fun-spot.com

Cost:	$3 to $35 as explained below; kids ride **free** with paying adult
Hours:	Daily 10:00 a.m. to midnight
Location:	Just off International Drive near the intersection of Kirkman Road and International

Fun Spot easily wins the Orlando go-kart sweepstakes with its intriguing, twisting, up and down, multilevel tracks. There are four of them here, with the 1,375-foot, three-level *QuadHelix* the most popular. There are also bumper cars, bumper boats, and a 101-foot high Ferris wheel that offers a panoramic view of the upper end of International Drive and Universal Orlando across the Interstate. A 10,000 square foot video arcade (tokens at 25 cents each or $25 for 120) and a snack bar round out the offerings at this compact amusement park.

Rides cost $3 each and go kart runs are $6, although most people will opt for a package deal. You can buy an armband that gives you unlimited access to all rides and the go kart tracks for $35. For $25 you get access just to the "kiddie" and "family" rides and for $15 your child can get unlimited access to six kiddie rides.

Nearby: Skull Kingdom, Universal Orlando, Vans Skatepark, Wet 'n Wild.

The Jesus Film Project Studio Tour

100 Lake Hart Drive, Orlando 32832
(800) 225-3787, (407) 826-2300
www.jesusfilm.org

Admission:	**Free**
Hours:	Tours Monday to Friday, 10:00 a.m. to 3:00 p.m.; 5 tours daily
Location:	In southeastern Orlando; call for directions or get map on web site

Campus Crusade for Christ (CCC) has set a goal to dub *Jesus*, a two-hour

1979 film based on the Gospel of Luke, into 1,800 languages. At 944 and counting, they're about halfway there. This modest but cleverly-designed 30-minute guided tour illustrates the challenges and payoffs of this ambitious project. At one point, a tour member gets to test his or her skill at dubbing the words of Peter; at another, in a simulated outdoor "theater," guests witness the reaction to a screening of the film at a remote village in India. Along the way, picture windows provide a glimpse into the actual translating, recording and editing process. At tour's end you can purchase the film in many different languages. Once a day, at 1:00 p.m., an extended tour encompasses other aspects of CCC.

Nearby: WordSpring Discovery Center.

Lakeridge Winery Tour

19239 U.S. 27 North, Clermont 34711
(800) 768-WINE; (352) 394-8627
www.lakeridgewinery.com

Admission:	**Free**
Hours:	Monday to Saturday 10:00 a.m. to 5:00 p.m.; Sunday 11:00 a.m. to 5:00 p.m.
Location:	About 5 miles north of SR 50 and 3 miles south of Florida Turnpike exit 285

Believe it or not, American wine making began in Florida, thanks to some French Huguenot settlers who started fermenting the local wild Muscadine grapes near present-day Jacksonville in about 1562. Viticulture was a thriving Florida industry until the 1930s, when a plant disease wiped out most of the grapes. Now, thanks to Lakeridge, the only winery in Central Florida, wine making is starting to make a comeback in the Sunshine State. Lakeridge currently produces some 200 thousand gallons a year with plans for expansion. Perhaps one day it will fill up all the acres abandoned by the citrus industry. (See Citrus Tower, above.)

The attractive Spanish-style building set atop a small hill on a bend in the highway has been cleverly designed to serve as both a working winery and a welcome center for passing tourists. Despite its out-of-the-way location and low-key promotion, Lakeridge attracts a steady stream of visitors. I wonder if it's the free wine?

Tours run constantly, as long as there are people arriving, and take about 45 minutes. After a short video about the history of wine making in Florida and Lakeridge's operations, you are taken on a short tour. It leads you, via an elevated walkway, over the compact wine making area at the back of the building, onto a terrace that overlooks the vineyards and the rolling, lake-dotted countryside of the Central Florida Ridge, and then back over the U-shaped wine making room.

After the tour, there is a 15-minute wine tasting that lets you sample some of Lakeridge's wines, including Crescendo, their *methode Champenoise* sparkling wine. You will also get to taste their mulled wine and, if you like, purchase a bag of spices to make your own. And speaking of purchases, all of Lakeridge's wines are available for purchase. In addition to a varying menu of specials, full cases are sold at a 20% discount. Buy three cases and get 25% off. Lakeridge also sells its own line of salad dressings, sauces, mustards, jams, and jellies.

The winery throws special events on a regular basis throughout the year, ranging from "Jazz at the Winery" to vintage auto shows. There is an admission of $2 for most of these events, although some are **free**.

Nearby: Citrus Tower, Presidents Hall of Fame.

Magical Midway

7001 International Drive, Orlando 32819
(407) 370-5353
www.magicalmidway.com

Cost:	Rides $3 to $7, $6 for go karts, $28 for unlimited rides and go karts
Hours:	Daily 10:00 a.m. to midnight
Location:	On I-Drive, two blocks south of Wet 'n Wild

Magical Midway is a smaller version of *Fun Spot,* described above, but due to the absence of kiddie rides it draws an older teen clientele. The main attractions are the two elevated wooden go kart tracks, but there are also midway-style rides including a scaled down version of Universal's *Dr. Doom* shot tower ($5). Since it's easy to burn through a lot of money paying for individual rides, the $28 ride-all-day option quickly begins to make sense.

There is also a giant sling shot that will shoot two riders ($25 each) some 370 feet into the air where they tumble and bounce for a while before being reeled back in. You can document your insanity on video for an extra charge. This one attracts far more observers than riders.

Nearby: Dottie's Comedy Theater, Ripley's Believe It or Not, Skull Kingdom, Titanic, Universal Orlando, Wet 'n Wild.

Medieval Life Village

4510 West Irlo Bronson Highway, Kissimmee 34746
(800) 229-8300; (407) 396-1518

Admission:	All ages $3.50, plus tax **Free** with tickets to *Medieval Times*
Hours:	Daily, open 2 hours before show time at *Medieval Times*
Location:	At the *Medieval Times* dinner attraction

What's a medieval castle without a village to supply all its needs? Fortunately, the owner of *Medieval Times,* the popular Kissimmee dinner attraction, is a Spanish count. So it wasn't too much of a stretch for him to clear out the attics and barns of his estates, buy up an old village on Majorca, and ship the whole lot to Central Florida.

The result is an intriguing re-creation of a twelfth century village, complete with a cadre of artisans and craftspeople plying their trades in much the way their medieval predecessors did. The buildings are modern construction, but the doors, the wooden windows, the furniture, and many of the other objects to be found in the village are all originals, some of them 800 years old.

The tiny village is set around a small courtyard and cobblestone street. Much of it is given over to a series of workshops and ateliers, including a basket shop, a carpenter's workshop, a metalsmith, and a blacksmith creating chain mail armor one link at a time. There is also a cloth weaver working at an 800-year-old loom. Many of the items produced here can be purchased in the gift shop.

One of the more interesting displays is "The Dungeon," a collection of implements of torture. A sign outside cautions that the display may not be suitable for small children and it is advice well worth heeding. The implements themselves (all apparently genuine) are ghastly enough but, for those with poor imaginations, mannequins have been added to illustrate the hideous uses to which these bizarre inventions were put. It may not be the best thing to see before sitting down to a meal and a night's entertainment.

Admission to the village is included in the price of your ticket to the dinner attraction (see *Chapter 10*), which is one of the best in the Orlando area. Whether the village is worth the admission if you are not seeing the show will depend on your interest in things medieval. There is a fair amount to see here, but much of it is unidentified and unexplicated. The artisans who "inhabit" the village, however, are friendly and knowledgeable and are a great source of information about the strange objects you'll encounter.

Nearby: Airboat Rentals U-Drive.

Old Town

5770 West Irlo Bronson Highway, Kissimmee 34746
(407) 396-4888
www.old-town.com

Admission:	**Free**. Rides are extra.
Hours:	Daily 10:00 a.m. to 11:00 p.m.
Location:	About 1 mile east of I-4, just past Mile Marker 9

Take away the window dressing and Old Town is just a mall filled with gift, novelty, and souvenir shops. But the window dressing is fun and obviously popular with the crowds that make Old Town a lively place to visit and shop during those sultry Florida evenings.

Behind a small, brightly lit amusement park facing route 192, a vaguely Western Main Street stretches through a few blocks of 70-plus shops, cafes, and entertainments to a tiny carousel, a mini roller coaster, and other rides on the edge of the Kissimmee night. It's pedestrians only, with frequent benches for weary strollers and a constant swirl of visitors from around the world.

The dozen or so rides are of the carnival midway variety and are paid for with tickets purchased from a booth at the front ($1 per ticket). Rides cost anywhere from two to five tickets, so a $25 ride-all-day pass will pay for itself fairly quickly. A tiny go-kart track collects a separate fee of $6 for a 13-lap, 4-minute ride. Old Town also boasts a haunted house, the **Haunted Grimm House**. Admission is $10 ($6.75 for kids 10 and under) for a 5- to 10-minute stroll through 20 rooms of shocks and surprises courtesy of special effects and a handful of live actors. If you don't plan on visiting the more elaborate *Skull Kingdom* (see below), and absolutely must visit a haunted house, the Grimm establishment is a satisfactory substitute. The **Wax Museum** ($5 for all ages) is a Madame Tussaud's wannabe featuring reasonable facsimiles of kings, queens, and movie stars.

Lazer Runner ($5), the resident laser tag game, works an interesting variation on the theme — the floors are inflated and the walls padded, allowing the shoeless players to dive and roll like action movie heroes as they fire off their laser weapons at all and sundry. For the fearless (or foolhardy, depending on your point of view), the **Human Slingshot** beckons. For $25 ($20 more for a DVD record), you can be shot into the sky in a seat powered by a giant rubber band.

Old Town lays on a number of **free** events to draw crowds and keep them entertained between bouts of shopping. An outdoor stage down one of the side streets offers musical entertainment on an irregular schedule. More predictable is the 8:30 p.m. **Friday and Saturday Night Cruise** of vintage automobiles. Over 350 cars show up on the average Saturday, and Old Town claims it's the largest such event in the world. It's great fun for anyone who grew up in the age of those great finned monsters. Live rock 'n' roll adds the perfect musical accompaniment to the nostalgia.

Nearby: Arabian Nights, SkyCoaster, G-Force.

Orlando Ghost Tours

(407) 247-0452
www.hauntedorlando.com

Admission:	Adults $25; children (7 to 12) $20; seniors, college students, and military $15
Hours:	Daily except Sunday at 8:00 p.m.
Location:	Meets at Church Street Marketplace, downtown Orlando

It turns out you don't need a centuries-old castle to have a haunted house. Orlando has plenty of haunts and most of them date to the early twentieth century. This low key operation will help you find them.

You meet your group of intrepid ghost hunters on downtown Church Street, steps away from the now-defunct entertainment complex known as Church Street Station, which turns out to be a hotbed of paranormal activity. The various buildings here, some of Orlando's oldest, are haunted by the spirits of newborns murdered by their prostitute mothers, a piano player (who, until the building closed recently, liked to play for late night guests), and a can-can dancer who died while preparing to perform at Rosie O'Grady's.

Then it's off to scope out hauntings in other downtown buildings. One of the most active locations is also one of the newest buildings. In fact, it's the fifth building to be built on the site, after a series of collapses and fires. As it turns out, this downtown corner was once a Seminole Indian burial ground and as anyone who goes to the movies knows, building there was a big mistake.

The evening wraps up inside an old courthouse (now the Orange County History Center), where the tour goes high tech. Tour guests are issued electromagnetic detectors (or, if you prefer, a laser thermometer) to detect paranormal activity. On the tour I took, my detector started "spiking" wildly. I had apparently sparked the interest of Emily, a little girl who met a sad end in the city's foster care system years ago. The guide explained that Emily is drawn to father figures. As to why a little girl is haunting a courthouse, speculation has it that this is the last place she saw her family intact.

Unlike other ghost tours I've taken, this one does not rely on lugubrious costumes or spooky speeches. Our guide was April, an attractive young woman with a degree in forensic anthropology, who brought a healthy dose of scientific scepticism to the proceedings.

If you're a "sensitive," you will definitely want to take this tour. If you "ain't afraid of no ghosts" (as the song says), this is a good chance to test the courage of your convictions.

Presidents Hall Of Fame

123 U.S. 27 North, Clermont 34712
(352) 394-2836
www.presidentshalloffame.com

Admission:	Adults $11.95, children (5 to 12) $6.95
Hours:	Daily 9:00 a.m. to 5:00 p.m.
Location:	About half a mile north of SR 50, near Grand Citrus Tower

Next to the *Grand Citrus Tower* (see above) sits a small porticoed house that is home to an even smaller porticoed house. This is *Presidents Hall of Fame*, a meticulous scale model of the White House that has been the life's work of Orlando resident John Zweifel and his wife Jan. Anyone who's into modeling or anyone who's helped a child build a doll house will want to visit this astonishing work.

Inside you'll find life-sized wax-museum-style statues of all the U.S. presidents, from Washington on down, that are a fascinating chronicle of the evolution of upscale American male clothing over the years.

In the first of the two display rooms in this small museum is a 16-foot square diorama depicting the building of the White House as it might have looked in 1797, three years before its completion. At a scale of three-quarters of an inch to one foot, we can watch the dozens of stonemasons, carpenters, and laborers ply their trade while George Washington himself surveys their progress. Washington, by the way, was the only president not to live in the White House, even though he supported the project.

The pièce de résistance, however, awaits in the much larger second room. Here you will find the 60- by 22-foot model of the White House executed in a scale of one inch to the foot. It took Zweifel, his wife, and hundreds of volunteers over 500,000 man-hours to bring the model to its present state and apparently they're not done yet, since the work is billed as an ongoing project. The result is impressive. They have re-created not just the main building but the East and West wings as well, all in astonishing detail.

As you enter the room, you see the front of the building. Peek through the windows and you can glimpse details of the rooms inside. But walk the length of the model and around to the back and the entire White House will be revealed to you. In doll house fashion, there is no rear wall and here the full extent of the Zweifels' accomplishment becomes apparent.

The scope of the re-creation and the attention to detail are astounding. You can spot pens on tables, cigar burns on tabletops, even the occasional gravy stain. The clocks tick, the phones ring, the television sets are on (picking up Orlando stations oddly enough). Along the wall behind you are dioramas of the Oval Office as decorated by a series of recent presidents.

The gift shop offers a surprising number of books about the White House and the presidents who have lived in it along with an assortment of more traditional souvenirs. A few items (not for sale) are worthy of *Ripley's Believe It or Not!* You can see, through magnifying lenses, the flags of all nations painted on a grain of wheat or a portrait of the Kennedys, John and Jackie, executed on the head of a pin. What possesses people to do this sort of thing?

Some of the exhibits go on tour from time to time and so may not be there when you visit (*Tribute to the Presidents*, for example, traveled to the 2000 Republican Convention). On the other hand, the *Presidents Hall of Fame* sometimes hosts exhibits on loan from presidential libraries and other museums.

Nearby: Citrus Tower, Lakeridge Winery.

Ripley's Believe It Or Not

8201 International Drive, Orlando 32819
(407) 363-4418
www.ripleysorlando.com

Admission:	Adults $16.95, children (4 to 12) $11.95, plus tax; parking is **free**
Hours:	Daily 9:00 a.m. to 1:00 a.m.; last ticket sold at midnight
Location:	Next to the Mercado on I-Drive

Is that an ornate Italian villa sliding into a Florida sinkhole on International Drive or is it just *Ripley's Believe It Or Not*? It's Ripley's, of course, and the zanily tilted building is only one of the illusions on display here (and one of the best).

Robert Ripley was a newspaper cartoonist whose series on oddities and wonders, man-made and natural, made him a very wealthy man and an American institution. The Orlando Ripley's is one of several monuments to Ripley's weird and wonderful collections, gathered in the course of visits to some 198 countries at a time when such globe-trotting travel was still a challenge. On display here are objects collected by Ripley himself, along with others gathered after his death, and a series of show-and-tell displays illustrating a variety of optical and spatial illusions.

Where else are you going to see a real two-headed calf? Or the Mona Lisa recreated in small squares of toasted bread? Or a three-quarter scale Rolls Royce crafted from over a million matchsticks? Most displays here are fascinating, although a few are not for the squeamish and some may strike you as tasteless. Best of all are the show-

and-tell displays, like an elaborately tilted and skewed room in which the balls on a pool table seem to roll uphill. There is also a giddily disorienting catwalk through a rock-walled tunnel. From the outside, it is obvious that the walls are moving, but step inside, onto the catwalk, and suddenly the walls seem to be rock solid and it is the catwalk that seems to be rotating.

Nearby: SeaWorld, Titanic, Train Land, Wet 'n Wild, WonderWorks.

Skull Kingdom

5933 American Way, Orlando 32819
(407) 354-1564
www.skullkingdom.com

Admission:	Day show (all ages) $9.50; night show (over 8 only) $14.95
Hours:	Daily 10:00 a.m. to 5:00 p.m. and 6:00 p.m. to midnight
Location:	Across from Wet 'n Wild

The art of stylish entertaining may be dying elsewhere but it's alive and decomposing at *Skull Kingdom* where gracious ghouls invite you in for a tour of their decrepit digs on I-Drive. If you've ever been to one of those haunted houses that spring up as fundraisers around Halloween, then you have a pretty good idea of what awaits you, although the experience here is probably a good bit more elaborate. For those new to the genre, the experience goes something like this: Once a group of likely victims, er guests, congregates, the doors open and the group is sent on a leisurely 20-minute stroll through two floors of mazes and cavernous rooms past all manner of yucky surprises. Most of the creatures you encounter are mechanical dummies but some are scarily real, and the living (or at least undead) entertainers carry off their tasks with great aplomb. If it's any consolation to the squeamish, the unwritten rule of the game is that the performers never actually touch you.

Skull Kingdom also has a spiffy new building, a brooding castle with an enormous skull shaped entrance, and it uses a bit more technology than similar attractions elsewhere — film, mechanical monsters, voiceover recordings, and the like.

Nearby: SkyVenture, Wet 'n Wild, Universal Orlando.

Spook Hill

www.historiclakewales.com/spookhill

Admission:	**Free**
Hours:	24 hours
Location:	South on 27 to 17A (before Lake Wales), turn left (east) and follow signs

I don't get it. A sign at this "attraction" (which is just a line drawn on a road in the small town of Lake Wales) talks about a legendary Indian chief, an epic battle with an alligator, and the belief of early pioneers that the place was somehow haunted. Then you are instructed to stop your car on the white line painted in the street, place it in neutral, and then marvel as the car mysteriously rolls backwards uphill!

The only problem with this scenario is that it seems to me screamingly obvious that your car is rolling downhill. Maybe I'm perceptually challenged. Or maybe the locals are hiding in the bushes laughing at tourists making fools of themselves on Spook Hill. But what the heck, it's a local legend, it's free, and it's on the way to Historic Bok Sanctuary if you're heading that way. Maybe you can explain it to me.

Nearby: Cypress Gardens, Historic Bok Sanctuary, Lake Wales Arts Center.

Titanic, The Experience

8445 International Drive, Orlando 32819
(877) 410-1912; (407) 248-1166
www.titanicshipofdreams.com

Admission:	Adults $21.25, children (5 to 12) $13.79, with tax
Hours:	Daily 10:00 a.m. to 8:00 p.m.
Location:	In the Mercado shopping and dining complex

Fans of the movie *Titanic* (and they are legion) will welcome the opportunity to visit this extremely well-done evocation of the most famous cruise ship in history. The exhibition takes the form of "guided tours" that depart every half hour or so and are led by actors representing historical characters, from the designers of the Titanic to crew members and passengers aboard the ship's ill-fated maiden voyage.

Among the highlights of the tour are re-creations of staterooms and other areas of the ship. And if the grand staircase looks smaller than the one in the film, that's because this one is accurate; the filmmakers took some liberties and made the staircase higher and broader. Then there are the artifacts, including actual chinaware, deck chairs, and life jackets from the ship. If you're in the right mood, these can be rather chilling. And some visitors may get a few goose bumps from seeing a costume worn by Leonardo himself in the movie.

But the real goose bumps come from the boarding passes you are handed at the start of your voyage into history. Each one bears the name of an actual Titanic passenger. At the end of the "voyage" you can consult a memorial wall and learn whether or not you survived. The historical character-guides handle their roles extremely well, giving equal time to historical trivia (like the fact that the ship's linoleum floors were the height of luxury at the time) and the somber human drama of the ship's tragic end.

Tickets are purchased at a sort of steamship office near the International Drive entrance to the Mercado. (Dollars off coupons are readily available.) Tickets in hand, you proceed to the Mercado's inner courtyard where you wait for the next "departure." The attraction's grand staircase has become a popular backdrop for weddings. For more information, visit www.titanicweddings.com

Nearby: Ripley's Believe It or Not, SeaWorld, Train Land, WonderWorks.

Train Land International

8990 International Drive, Orlando 32819
(407) 354-1400

Admission:	Adults $8, children (3 to 12) $6, seniors (50+) $6
Hours:	Sunday to Thursday 10:00 a.m. to 6:30 p.m.; Fri-

day and Saturday to 7:00 p.m.

Location: Just south of Pointe★Orlando shopping mall

If you think your old HO-gauge model train set was pretty nifty, you may want to do a reality check at Train Land. This combination train store/museum boasts one of the largest G-gauge layouts in the world — and G-gauge is four times bigger than HO.

The layout occupies 4,800 square feet of space in its own room and required more than 3,000 feet of track and some 4,700 man-hours to complete. The result is impressive, rising high overhead and twisting and turning through mountain passes, quaint small towns, industrial zones, and idyllic farm valleys. There's even a spur line to Santa-Land. The elaborate landscape is microscopically imagined with a wealth of telling details. The rivers have fish in them and the mountaintops are home to Bigfoot and the Abominable Snowman.

The Trolley and Train Museum is a labor of love, as you will quickly discover if you fall into conversation with one of the managers on duty. They take great pride in their creation and obvious joy in sharing its wonders with visitors. Model train devotees will find them a virtually inexhaustible font of modeling tips and train lore.

Nearby: Ripley's Believe It or Not, SeaWorld, Titanic, WonderWorks.

Warbird Air Museum

6600 Tico Road, Titusville 32780
(321) 268-1941
www.vacwarbirds.org

Admission: Adults $12, children (4 to 12) $5, military and seniors (55+) $10, plus tax; group and family rates are available

Hours: Daily 10:00 a.m. to 6:00 p.m., except Thanksgiving, Christmas, New Year's Day

Location: On SR 405, on the way from Orlando to Kennedy Space Center, via routes 528 and 407; from I-95, take Exit 215

The Valiant Air Command is a non-profit group dedicated to preserving historic aircraft and, not incidentally, putting on some smashing aerial demonstrations. This small museum, located on the grounds of the Space Coast Regional Airport, shows off their collection when it's not airborne. An anteroom to the hangar contains a grab bag of military and aviation memorabilia, most of it from World War II. There's a little bit of everything, from propaganda posters, to uniforms, to weapons and war trophies, to model airplanes. Overhead hangs a replica of a 1907 Epps Monoplane. Your interest in all this will no doubt depend on your personal connection to the subject matter.

In the hangar, however, just about everyone will find something worth oohing and aahing over. While there are a few WWII planes, the bulk of the collection dates from the fifties. The collection changes from time to time but there will be enough Dakotas, Messerschmitts, Wildcats, Crusaders, and Hueys to keep the military aircraft buff happy. There's even an F-5 once used by NASA in attempts to break the sound barrier. If seeing all these planes makes you itch to get airborne, that can be arranged thanks to Warbird Flights, a separate company operating out of the Warbird Museum. Their services are described in *Chapter 16: Moving Experiences.*

Nearby: Astronaut Hall of Fame, Enchanted Forest, Kennedy Space Center, Police Hall of Fame.

The Water Ski Experience
1251 Holy Cow Road, Polk City 33868
(863) 324-2472
www.waterskihalloffame.com

Admission:	Adults $5, seniors (65+) $4, children (6 to 12) $3
Hours:	Monday to Friday 10:00 a.m. to 5:00 p.m.
Location:	From I-4 Exit 44, go north on SR 559, then right on CR 557A

If water skiing is your thing, then you might find a visit to this museum rewarding. Here you can gawk at the first ever pair of water skis, which dates back to 1922 and to the "father" of water skiing, Ralph Samuelson. There are also displays of antique outboard motors, water skis, and memorabilia of all sorts, with an accent on trophies. The Time Line Wall illustrates key developments in the history of the sport and the library boasts over a thousand videos that you can see on request. The earliest footage, silent and in black and white, dates from 1939.

Nearby: Fantasy of Flight, Frank Lloyd Wright buildings, Polk Museum of Art.

White 1
233 North Hoagland Avenue, Kissimmee 34741
(727) 365-1713
www.white1foundation.org

Cost:	Donations requested and urgently needed
Hours:	Monday to Friday 9:00 a.m. to 5:00 p.m.; Saturday and Sunday by appointment
Location:	At the Kissimmee Airport, south of US 192

World War II aviation buffs will want to make a beeline for this fascinating work in progress. A small cadre of vintage fighter plane restorers is laboring to bring back to life one of the most feared planes of the Luftwaffe, the Weisse Eins, or White 1. Manufactured by the fabled Focke-Wulf firm, its official designation is FW-190F, but it was better known by its nickname the "Butcher Bird." The White 1 was the Swiss Army knife of Nazi military aviation, functioning variously as a fighter, a bomber, and even as a torpedo plane. In its day, it was the fastest military plane aloft.

The bits and pieces of plane that sit in this nondescript hangar are what's left of Number 931862, which was shot down on February 9, 1945 during the Battle of Fordefjord in Norway. The small team that works here pieces the plane back together as time and money permit. Their goal is to fly it once again, powered by an original BMW 801 radial engine. If they are successful, it will be the only White 1 in existence.

Visitors can stop by to watch the restoration in progress and gawk at some of the WWII pilot flight gear and survival gear on display. The web site offers various ways to become part of the effort through donations to the project. Give enough and you might get a chance to sit at the throttle.

Nearby: Stallion 51, Warbird Adventures.

WonderWorks

9067 International Drive, Orlando 32819

(407) 351-8800

www.wonderworksonline.com

Admission:	Adults $19.95, children (4 to 12) and seniors (55+) $14.95, plus tax; with magic show, adults $37.95, children and seniors $27.95
Hours:	Daily 9:00 a.m. to midnight
Location:	On International Drive, next to Pointe★Orlando

If you liked the subsiding building that houses *Ripley's Believe It Or Not*, wait 'til you see *WonderWorks*. The fantasy here is that a mysterious neoclassical building has crashed out of the sky, upside down, right in the middle of Orlando's glitziest tourist strip. Inside, the normal laws of physics are likewise turned upside down. The exterior of *WonderWorks* may be its best feature; it has become Orlando's most-photographed building.

In fact, *WonderWorks* is packed with the kind of games and gimmicks (over 100) used by science museums to teach basic principles of physics, and it turns them into a highly enjoyable interactive amusement arcade. Here, on three noisy levels, you can experience an earthquake or a hurricane and get some idea of what it would be like to fly a fighter jet or land the Space Shuttle. Then test your reflexes, your pitching arm, the strength of your grip, and your visual acuity. Or maybe you'd just prefer to play around with soap bubbles as big as you are.

One of the most popular attractions, often spawning long lines, is a station where you can design your own roller coaster then climb into a simulator and find out what it would feel like to ride it.

There's plenty more to keep you amused and entertained for as long as you'd like to hang out. The "world's largest" laser tag arena occupies the third level. Single games are $5 and replays $3; unlimited play from 9:00 p.m. to midnight, Monday through Thursday, is $15. Next door is Pointe★Orlando, an elaborate shopping, dining, and movie venue that is an attraction in its own right.

WonderWorks is also home to a nightly magic show that comes with all-you-can-eat pizza and all-you-can-guzzle beer, wine, or soda. Special combination packages include both the show and the attraction. Show times are 6:00 p.m. and 8:00 p.m. A great way to experience *WonderWorks* is to catch the magic show first and then while away the rest of the evening exploring the attraction. The magic show is reviewed in *Chapter 10: Dinner Attractions*.

Nearby: Ripley's Believe It Or Not, Titanic, Train Land, SeaWorld.

WordSpring Discovery Center

11221 John Wycliffe Boulevard, Orlando 32832
(800) 992-5433; (407) 852-3626
www.wycliffe.org/wordspring

Admission: Adults $6, seniors (55+) $5, students (grades 1 to 12) $4, family (parents and all children) $20, children under 6 free.

Hours: Monday to Friday 9:00 a.m. to 4:00 p.m.; first and third Saturday of the month 10:00 a.m. to 4:00 p.m.

Location: In southeastern Orlando; call for directions or get map on web site.

If you thought the Bible had long since been translated into every conceivable language, think again. Of the world's estimated 6,800 languages, only an estimated 392 have the entire Bible. Another 1,000 or so have a complete New Testament and 883 have at least one book of the Bible. Some 3,000 languages still do not have their own version of the Bible.

Wycliffe Bible Translators seeks to fill in most of the gaps and this compact and colorful multimedia museum chronicles the process and the challenges involved. Many of the interactive stations are designed with kids in mind, but adults will find them a lot of fun, too. At one, you can type in your name and get a printed certificate showing how it would look in six different languages from ancient Egyptian hieroglyphics to Klingon. At another, you can send an electronic postcard with your photo via email. Or you can listen in on Mazateco, a tonal Mexican language that can be spoken or whistled.

There are a number of special activities. Monday to Friday, at 10:00 a.m., there is a **guided tour** of the entire Wycliffe facility. At 1:00 p.m. on the same days, **Face To Face** features talks by various people involved in the Bible translation process. **A to Z Adventures** ($3 per child), which is presented once a month, gives kids a window on the cultures of different countries around the globe. If you'd like to return regularly for these activities and events, there is an annual pass available for just $12 for adults, $10 for seniors, and $6 for students.

There is a modestly priced cafeteria (open from 11:30 a.m. to 1:00 p.m.) and a small gift shop selling handicrafts from around the world at very reasonable prices. Surprisingly, there were no foreign language Bibles on sale when I last visited, with the exception of the surprise bestseller, *Da Jesus Book*, the Bible translated into very readable Hawaiian pidgin.

Nearby: Jesus Film Studio Tour.

Chapter Twelve:

Do It!

A VACATION IN ORLANDO DOESN'T MEAN ALWAYS BEING A SPECTATOR. THERE are plenty of activities that will put you right in the middle of the action. In this chapter, I will discuss some of them. Of course, there are many sports-oriented activities as well. They are discussed in *Chapter 17: Sports Scores*.

Bird Watching

Central Florida offers some excellent opportunities for birders, experienced or not. For the novice, there's the spectacle of the spring nesting season at Gatorland, described in *Chapter 4*. More experienced birders will want to head for the Merritt Island Wildlife Refuge (*Chapter 14*); during the winter months it is one of the country's premier birding destinations.

Bird watching is pretty much a do-it-yourself activity, but there are some organized activities. Several area Audubon Societies offer periodic field trips, which are listed on their web sites:

Orange Audubon Society
www.orangeaudubonfl.org
Kissimmee Valley Audubon Society
www.kissimmeeaudubon.org
Ridge Audubon Society (Lake Wales area)
www.ridgeaudubon.org
Indian River Audubon Society (Kennedy Space Center area)
www.spacecoastaudubon.org

A wealth of other information about birding in Florida can be found at the following web sites

www.americanbirdcenter.com/abc-florida.html
www.camacdonald.com/birding/usflorida.htm

Boat Rides

There are many places in the Orlando area where you can take a pleasant water-borne ride — as a passenger. You will find them listed in *Chapter 16: Moving Experiences*. However, there are a few places that let you take control.

Airboat Rentals U Drive

4266 West Irlo Bronson Highway, Kissimmee 34746
(407) 847-3672
www.airboatrentals.com

Cost:	$7 to $30 an hour
Hours:	Daily 9:00 a.m. to 5:00 p.m.; last boat leaves at 5:00 p.m.
Location:	East of *Medieval Times*, near Mile Marker 15

Just east of the *Medieval Times* dinner attraction, US Highway 192 crosses Shingle Creek. You'd never notice if it weren't for this unassuming rental operation. Here in the middle of Kissimmee's major commercial strip is a little fragment of old Florida wetlands that you can explore in that most traditional of vehicles, the airboat.

The four-person airboats, which rent for $30 an hour, are so easy to drive that even a child can pilot them (as long as an adult is present). The driver sits in a slightly elevated seat right in front of the shielded, rear-facing propeller. A lever, operated with the left hand, steers the boat right and left; the throttle is on the right.

You can explore upstream (under the highway bridge) for about a mile and a half before the water gets too shallow for even the low-draft airboat. Or you can head downstream for about two miles toward Lake Kissimmee. Since the airboats do about 8 to 10 miles per hour, this makes a comfortable hour's outing.

There are other boats available. A six-seat rowboat powered by a tiny electric outboard is $25 an hour or $60 for the day; rent a fishin' pole for another $5. Canoes are $7 an hour or $25 a day. Alligators are spotted here occasionally; river otters are seen more frequently: A family of six or seven frequents the area near the dock.

Nearby: Kissimmee Lanes, Medieval Times, Pirate Island Adventure Golf.

Lake Eola Swan Boats

Lake Eola Park, Orlando
(407) 232-0111

Cost:	$12 per half hour, including tax
Hours:	Weekdays noon to 6:00 p.m., weekends 10:00 a.m. to 8:00 p.m.
Location:	Downtown, near the intersection of Rosalind Avenue and Robinson Street

Right in the heart of Orlando's super-serious business district is this charming bit of whimsy. Lake Eola is Orlando's signature park, with its spectacular floating fountain. Along its shore, at a tiny kiosk called the Lake Eola Cafe, you can rent paddle boats decked out as graceful white swans and take them for a spin on this picture postcard lake. A sunset cruise on a swan makes a lovely way to get your evening off to a flying ... er, floating start.

Nearby: Orange County Regional History Center.

Bowling

This all-American pastime is alive and well in central Florida and if you've never tried your hand at it, a Florida vacation might be a good excuse. It's not that hard to master the basics and bowlers are a friendly lot willing to offer helpful hints to beginners. I have singled out two locations that are ultra-convenient for most tourists; however, there are many others in the Orlando area. If you'd like to sample them, you can get good information at www.floridabowling.com and www.bowlorlando.com, which sometimes features money-saving coupons.

Kissimmee Lanes

4140 West Vine Street, Kissimmee 34742

(407) 846-8844

www.amf.com/kissimmeelanes

Cost:	All ages $4.00 per game ($3.25 before 6:00 p.m. Monday to Friday; $3.75 after 9:00 p.m.)
Hours:	Monday to Thursday noon to midnight; Friday noon to 2:00 a.m.; Saturday 9:00 a.m. to 2:00 a.m.; Sunday 9:00 a.m. to 11:30 p.m.
Location:	East of *Medieval Times* on US 192

This is a friendly neighborhood place that draws a lot of tourists to its 32 lanes. There is a full snack bar and a bar to slake that deeper thirst. The web site often has dollars-off coupons for both bowling and food. Shoe rental is $4.

Nearby: Airboat Rentals U-Drive, Medieval Times, Pirate Island Adventure Golf.

World Bowling Center

7540 Canada Avenue, Orlando 32819

(407) 352-2695

Cost:	Adults $4, children $3, seniors (60+) $3 per game
Hours:	Daily noon to 11:00 p.m.
Location:	Near *Pirates Dinner Adventure*

Here is a moderately-priced, basic 32-lane bowling alley right in the heart of the I-Drive district. What makes World Bowling Center a bit out of the ordinary is the wacky decor, which features murals of astronauts bowling, among other whimsical touches. Prices are always the same, regardless of the time of day. However, on Sundays the adult price drops to $3 per game. Shoe rental is $3.

Nearby: Pirates Dinner Adventure, Magical Midway, Ripley's Believe It Or Not, Titanic, Wet 'n Wild.

Canoeing & Kayaking

What easier way to appreciate the pristine wilderness of the "real Florida" than to glide gently past it in a canoe? Surprisingly close to downtown Orlando are a number of canoeing trails that offer a glimpse of a Florida few tourists see. The shoreline will vary from well-manicured backyards to impenetrable jungles depending on where you canoe, and much of the scenery is drop-dead gorgeous. In many places, the landscape is little changed from the days Florida was first settled by humans. There are plenty of turtles and birds to be seen and you might even glimpse an alligator.

The two closest spots to Orlando are the Wekiva River basin to the north of the city and the Little-Big Econ Wilderness Area to the east. Most of the outfitters listed below will offer drop-off and/or pickup service. Plan on starting fairly early in the morning and ending in mid-afternoon. Some places offer overnight trips and will rent you camping gear. A typical four- or five-hour outing will cost about $25 to $35; hourly rates, where available, start at about $16.

I have restricted listings to the immediate Orlando area, but if you're willing to drive a bit, there are many more streams to explore. A good source of information is the **Florida Professional Paddlesports Association** at www.paddleflausa.com

Adventures in Florida

2912 East Marks Street, Orlando 32803
(407) 924-3375
www.adventuresinflorida.com

This eco-tour company offers day-long canoe or kayak expeditions, lunch included, to the Little-Big Econ area and the Wekiva basin ($40 to $75 per person). On nights of the full moon they organize nighttime paddles. They also offer a number of week-long expeditions (about $1,300 per person), including one in Central Florida that includes a lot of kayaking and snorkeling with a manatee. If you know a place you'd like to explore, they can also arrange for rentals, drop off, and pick up.

Hidden River Park Canoe Rentals

15295 East Colonial Drive, Orlando 32826
(407) 568-5346

This RV and camping resort on the eastern edge of Orlando rents canoes and kayaks that put in on the Big Econlockhatchee River. If you simply rent a canoe ($25 for the day), you will have to paddle back, but if you organize a "trip" (two canoe minimum, $25 per canoe) they will pick you up. Overnight trips can also be arranged, including a 35-mile voyage to the St. John's River.

King's Landing Canoe Rental

5722 Baptist Camp Road, Apopka 32712
(407) 886-0859
members.aol.com/kingslndng/

If you want to explore Rock Springs Run in Kelly Park, this is a good choice.

For $25, you can enjoy a leisurely four-hour paddle downstream to the take out pc at Wekiva Marina (see below), or dawdle for a picnic lunch along the way. For more on Kelly park, see *Chapter 14: Gardens & Edens.*

Wekiva Falls Resort
30700 Wekiva River Road, Sorrento 32776
(407) 830-9828; (352) 383-8055

After paying a $6 day guest fee to this funky RV resort, canoe rentals are an extremely modest $5 for all day, or $3 for two hours. From here you can explore the Wekiva River, but there is no pick up service; you paddle out and paddle back.

Wekiva Marina
1000 Miami Springs Drive, Longwood 32779
(407) 862-1500
www.geocities.com/wekivamarina

Located about half a mile downstream from where the Wekiva River and Rock Springs Run join, this outfitter rents canoes ($20 a day) or lets you launch your own canoe, kayak, or motorboat (up to 25hp) for a $3 launch fee. Wekiva Springs State Park is a mile upstream; there is no pick up service. You'll be able to stock up on essentials, like beer and bait, before you head out.

Wekiwa Springs State Park Nature Adventures
1800 Wekiwa Circle, Apopka 32712
(407) 880-4110 for rental info; (407) 884-2008 for park info
www.canoewekiva.com

There is a $5 per vehicle charge for entry into this charming park (See *Chapter 14: Gardens and Edens*). The rental concession is at the headwaters of one source for the Wekiva River and offers single and double kayaks as well as canoes. Canoe rentals start at $12 for two hours plus $3 for each additional hour; kayaks are $15 for the first two hours. Several set trips ($35 to $40) offer pick up service; otherwise, you must return canoes to the landing. They will also completely outfit a canoe for an overnight camping trip for $132.

Climbing
Central Florida is pretty flat, but if you get an itch to scale a sheer cliff face there's a place just north of Orlando that can accommodate you.

Aiguille Rock Climbing Center
999 Charles Street, Longwood 32750
(407) 332-1430
www.aiguille.com

Cost: Adults $15, students with ID $10.75, bouldering only $8.25, equipment rentals extra

Hours: Monday to Thursday 10:00 a.m. to 10:00 p.m.,
Friday 10:00 a.m. to 11:00 p.m., Saturday 9:00
a.m. to 11:00 p.m., Sunday noon to 7:00 p.m.

Location: From I-4 Exit 94 drive east on SR 434 for 3
miles, then right on Ronald Reagan, right on
Marvin, and right on Charles.

Located in a spacious former warehouse, Aiguille offer 25 rope stations on cliff faces of up to 36 feet in height, studded with colorful hand holds and with plenty of challenging overhangs. You can boulder (climb up to 11 feet off the ground) by yourself, but if you want to go higher you'll need a belayer to hold your support rope. If you don't have a buddy along, you can hire a staffer for this chore for $25 an hour, but only with two weeks notice. There's plenty of room for non-climbers to relax and watch the show, which can be pretty entertaining. If you get inspired to give it a try, lessons are offered.

Nearby: Sanford Orlando Kennel Club.

Fishing

The best time to go fishing, the conventional wisdom has it, is when you can. And you can go fishing in Central Florida. Boy, can you ever. If you just want to throw a line in the water and drift into a semi-trance, you can do that just about anywhere. If you'd like to do some real fishing, I strongly suggest you hire a guide. There are a number of reasons for this:

- A guide has the in-depth local knowledge you lack.
- A guide may be your only means of access to private lakes that have not been overfished.
- A guide will provide tackle and bait.
- Many of Orlando's fishing guides are attractions in themselves, practitioners of a lifestyle that has all but disappeared in our homogenized fast-food culture.

Throughout much of the American Southeast, bass fishing is virtually a state religion, and most of the Orlando area fishing guides seem to specialize in this feisty game fish. There are, however, other fish to be caught hereabouts. Here is a list of Central Florida species, with notes on their seasons:

American shad: Optimum, February and March, so-so January, April, and May.

Bluegill: Optimum, April to June, so-so the rest of the year.

Channel catfish: So-so all year.

Crappie: Optimum, December to March, so-so April and May.

Largemouth bass: Optimum, January to March, so-so the rest of the year.

Shellcracker: Optimum, May to July, so-so the rest of the year.

Sunshine bass: Optimum, December to February, so-so March, April, October, and November.

Striped bass: Optimum, December to February, so-so March, April, October, and November.

What you go after, then, will be a function of the time of your visit and your guide's predilections. Where you go will depend to a fair extent on the guide you hire and his location; each has his favorite (or even exclusive) areas. Among the more popular fishing spots are the Clermont chain of lakes (west of Orlando), the Wekiva River and the St. John's River (north of Orlando), and West Lake Tohopekaliga (in Kissimmee). Serious fishermen will want to pick up a copy of Kris Thoemke's *Fishing Florida* (Falcon Press, $18.95), which provides lake by lake, stream by stream commentary.

Guides do not come cheap; $325 for a full day and $225 for a half day is fairly standard, although some services charge as much as $350 for a full day and $250 for a half. The price covers two people, plus tackle and, sometimes, bait. If all you have time (or money) for is a half-day, make it the morning. Of course, you will also need a Florida State fishing license. A 7-day license for a nonresident is $16.50, an annual one is $31.50. You can get one at any fishing camp, or your guide will help you obtain one.

A #1 Bass Guide Service
P.O. Box 421257, Kissimmee 34742
(800) 707-5463
www.a1bassguideservice.com

A Pro Bass Guide Service
398 Grove Court, Winter Garden 34787
(800) 771-9676; (407) 877-9676

Ace Bass Guide Service
(321) 695-5042

Bass Anglers Guide Service
6526 SR 535, Windermere 34786
(407) 257-2241
www.fishing-boating.com/bassanglers

Bass Challenger Guide Service
(800) 241-5314; (407) 273-8045
www.basschallenger.com

Bass Fishing Unlimited, Bob Lawson
(407) 957-8900

Bass-n-Action
966 Humphrey Boulevard, Deltona 32738
(407)-739-5555
www.bass-n-action.com

Bear's Bass Guide Service
(800) 218-3351
www.bearbass.com

Big Toho Marina
101 Lake Shore Boulevard, Kissimmee 34741
(407) 846-2124
www.bigtoho.com

Champion Pro Guide Services
(407) 738-7652
www.championbass.com

Fishin' Fun
1699 Ruston Lane, Kissimmee 34746
(888) 621-1184; (407) 933-0951
www.captain-jac.com

Fishing Charters, Inc.
P.O. Box 700361, St. Cloud 34770
(800) 244-9105
www.fishingchartersinc.com

Gator Rod Charters
857 South Marshall Lake Road, Apopka 32703
(866) 460-3474; (407) 257-2941
www.gatorrodcharters.com

Gators Big Bass Guide Service
2824 Conway Gardens Road, Orlando 32806
(407) 856-7961
www.gatorbass.com

Highland Park Fish Camp
2640 West Highland Park Road, DeLand 32720
(800) 525-3477; (386) 734-2334
www.hpfishcamp.com

Lake Charters Guide Service
1650 Justin Matthew Way, St. Cloud 34769
(877) 326-3575; (407) 891-2275
www.lakecharter.com

Lake Toho Tackle Company
1879 Kings Point Boulevard, Kissimmee 34744
(407) 928-2529
www.billwhipplefloridafishingguide.com

Richardson's Fish Camp
1550 Scotty's Road, Kissimmee 34744
(407) 846-6540

Spotted Tail Fishing Charters
284 Clearview Road, Chuluota 32766
(407) 977-5207
www.spottedtail.com

Tom and Jerry's Pro Guide Services
(800) 328-5686
www.tomandjerrys.net

Trophy Bass Only
(407) 831-8512
www.trophybassorlando.com

Go Karts

Go karts, for the uninitiated, are miniaturized racing cars and they've been around for 50 years. Originally marketed as do-it-yourself kits to hobbyists, go karts have become a popular form of recreation that appeals to kids and grown ups alike, with commercial tracks popping up to let casual enthusiasts have a go.

Powered by small gas engines, karts can reach speeds of up to 50 miles an hour, although the karts you'll encounter in Orlando, seldom top 25 mph. Go kart tracks range from simple concrete tracks marked off by old tires to elaborate, multi-level wooden courses.

Fun Spot

5551 DelVerde Way, Orlando 32819
(407) 363-3867
www.fun-spot.com

Cost:	$6 per ride, $35 unlimited rides
Hours:	Daily 10:00 a.m. to midnight
Location:	Just off International Drive near the intersection of Kirkman. Look for the Ferris wheel.

Fun Spot easily wins the Orlando go kart sweepstakes with its intriguing, twisting, up and down, multilevel tracks. There are four of them here, with the 1,375-foot QuadHelix the most popular. Fun Spot is also a small amusement park and is reviewed in *Chapter 11: Another Roadside Attraction.*

Nearby: Skull Kingdom, Universal Orlando, Vans Skatepark, Wet 'n Wild.

Kissimmee Go Karts

4708 West Irlo Bronson Highway, Kissimmee 34746
(407) 396-4800

Cost:	$4 per lap, 5 laps for $16, 10 for $22
Hours:	Daily usually 11:00 a.m. to 11:00 p.m.
Location:	1 mile east of SR 565 at Mile Marker 13

Nothing fancy here, just go karts conveniently located on Kissimmee's main tourist strip. Go karts come in three sizes here — a large and a small single-seater and a two-seater — and the price is the same for all sizes of kart. The almost one-mile track snakes around three loops with a bridge and overpass arrangement allowing the karts to end up where they started.

Nearby: Airboat Rentals U-Drive, Medieval Times, Pirate Island Adventure Golf.

Li'l 500

150 Atlantic Drive (at US 17-92), Maitland 32751
(407) 831-2045

Cost:	$4 to $5 per ride, depending on track
Hours:	Monday to Thursday 10:00 a.m. to 11:00 p.m., Friday and Saturday 10:00 a.m. to 11:30 p.m.,

Sunday 2:00 p.m. to 10:00 p.m.

Location: From I-4 Exit 92 drive east on SR 436, then south on US 17-92 1.5 miles

Located north of Orlando, outside the tourist zone, this family-oriented attraction offers three separate tracks. The Family Track is strictly for little kids, while the Moto Track and Fastrac appeal to teens and adults.

Nearby: Birds of Prey Center, Holocaust Memorial, Enzian Theater, Maitland Historical Museums.

Magical Midway

7001 International Drive, Orlando 32819

(407) 370-5353

www.magicalmidway.com

Cost: $6 for one ride, $23 for three hours, and $28 for all day

Hours: Daily usually 11:00 a.m. to 11:00 p.m.

Location: On I-Drive, two blocks south of Wet 'n Wild

Magical Midway is a smaller version of Fun Spot, but due to the absence of kiddie rides it draws an older teen clientele. The main attractions are two elevated wooden go kart tracks. There are also midway-style rides including a scaled-down version of Universal's *Dr. Doom* shot tower.

Nearby: Dottie's Comedy Theater, Tiki Adventure Golf, Wet 'n Wild.

Naskart Family Raceway

5071 West Irlo Bronson Highway, Kissimmee 34746

(407) 397-7699

Cost: $10 for a 30-lap ride

Hours: Daily 11:00 a.m. to 11:00 p.m.

Location: Between Mile Marker 10 and 11 on US 192

There are no video arcades or other distractions at Naskart. Go karts are the central and only attraction at this small venue on the busy 192 tourist strip. There are two fairly short tracks. The "Naskar" track features fully enclosed stock-car-like karts (the roof closes over your head) and an oval track, while the "Indy" track offers one- and two-seater karts and a winding course. A new feature is toy go karts so even little kids can get into the action.

Nearby: Arabian Nights, Old Town, SkyCoaster & G-Force.

Old Town

5770 West Irlo Bronson Highway, Kissimmee 34746

(407) 396-4888

www.old-town.com

Cost: $6 for a 13-lap, 4-minute ride

Hours: Daily noon to 11:00 p.m.

Location: Between Mile Marker 10 and 11 on US 192

Go karts are a small feature of this attraction (described in the previous chapter). The single, small, concrete track has a few ups and downs.

Nearby: Naskart Family Raceway, SkyCoaster & G-Force.

Golf

For golfers, Central Florida is a sort of demi-paradise, with 123 courses within a 45-minute drive of downtown Orlando. With that many, choosing one can be a daunting task. You can simplify matters by using the services of Tee Times USA, (888) 465-3356, (386)439-0001, or www.teetimesusa.com. They will help you pick a course and make the reservations for you; they'll even fax driving directions to your home or hotel. It's a free service and you will pay the regular greens fees. You'll get the best choice of courses and times if you book several months in advance, but they can arrange next-day tee times as well.

I have listed here golf courses in Orange and Osceola counties on the theory that most of my readers will be staying in Orlando (Orange County) or Kissimmee (Osceola County). If you want to explore farther afield, call (800) 864-6101 before you leave for Florida and order a copy of *Golfer's Guide* for the Orlando and Central Florida area. There is a $3 charge that can be paid for over the phone with a credit card. Or call the Orlando Convention and Visitors Bureau, (800) 972-3304, to find out where you can pick up a free copy in the Orlando area. You will also find an extensive listing of golf courses of all types in the Yellow Pages in your hotel room.

All these courses are in the (407) area code.

Municipal Courses

Dubsdread Golf Course, Orlando, 246-2551
Winter Park Municipal, Winter Park, 623-3339

Public Courses

Boggy Creek, Orlando, 857-0280
Crystalbrook Golf Club, Kissimmee, 847-8721
Eagle Creek Golf Club, Orlando, 273-4653
Eaglewood Golf Club, Orlando, 351-5121
Forest Lake Golf Course, Ocoee, 654-4653
Hunters Creek Golf Club, Orlando, 240-4653
Remington Golf Club, Kissimmee, 344-4004
Ritz-Carlton Golf Club 393-4900
Shingle Creek Golf Club, Orlando, 996-9933
Walk-N-Sticks Golf Club, Kissimmee, 348-9555
Winter Pines Golf Club, Winter Park, 671-3172

Resort Courses

Eagle Pines (WDW), Lake Buena Vista, 939-4653
Falcon's Fire Golf Course, Kissimmee, 397-2777

Grand Cypress Resort, Orlando, 239-4700
Hawk's Landing Golf Club, Orlando, 238-8660
International Golf Club, Orlando, 239-6909
Orange Lake Country Club, Orlando, 239-1050

Semi-Private Courses

Bay Hill Club, Orlando, 876-2429
Cypress Creek Country Club, Orlando, 351-2187
Eastwood Golf Club, Orlando, 281-4653
Kissimmee Bay Country Club, Kissimmee, 348-4653
Kissimmee Golf Club, Kissimmee, 847-2816
Lake Orlando Golf and Country Club, Orlando, 298-4144
Meadow Woods Golf Club, Windermere, 850-5600
Metro-West Country Club, Orlando, 299-1099
The Oaks, Kissimmee, 933-4055
Wedgefield Golf and Country Club, Orlando, 568-2116

Guns

Nothing is quite so American as the belief in the inalienable right to bear arms. If shooting off something that packs a kick is your idea of the pursuit of happiness, your visit to Orlando offers a good opportunity to indulge yourself.

The Shooting Gallery

2911 West 39th Street, Orlando 32839
(407) 428-6225

Cost:	$16 to $33 per hour, plus ammo and targets
Hours:	Daily 10:00 a.m. to 8:00 p.m.
Location:	From I-4 Exit 79, go south on John Young Parkway a quarter mile to Cox Plaza on your left

At The Shooting Gallery you can rent any of a wide selection of handguns or automatic machine guns to experience the thrill of slamming hot lead into the paper thin body of an imaginary enemy. Instruction is available (briefly) if you need it, but the experience here is pretty much point and shoot simplicity itself.

There are six booths looking down the shooting range where paper targets in the form of human silhouettes hang from wires. There is a range rental of $8 per hour with handguns going for $8 and submachine guns for $25. Ammo and targets cost extra. To give you an idea, the typical machine gunner will go through four to five 50-round boxes of ammo at $11 a box in an hour. Targets of Osama bin Laden are $2. If business is light, they will often let you overstay your hour at no extra charge.

The Shooting Gallery is located in a downscale strip mall across the street from an Orange County correctional facility and is surrounded by bail bondsmen. Are they trying to tell us something?

Nearby: Holy Land Experience, Millenia Mall.

Hang Gliding

Hang gliding was invented in Australia, which may be why you hear so much Aussie slang among Orlando-area hang gliding enthusiasts. There are two hang gliding venues to Orlando's south and west. Both have an appealing, low-key, good-vibes atmosphere and, thanks to tandem (two-person) gliders, both are well equipped to introduce the novice to this exciting experience. A word of warning: hang gliding can induce motion sickness, especially when the air is choppy.

An experienced pilot goes aloft with you and keeps you safe, but you can do much of the actual flying if you wish. Flights last about 20 minutes, 10 up and 10 down. Experienced hang gliders can sharpen their skills and rent gliders if they haven't brought their own.

Wallaby Ranch

1805 Deen Still Road, Davenport 33897
(800) 925-5229, (863) 424-0070
www.wallaby.com

Cost:	$95
Hours:	Daily 8:00 a.m. to sunset
Location:	From I-4 Exit 55, drive north on US 27 and turn left at Deen Still Road; drive 1.7 miles to the poorly signed driveway on your left.

This is a hang gliding club with regular, and very friendly, get togethers. Of the two, it is the larger and has fairly extensive facilities. There is a barbecue and a tented eating area as well as a treehouse for kids and overnight accommodations.

The 500-acre facility has plenty of room for running and mountain bike trails. There is also a pool, a trampoline, and a climbing wall. If you come to the Orlando area regularly, you can store your hang glider here.

Nearby: Seminole-Lake Gliderport, QuestAir.

QuestAir

6548 Groveland Airport Road, Groveland 34736
(352) 429-0213
www.questairforce.com

Cost:	$125
Hours:	Daily 8:00 a.m. to sunset
Location:	Take State Road 50 (East Colonial Drive) west to State Road 33 and turn left. Look for sign on your left.

Tucked away in a bucolic setting west of Orlando, this small operation offers rides in ultra-light aircraft as well as tandem hang gliding experiences. There is primitive camping available for hang gliders.

Nearby: Seminole-Lake Gliderport, Wallaby Ranch.

Horseback Riding

There are a few places to go horseback riding in the Orlando area. Most stables offer leisurely trail rides of about an hour or so. Lessons are available at these stables.

Devonwood Farms

2518 Rouse Road, Orlando 32817
(407) 273-0822
www.devonwoodfarms.com

Cost:	$48 per hour for private lessons
Hours:	Tuesday to Friday 11:00 a.m. to sunset
Location:	Half way between East Colonial Drive and University Boulevard in eastern Orlando

Offers lessons in both English-style and western riding. A one-week summer camp is $300 per rider, $500 for two weeks.

Grand Cypress Equestrian Center

1 Equestrian Drive, Orlando 32836
(407) 239-1938
www.grandcypress.com/equestrian_center

Cost:	$45 to $85 (Western) to $100 (English), plus tax
Hours:	Daily 8:30 a.m. to 6:00 p.m. (to 5:00 p.m. on weekends)
Location:	On SR 535, about 4 miles from I-4 Exit 68

Both Western and English-style riding. They offer birthday parties with pony rides for $25 to $35 per child.

Horse World

3705 South Poinciana Boulevard, Kissimmee 34758
(407) 847-4343
www.horseworldstables.com

Cost:	$39 (beginners, 60 minutes) to $69 (advanced, 75 minutes), plus tax
Hours:	Daily 9:00 a.m. to 5:00 p.m.
Location:	About 12 miles south of Highway 192

Western-style riding on 750 acres. Riding lessons are offered and they rent facilities for group events such as picnics.

Rock Springs Riding Ranch

31700 CR 433, Sorrento 32776
(352) 735-6266
www.rsrranch.com

Cost:	$30 to $80 for one- to three-hour guided trail rides; $150 for all day

Hours: Daily 8:00 a.m. to 5:00 p.m.
Location: North of Orlando in the Rock Springs Run State Reserve

Western-style trail riding in a beautiful state park. See *Chapter 14: Gardens and Edens* for more on Rock Springs Run State Reserve.

Jet Ski Rentals

Jet skis, those noisy motorcycles of the seas, are becoming increasingly popular (much to the dismay of those who prefer their lakes quiet and peaceful). If you'd like to take one out for a spin, there are a number of places that will accommodate you. No experience is necessary and driving a jet ski is the soul of simplicity. Rentals start at about $50 for 30 minutes and go as high as $100 an hour for really fast three-seater machines. Some places may offer other activities such as wakeboarding, water skiing, or fishing.

Buena Vista Watersports

13245 Lake Bryan Drive, Lake Buena Vista 32830
(407) 239-6939
www.bvwatersports.com

Kissimmee Water Sports

4914 West Irlo Bronson Highway, Kissimmee 34746
(407) 396-1888

Miniature Golf

Just as the amusement park was revolutionized by Walt, miniature golf, once a homey mom-and-pop sort of attraction, has become a multilevel "themed" extravaganza with entrepreneurs competing with each other to create the most unusual, most atmospheric, most elaborate course yet. And the Orlando area boasts some of the finest examples of the genre. For most visitors, there's nothing quite like this back home, and I think a visit to at least one miniature golf attraction should be included in every Orlando vacation.

Most of the courses are concentrated in the International Drive area of Orlando and along US 192 in Kissimmee. During the warmer months, it's best to avoid the torrid heat of the day and play at night. Don't worry, they all stay open late. Discount coupons to most (if not all) of these courses can be found in brochure racks and throwaway magazines.

Bonanza

7761 West Irlo Bronson Highway, Kissimmee 34746
(407) 396-7536

Behind that towering rock formation over the Magic Mining Company restaurant ("Steaks & Seafood") lies a cleverly laid out miniature golf course with a Gold Rush theme. There are two complete 18-hole courses, "The Prospector" (the easier of the two) and "The Gold Nugget." Putt your way over this three-story mountain past cascading waterfalls, old mining sluices, trestle bridges, mountain pools, and cool grottoes. The course is compact, well maintained, and a lot of fun.

Prices: $8 adults, $7 children under 9. The second 18 holes are half price.

Congo River Golf

5901 International Drive, Orlando 32819
(407) 248-9181
6312 International Drive, Orlando 32819
(407) 352-0042
4777 West Irlo Bronson Highway, Kissimmee 34746
(407) 396-6900
531 West SR 436, Altamonte Springs 32714
(407) 682-4077
www.congoriver.com

Here you can putt your way up, through, around, and over Livingston Falls in a setting that evokes a storybook Africa and the memory of Stanley and Livingston. There are two complete 18-hole courses, with the "Stanley" course being the easier of the two. If you find yourself having difficulties making par, it's "Livingston," I presume. The holes on both courses are lined with small rocks and large boulders, making for erratic and unpredictable bounces. The 6312 International Drive location offers views onto Wet 'n Wild's lake (see *Chapter 9*), where you will see screaming riders in inner tubes being towed by jet skis.

Prices: $11.50 for 36 holes, $9 for 18, $4.50 for replays. The Altamonte Springs location only has 18 holes and the fee is $8.

Hawaiian Rumble Adventure Golf

8969 International Drive, Orlando 32819
(407) 351-7733
13529 South Apopka-Vineland Road, Orlando 32830
(407) 239-8300
www.hawaiianrumbleorlando.com

There are two courses here, Kahuna and Lani, with Lani being the more difficult of the two. The courses wind around and through a towering central volcano with thundering waterfalls substituting for lava. Each location has a small Internet cafe.

Prices: $10 adults, $8 children (4–10); 36 holes are adults $15 and children $12.

Pirates Cove

8601 International Drive, Orlando 32819
(407) 352-7378
Crossroads Center, Lake Buena Vista 32836
(407) 827-1242

2845 Florida Plaza Boulevard, Kissimmee 34746
(407) 396-7484
www.piratescove.net

Adventure on the high seas is the theme here with two 18-hole courses named after Blackbeard and Capt. Kidd. "Blackbeard's Challenge" is the more challenging of the two. The design and execution of these courses is on a par with that seen at Congo River (see above). I give Pirates Cove a slight edge, however, with the Lake Buena Vista location my personal favorite. It boasts extra height and higher waterfalls, not to mention its location next to a number of excellent restaurants and Downtown Disney. At all locations, the courses are punctuated with signs offering the real-life history of their namesake pirates. (Will this edutainment never stop!)

Prices: Adults $10, children (4-12) $9. Unlimited play $12.

Pirates Island Adventure Golf

4330 West Irlo Bronson Highway, Kissimmee 34746
(407) 396-4660

Once again the theme is piracy and once again the two 18-hole courses are named for Blackbeard and Capt. Kidd. This is one of the handsomest courses in the Orlando area, with a spectacular central waterfall cascading down in stages to a series of lagoons complete with artificial mist. The course is beautifully maintained, with smooth brick borders on each hole. There's edutainment here, too, with signs providing capsule biographies of well-known (and not so well-known) pirates.

Prices: Each course is $10 for adults, $9 for children; all-day unlimited play costs $12 for all.

Putting Edge

Festival Bay Shopping Center at I-Drive and Oak Ridge, Orlando 32819
(407) 248-0700
www.putting-edge.com

Here's an interesting take on the mini-golf theme. The greens are black and you play in the dark. Well, not completely. Ultra-violet light turns this compact 18-hole indoor course into a psychedelic wonderland. Even the balls and putters glow in the dark and once you get used to it, it's surprisingly each to play.

Prices: Adults $9, youths (7 to 12) $8, children 6 and under $6.50; second round is half price. Party packages are $12 to $21 per person.

River Adventure Golf

4535 West Irlo Bronson Highway, Kissimmee 34746
(407) 396-4666

The spinning waterwheel that serves as this course's billboard says it all. A river bubbles up at the top of an artificial hill and tumbles down through a number of rocky streams to a placid lagoon below. There's just one 18-hole course with plenty of greenery. Hedges and ivy-covered rock outcroppings abound. This is yet another impeccably maintained course, with signs that announce not just the hole number and par but the distance to the hole as well. There's a "19th hole" where you can putt for a free game.

Prices: $8 for everyone 4 and older. The second game is $4. Play all day for $14. Children under 4 play **free** with a paying adult.

Tiki Island Adventure Golf

7460 International Drive, Orlando 32819
(407) 248-8180

Here's another volcano-themed course, with a four-story caldera "erupting" on a regular schedule, as cooling waterfalls cascade around you. A river runs through it, too, complete with flamingo paddle boats. There are two 18-hole courses, Tiki Falls and Volcano Voyage.

Prices: Adults $10, children (4–12) $9 for each course; the "Big Kahuna" package ($13 and $12 respectively) lets you play both courses.

Paintball

Hunkered down under a moonlit sky behind a sandbag bunker with a remorseless "enemy" bearing down on you or running like mad through the scrub forest from barricade to barricade, with bursts of gunfire going off all around, you begin to understand why paintball has been called "the ultimate adrenaline rush."

Paintball lets you play John Wayne (or Rambo, or Chuck Norris) in refereed "battles" that last about 15 minutes and pit two teams of five to eight players against each other. The challenge — and the fun— comes in the form of the tiny paintballs that give the game its name. Fired from small CO_2 powered guns, they zip along at 190 miles an hour, splatting against whatever they come in contact with, leaving a telltale mark. They hit with quite a sting and raise a lovely red welt so when you get hit, you'll know it. The games are highly structured with an emphasis on good sportsmanship and safety. Anyone breaking the rules will be removed from the game. According to paintball promoters, paintball causes fewer participant injuries than bowling and golf. And, lest you think paintball is a game just for young boys and grown men who act that way, a surprising number of women play — and play hard.

Most games are played outdoors, although there are some indoor courses. Some fields use inflatable barricades to provide cover, others use hard plastic; best of all, in my opinion, are the woods courses, in which most, if not all the cover, is natural. The fields I have played are very imaginatively designed, well executed, and meticulously maintained. The length of game session varies and sessions can last four or five hours. Night games are especially exhilarating and highly recommended.

There are a number of paintball fields in the Orlando area. Most are fairly modest operations and locations can change regularly and without notice. So can hours of operation. Schedules are somewhat loose and fields are sometimes booked by local groups. There's always a possibility that you'll be able to join a private group, so it's worth dropping by or calling in to check. Kids as young as ten can play at some courses with signed parental approval.

Prices vary from place to place. Some charge a basic fee, others don't. The real money is in the paintballs, which can cost upwards of $60 a case of 2,000 rounds. Most places sell them in batches of 500. If you don't have your own paintball gun, not to worry. You can rent one for $10 or so; many rental packages include ammo. Budget a minimum of about $40 per person for your paintball adventure. Make sure to dress down for your game and make sure to wear the required footgear, either boots or athletic shoes. Some places rent jumpsuits, many of them camouflaged; they are highly recommended. They provide concealment and some protection from the sting of a direct hit.

Since the paintball scene changes so often, I strongly recommend you call to check location, hours, and pricing before driving long distances. Note that the addresses given may be the office location and not the field location.

Epik Paintball

14200 East Colonial Drive, Orlando 32826
(407) 273-6899
www.epikpaintball.com

Associated with a paintball shop of the same name, this 40-acre complex of fields is located to the east of downtown Orlando on heavily traveled State Route 50. There are air bunkers, hyperball, and woods fields available. Games are held weekends and on two weekday nights. When school's out, they go to a seven-day schedule.

Orlando Paintball

7215 Rose Avenue, Orlando 32810
(407) 294-0694
www.orlandopaintball.com

A 300,000 square foot, air-conditioned, indoor playing area housed in a former shipping warehouse well off the tourist track on the northeast side of Orlando. Indoor paintball is a different experience and is best in the cooler months or when it's raining. The floor here is well cushioned with sawdust, and the low-tech layout of plywood and rubber tire barricades is imaginative and challenging with many dangerous cul de sacs to trap the unwary. This is sort of the urban guerilla version of paintball and vaguely reminiscent of those post-apocalypse shoot-em-up movies. This is another location that's hard for out-of-towners to find. Call for directions.

Osceola Extreme Sports

3831 West Vine Street, Kissimmee 34741
(407) 933-7785
www.oes.cc

These outdoor courses offer a variety of playing areas, including two woods courses. The fields are located 4.5 miles south of US 192 (Irlo Bronson Highway), on Poinciana Boulevard, just before you get to Green Meadows Farm. There was no sign (or driveway!) the last time I visited, so be on the lookout on your right and drive carefully into the makeshift lot.

Plane Rides

It may be hard to believe, but it is actually possible when in Orlando to take the controls of an airplane and actually fly it — no experience necessary. You even have your choice of planes.

Stallion 51

3951 Merlin Drive, Kissimmee 34741
(407) 846-4400
www.stallion51.com

Cost:	$2,150 (half hour) to $2,950 (one hour)
Hours:	Monday to Friday, by appointment
Location:	At the Kissimmee Airport off North Hoagland Boulevard

Orlando's theme parks have their share of thrill rides, but none of them have anything that can match this.

At the Kissimmee Airport, you can strap yourself into a beautifully maintained and painted P-51 Mustang and spend an hour soaring and swooping central Florida. These World War II vintage warbirds are powered by V-12 Rolls Royce engines and are capable of speeds up to 500 mph, although you'll be held to a more sensible 280 or 300 mph. You're not alone, of course. These Mustangs have dual-control cockpits and you ride in back, but you will have actual control of the plane at least 90% of the time — if you want to, that is.

For the penny-pinchers, there is a less pricey alternative, a flight in a T-6 Texan Mustang trainer that costs just $400 for a half hour and $600 for a full hour. The company bills this as the stepping stone from general aviation flying to vintage warbirds.

To make doubly sure you get your money's worth, your flight is meticulously documented on video using cameras mounted on the stabilizer and the glareshield. You also get a pre/postflight briefing, a cockpit briefing, a photo, and a certificate as part of the package. If you decide you're cut out to be an aerial ace, ongoing training is a mere $3,250 an hour ($700 an hour for the T-6 Texan).

Nearby: Green Meadows Farm, Warbird Adventures, White One.

Warbird Adventures

233 North Hoagland Avenue, Kissimmee 34741
(407) 870-7366
www.warbirdadventures.com

Cost:	$190 (15 minutes) to $560 (one hour)
Hours:	Daily, except Sunday, by appointment
Location:	At the Kissimmee Airport, south of US 192

If you blanched at the cost of flying one of those Mustangs at Stallion 51 (see above), you'll be glad to know that just a short distance away, in more modest surroundings, you can fly their baby brothers at a fraction of the cost. The North American T-6/SNJ/Harvards flown here were the premier fighter-trainers of World War

II, renowned for their excellence for teaching pilots and preparing them for bigger planes (like the Mustang).

The experience is similar to that offered at Stallion 51, except that here you get to pilot from the front seat. The planes are also not quite as zippy, although that will hardly matter to most folks. The Pratt and Whitney 1340 radial engines are capable of speeds up to 240 mph, although typical cruising speed during these flights is 160 mph. The three planes in the fleet are painted with the markings of the Navy, Marines, and the Army Air Corps; you have your pick.

Warbird Adventures uses an a la carte approach to pricing. It costs $190, $320, and $560 for 15-, 30-, and 60-minute flights, with additional charges for options like aerobatics ($35, included in the 60 minute flight), a DVD of your flight ($50), and so forth. Flights are timed from takeoff to landing.

Nearby: Green Meadows Farm, Stallion 51, White One.

Skating & Skateboarding

Orlando and the surrounding suburban areas offer a good selection of roller skating and skateboarding venues. You can even go ice skating when you tire of the heat and humidity! With the exception of Vans Skatepark, which pretty much goes full-throttle all the time, they have patchwork schedules. It's best to call ahead or check schedules on the web sites given below.

Ice Den

8701 Maitland Summit Boulevard, Orlando 32810
(407) 916-2550
www.rdvsportsplex.com

Cost:	$6 to $8 depending on venue and time
Hours:	Vary by day
Location:	From I-4 Exit 90 go west on Maitland Boulevard about a mile to Maitland Summit on your right

Located in a sprawling modern fitness complex on the north end of Orlando, the Ice Den is a compact ice skating rink with two-hour public skating sessions on an idiosyncratic schedule. Skate rentals are just over $2 and there is a snack bar.

Nearby: Orlando Paintball.

Ice Factory of Central Florida

2221 Partin Settlement Road, Kissimmee 34744
(407) 933-4259
www.icefactory.com

Cost:	$6 per session skate rentals $3
Hours:	Friday to Tuesday; call for precise hours
Location:	From Florida's Turnpike Exit 244, go straight from the toll plaza on Shady Lane, then left on Partin Settlement Road

There are two rinks here, a large main rink and a smaller "studio" rink. Saturday nights are family nights, with a group of five getting admission and pizza for $35.

Nearby: Boggy Creek Airboat Rides, Bob Mackinson Aquatic Center, Osceola County Stadium (Houston Astros).

Orlando Skate Park
400 Festival Way, Orlando 32803
(407) 898-9600
www.orlandoskatepark.org

Cost:	$6 per 3-hour session; $15 for all day; $30 for unlimited sessions in a month; BMX sessions $8
Hours:	Monday to Friday 11:00 a.m. to 10:00 p.m., Saturday and Sunday 9:00 a.m. to 9:00 p.m.
Location:	From I-4 Exit 84, go east on Colonial about 3 miles, then right on Maguire to the corner of Livingston

This is a well-designed outdoor skateboarding park that looks like a large, empty swimming pool. Depths range from 5 to 11 feet, with interesting variations in terrain along the bottom. There's even a transfer ridge. The mandatory waivers can be downloaded from the web site. Sessions for BMX bikes are held Wednesday and Sunday evenings. A variety of membership options will appeal to enthusiasts who will be in Orlando for a while.

Nearby: Orlando Museum of Art, Orlando Science Center.

Semoran Skateway
2670 Cassel Creek Boulevard, Casselberry 32707
(407) 834-9106
www.semoranskateway.com

Cost:	$5 to $9.25; basic skate rental included in most admissions
Hours:	Vary by day
Location:	Just west SR 436 (Semoran Boulevard), near lake Howell

Roller skating pure and simple is what's on tap at this venue, which lies somewhat north of the beaten tourist track. There's a large rink, a good snack bar, and upbeat music. It's a real neighborhood place and crowded at most sessions, so grown ups might want to take advantage of the adult skates on Sunday evening and Tuesday morning. Monday, Wednesday, Thursday, and Tuesday afternoons are reserved for private parties; Saturday is Christian Music Night.

Nearby: Orlando Jai-Alai.

Skate Reflections
1111 Dyer Boulevard, Kissimmee 34741
(407) 846-8469; (407) 239-8674 (from Orlando)

www.skatereflections.com

Cost:	$6 to $7 plus $1 skate rental, varies by session
Hours:	Vary by day
Location:	Just south of Highway 192

This roller skating rink specializes in good clean fun with strict rules against smoking and gum chewing and a dress code that bans such things as "muscle shirts" and "obscene wording" on clothes. The large rink is impeccably maintained with subdued disco lighting and a snack bar area with plenty of seating. Monday, Tuesday, and Thursday nights are reserved for private parties. Once a month they have a Christian Music Night.

Nearby: Green Meadows Farm, Kissimmee Lanes, Medieval Times.

Vans Skatepark

5220 International Drive, Orlando 32819
(407) 351-3881

Cost:	$12 to $15 per session ($5 to $7 for members); membership $25 per year
Hours:	Daily 10:00 a.m. to 11:00 p.m.
Location:	Off I-Drive, near Prime Outlets

Part of a nationwide chain, Vans Skatepark in Orlando is the second largest indoor skateboard facility in the world. This is the place to come to practice your skateboarding and extreme skating skills on a bewildering array of ramps, jumps, and chutes, ranging from beginner to professional level. An elevated walkway affords easy viewing and makes a visit to Vans a fun excursion even for those who would never think of attempting the wild stunts going on below.

Sessions last two hours, with the more expensive ones on Saturdays, Sundays, and holidays. For an avid skateboarder, an annual membership will pay for itself fairly quickly. Safety gear is mandatory and if you don't have your own you can rent helmet, elbow, and knee pads for $5 a session. You can also rent a skateboard for $5.

Nearby: Fun Spot, Universal Orlando, Wet 'n Wild.

Skydiving

Florida Skydiving Center

Lake Wales Airport
440 South Airport Road, Lake Wales 33853
(863) 678-1003
www.floridaskydiving.com

Ever feel like throwing yourself out of a plane? Then this is the place to come and test your resolve. Actually, it's remarkably easy, since someone else throws you out. Allow me to explain: Would-be skydivers can experience the joys of freefall on a "tandem jump." That means you are strapped securely to a certified instructor, who knows the ropes and controls the jump. After a flight to 13,500 feet, the fun begins, with a full minute of freefall and about five minutes under a parachute to landing. No experience is necessary, but jumpers must be at least 18 years of age and weigh no more than 230 pounds.

The cost, including tax, is $179. If you want your dive immortalized on video or DVD, add another $95. If you can talk two or more of your friends into jumping with you, you'll all receive a discount — $10 per person. For groups of seven or more people, the discount goes to $20 a head. Licensed skydivers with their own gear can jump for just $22.

The first jump is scheduled for about 8:00 a.m. and the last usually goes at sunset. But since the entire experience takes about four to six hours, including a very thorough pre-jump briefing, plan on arriving early. The best idea is to reserve your jump a few days in advance. Florida Skydiving Center is open daily year round but hours vary seasonally.

Nearby: Historic Bok Sanctuary, Lake Wales Arts Center, Spook Hill.

Skydive Deland

1600 Flightline Boulevard, DeLand 32724
(386) 738-3539
www.skydivedeland.com

Skydive Deland operates in much the same way as the Florida Skydiving Center. Here the price of a tandem jump is $169, with groups of four to six people paying $155 each and groups of seven or more paying $145. The cost of a video or DVD record of the experience is $85. These prices reflect a 5% discount for payment in cash.

If you are trying to decide which of these two skydiving venues to use, it turns out that both are almost exactly the same distance from the Universal Orlando theme park complex. Lake Wales is closer to the Disney World area. Deland is to the north, while Lake Wales is to the south.

Swimming

Unless you are staying at one of the large resorts, the swimming pool at your hotel may seem a bit cramped. And even then, the pool may be so crowded that you won't be able to do much more than splash about. Fortunately, there are two municipal swimming centers that offer some room for dedicated lap swimmers.

Bob Mackinson Aquatic Center

2204 Denn John Lane, Kissimmee 34744
(407) 870-7665
www.kissimmeeparksandrec.com/aquatics.html

Cost:	$4 per day for non-residents of all ages
Hours:	March to September; hours vary with the season; call
Location:	From Kissimmee follow US 192 (Vine Street)

east, veer left onto Boggy Creek Road, then left
onto Denn John Lane

This outdoor facility features an eight-lane competition pool with diving boards, a shallow depth play pool with a water playground, and a 150-meter water slide with plunge pool.

Nearby: Boggy Creek Airboat Rides, Osceola County Stadium (Houston Astros).

YMCA Aquatic and Family Center of Orlando

8422 International Drive, Orlando 32819
(407) 363-1911
www.centralfloridaymca.org

Cost:	$12 per day for non-residents of all ages
Hours:	Monday to Friday 6:00 a.m. to 9:00 p.m., Saturday 8:00 a.m. to 5:00 p.m., Sunday noon to 4:00 p.m.
Location:	From I-4 Exit 74 drive east and turn right onto International Drive, then right onto Jamaican Court

This elaborate indoor complex, which hosts regular swim meets and competitions, has three heated pools, including a diving well. All pools have lanes set aside for long distance lap swimmers.

Nearby: Pirate's Dinner Adventure, Ripley's Believe It Or Not, Sleuths, Titanic.

Thrills

A number of Orlando area attractions appeal to the thrill seekers in the crowd. Even if you are not the kind of person who wants to jump from an enormous height or hit mach 4, you may be the type who likes to watch.

SkyCoaster & G-Force

2850 Florida Plaza Boulevard, Kissimmee 34746
(407) 397-2509

Cost:	*SkyCoaster:* $40 for one person, $70 for two, $90 for three *G-Force:* Driver $30, rider $10
Hours:	Daily noon to midnight on weekends, varies during the week
Location:	On US 192 near Old Town, between Mile Markers 9 and 10

Those odd looking white towers, floodlit at night, that stick up over the Kissimmee tourist strip will lead you to *SkyCoaster* where you can swing high and low over an artificial lake. The experience begins when you are strapped into a full body harness, on your stomach, in a prone position. Up to two friends can ride with you, with discounts for the additional riders.

Next you are hoisted 300 feet in the air to the rear tower and . . . well, dropped. But this is not bungee jumping. There is no gut-wrenching jolt at the bottom. Instead you glide suspended on stainless steel airline wire along a path mathematicians call an "arcuate curve" between the other two towers. The result is a remarkably smooth and — once you recover from the initial shock — relaxing ride. After about three swings of ever decreasing arc, you are lowered to a platform and released. For $16 you can have your adventure immortalized on video.

Nearby, is **G-Force**, a drag racing simulation that uses real (but highly modified) race cars. You and a passenger sit in one of two cars and "compete" with the fellow next to you. The key to winning is having the best reaction time when the "GO" signal flashes. Once you hit the accelerator, the air-powered system built into the cars takes over and shoots you down the drag strip to a speed of 110 miles per hour in 1.8 seconds. It's quite a rush. There are several ways to immortalize your adventure; the most popular is a DVD and t-shirt combination for $15, which must be purchased before your flight.

Nearby: Naskart Family Raceway, Old Town.

SkyVenture

6805 Visitors Circle, Orlando 32819
(407) 903-1150
www.skyventureorlando.com

Cost:	All ages $39.95, plus tax
Hours:	Daily 10:00 a.m. to midnight; reservations suggested
Location:	Off I-Drive, opposite Wet 'n Wild

The folks who brought you SkyCoaster bring you this freefall skydiving adventure. SkyVenture is housed in an odd looking tower that packs quite a punch. Inside is a powerful fan that creates a 120 mile per hour rush of air in a vertical wind tunnel.

Following a course of instruction in the fine art of skydiving, you are suited up and walked high into the tower where, along with your instructor, you step out into mid air and learn to fly. The upwards rush of air keeps you aloft as your instructor takes your hand and shows you how to negotiate the updraft. Around you, a 360 degree virtual reality display heightens the sensation of free falling thousands of feet above the ground below. The entire experience takes about an hour, although the free fall portion lasts only about two minutes, which they say is about as much as first-timers can take. A video of your adventure costs $16 (VHS) or $21 (DVD).

Nearby: Fun Spot, Skull Kingdom, Universal Orlando, Wet 'n Wild.

Wakeboarding & Water Skiing

Central Florida is dotted with lakes, many of which make ideal venues for waterskiing and wakeboarding. Unfortunately, unless you happen to have friends with lakeside property and a properly equipped boat, getting in on the action is hard. Here are some helpful alternatives.

Buena Vista Watersports

13245 Lake Bryan Drive, Lake Buena Vista 32830
(407) 239-6939
www.bvwatersports.com

Cost:	$70 for half an hour, $130 for an hour, including driver and gas
Hours:	Daily 10:00 a.m. to 6:00 p.m.
Location:	From I-4 Exit 68 take SR 535 south; Buena Vista is on your left

Water skiers and wakeboarders can rent a boat and driver at this location on a small lake very conveniently located in the tourist district. If you don't feel confident enough to take a spin on skis, you can opt for a tube ride. All you need to do is sit down and hang on tight!

Nearby: Dixie Stampede, Hawaiian Rumble Adventure Golf, Lake Buena Vista Factory Outlets, Medieval Times.

Orlando Watersports Complex

8615 Florida Rock Road, Orlando 32824
(407) 251-3100
www.orlandowatersports.com

Cost:	Rates range from about $20 for an hour to $37 for an all-day pass. Weekly passes are $196 and annual passes go for $1,000.
Hours:	Daily 11:00 a.m. to 9:00 p.m.; closes at 8:00 p.m. from October through February
Location:	From I-4 Exit 74 take Sand Lake Road east, turn right on Orange Blossom Trail, left on Landstreet Road, and left on Florida Rock Road

Sort of a cross between (or among) water skiing, surfing, and skateboarding, wakeboarding is an increasingly popular sport, and this 50-acre facility has quickly become its Central Florida epicenter. Here you can take advantage of two "cable-ways," overhead tracks that take the place of the more traditional speedboats and tow you along an oval course past (or over) a series of ramps and obstacles at speeds of up to 36 miles per hour. You can choose from the double skis popular with beginners or a variety of special discs and trick skis, but the platform of choice seems to be the wakeboard.

Although beginners are welcome (or at least tolerated), this place has become a hot spot for pros and semi-pros looking to brush up on their skills. The level of ability on display can be pretty intimidating for novices. If you'd just like to come and watch, that's okay, too. There is a snack bar and a terrace-like dining area with a good view of the action. A pro shop offers the latest in equipment and accessories.

Note: Professional events are held here from time to time, which will limit your access to the facilities.

Although the complex can be seen quite easily from the toll road to the airport, it's a little tricky to find. Perhaps the easiest route for tourists is to head south from Sand Lake Road on Orange Blossom Trail (US 17/441). Just before the junction with Florida's Turnpike, turn left on Landstreet Road and drive about two miles through a heavily industrial area before turning left onto Florida Rock Road.

Nearby: Florida Mall, SeaWorld.

Chapter Thirteen:

A Who's Who of Zoos

ANIMALS HAVE ALWAYS HELD A FASCINATION FOR US HUMANS, ESPECIALLY THE younger members of our species. So it's hardly surprising that in a tourist-saturated area like Orlando, you'd find a number of attractions built around this ancient allure. The attractions I describe in this chapter run the gamut from a true zoological park, to roadside attractions, to Gatorland clones, to conservation and preservation efforts; what they have in common, of course, is animals even though the context may differ from place to place. Other animal-themed attractions such as SeaWorld, Discovery Cove, Busch Gardens, and Gatorland are described in earlier chapters.

Amazing Exotics
17951 SR 452, Umatilla 32784
(352) 821-1234
www.amazingexotics.com

Admission:	$54 and up
Hours:	Daily by appointment
Location:	North of Eustis on SR 452

What Discovery Cove (*Chapter 3*) is to dolphins, Amazing Exotics is to servals, lynxes, lemurs, and tigers. If you ever thought what fun it would be to have a tiger sink its teeth into you, this is the place to come.

Amazing Exotics, located on a sprawling ranch on the northern fringes of the Orlando area, began as a rescue facility for macaque monkeys that escaped during the filming of the *Tarzan* movies in nearby Silver Springs. Today it is a nonprofit educational facility dedicated to caring for a variety of exotic animals (many of them show biz retirees) and training animal handlers for zoos and other animal preserves. One way the facility pays its way is by offering instructional tours and close-up animal encounters with wild beasts to folks like you and me.

The priciest option here, and the one I chose, is the **Safari Tour**. Your adventure begins in a suitably hair-raising fashion. You are handed a multi-page legal disclaimer in which you attest to your understanding that you might be maimed or even killed during your visit and that this is just fine by you. And just to make sure, they require that you initial each and every bloodcurdling paragraph. Of course dealing with any wild animal carries risks, but I suspect the real vicious animals in this scenario are the ones in three-piece suits with "esquire" at the end of their names.

After you've cheerfully signed away your right to sue, a charming young animal handler, most likely a recent graduate of Amazing Exotics' training program, takes small groups of people on a tour of the compound's extensive collection of animals. It's a bit like a visit to the zoo except that all of the animals here have a personal story — one is a rescued throwaway, another a former Las Vegas star — and a personal relationship with your tour guide. The narration has the usual tidbits of natural history lore but the emphasis is on the nuts and bolts and challenges of caring for these animals. It's an insider's viewpoint and it offers the visitor an unusual perspective on the ironies of working with caged wild animals. The guide's enthusiasm is contagious and I'm sure many guests contemplate a career change at some point during the tour.

But the main attraction, and the reason people shell out serious money to take the Safari Tour, is the chance to get up close and personal with animals that few people are lucky enough to approach closely, let alone touch. There are two separate animal encounters, with primates and large cats. Which exact animals you might interact with when you visit is hard to predict. It will depend to some extent which animals are how old at the time of your visit and which animals seem to be in the right mood to tolerate a bunch of fawning tourists. (One of the major elements in the training program is the fine art of how to "read" an animal's facial expression and body language.)

The primate encounter, which takes place indoors, involves five or six small primates. On the tour I took that meant a brown lemur, two small siamang apes, and two capuchin monkeys, one of them a minuscule specimen that had been born prematurely and would never reach full size. We adults sat crossed-legged on the floor while the primates literally bounced off the walls and off us, landing on our heads and shoulders, licking our hair and swinging from our arms. It was as much fun as, well, a barrel full of monkeys.

The finale is the big cat encounter. During our tour I had heard of a five-month-old tiger cub named Apollo and asked if we could visit with him as our big cat encounter. All the other tour guests seconded the motion and, after some discussion, it was decided that Apollo and his handler could oblige us. While the small cats ignored us, Apollo seemed to see us as a chance to practice bringing down large prey and he made regular attempts on our legs. He sure looked adorable and cuddly but he was a wiry little guy with incredibly sharp teeth. Petting a tiger cub had long been a dream for me, so the scrape on my calf was a small price to pay. (In fact, I went out of my way to brag about it in the days that followed, much to my wife's embarrassment.)

Amazing Exotics is the antithesis of a theme park, which is a major part of its immense charm. Staff members wear faded blue jeans with gaping holes at the knees or wander about stripped to the waist, showing off rippling muscles and lavish tattoos.

The facility is hoping to expand and perhaps things will be less casual by the time you visit, but I certainly hope not.

The three-hour Safari Tour described above costs $94. The two-hour **Encounter Tour** includes the tour and a hands-on encounter with two to three small primates and costs $54.

For those who have visited before or who have very specific interests, Amazing Exotics offers a number of options that skip the tour and focus on the animal encounters. They are the **Tiger Encounter** ($74) and the **Primate Encounter** ($25 for each primate).

Since Amazing Exotics is a bona fide nonprofit organization, no tax is added to these prices and the admission price is treated as a contribution, making it tax deductible (at least for US citizens). Reservations are mandatory. When you call, you will be booked for a specific time and you are expected to arrive promptly. Since slots for the Safari and Encounter Tours are strictly limited, it is advisable to book as far in advance as possible.

To reach Amazing Exotics from Orlando drive north on US 441, to SR 19 north, to CR 452. When you see the sign that welcomes you to Marion County, look for the entrance on your right. Depending on where in Orlando you start your journey, the trip should take about an hour and a quarter to an hour and a half.

Nearby: Not a thing. This really is the country.

Audubon Center for Birds of Prey

1101 Audubon Way, Maitland 32751
(407) 644-0190
www.audubonofflorida.org

Admission:	Adults $5; children (3 to 12) $4; under 3 **free**
Hours:	Tuesday to Sunday 10:00 a.m. to 4:00 p.m.
Location:	East of I-4, near Exit 88

One of the most enchanting animal encounters to be found in the Orlando area is also one of the cheapest. The Center for Birds of Prey is an endeavor of the Florida Audubon Society. Each year it takes in about 700 wounded and orphaned raptors from all over Florida, tends to their wounds, and nurses them back to health with the ultimate goal of releasing them back into the wild. About 40% make it.

You won't be able to see the rehabilitation process; these birds are shielded from public view lest they become habituated to humans, thus lessening their odds for survival back in the wild. You will be able to see from a distance the "flight barn" and the "rehabilitation mews," odd looking structures with slatted wooden walls, in which injured birds are nursed back to health, and view a behind-the-scenes video.

You can also see, in a series of attractive aviaries, birds whose injuries are so severe that they cannot be released. Here they lead the good life (at least they eat well and regularly) and perform a useful role in educating Florida school children and others about the wonders of wildlife and the need to protect it. There are about 20 different species of raptors housed here. They range from tiny screech owls to vultures. There are also a fair number of ospreys, red-tailed hawks, kites, and others. A pair of bald eagles, Prairie and T.J., are particularly fascinating. A short video tells the story of their offbeat love affair and touching attempts to have young.

A visit here can be an educational as well as an uplifting experience. While here, I learned for the first time of the 1916 Migratory Bird Treaty Act that made it illegal to own or transport even a single feather from these birds. The Center collects every feather from molting birds, as well as feathers from specimens that don't survive. They are turned over to the government, which in turn distributes them to Native American tribes for whom the feathers of eagles and other species have ritual significance.

A boardwalk leads down to a charming gazebo set in the wetlands along the shore of Lake Sybelia. A small museum tells the history of the Florida Audubon Society. Guided tours are available by reservation for groups of 10 or more and it's a good idea to call ahead to find out when volunteers will be on hand to answer questions. If a group comes through while you are visiting, feel free to join it. Finding Birds of Prey is a little tricky but it's worth it. Call ahead for detailed directions.

Nearby: Maitland Art Center, Maitland Historical Museum.

Back to Nature Wildlife Refuge

18515 East Colonial Drive, Orlando 32820
(407) 568-5138
www.btn-wildlife.org

Admission:	**Free**. Donations requested
Hours:	Daily 9:00 a.m. to 4:00 p.m.
Location:	East of central Orlando

Located incongruously next to an auto repair shop, with which it shares an office, this nonprofit organization is dedicated to the four R's — Rescue, Raise, Rehabilitate, and Release. In the average year, it plays host to some 2,500 critters, but unlike Birds of Prey (see above), Back To Nature Wildlife Refuge takes on all comers, except common household pets like dogs and cats. The ultimate goal is to release their charges back into the wild, a goal that often proves elusive. What you will see when you visit are the animals that, for a variety of reasons, will be living out their lives in captivity. Many of the cages are marked with the nicknames and histories of their occupants.

The tales told about these animals are a litany of abuse, abandonment, stupidity, and the random cruelty of nature and (more often) mankind. There are "throw away" pets sold by unscrupulous dealers and abandoned when their owners discovered that porcupines, raccoons, and wild African cats don't make the charming pets they'd imagined. Then there are the birds and beasts damaged by pesticides or wounded by bullets. There are also many animals orphaned in the wild or born with disabilities that would have quickly killed them had they not been rescued first. Among the more impressive residents here are cougars, bobcats, bald eagles, and a hybrid wolf. A small nursery looks after the littlest guests, including baby raccoons and fledgling birds.

Back To Nature is a labor of love of David and Carmen Shaw and a dedicated group of volunteers. Donations are requested subtly via donation boxes scattered throughout the property. Many of the animal enclosures bear the names of donors who made them possible. It is unlikely you will leave without becoming a donor.

Nearby: Fort Christmas Historical Park, Jungle Adventures, Orlando Wetlands Park.

C.A.R.E. Foundation

4609 West Ponkan Road, Apopka 32712
(407) 247-8948
www.thecarefoundation.org

Admission:	**Free**; donations requested
Hours:	By appointment only
Location:	Just off SR 441 and SR 429

C.A.R.E. stands for Creating Animal Respect Education. Like Back To Nature, above, it is a scrappy little nonprofit organization dedicated to rescuing abandoned animals, with an accent on "exotics." It is also a working educational facility with a full schedule of programs on Florida wildlife that it provides for both the tourist trade and local schoolchildren, so advance reservations are a must. You will find it down a dirt road on ten acres of Florida pine woods, in a ramshackle collection of barns and volunteer-built animal pens. It's worth seeking out.

Among the more impressive animals here are an immense Siberian tiger, a jaguar, and several gorgeous Florida panthers. There are also homelier charges like Daphney, a duck with a broken beak, and Truffles, a Vietnamese potbellied pig, who have become the best of friends.

Visitors are treated to a guided tour by a friendly and knowledgeable volunteer. You'll learn the stories behind the animals and may even get to pet one or two. One of the most enjoyable aspects of the tour is just getting to see the obvious affection and interaction between the volunteers and their charges; it's really something to see a panther light up and start purring when her best friend approaches the enclosure.

At press time, they were just moving to their new facility and construction was still in progress, but the plans call for one area for their "exotic" charges — Florida native wildlife such as panthers, the mischievous raccoon siblings Thelma and Louise, alligators and some impressive snapping turtles — and another for the miscellaneous abandoned pets and farm animals the organization takes under its wing. C.A.R.E. helps support itself by taking its animals to Orlando area resorts, festivals and such for educational displays. Check the web site for a calendar of upcoming public events.

Nearby: Central Florida Zoological Park, Kelly Park, King's Landing Canoe Rental, Rock Springs Run State Reserve, Wekiwa Springs State Park.

Central Florida Zoological Park

3755 NW Highway 17-92, Sanford 32747
(407) 323-4450
www.centralfloridazoo.org

Admission:	Adults $9, children (3 to 12) $5, seniors (60+) $7, half price for all Thursdays 9 a.m. to 10:00 a.m.; **free** parking

Hours: Daily 9:00 a.m. to 5:00 p.m. Closed
                      Thanksgiving and Christmas

Location: From I-4 Exit 104 drive south on US 17-92 and
                      follow signs, less than a mile.

The Central Florida Zoo can't hold a candle to its bigger cousins in the Bronx and San Diego, but it does wonders with what it has. The collection is small, with an understandable strength in local species, many of which will be found in the excellent herpetarium (snake house). Among the more "exotic" species are kangaroos, two elephants, a clouded leopard, and cheetahs in a lovely habitat viewed through one-way glass. Other impressive specimens include a rare and endangered Amur leopard and some delightfully colorful Hyacinth macaws.

What makes this zoo special is its design and layout. Lovely boardwalks carry you between exhibits arrayed under a sheltering canopy of oaks. Especially nice is the **Florida Nature Walk** that snakes through a wooded and swampy area of the zoo grounds. Signs along the way do an excellent job of explicating Central Florida fauna and explaining the way in which minor differences in altitude produce major differences in plant life. The **Butterfly Sensory Garden** has been planted with flowers and herbs that attract these colorful insects for your delight.

On weekends and holidays there are animal demonstrations involving the elephants, along with primate and feline feeding programs. Volunteer "docents" also roam the park with one of some 40 species used for educational purposes. You may get a chance to touch a boa or pet a possum. The zoo has a bare-bones snack bar, serving inexpensive hot dog and burger fare, with a lovely outdoor seating area nearby. Across from the entrance, there are sheltered picnic tables and barbecue pits, as well as a small carousel ($2) and an eight-minute, three-quarter-mile miniature train ride (adults $3, children $2).

Nearby: C.A.R.E., Kelly Park, King's Landing Canoe Rental, Rock Springs Run State Reserve, Wekiwa Springs State Park.

Green Meadows Farm

1368 South Poinciana Boulevard, Kissimmee 34741
(407) 846-0770
www.greenmeadowsfarm.com

Admission: $19, including tax, for all those 3 years old and up;
                      Florida residents $17; seniors (55+) $15; annual
                      pass $40

Hours: Daily 9:30 a.m. to 4:00 p.m.

Location: Six miles south of Highway 192

This is where kids meet kids — and piglets, and ducklings, and chicks. If you have little ones between the ages of three and seven, this cleverly conceived and well-run petting farm is sure to be a favorite memory of their Orlando visit. Better yet, let their grandparents take them! Green Meadows is an ideal place for this sort of trans-generational bonding experience. Meanwhile, you and your spouse can take the in-room jacuzzi out for a spin.

The ethos of Green Meadows Farm is pretty well summed up by the quote from Luther Burbank that greets you on your arrival: "Every child should have mudpies, frogs, grasshoppers, waterbugs, tadpoles, mud turtles, elderberries, wild strawberries, acorns, chestnuts, trees to climb, animals to pet, hay fields, pine cones, rocks to roll, lizards, huckleberries, and hornets. Any child who has been deprived of these has been deprived of the best part of their education."

Green Meadows Farm is spread out over 50 acres under the dappled shade of moss-draped southern oaks. The farm is experienced via a guided tour that lasts about two hours. If the park is busy, you may be asked to wait until the next tour begins but on slower days you'll be escorted to the tour in progress. ("When you get back to the chickens, you'll know the tour's over.") If you like, you can simply stay with the tour and repeat it over and over.

The tour includes a short ride on the farm train and a bumpy tractor-powered hayride, but the real stars of the show are the animals. This is not a working farm but more of a "farm zoo" with widely spaced pens holding a fairly representative cross section of American farm animals. There are also a few more exotic species, like llama, buffalo, and ostriches, that are showing up on your trendier farms. Visitors can enter most of the pens for a close-up encounter. This is the city kid's chance to hold a chicken, pet a baby pig, feed a goat, milk a cow, chase a goose, and meet a turkey that has yet to be served at Thanksgiving. Squawking guinea hens and stately peacocks (including a stunning all-white specimen) roam freely about the grounds. And, of course, there is a pony ride. The little ones love every minute. For doting parents and grandparents, it's a photographic field day.

The tour guides are the antithesis of theme park attendants. There are no spiffy uniforms or carefully rehearsed spiels here. These folks look and talk like they're down on the farm, dirty jeans and all. It's truly refreshing. But don't expect to escape the edutainment. You'll be treated to spot quizzes ("Who can tell me what a baby goose is called?") and little known facts ("The pig is a very clean animal.") as the guide shepherds you from pen to pen. Thanks to this tour I now know that the gestation period of a pig is three months, three weeks, and three days.

Of course everyone's favorites are the farm babies; you can increase your odds of seeing them by visiting during spring or around harvest time. During October there is pumpkin picking, another winner with the wee set.

There's little in the way of food. At the General Store, sandwiches are about $3 and ice cream bars about half that. Soft drinks are available from vending machines. You can also bring a cooler and have a picnic. Judging from the number of tables provided, quite a few people do just that.

Remember to wear sensible shoes — this is a farm, after all, and after a rain, it can get muddy. The tour is long and covers a fair amount of ground. You can rent a "little red wagon" for $3 in which to lug the kids.

Nearby: Old Town, Osceola Environmental Study Center, Osceola Extreme Sports.

Jungle Adventures

26205 East Colonial Drive, Christmas 32709
(407) 568-2885
www.jungleadventures.com

Admission: Adults $17.50, children (3 to 11) $8.50, seniors
             (60+) $14, all plus tax
Hours: Daily 9:30 a.m. to 5:00 p.m.
Location: On SR 50, about 17 miles east of Orlando

It's hard to miss Old Swampy. He's a 200-foot foam and cement alligator stretched smilingly alongside SR 50 on the way to the Space Coast. Step into (or more precisely, around) his jaws and you enter Jungle Adventures, a small attraction that has some things in common with Gatorland (see *Chapter 4*) but a few surprises of its own.

At its most basic, Jungle Adventures is a small zoo with a familiar cast of characters — two black bears (Boris and Natasha), some spider monkeys, some crocs, macaws and cockatoos, bobcats, wolves, and coatimundi. The zoo's most distinguished specimens are its hybrid panther-cougars, including siblings Sparkles and Junior. But mostly there are alligators. Jungle Adventures is part of a larger alligator farming operation. There are some 200 gators living in the 20-acre park but just a stone's throw away are 10,000 more being grown out for their skin and meat.

What sets Jungle Adventures apart, and makes a visit worth consideration, are its fascinating setting and its shows. The setting is in the midst of a swamp, with the main zoo across a bridge and completely surrounded by water fed from a sulfurous spring. At first it seems that there's something terribly wrong with the water; it's completely covered by what looks like a chartreuse slime. Actually, it's duckweed, a tiny four-leafed water plant that grows in the billions. It adds a marvelously primordial touch to the alligators that swim through it, coating their horny hides with gooey green. Two short **jungle nature trails** take you around the back of the animal cages and let you take a close look at the natural Florida setting from the safety of a boardwalk.

The shows at Jungle Adventures are refreshingly low key, one might almost say amateurish, although in the very best sense of the term. There are three shows and a boat ride that are timed so that you can move seamlessly from one to the next. A complete cycle takes about two and a half hours and there are four cycles each day.

The 15-minute **pontoon boat ride** circles the island zoo as gators swish thorough the duckweed, leaving a telltale trail in the green coating on the water's surface. Along the way, your guide tells tales of Jungle Adventures' past and present, and its future plans. An eclectic **animal show** features a small alligator, which everyone gets a chance to hold while their picture is taken. Next comes a snake or two, draped languorously on the presenter's shoulders. And if you're really lucky, you'll get a chance to pet a cougar.

In the **Indian Village** tour, you will hear fascinating lore about the Calusa, Seminole, and Cherokee tribes and have the opportunity to buy Native American flutes, necklaces, and dream-catchers.

Finally, there is an **alligator feeding show** reminiscent of the *Jumparoo* at Gatorland. Sometimes, the gators are fed from a dock-like platform over the water, but from time to time the handler chooses to work the shore, drawing the enormous reptiles from the green waters to leap and snap just a few feet away from the audience.

On a more downbeat note, it must be said that Jungle Adventures is showing its age. On a recent visit, there were many signs of "deferred maintenance" and the level of animal care left something to be desired in my opinion. I suspect this has more to do with budgetary restraints than willful neglect, but those who might be put off by this are hereby forewarned.

Nearby: Back To Nature Wildlife Refuge, Fort Christmas Historical Park, Orlando Wetlands Park.

Reptile World Serpentarium

5705 East Irlo Bronson Highway, St. Cloud 34771
(407) 892-6905

Admission:	Adults $5.75, students (6 to 17) $4.75, children (3 to 5) $3.75; prices include tax
Hours:	Tuesday to Sunday 9:00 a.m. to 5:30 p.m.
Location:	East of St. Cloud, about 9 miles east of Florida Turnpike Exit 244.

This unassuming cinder block and stucco building houses an impressive collection (over 50 species) of snakes from around the world, ranging from the familiar and innocuous to the exotic and deadly. Here you'll find the Australian taipan, considered by some to be the world's deadliest snake, as well as a splendid 18-foot king cobra. All told, there are six species of cobra and 11 kinds of rattlesnakes. There are also snakes you may never see elsewhere, like the brilliant pea green East African green mamba and its less startling but nonetheless beautiful West African cousin. The snakes are housed in modest glass-fronted pens along a darkened corridor. Snakes are the main course, but there are also a 14-foot gator sulking in a shallow, murky pool, a passel of iguanas, and a pond full of turtles.

If all Reptile World had to offer was its snake displays, it might be recommended only to the certified snake fancier. But this is a working venom farm (if that's the right term). Though there may be only 50 snakes on public display, behind the scenes are hundreds of venomous snakes just waiting to be milked for their valuable venom. Reptile World ships this precious commodity worldwide for use in medical and herpetological research. The regular milking of these dangerous snakes is done in public and makes Reptile World more than just another snake house.

Venom shows are scheduled at noon and 3:00 p.m. daily. Sometimes the shows start a bit late, but any wait will quickly be forgotten once the show starts. After bringing out a large snake for guests to hold, owner George Van Horn retreats behind a glass wall to take care of business. About half a dozen snakes are plucked from their boxes and coaxed into sinking their fangs through a clear membrane stretched over a collection glass. The glasses range in size from small test tubes used for coral snakes to hefty pilsner glasses used for large rattlers and cobras. The view can't be beat; you are just three feet away from these fanged wonders and will be thankful for the glass window between you and the snakes.

The entire show is fascinating but the large snakes are the most impressive. The Eastern diamondback rattlesnake, the largest of its kind, bares huge fangs and spits copious venom into the collection glass. The black and white spitting cobra requires special care. As its name suggests, it spits its venom into its victim's eyes and the recommended treatment is to wash the eyes with urine. The monocled cobra, so called because of the eye-like marking on the back of its head, emerges from its box with hood flaring and head darting rapidly about. This is serious, not to mention dangerous business. Van Horn once received a near-fatal bite from a king cobra while 30 school children looked on enthralled, convinced it was part of the show.

Reptile World is on the extreme outer fringe of the Orlando tourist circuit. For anyone who has ever been fascinated by snakes, it's well worth the detour. By all means time your visit to the venom shows.

Chapter Fourteen:

Gardens & Edens

FOR THOSE WHO FEEL THE ORLANDO THEME PARK EXPERIENCE IS "SO PLASTIC!,"
help is at hand. Within the Orlando metropolitan area, or just a short ride away, are private gardens, public parks, and wilderness tracts where cool waters, fresh breezes, and quiet forests await to soothe the simulation- and stimulation-weary tourist.

Here I describe the Harry P. Leu Gardens, right in the heart of Orlando, and the spectacular Historic Bok Sanctuary in Lake Wales, a short drive from Orlando. Of course, these attractions involve the cunning hand of man and are, in a way, just as artificial as any theme park — although some would argue they are a good deal more beautiful.

Then there are the state, county, and city parks, many of which have been only slightly modified by humans. It comes as a surprise to many visitors that the "real Florida" (to use a phrase pushed by the state's public relations campaigns) lies all around them. Just a short drive from your motel, you can hike miles and miles of pristine trails and never see another human, or swim in a crystal clear spring bubbling up from deep in the earth, or canoe down a river that still looks much as it did when the first Europeans arrived in this part of Florida.

This is nature, let us not forget, so in addition to sunscreen, a good bug repellent will come in handy for hikers. Be aware too that deer ticks carrying Lyme disease are found here. Common-sense precautions should be used with wildlife — don't pick anything up and don't feed the alligators (it's against the law!). The words to live by when visiting these beautiful areas are: "Take nothing but pictures, kill nothing but time, leave nothing but footprints."

The parks listed here are just the beginning. If this type of unspoiled recreation is to your taste, you may want to venture farther afield — to Blue Springs State Park to the north, where manatees come to warm up in the winter, or to Homosassa Springs State Park to the west, or to Lake Kissimmee State Park to the south. An excellent (and free) guide to Florida's state parks is available from the Department of

Environmental Protection, Division of Recreation and Parks, MS#535, 3900 Commonwealth Boulevard, Tallahassee, FL 32399-3000. Or ask for *Florida State Parks . . . the Real Florida* at the ranger station of any state park. For more on Orlando's city parks, go to the city's web site, www.cityoforlando.net, and click on "Parks."

Big Tree Park

General Hutchinson Parkway, Longwood 32750
No phone

Admission:	**Free**
Hours:	Daily 8:00 a.m. to sunset
Location:	Take I-4 Exit 94, drive east on SR 434; turn left on Route 17-92 and left on General Hutchinson

Pay a brief visit to this small Seminole County park to gawk at the oldest cypress tree in the U.S. "The Senator" (nicknamed to honor the senator who donated the land) stands 126 feet high and measures 47 feet around. It's estimated that the behemoth is some 3,500 years old.

Enchanted Forest Sanctuary

444 Columbia Boulevard, Titusville 32780
(321) 264-5185
www.eelbrevard.com

Admission:	**Free**
Hours:	Daily 9:00 a.m. to 5:00 p.m.
Location:	From I-95 Exit 215 drive east on SR 405 for 3.7 miles

The Environmentally Endangered Lands Program of Brevard County has created this picture perfect learning vehicle to teach people about the unique and subtle topography of coastal Florida. There are attempts to do this in other parks around the region, but none that I've seen do it as well as the Enchanted Forest.

Some 3.7 miles of self-guided trails through a portion of this 393-acre preserve take the visitor through six distinct environments, from scruffy, sandy scrub ridges to lush tropical forests that seem, well, enchanted. You can use the laminated trail guides to educate yourself to what you're seeing or just use the beautifully maintained trails for rest, relaxation, or exercise. A small interpretive center offers cleverly designed exhibits that further explain the surprising way in which a few feet of elevation in the Florida ecosystem can mean a startlingly different plant environment. There's also a gift shop.

Nearby: Police Hall of Fame, Kennedy Space Center, Warbird Air Museum.

Forever Florida and Crescent J Ranch

4755 North Kenansville Road
St. Cloud, FL 34773
(866) 854-3837

(407) 957-9794
www.floridaeco-safaris.com

Admission:	**Free** admission and parking; there is a charge for most activities
Hours:	Daily 8:00 a.m. to 9:00 p.m.
Location:	Take US 192 east from Kissimmee for about 24 miles to Holopaw; turn south on US 441 for about 7 miles to the entrance on your left. (The address given above is the corporate office.)

Did you know that wild hogs kill more people than any other wild animal? Did you know that red carpet lichen grows only where the air is especially pure? Did you know that the berries of poison ivy plants are the sole source of vitamin C for the animals of Florida's forests? These are just a few of the fascinating facts you'll learn as you explore a patch of the "real Florida" that is as much a family affair as it is a tourist attraction.

Forever Florida was founded by Dr. Bill Broussard as a living monument to his son Allen, a devoted ecologist who died well before his time. The attraction combines Dr. Broussard's ranch (he's a tenth generation rancher as well as an ophthalmologist) with a swampy wilderness tract next door that had been sold in parcels as part of a classic Florida land scam back in the sixties. It was in these woods, that young Allen fell in love with Nature and found his vocation. Also part of Forever Florida is the former country retreat of another doctor, whose house will be converted into a bed and breakfast and whose private grass airstrip welcomes fly-ins so long as they call ahead.

You begin your visit to Forever Florida at the **Visitor Center**, which contains a gift shop and restaurant. Near the Visitor Center are a free **petting zoo and pony rides** ($8 by reservation). But the real attraction here is access to the nearby wilderness, much of which has remained untouched by the hand of man, despite the fact that this part of Florida was a thriving logging center in the nineteenth century.

You can reach the wilds in a number of ways: by foot, on horseback, or on a wacky-looking green "Swamp Buggy" designed by Dr. Broussard and unique to Forever Florida. Most people choose the last alternative.

Your tour vehicle is a 32-seat open-sided coach raised well above the ground on large tractor tires. The bucket seats are comfortable and the tour guides extremely knowledgeable experts, many with degrees in biology or ecology.

There are tours at 10:30 a.m. and 1:30 p.m. On the tour I took, we sighted white-tailed deer, armadillos, gators, wild turkey, and gopher tortoises. We even sighted some of those elusive wild hogs, albeit in hog traps. One lucky tour group sighted the Florida panther that roams this preserve. There are fewer than 30 left in the wild, so don't count on seeing one on your visit. Photographers should make sure to bring along their best telephoto lenses.

The highlight of the tour is the narration by your guide. These folks love this scruffy patch of Florida wilderness and it shows. They mix an in-depth knowledge of the local ecology with a passion for its preservation. You will leave this tour knowing why you should never buy cypress mulch for your garden and why wild hogs (descended from those abandoned by the Spaniards when they discovered there was no gold in Florida) should be removed from the Florida ecosystem. In fact, you will see ample evidence of the damage the preserve's estimated 800 hogs inflict on the local ecology. Those trapped hogs, by the way, are fattened up on yummy farm feed and then relocated elsewhere or given away to local groups for barbecues.

The **motorized tours** cost $25 ($20 for children 6 to 12; kids under six are **free**) and last about two hours. The **guided horseback tours** are offered daily, by reservation only, and cost $37.50 for one hour, $57 for two, and $73 for three; the three-hour tour includes lunch. There is no reduced price for children (age 10 and up only) on these tours. The hiking fee is a flat $5 per person per day, but at least one member of the group must be a member of a nationally recognized group such as the Audubon Society. This rule was instituted to cut down on littering by ignorant tourists.

The **Cypress Restaurant** offers a straightforward and familiar menu of country-style cooking, although you are not likely to find the Fried Gator Tail Plate on too many other local menus. It's open 9:00 a.m. to 5:00 p.m. daily and until 8:00 p.m. on Friday and Saturday. The gift shop sells clothing, some interesting crafts, and books on Florida ecology and cooking.

Forever Florida offers an evolving menu of special events and programs. One recent offering was a two-night sleepover for kids that included a nighttime outing to find nocturnal critters. To celebrate Earth Day, the preserve hosted "Cracker Survivor Island" inspired by the TV show. Typically, when a special event is on, there will be a modest parking charge. Call ahead or check the web site to see what's going to be on during your visit.

Historic Bok Sanctuary

1151 Tower Boulevard, Lake Wales 33853
(863) 676-1408
www.boksanctuary.org

Admission:	Adults $10, children (5 to 12) $3
Hours:	Daily 8:00 a.m. to 6:00 p.m. (last admission at 5:00 p.m.)
Location:	Off Burns Avenue in Lake Wales. Take US 27 South to Mountain Lake Cutoff and follow the signs

Once upon a time, before the age of Leona Helmsley and Donald Trump, the wealthy knew how to spend their money. One such individual was Edward W. Bok, a Dutch immigrant born in 1863 who came to the United States at the age of six and made his fortune as a writer and magazine publisher. In the twenties, after his retirement, he set out to create an Eden on an unprepossessing patch of land whose only claim to fame was that it was reputedly the highest point on the Florida peninsula. He enlisted Frederick Law Olmstead, Jr. (son of the creator of New York's Central Park and a major landscape architect in his own right) to do the landscaping and hired noted architect Milton B. Medary to build a setting for a very special musical instru-

ment. In 1929, he presented the result as a gift to the American pe
is the Bok Tower and its magnificent carillon that stands majestica'
an artfully designed wooded park, specifically conceived as a refuge from
of "the world."

Historic Bok Sanctuary, now a National Historic Landmark, is a very special and a very quiet experience. Unlike nearby Cypress Gardens, where the landscaping is over-the-top and in-your-face, the effect here is far more subtle, almost ethereal. The bark-chip covered paths through the woods are meant for leisurely strolls and quiet moments alone with one's thoughts. The vistas, powerful as they are, are contemplative and softly romantic.

Olmstead's design is devilishly clever in the way he leads you to the tower. He only lets you see it when he wants you to. Your first glimpse is across a reflecting pool, framed by palm fronds and Spanish moss. Then it vanishes as you walk through a palm-fringed glade to approach more closely. Suddenly, the tower rises above you, standing on an island barely larger than its base, surrounded by a moat crossed by marble bridges and guarded by massive wrought iron gates. It's as if you have come upon a magical remnant of an ancient city in a storybook land, part cathedral, part castle keep.

The storybook aspect is heightened by the pink and gray Georgia marble that forms the tower's base and accents its flanks, the odd and complex sundial mounted on the side of the south wall, the highly polished brass door on the north, the mysterious red door behind the ornately carved balustrade above the sundial, by the very fact that you cannot cross the moat for a closer look. It must be a wondrous experience on a foggy morning.

The tower was never intended to welcome guests; the only way to get a look inside is to see the orientation film screened at the **Visitors Center** on a regular schedule. The tower exists solely to house the 60 precisely tuned bronze bells operated by a massive keyboard played with the fists. The carillon occupies the upper third of the structure. The unique sound produced by this massive instrument rolls out across the surrounding woods through 35-foot high grilles in the form of Art Deco mosaics of drooping trees and animals in colorful shades of turquoise and purple.

Every afternoon at 1:00 and 3:00 there is a 45-minute carillon recital. Many of the pieces played were composed specifically for carillon, others have been adapted to the unique requirements of the massive instrument. A schedule of "Daily Carillon Music" lists the day's program, everything from old folk tunes to opera. It's a wonderful experience on a warm, sunny day and, unless you're a carillon connoisseur, probably unlike any other concert you've ever heard. When the performance is live (rather than recorded), a video monitor mounted in what appears to be a small green shelter lets you watch the carillonneur play.

Tip: Most people sit on the grass or on benches under the shady oak trees near the tower's base during the recitals. You will have a better musical experience if you move somewhat farther away. Stroll down the slope away from the tower until the tower's mosaic grilles reappear over the tops of the oak trees. Then find a spot with an unobstructed view of the top of the tower. This way, the music will roll over the tree tops and cascade down the slope towards you.

Don't leave without exploring the rest of the grounds. Past the reflecting pool that marked your approach to the tower lies an "exedra," a semicircular marble bench that looks out from the top of Iron Mountain to the west. At the northern edge of the grounds is a more recent, and ingenious, addition, the **Window By The Pond Nature Observatory**. It's a small wooden building on the lip of a pond. You sit behind a large picture window, unseen by the wildlife outside. A sign notes that this is nature's show and that the performance schedule is erratic. On the back wall are drawings of the local animals you might glimpse from your hiding place.

From here you can take a one-mile hike through the **Pine Ridge Preserve**, one of the few remaining fragments of the sort of longleaf pine forest that once covered millions of acres of the southeastern United States. Preserving this patch of woods is not as easy as it may sound. A carefully orchestrated series of controlled burns is used to mimic ageless natural processes. Otherwise, evergreen oaks would invade the habitat and eventually kill the pines with their shady branches. An informative brochure that explicates the habitat can be found at the trailhead.

The **Visitors Center** houses a modest but finely executed exhibit that provides background on Bok, the tower, and the carillon it houses. The cafeteria-style **Carillon Cafe** serves simple sandwich platters and hot dogs. There is also a tasteful gift shop where you can get cassettes and CDs of Bok Tower carillon recitals. It carries a good selection of books about gardening, wildlife, conservation, and Florida's natural wonders. Framed photos and posters of the gardens make nice souvenirs.

In 1970, the Bok Tower Gardens Foundation acquired the nearby **Pinewood Estate**, formerly known as "El Retiro," a palatial summer home built for a steel mogul. Although it dates to only 1929, it has the look of a much older Mediterranean villa and has been meticulously restored inside. Both the house and the grounds were designed by architects associated with the Olmstead firm. You can tour the house by appointment.

There are daily tours November to April; the rest of the year, tours are offered only Wednesday through Sunday. Tours are limited to 16 guests. The price is $6 for adults, $3 for children 5 to 12. From Thanksgiving to Christmas, the house is decorated for the holidays and is open without reservations. To check the tour schedule (always a good idea) and make reservations, call (863) 676-1408.

The Sanctuary is accessible to the physically challenged. It offers complimentary wheelchairs and strollers and mobility vehicles for a fee.

Nearby: Cypress Gardens, Florida Skydiving Center, Lake Wales Arts Center, Spook Hill.

Kelly Park, Rock Springs

400 East Kelly Park Road, Apopka 32712
(407) 889-4179
http://parks.orangecountyfl.net

Admission:	Adults and children $1, children under 5 **free**
Hours:	Daily 9:00 a.m. to 7:00 p.m. in summer; 8:00 a.m.

to 6:00 p.m. in winter

Location: Take Rock Springs Road north from Apopka;
                          right onto Kelly Park Road and follow signs

This 248-acre Orange County park is built around one of the Apopka area. crystal clear springs. As its name suggests, Rock Springs bubbles up from a cleft in a rock outcropping and, instead of spreading out into a pool, becomes a swiftly running stream that quickly slows to a meander. The activity of choice here, and the major reason for the park's obvious popularity, is riding down the stream in an inner tube or on a float.

Kids, and not a few grown-ups, jump into the headwaters by the dozens and bob and splash their way downstream for about a mile. The trip takes about 25 minutes at a leisurely float. There are exits from the river along the way, and an excellently maintained network of boardwalks (with flooring designed to protect the barefooted) lets you carry your tube back to the beginning for another go. You can also go down without a tube but, for most adults at least, the stream is too shallow for swimming during most of its course. At the middle of the tubing course, the stream blossoms into a series of lagoons and pools that form the centerpiece of the park. This is the place to come for a cooling, if somewhat crowded, swim. Or join the sunbathers thronging the shores and islands. This is a great park for kids and, if you don't have any, you may feel a bit overwhelmed by other people's.

Tubes are not available in the park, so unless you bring your own, stop at one of the tube rental shops near the park entrance. The cost is modest, about $5 for a day's rental.

Most of the rest of the park is given over to nicely shaded picnic tables, most with a barbecue nearby. The park also offers camping sites ($10 a night for Orange County residents, $15 for all others); electricity is another $3. Your admission receipt lets you leave the park and return the same day. No pets are allowed in the park, and there's no fishing here.

Nearby: C.A.R.E., Central Florida Zoological Park, Kelly Park, King's Landing Canoe Rental, Rock Springs Run State Reserve, Wekiwa Springs State Park.

Leu Gardens

1920 North Forest Avenue, Orlando, 32803
(407) 246-2620
www.leugardens.org

Admission: Adults $5, children (grades K-12) $1
Hours: Daily 9:00 a.m. to 5:00 p.m. Closed Christmas day.
Location: Take I-4 Exit 85 (Princeton Street), go east to
                          Mills (US 17-92) and turn right. Turn left on Vir-
                          ginia Drive and follow signs

Strolling through Harry P. Leu's magnificent formal gardens on the shores of Lake Rowena, it's hard to believe that you're in the heart of the city, just a short drive from the bustling "Centroplex" as Orlando rather inelegantly refers to its central business district.

There's nothing inelegant about this luxurious estate, however. Deeded to the city by a local industrial supplies magnate and amateur botanist, the 50 acres of manicured grounds and artfully designed gardens offer a delicious respite from the cares of the world.

Camellias were Harry Leu's first love and the place is full of them — over 2,000, making this the largest documented collection of camellias in North America. But there are many other trees, flowers, and ornamental plants to catch the fancy of amateur gardeners, who will appreciate the meticulous signage that provides the full scientific name for the thousands of species represented. They can flag down a passing staff member, who will be more than happy to answer their questions. The rest of us will simply enjoy strolling through this artfully constructed monument to the gardener's art, stopping now and then to smell the roses.

The estate is given over to a number of gardens that blend seamlessly one into another. Camellias bloom under tall Southern oaks dripping with Spanish moss in the North and South woods, while the palm garden allows botanists to test the hardiness of various species during the nippy Central Florida winters. In the center is a formal rose garden that is at its best from April through October. The Tropical Stream Garden features tropical vines and plants that are native to or can be grown in Florida. By the lake, the Native Wetland Garden is home to swamp hibiscus, lizard's tail, loblolly, and dwarf wax myrtle, all under the shade of stately cypress trees.

Another not-to-be-missed highlight is the 50-foot floral clock. The mechanism was purchased in Scotland and now sits on an intricately planted sloping hill at the foot of a formal garden. Later, a stroll down to the lake takes you past the Ravine Garden, lush with tropical plants. At the water's edge a spacious wooden terrace offers a peaceful spot to sit and admire the wading birds. Benches and a gazebo encourage you to sit and stay awhile. Your patience may be rewarded with a glimpse of Lake Rowena's resident eight-foot alligator.

Every half hour from 10:00 a.m. to 3:30 p.m., except in July when it is closed, volunteers conduct tours through the **Leu house**. Don't miss it. You'll be treated to a wonderfully gossipy recounting of the building's evolution, through several changes of ownership, from humble farm house to rich man's estate, spiced with tales of a sheriff gunned down in the line of duty and a home-wrecking New York actress. (That's her as Cleopatra in the photo in the living room.) Nearby is a cemetery in which the unfortunate lawman lies buried with many of his kin.

The antebellum-style **Garden House**, where you pay your modest admission to the gardens, houses a 900-volume horticultural library (open to visitors) and spacious meeting rooms. The terrace at the back of the building offers a stunning view of the lake. There are frequent arts and crafts exhibits in the Garden House, as well as a regular schedule of musical events. Wheelchairs are available free of charge. Pets are not allowed in either the gardens or the houses.

Nearby: Mennello Museum of Folk Art, Orlando Fire Museum, Orlando Museum of Art, Orlando Science Center.

Little Econ Greenway

2451 North Dean Road, Orlando 32817

(407) 254-9030

http://parks.orangecountyfl.net

Admission:	**Free**
Hours:	Daily sunrise to sunset
Location:	Off East Colonial Drive, approximately 10 miles east of I-4 Exit 84

Five miles of paved path wind alongside the Little Econlockhatchee River offering a smooth ride for cyclists, skaters, and hikers alike. Ospreys and red-tailed hawks, as well as alligators can be sighted here and a special garden has been planted to attract butterflies. You can enter the trail at Colonial and Central Park Avenue on the west and hike to the eastern end, in Jay Blanchard Park, where a YMCA branch offers a smoothies bar to slake your thirst. Tell them you'd like to be a guest and they will give you a day's free access to their well-equipped gym and outdoor pool. Plans are on the boards to extend the trail in each direction to create a ten-mile path that will link with other extensive trail networks.

Merritt Island National Wildlife Refuge

State Route 402, east of Titusville

(321) 861-0667

www.fws.gov/merrittisland/

Admission:	**Free**
Hours:	Monday to Friday 8:00 a.m. to 4:30 p.m.; Saturday and Sunday 9:00 a.m. to 5:00 p.m.
Location:	Just east of Titusville on State Route 406; from I-95, take Exit 229

Hard by Kennedy Space Center, surrounding it in fact, are 140,000 acres of pristine Florida coastal wilderness, home to some 500 species, including 21 on various endangered and threatened species lists. With the possible exception of the West Indian manatee, the stars of the show here are the 311 species of birds that either make the Refuge their home or pass through en route to other climes. As a result, the Refuge is one of the prime birding spots in the Southeast and a must-see attraction for anyone with even a modest interest in bird watching. From the majestic American bald eagle, to the colorful Florida scrub jay, to the many varieties of ducks and wading birds that frequent the salt marches, a visit here will provide ample opportunities to add to your list of species spotted. In between birds, be on the lookout for alligators cruising through the shallows, and if you're really lucky you might catch a glimpse of an elusive bobcat bounding across the road.

The aforementioned manatees gather at the Haulover Canal linking the Indian River with Mosquito Lagoon. They appear with such regularity at a certain spot that the Park Service has erected a **Manatee Observation Deck** to give visitors a better look. A stop here makes a perfect counterpoint to the manatee exhibit over at SeaWorld.

The **Black Point Wildlife Drive**, a self-guided driving tour of the Refuge's natural marshes and man-made impoundments, is a popular diversion. Maps and recorded guides are available at the Visitors Center. About half way through, you can park and set off on the 5-mile **Cruickshank Trail** for a closer look at this magnet for migratory birds. The adjacent **Canaveral National Seashore** ($5 per vehicle charge) offers miles of pristine beaches along the Atlantic. You can spend a very full day or two exploring the rich variety of a landscape that has changed little since the days of Ponce de Leon.

Nearby: Kennedy Space Center.

Orlando Wetlands Park

25155 Wheeler Road, Christmas 32709
(407) 568-1706

Admission:	**Free**
Hours:	Daily, January 21 to September 30 only, sunrise to sunset
Location:	East on SR 50, then left on CR 420 (Ft. Christmas Road); go 2.3 miles and turn right onto Wheeler Road

Tucked away on the far eastern fringes of Orlando is an ingenious combination of the practical and the aesthetic. To the untrained eye, the "Iron Bridge Easterly Wetlands" that comprise this park look like a preserved sliver of the "real" Florida. It is, in fact, part of the City of Orlando's wastewater treatment system. Every day, 16 million gallons of highly treated reclaimed wastewater from parts of Orange and Seminole counties are pumped into this 1,650-acre, man-made wetlands where aquatic plants continue the process of removing nutrients as the water slowly makes its way to the St. John's River. If visions of open sewers spring to mind, banish them. The result is enchanting, combining open fields, gently rolling woods, a small lake, and a thick forest.

In the parking area, go to the wooden announcement board. There you can sign in (don't forget to sign out!) and pick up a park map and a *Field Checklist of Birds.* The best way to get acquainted with the park is to walk (or jog) the four-mile "walk/jog loop." If you'd like, you can veer off onto a more primitive hiking trail through the woods; it eventually rejoins the main trail. The map thoughtfully points out the best bird-watching spots along the park's 20 miles of raised roads. More than 150 species frequent the park. The *Checklist* lists them and the seasons in which they visit and notes whether they are common, uncommon, or rare.

Biking is permitted on the berm roads and there is a sheltered picnic area in a broad grassy area near the parking lot. The Florida Trail skirts the property, allowing serious hikers to extend their explorations. The Orlando Wetlands Park is a bit out of the way (it is about a 40-minute drive east of the city), but a visit will reward bird watchers and those looking for a more exciting jogging trail than the motel parking lot.

Nearby: Back to Nature Wildlife Refuge, Fort Christmas Historical Park, Jungle Adventures, Tosohatchee Wildlife Management Area.

Osceola Schools Environmental Study Center

4300 Poinciana Boulevard, Kissimmee 34758
(407) 870-0551

Admission:	**Free**
Hours:	Saturday 10:00 a.m. to 5:00 p.m.;
	Sunday noon to 5:00 p.m.
Location:	13 miles south of Highway 192

During the week, this 19-acre patch of Reedy Creek Swamp serves as an educational resource for the school children of Osceola County. On weekends, it's open to the public and well worth a visit from the wildlife-loving tourist. In the winter and spring, you might even be able to spot a nesting bald eagle.

Begin at the Visitors Center, which houses one of the best introductions and reference guides to Central Florida wildlife you are likely to find. If you've spotted some critter that you couldn't identify, you'll probably find it here. Most impressive are the taxidermy of birds like the bald eagle and osprey. There are also stuffed panthers and black bears. Most of these specimens were killed accidentally, typically by an automobile. Now they help teach school kids. These three-dimensional examples are supplemented by quite lovely color photographs of the native species taken right here at the Study Center. On another wall are photos of the local flora. Add to this charts of bird silhouettes and animal tracks and you have a remarkably complete resource for enjoying the Florida wilderness. Pick up a free copy of *The Reedy Creek Swamp Nature Guide* and the trail guides to guide the rest of your visit.

There are three short trails to explore. An 1,800-foot raised walkway takes you into Reedy Creek Swamp and its 400-year-old cypress trees. At the end, an observation platform lets you eavesdrop on the osprey nests. The short Pine Woods Trail features a reconstruction of the portable logging railroads that once ferried felled trees out of the swamp. The rails were made by Krupp, the famous German industrial giant. Another trail leads to a modest Indian mound formed by snail shells discarded by the aboriginal inhabitants. A small picnic area is available.

Nearby: Green Meadows Farm, Old Town, Osceola Extreme Sports.

Rock Springs Run State Reserve

31799 SR 433, Apopka 32712
(407) 884-2008
www.floridastateparks.org/rockspringsrun/

Admission:	$2 per vehicle (up to 8 people); $1 for walk-ins and bicyclists
Hours:	Daily 8:00 a.m. to sunset
Location:	From I-4 Exit 101C, take SR 46 West about 7 miles; turn left onto route 433

This sprawling park is bounded by Rock Springs Run and the Wekiva River, which might suggest that water activities abound. Not so. There is no water access and a sign at the gate directs you to nearby resorts and parks if that's what you have in mind.

What the Reserve has to offer, in abundance, is solitude and well-maintained hiking trails that meander through 8,750 acres of the kind of terrain that's referred to as "Florida's Desert." Depending on how far you trek, you'll see sand pine scrub, pine flatwoods, bayheads, hammocks, and a few swamps. Depending on how lucky you are, you may glimpse a black bear. If you do, report the sighting by calling (407) 884-2008.

There is one "primitive" camping site in the Reserve for those hardy enough to backpack to the far side of the park. Or you can ride your horse there. The camping fee is $4 per person (adult or child) and $5 per horse. If riding is your cup of tea, the Rock Springs Run Riding Stables has horses for hire. (See *Chapter 12: Do It!*)

Nearby: Kelly Park, King's Landing Canoe Rental, Wekiva Falls Resort, Wekiwa Springs State Park.

Sylvan Lake Park
845 Lake Markham Road, Sanford 32771
(407) 322-6567
www.seminolecountyfl.gov/lls/parks/

Admission:	**Free**
Hours:	Daily 8:00 a.m. to 10:00 p.m. Closed Thanksgiving and Christmas
Location:	From I-4 Exit 101A, drive west on SR 46 3.2 miles, turn left onto Lake Markham Road. Park is less than a mile on left

This Seminole County park offers cut-rate tennis and racquetball, along with four soccer fields. Tennis courts are $2 an hour before 5:00 p.m. and $4 per hour thereafter; racquetball courts are $4 an hour at all times; soccer fields go for $10 an hour before 5 p.m. and $20 per hour thereafter. Use of the facilities is open to all, even to tourists, but you must call for reservations.

Otherwise, the park offers picnicking, a jogging trail, and an intricate network of boardwalks that take you through the woods and across the swampy fringes of Sylvan Lake, where you can sit in a spacious gazebo and bird watch or just while away the time. A small dock offers fishing or a place to launch your own canoe or other non-motorized boat.

Tibet-Butler Preserve
8777 State Road 535, Orlando 32836
(407) 876-6696

Admission:	**Free**
Hours:	Wednesday to Sunday 8:00 a.m. to 6:00 p.m.
Location:	About five miles north of I-4 Exit 68

Just a stone's throw from Walt Disney World and SeaWorld, amid the gated communities of Orlando's burgeoning southwest district, lies this 440-acre patch of Florida wilderness. The spiffy new Vera Carter Environmental Center building, with its state-of-the-art interpretive displays, is the kickoff point for four miles of beautifully maintained trails and boardwalks that meander through bay swamps, marshes, cypress swamps, pine flatlands, and Florida scrub. The park borders the Tibet–Butler chain of lakes from which it takes its name, but you can't get down to the water. You can get close, though, on a lovely pavilion at the end of Osprey Overlook Trail. This is a great spot for bird watching and an excellent place to escape the bustle of tourist Orlando. The Preserve is home to bobcats and foxes, although it is unlikely you'll spot any of these elusive creatures. Special programs and guided nature hikes are offered from time to time. Call for details.

Nearby: SeaWorld, Discovery Cove.

Tosohatchee Wildlife Management Area

3365 Taylor Creek Road, Christmas, 32709
(407) 568-5893

Admission:	$3 per vehicle (up to 8 people)
Hours:	Daily 8:00 a.m. to sunset
Location:	3 miles south of SR 50 in Christmas

If you really want to get away from it all, this mammoth (28,000-acre) wilderness area is an excellent choice. I visited one Wednesday afternoon and was the only person there. The park borders 19 miles of the St. John's River and includes wetlands, pine flatwoods, and hammocks. The name is a contraction of Tootoosahatchee, an Indian word for "chicken creek," and the eponymous stream flows through the northern portion of the reserve.

Hiking, biking, and horseback riding are the activities of choice here. If you want the purest experience of this enchanting and sometimes spooky ecosystem stick to the primitive Florida Trail, marked with white (or sometimes blue) blazes. The trails marked with rectangular or diamond-shaped orange blazes allow bikes and horses (bring your own horse; there are none for hire here). Walking softly and quietly will increase your chance of spotting wildlife. There are white-tailed deer, bobcat, gray fox, and several varieties of raptors to be seen here. The Florida panther is said to put in a rare appearance. More likely, you will flush large vultures or hawks as you proceed through the semi-gloom of the forest past tea-dark streams and pools, their still surfaces like obsidian mirrors.

If a casual visit is not enough, why not spend a few days? The camping here is "primitive," that is no recreational vehicles or pop-up tent trailers are allowed. Most of the campsites have nearby parking areas but for the truly adventuresome, there are two backpacking campsites, one of them seven miles from the nearest road. Campers must make reservations by phone at least two weeks (but no more than 60 days) in advance. There is a fee of $4.50 per person per night (all ages). The regular admission fee is waived for campers.

When you arrive, sign in and pay your vehicle fee (envelopes are provided). You must also sign out to let the park caretaker know that you are not lying wounded in some far flung corner of the wilderness. Also, be aware that hunting is allowed in this park. The deer season runs from late September to about Thanksgiving. The wild hog (yes, wild hog) season is in January and wild turkey have their turn in March and April. All of these hunting seasons have gaps, that is, periods of three days to two weeks when hunting is not allowed. Hikers are advised to steer clear of the woods when hunting is allowed; call to check the schedule, which is also posted at the sign-in area. If you want to hunt, you have to get a special permit from the state even if you are a local resident.

Nearby: Back to Nature Wildlife Refuge, Fort Christmas Historical Park, Jungle Adventures, Orlando Wetlands Park.

Turkey Lake Park
3401 Hiawassee Road, Orlando 32835
(407) 299-5581, (407) 299-5594
www.cityoforlando.net/fpr

Admission:	$4 per car ($2 if it's just the driver)
Hours:	Daily 8:00 a.m. to 5:00 p.m. November to March; 8:00 a.m. to 7:00 p.m. April to October
Location:	From I-4 Exit 75 take Kirkman north, turn left onto Conroy then right onto Hiawassee to park entrance, about 4 miles total

Just a stone's throw from the hurly-burly of Universal Orlando, the city of Orlando has created a 300-acre oasis along the shores of Turkey Lake. Officially called the Bill Frederick Park at Turkey Lake, this beautifully landscaped and maintained park offers picnicking, hiking along seven miles of nature trails, biking along a three-mile bike path, and a number of other diversions. The picnic areas are close to the lake with beautiful shaded tables and "picnic pavilions" (additional charge). There are nearby kiddie play areas and sandy "beaches" but no lake swimming. Instead there is a large pool overlooking the lovely lake. A fishing pier lets you test your angling skills against largemouth bass and other species. If you prefer to fish from a boat, you can rent one for $15.00. Thursday through Sunday from 7:00 a.m. to 11:00 a.m. Call (407) 299-1248 to make a reservation.

Across the park, an "all children's" playground offers an enormous wood and car-tire wonderland that will offer little ones hours of exploration and fun. Shaded gazebos nearby keep Mom and Dad out of the sun. No eating here, however, as food draws rats and other not-so-welcome wildlife. Next door is a "Cracker" farm featuring an authentic 100-year-old barn, to give kids an idea of what pioneer Florida looked and felt like.

There's camping here, too. Cabins that sleep up to 10 are available for $35 per night. "Family" camp sites for trailers and RVs are $15 per night including electricity and water. If you need a sewer hookup as well, the price is $18. The area is beautifully shaded, with picnic tables and barbecue pits. A "primitive" camping area nearby is less shady, but at $7 per four-person tent, the price may be right. Camping requires reservations.

Nearby: Universal Orlando.

University of Central Florida Arboretum

UCF Campus
4000 Central Florida Boulevard, Orlando 32816-2368
(407) 823-2978

Admission:	**Free**
Hours:	Daily 9:00 a.m. to 6:00 p.m.
Location:	On the UCF campus in east Orlando; ask at the campus information booth for directions and parking information

The University of Central Florida has a quite extensive "collection" of trees and other flora, and it is displayed in this tranquil oasis in the midst of its ultramodern campus on the eastern fringes of Orlando. The emphasis is on Florida species but the collection ranges far and wide. A maze of nature trails takes the visitor through a number of plant "communities," including oak hammock, cabbage palm, and pond pine. Informative signage identifies individual species and, when appropriate, gives tips to gardeners. Best of all, secluded tables and benches, some with thatched shelters offer quiet spots for contemplation or study.

Nearby: Back to Nature Wildlife Refuge.

Wekiwa Springs State Park

1800 Wekiwa Circle, Apopka 32712
(407) 884-2008
www.floridastateparks.org/wekiwasprings/

Admission:	$5 per vehicle (maximum of 8 people); single occupant vehicles $3; pedestrians, bicyclists $1
Hours:	Daily 8:00 a.m. to sunset
Location:	From I-4 Exit 94 take route 434 West to Wekiva Springs Road, then about 3 miles to the park entrance

This gem of a park boasts what must be the most beautiful spot to take a swim in all of Central Florida. The spring that gives the park its name bubbles up at the base of an amphitheater of greensward, forming a crystal clear circular pool of pure delight. The water is a steady 72 degrees year-round, making for a bracing dip in the heat of summer and a heated pool for snowbirds in the winter. The pool is fairly shallow, seldom more than five feet deep. Bring a snorkel and mask for a peek down into the spring itself.

The spring is one source of the Wekiva River, which flows from here northeast to the St. John's River. If you wish, you can rent a canoe to explore this lovely stretch of river. (See the canoeing section of *Chapter 12: Do It!*) The river is gorgeous from a canoe but some daring souls snorkel it. The park police tell me this is a foolhardy venture given the population of large alligators who have lost their fear of man, thanks to being fed by ignorant tourists. Shortly before one of my visits to the park, an 11-foot gator was pulled from the waters of nearby Wekiva Marina. Because of its aggressive behavior and total lack of fear of humans, the trapper was forced to kill it.

If you get hungry after your swim, there's a bare-bones snack bar at the top of the hill. But a better choice might be the picnic area at the other end of the park, where you'll find a couple of dozen picnic tables artfully sited around the shores of Sand Lake. There are alligators here, so be careful.

In between there are some beautifully maintained trails. If you begin from the spring-fed swimming pool, a boardwalk takes you from the swampy jungle of the river's edge to the sandy pine forest of the drier uplands. This is one of the nicest spots I found in Central Florida for a visitor to get a quick appreciation of just how different Florida's ecosystems are. There's plenty of wildlife, too. I've spotted white-tailed deer fawns leaping through the woods and armadillos grubbing in the underbrush.

Family campsites are available by reservation if you'd like to stay longer. The fees for up to eight people are $20 per site per night. Primitive camping is $4 per person per night. The park requires written proof that pets have had a rabies vaccination. Call Reserve America, (407) 326-3521, for campsite reservations. Call the park at (407) 884-2008 for more information.

Nearby: Central Florida Zoological Park, Rock Springs Run State Reserve, Wekiva Falls Resort.

World of Orchids

2501 Old Lake Wilson Road, Kissimmee 34747
(407) 396-1887
www.aworldoforchids.com

Admission:	**Free**
Hours:	Monday to Saturday 9:30 a.m. to 4:30 p.m.
Location:	From I-4, take US 192 West and turn left on Old Lake Wilson, about one mile

World of Orchids is actually a working greenhouse that will ship its orchids and other plants nationwide. To educate and enchant the public, they have constructed a vast greenhouse covering some three-quarters of an acre. In the carefully controlled warm, humid air hundreds of orchids are displayed in a natural jungle setting, complete with waterfalls, babbling streams filled with koi fish, and squawking parrots. The total number of orchids varies seasonally and can double at certain times of the year.

Nearby: Arabian Nights, Bonanza Golf.

Chapter Fifteen:

Artful Dodges

THOSE WHO ASSUME THAT ORLANDO, WITH ITS HIGH CONCENTRATION OF THEME parks and "mindless" entertainments, is a cultural wasteland have got it dead wrong. In fact, the Orlando area boasts some world-class museums, a lively and growing theater scene, and a number of modest local history museums.

HISTORICAL & SCIENCE MUSEUMS

Fort Christmas Historical Park & Museum

1300 Fort Christmas Road, Christmas 32709

(407) 568-4149

http://parks.orangecountyfl.net

Admission:	**Free**
Hours:	Museum is open Tuesday to Saturday 10:00 a.m. to 5:00 p.m.; Sunday 1:00 p.m. to 5:00 p.m. Park is open daily 8:00 a.m. to 8:00 p.m. (to 6:00 p.m. during winter months)
Location:	Two miles north of SR 50, a major artery between Orlando and the Kennedy Space Center

This is not the actual Fort Christmas but a re-creation. The original was built a short distance away in 1837 during the Second Seminole Indian War (1835-1842) and has long since rotted away. The re-created fort, with its log cabin-like blockhouses and pointed palisades, is remarkably evocative of a frontier that most Americans associate with the West, not the South.

Display cases in the blockhouses provide a fragmentary history of the Seminole Wars, the culture they destroyed, and the early days of white settlement. In the nearby Visitors Center, which is built in the style of a "Cracker" (old-time Florida cowboy) farm house, you can get a pamphlet that explicates the museum's exhibits and provides a short history of the Seminole Wars. Scattered about the property is a small but growing collection of original Cracker architecture that you can poke through at your leisure. Yesterday, disreputable shacks. Today, cherished history.

Fort Christmas is also a county park complete with picnic tables (many with barbecues), a shaded playground, a baseball diamond, and tennis, volleyball, and basketball courts.

Nearby: Back to Nature Wildlife Refuge, Jungle Adventures, Orlando Wetlands Park, Tosohatchee Wildlife Management Area.

The Holocaust Memorial

851 North Maitland Avenue, Maitland 32794
(407) 628-0555
www.holocaustedu.org

Admission:	**Free**
Hours:	Monday to Thursday 9:00 a.m. to 4:00 p.m.; Friday 9:00 a.m. to 1:00 p.m.; Sunday 1:00 p.m. to 4:00 p.m.
Location:	At Maitland Boulevard and Maitland Avenue, about a mile east of I-4 Exit 90

The Holocaust Memorial Resource and Education Center houses a modest and moving museum commemorating one of the darkest moments in human experience — the martyrdom of the six million Jews ruthlessly exterminated by the Nazis in the 1930s and 1940s.

A small chapel-like room houses "The Holocaust in History," a permanent collection of multimedia displays documenting the horrors of institutionalized hate. A separate room houses rotating exhibits on aspects of the Holocaust; these change every three to four months. A rapidly expanding 6,000-volume library is devoted exclusively to Holocaust history.

A visit here can be a profoundly disturbing experience, which is not to say it is something to shy away from. Stepping out once again into the Florida sunshine, we are reminded that we have been blessed to live on one of history's peaks — a lesser peak, it might be argued, but a peak nonetheless. A visit here will put the pleasures of your Orlando vacation in a richer perspective.

Nearby: Maitland Art Center, Maitland Historical Museum, Waterhouse Residence, Birds of Prey Center.

Maitland Historical & Telephone Museum

221 West Packwood Avenue, Maitland 32751
(407) 644-1364
www.maitlandhistory.org

Admission:	Adults $3, children under 18 $2
Hours:	Thursday and Friday noon to 4:00 p.m.; Saturday and Sunday 10:00 a.m. to 4:00 p.m.

Location: From I-4 Exit 90 go east on Maitland Boulevard,
                     then turn right onto Maitland Avenue and right
                     onto Packwood.

This modest museum, housed in a former residence next to the Maitland Art Center (see below), houses memorabilia of the tiny town of Maitland, which began its life as Fort Maitland in 1838, serving as a way station between larger forts in Sanford and Orlando. There is a timeline of Maitland history supplemented by changing exhibits focusing on a theme. Past exhibits have highlighted Maitland's Girl Scout history and toys, games, and leisure activities of the late 1800s and early 1900s.

The real attraction here, however, is the **Telephone Museum** housed in a building out back. Telephone service in this part of Florida began in 1909, when the Galloway family grocery store installed 10 phone lines so their good customers could order by phone. The service mushroomed into what came to be known as the Winter Park Telephone Company, which remained independent and family-owned until 1976 when it was sold to the company that became Sprint. There are several old magneto switchboards here, dating back to 1900, and a large collection of phones, from the old-fashioned, wall-mounted, hand-cranked varieties to a sleek one-piece 1970 Swedish Ericofon. Also on display are samples of copper wiring and other telephony paraphernalia, including wooden conduits once used to snake wire beneath city streets. Some more recent switching equipment is housed here and volunteers hope to get it working again for demonstration purposes.

There are very few explanatory labels, so ask for a guided tour. On my visit, I was escorted by a charming lady who once worked for the Galloways themselves.

Nearby: Maitland Art Center, Waterhouse Residence, Birds of Prey Center.

Orange County Regional History Center

65 East Central Boulevard, Orlando 32801
(800) 965-2030; (407) 836-8500
www.thehistorycenter.org

Admission: Adults $7, seniors (60+) $6.50, children (3 to 12)
                     $3.50
Hours: Monday to Saturday 10:00 a.m. to 5:00 p.m.;
                     Sunday noon to 5:00 p.m.
Location: In downtown Orlando; from the north take I-4
                     Exit 84, from the south Exit 83A

Unlike most county historical museums, which are dusty hodgepodges of miscellaneous objects displayed in a donated and threadbare house of "historical" interest, Orange County's museum is housed in a magnificent 1927 courthouse, its collection attractively and professionally displayed. This is one of the best looking local history museums I have visited and well worth a look if you venture downtown.

The impressive ground floor entrance features a marble inlay map of the world with Orlando at the center; above is a wonderfully zany multimedia sculptural dome dotted with references to Central Florida's natural, cultural, and social history. Your best bet is to head for the fourth floor, enjoy the short orientation film, and then work your way down through a chronologically arranged series of exhibit rooms.

After an introduction to Florida's natural environment and its first Paleo-Indian inhabitants, the focus shifts to the settler period in which both the Europeans and the Seminoles, the latter forced from their homelands in Georgia and the Carolinas, were newcomers. A fascinating display on tourism takes us back to the 1920s and the first RVs, converted Model Ts that brought penny-pinching "tin can tourists." The then governor of Florida said of these pioneers, "They came with one pair of underwear and one twenty dollar bill and changed neither." How times change!

Other highlights are a perfectly preserved courtroom, a reminder of the building's previous life, and a display on the pre-World War II training of military pilots, when Central Florida was so little-known that it was the perfect place for a top-secret government base.

The History Center is one of the high points of Orlando's revitalized downtown. In front is a small but lovely park. The Public Library, with free Internet access, is on one side and Wall Street Plaza, a charming pedestrian street with cafes and restaurants, on the other.

Nearby: Lake Eola Swan Boats, Leu Gardens, Orlando City Hall Galleries.

Orlando Fire Museum

814 East Rollins Street, Orlando 32803
(407) 898-3138; (407) 246-2390

Admission:	**Free**, donations requested
Hours:	Thursday to Saturday 9:00 a.m. to 2:00 p.m.
	Group tours by appointment
Location:	From I-4 Exit 85, go east and follow Loch Haven
	Park signs about one quarter mile

The charming brick 1926 Fire Station #3 has been lovingly moved to this secluded location behind the Orlando Shakespeare Festival in Loch Haven Park. Here fire buffs can enthuse over meticulously restored fire engines, including a 1911 horse-drawn steam pumper, a 1915 LaFrance Fire Engine, and a 1919 LaFrance Ladder Truck. Photos and documents arranged chronologically around the walls document the department's proud history. Upstairs, in a room used for fire department training, are displays of fire fighters' gear, from dress uniforms to bomb suits, and a memorial to those who have sacrificed their lives in service to the community.

You have to pass through the lobby of the Orlando Shakespeare Festival to reach the museum, tucked away in a quiet courtyard, but it's worth seeking out.

Nearby: Leu Gardens, Mennello Museum of Art, Orlando Museum of Art, Orlando Science Center.

Orlando Science Center

777 East Princeton Street, Orlando 32803
(407) 514-2000
www.osc.org

Admission:	Adults $14.95, seniors (55+) $13.95, youths (3 to

11) $9.95; after 4:00 p.m., prices are $9.95 for
adults and $4.95 for youths

Hours: Monday to Thursday 9:00 a.m. to 5:00 p.m.; Friday and Saturday 9:00 a.m. to 9:00 p.m.; Sunday noon to 5:00 p.m.

Location: From I-4 Exit 85, go east and follow Loch Haven Park signs about one quarter mile

The Orlando area is gaining a reputation as another high-tech business corridor with specialties in laser and simulation technologies. The Orlando Science Center's smashing new home is a fitting monument to the technological explosion going on around it and should serve as a launching pad for future generations of scientists. The accent is on kids and science education but, thanks to its ingenious hands-on approach, the Center offers plenty to keep even the dullest adult occupied.

The Center's 42,000 square feet are crammed with eye-catching exhibits that illustrate the many faces of science and how it interacts with our everyday life. Power Station teaches about energy, LightPower about lasers and optics, The Cosmic Tourist about earth and the solar system, and Body Zone about health and fitness. There's even a section, ShowBiz Science, that explains the technology underlying some of the man-made wonders you've been gaping at during your Orlando visit.

The 310-seat CineDome features large-format movies and planetarium shows on a screen eight stories high, with a state-of-the-art sound system. This is one of the largest such theaters in the world and seeing a nature movie on the vast curved screen is an experience not easily duplicated elsewhere. The films are included in the price of admission, or you can see them separately for $8 for adults, $7 for seniors and $5 for youths.

There's a spacious cafeteria so you can plan a visit around lunchtime and then spend the rest of the day exploring the wonderful world of science, with side trips to the nearby museums.

Nearby: Leu Gardens, Mennello Museum, Orlando Fire Museum, Orlando Museum of Art.

Spence-Lanier Pioneer Center

750 North Bass Road, Kissimmee 34746
(407) 396-8644

Admission: Suggested donation, adults $2, children $1

Hours: Thursday to Saturday 10:00 a.m. to 4:00 p.m., Sunday 1:00 p.m. to 4:00 p.m.

Location: Just south of Irlo Bronson Highway (US Route 192)

Sometimes referred to as the Pioneer Museum, this open-air venue is a labor of love of the Osceola County Historical Society. The highlights are two old wooden buildings, rescued from oblivion and moved to this site as reminders of Central Florida's not too distant but nonetheless vanished past.

The Lanier House, which has been dated to about 1887, is a Cracker-style residence made from broad cypress boards that have aged to a lovely cafe au lait shade of beige. The broad, shaded porches and airy central breezeway, or "possum trot," were designed to let air circulate through the four rooms. The spare interior rooms, including a kitchen with a wood stove, touchingly evoke the rhythms of life in a simpler time. Next door is the smaller, two-room 1890 Tyson Home, now used to re-create a turn of the century general store. Books of local history and locally produced crafts are sold here.

A nearby modern prefab building holds a growing and random collection of antiques and memorabilia donated by the local community. Many of these touchstones to the past seem to have been passed from generation to generation before finding their way here. This is the living, collective memory of Osceola County and reflects not just Florida history but the many ways in which foreign and national events impinged on small towns like Kissimmee.

Across the street from the four-acre site of the museum is the **Mary Kendall Steffee Nature Preserve**. This 7.8-acre patch of wilderness lies in the very heart of tourist Kissimmee and yet remains remarkably isolated. A short walk on marked trails brings you to a raised boardwalk that juts out into Shingle Creek Swamp. A shaded seating area beckons the footsore. Aside from the intermittent drone of small planes landing at the nearby Kissimmee Airport, this is an oasis of tranquillity where you can glimpse the occasional eagle or other large raptor. You will need a key to the gate, which you can get at the office behind the preserved houses. The office will lend you a trail guide or you can purchase a copy for $2.

Nearby: Medieval Times, River Adventure Golf.

Waterhouse Residence & Carpentry Museum

820 Lake Lilly Drive, Maitland 32751
(407) 644-2451
www.maitlandhistory.org

Admission:	Adults $3, children under 18 $2
Hours:	Thursday and Friday noon to 4:00 p.m.; Saturday and Sunday 10:00 a.m. to 4:00 p.m.
Location:	From I-4 take Exit 90 East onto Maitland Boulevard, then turn right onto Maitland Avenue and right onto Lake Lilly Drive

William H. Waterhouse, a home builder and cabinetmaker by trade, came to Central Florida in the early 1880s and put his obvious skills to use building a handsome family residence overlooking tiny Lake Lilly. Today, it serves as a monument to gracious living in a simpler, less stressful time.

Lovingly restored and maintained by volunteers, the house contains many items of furniture fashioned by Mr. Waterhouse in the carpentry shop behind the home. The home itself is furnished throughout and looks as if the Waterhouse family had just stepped out for a moment. Do-it-yourselfers will marvel at the fine detail work and the lavish use of heart of pine, a favorite of builders of the period because it was impervious to termites. It is rare today because few loggers are patient enough to let pines go unharvested long enough for this prime lumber to develop.

Tours are conducted by knowledgeable volunteers who will provide you with many insights into this charming home and the people who lived here. If you arrive when a tour is in progress, you may find the door locked. Just take a seat in the comfortable chairs on the porch; a volunteer will be with you shortly. Tours last about 30 to 40 minutes.

The museum offers two children's programs that transport kids back to the late 1800s. *Carpentry Crew* ($12) showcases woodworking and building techniques while *Hats and Teas* ($10) focuses on social etiquette. These programs are designed for kids in grades three and up. Call for more information and to make reservations, which are required.

Nearby: Maitland Art Center, Maitland Historical Museum, Birds of Prey Center.

Wells' Built Museum of African American History

511 West South Street, Orlando 32805
(407) 245-7535

Admission:	Adults $5, students and seniors (60+) $3, children (4 to 14) $2
Hours:	Monday to Friday 10:00 a.m. to 5:00 p.m.; Saturday 10:00 a.m. to 2:00 p.m.
Location:	Just west of I-4 near Church Street

Dr. William M. Wells was a prominent African-American physician in Orlando during the first half of the 20th century. He created the South Street Casino to host touring black bands and, since Orlando was rigorously segregated, he opened the Wells' Built Hotel next door to house the musicians. Ella Fitzgerald, Count Basie, Ray Charles, Cab Calloway, Ivory Joe Hunter, and many other musical greats played the Casino and stayed at the hotel over the years. White Orlando didn't know what it was missing.

The Casino is gone now, but the hotel remains. It has been converted into a modest museum housing memorabilia of Orlando's African-American community and displays on the Civil Rights movement in Orlando, along with some African art on loan from local collectors.

Dr. Well's home has been moved to the site of the Casino. It is being restored and will open to the public sometime in 2007.

Nearby: Orange County History Center, Orlando City Hall Galleries.

Winter Garden Heritage Museum & History Center

1 North Main Street, Winter Garden 34787
(407) 656-3244
www.wghf.org

Admission:	**Free**
Hours:	Daily 1:00 p.m. to 5:00 p.m.
Location:	In the center of downtown Winter Garden, 12 miles west of Orlando via SR 50

This is actually four attractions in one, all located within easy walking distance of one another in "historic" downtown Winter Garden, which looks much the way it did back in the 1920s and 30s. The **History Center** serves primarily as a research resource for Winter Garden family and business history, but it also presents displays of local history that change every three months. The **Heritage Museum**, located in the picturesque old train station, is typical of other local history collections, although the museum does boast the "largest collection of antique citrus labels from West Orange County." Otherwise, the gown worn by a local matron to President Eisenhower's inaugural is fairly typical of the artifacts on display.

Railroad buffs will most definitely want to visit the **Railroad Museum**, around the corner on South Boyd Street in yet another old train station, the "Tug and Grunt," so called for its role as a freight line and low-cost passenger line for locals. It still gets daily freight runs from nearby Ocoee. The collection is catch as catch can, but claims to be one of the largest of its kind. Back on Main Street, the **Garden Theatre** has been restored to its 1930s glory, with an auditorium decorated to evoke an Italian courtyard, complete with twinkling stars overhead. It now hosts local dance and theatre troupes and occasional showings of classic films.

Nearby: Orlando City Hall Galleries, Wells' Built Museum.

Winter Park Historical Association Museum

200 West New England Avenue, Winter Park 32790
(407) 647-8180

Admission: **Free** (Donations requested)
Hours: Thursday and Friday 11:00 a.m. to 3:00 p.m.; Saturday 9:00 a.m. to 1:00 p.m.; Sunday 1:00 p.m. to 4:00 p.m.
Location: In downtown Winter Park next to the park

This fledgling historical museum is housed in one room around the corner from the building in which Winter Park's Saturday Farmer's Market is held. The display is simple, relying heavily on photographs of now-vanished buildings and assorted household items and artifacts that speak less of Winter Park than of American consumerism.

The best part of this museum is the central display area, a sort of room within a room. It houses changing exhibits artfully put together by a local architect and interior decorator using donated and loaned furniture and artifacts. Past exhibits have included a Victorian parlor decked out for a Christmas celebration and an upper middle-class kitchen circa 1932. The exhibit changes every six months or so.

While perhaps not worth a special trip, you may want to consider a visit if you are touring the many other attractions in Winter Park.

Nearby: Morse Museum, Cornell Museum, Albin Polasek Galleries, Winter Park Scenic Boat Tour.

ART MUSEUMS & GALLERIES

Visitors to Orlando will find plenty of opportunities to buy schlocky "art" aimed at the tourist trade, but if you'd prefer to admire fine art without having to buy it, there are a growing number of venues to choose from.

Albin Polasek Galleries

633 Osceola Avenue, Winter Park 32790
(407) 647-6294
www.polasek.org

Admission:	Adults $5, seniors (60+) $4, students $3, under 12 **free**
Hours:	Tuesday to Saturday 10:00 a.m. to 4:00 p.m.; Sunday 1:00 p.m. to 4:00 p.m.; closed during July and August
Location:	From I-4 Exit 87, follow SR 426 East about 3 miles

The studio-home and gardens of the late Czech-American sculptor, Albin Polasek, have been turned into a loving memorial by his widow. The quietly luxurious home was designed by Polasek himself and constructed in 1950 overlooking Lake Osceola. Today it is on the Register of Historic Places and houses some 200 of his works. The paintings are originals while most of the sculptures are reproductions.

Polasek was a devout Roman Catholic and a self-taught woodcarver who, as a young immigrant, found work carving religious statues in the Midwest. Later, he received formal art training and eventually became a highly respected academic artist. The work on display here ranges from the mawkish to the quite impressive. He was a better sculptor than painter and some of his bronzes, like The Sower and Man Carving His Own Destiny, possess real power. The former is a classically inspired bronze, the latter depicts a muscular figure in the process of carving itself out of stone.

One of his most affecting pieces is The Victorious Christ, a larger than life sculpture of the crucified Christ gazing heavenward. The original hangs in a cathedral in Omaha, Nebraska. There are two reproductions here. One dominates his two-story studio but the real stunner is the bronze version in the back garden. Mounted on a large wooden cross and sited under a theatrically towering oak tree, facing the lake, it is a powerful work.

Nearby: Cornell Fine Arts Museum, Morse Museum of American Art, Winter Park Scenic Boat Tour.

Cornell Fine Arts Museum

1000 Holt Avenue, Winter Park 32789
(407) 646-2526
www.rollins.edu/cfam

Admission:	Adults $5
Hours:	Tuesday to Saturday 10:00 a.m. to 5:00 p.m.;

Sunday 1:00 p.m. to 5:00 p.m.

Location: On the campus of Rollins College, at the foot of Holt Avenue

The Cornell Fine Arts Museum has luxurious digs overlooking Lake Virginia on the Rollins College campus. The collection's emphasis is on European and American painting of the last three centuries. It is the oldest art collection in the state and boasts a permanent collection of over 5,000 objects, ranging from Old Masters to twentieth century abstractionists.

Typically, two of the museum's six galleries are given over to special exhibitions, such as recent ones showcasing contemporary prints and Winslow Homer's illustrations of the Civil War, while two other galleries feature some choice examples from the permanent collection. The remaining space is given over to the print collection and educational activities. Many exhibits are locally curated and draw either from the permanent collection or from private and public collections in Florida, offering the art lover the opportunity to view works that would otherwise be impossible to see. For other exhibits, the Cornell joins forces with smaller museums across the country to mount distinguished traveling shows. Exhibits, which run from six to eight weeks, range from retrospectives of a single artist, to highlights of distinguished private collections, to surveys of important movements, to themed shows illuminating genres and techniques.

Nearby: Albin Polasek Galleries, Morse Museum, Winter Park Scenic Boat Tour.

Frank Lloyd Wright Buildings at FSC

111 Lake Hollingsworth Drive, Lakeland 33801

(863) 680-4110

www.flsouthern.edu/fllwctr

Admission: **Free**

Hours: Visitor Center is open Monday to Friday 10:00 a.m. to 4:00 p.m.; Saturday 10:00 a.m. to 2:00 p.m.; Sunday 2:00 p.m. to 4:00 p.m.; grounds are accessible 24 hours a day

Location: On the shores of Lake Hollingsworth

Devotees of Frank Lloyd Wright (and they are legion) will want to make a pilgrimage to Lakeland, about 54 miles west of Orlando, to marvel at the largest group of Wright buildings in the world. Wright designed 18 buildings for Florida Southern, a liberal arts college affiliated with the Methodist Church. Twelve were built.

To get there from Orlando, drive west on I-4 and take Exit 32. Follow US 98 South. From Tampa take Exit 22 and follow US 92 East. The two routes join in downtown Lakeland. When they part ways again, follow route 98 and, shortly, turn right onto Ingraham Avenue. Follow Ingraham until it deadends at Lake Hollingsworth Drive (you'll see the campus of Florida Southern College on your right).

Turn right onto Lake Hollingsworth, then right again onto Johnson Avenue. Look for the parking lot on your right opposite the William F. Chatlos Journalism

Building. If the visitor center isn't open when you drop by, look for a red and white sign; on it is a clear plastic box containing brochures that outline a self-guided walking tour that circles the grounds.

The buildings were designed for a tight budget (in fact, much of the early construction was done by students in the forties) but the results are impressive. Many buildings are unlocked and open to the casual visitor. Inside, look for the tiny squares of colored glass embedded in the exterior walls — a delightfully whimsical touch. Take a moment to sit in the quiet splendor of the Annie Pfeiffer Chapel; the smaller but equally arresting Danforth Chapel is nearby. One of the most interesting buildings to be seen here is the only planetarium Wright ever designed.

The buildings are starting to show their age, but Wright's designs are so idiosyncratic, his decorative elements so unique, that this extensive example of his "organic architecture" seems to exist outside the time/style continuum we carry around in our heads. Instead, it is easy to imagine you are in a city built a long time ago in a galaxy far, far away.

The buildings are linked by one and a half miles of covered esplanades that Wright, in his charmingly perverse way, scaled to his own rather short height. "It makes it kind of difficult to recruit a basketball team," a college executive confided. But for those who fit underneath, the effect is rather cozy and Florida Southern students must say a silent prayer of thanks to Wright as they scurry between classes during an afternoon downpour.

Nearby: Fantasy of Flight, Polk Museum of Art, Water Ski Experience.

Lake Wales Arts Center

1099 State Road 60 East, Lake Wales 33853
(863) 676-8426
www.lakewalesartscenter.org

Admission:	**Free** to exhibits; admission to events varies
Hours:	Monday to Friday 9:00 a.m. to 4:00 p.m.; Saturday 10:00 a.m. to 4:00 p.m.; Sunday 1:00 p.m. to 4:00 p.m. (September to May)
Location:	Take U.S. 27 south to SR 60 and turn left

If the Lake Wales Arts Center looks like an old Spanish mission, that's because it used to be a Catholic church. Today it is home to a smorgasbord of art exhibits, concerts, and cultural enrichment programs. A rotating series of month-long art exhibits feature group shows of abstract and figurative art, with an emphasis on Florida artists. The Masterworks Series features one-night stands by musicians from around the world, while the Entertainment Series showcases jazz and contemporary music. Local residents can become members and receive discounts and other privileges.

Nearby: Cypress Gardens, Historic Bok Sanctuary, Spook Hill.

Maitland Art Center

231 West Packwood Avenue, Maitland 32751
(407) 539-2181

www.maitlandartcenter.org

Admission: For the gallery, adults $3; seniors (65+), Maitland residents, and students (12 to 22) $2

Hours: Monday to Friday 9:00 a.m. to 4:30 p.m.; Saturday and Sunday noon to 4:30 p.m.

Location: From I-4 take Exit 90. Go east on Maitland Boulevard, then turn right onto Maitland Avenue and right onto Packwood

The Maitland Art Center is both a gallery and a working art school. It was founded in the late 1930s by the artist and architect André Smith as a "laboratory" for the study of modern art. Smith built a charmingly eccentric complex of tiny cottage/studios for visiting artists. He decorated the modest buildings with cast concrete ornaments and detailing heavily influenced by the art of the ancient Aztecs and Maya.

Today the gallery plays host to a regular succession of exhibits by local and national artists, exhibits of private collections, and arts and crafts workshops that are open to the public.

After visiting the gallery, take some time to stroll the grounds. The place must have been idyllic in its heyday, before Maitland became quite so built up. Across the street from the gallery and studios is a roofless outdoor concrete chapel with a latticework cross. Shaded by oaks dripping in Spanish moss and surrounded by lush vegetation, the chapel offers a peaceful corner for contemplation. It is also the setting for some spectacular weddings. Right next to it is an open courtyard whose exuberant decoration owes a debt to the boisterous paganism of pre-Columbian Mexico; it makes for quite a contrast.

Nearby: Maitland Historical Museum, Waterhouse Residence, Birds of Prey Center.

Mary, Queen of the Universe Shrine

8300 Vineland Avenue, Orlando 32821

(407) 239-6600

www.maryqueenoftheuniverse.org

Admission: **Free**

Hours: Weekdays 10:30 a.m. to 4:00 p.m. (closed Wednesday); Saturday and Sunday to 6:00 p.m.

Location: Near I-4 Exit 68

This Roman Catholic shrine had humble beginnings as a tourist ministry; today it is a large modern cathedral named by the Pope as a "house of pilgrimage." There is some striking architecture and religious art to be seen here, especially a lovely, abstract, blue stained-glass wall in a chapel dedicated to Our Lady of Guadalupe. A small museum off the gift shop hosts rotating exhibits of religious relics and art from around the world.

Nearby: Discovery Cove, Dixie Stampede, SeaWorld.

Mennello Museum of American Folk Art

900 East Princeton Street, Orlando 32803

(407) 246-4278

www.menellomuseum.com

Admission: Adults $4, seniors (60+) $3, students $1, children under 12 **free**.

Hours: Tuesday to Saturday 10:30 a.m. to 4:30 p.m.; Sunday noon to 4:30 p.m.

Location: In Loch Haven Park, near I-4 Exit 85

Art collectors Marilyn and Michael Mennello fell in love with the work of "naïve" artist Earl Cunningham and purchased virtually his entire life's output. The City of Orlando, meanwhile, had been collecting Florida and southern folk art as part of its Public Art Collection. Now these two visionary endeavors have been brought together in a small gem of a museum located in a renovated private residence overlooking picturesque Lake Formosa in Loch Haven Park.

Cunningham was a Maine sea captain who gradually worked his way south, all the while painting imaginative and idealized coastal landscapes with a Caribbean sense of color. His works form the backbone of the Mennello Museum's collection. They are displayed using a clever halogen lighting system, designed by the museum's director, that heightens the colors in the paintings to almost neon intensity. Other rooms in the museum showcase items from the Orlando city collection and traveling exhibits of other folk artists.

Nearby: Leu Gardens, Orlando Fire Museum, Orlando Museum of Art, Orlando Rep, Orlando Science Center, Orlando-UCF Shakespeare Festival.

Morse Museum of American Art

445 North Park Avenue, Winter Park 32789

(407) 645-5311

www.morsemuseum.org

Admission: Adults $3, students $1, children under 12 **free**; **free** to all Friday 4:00 p.m. to 8:00 p.m. September through May

Hours: Tuesday to Saturday 9:30 a.m. to 4:00 p.m. (Friday to 8:00 p.m. September through May); Sunday 1:00 p.m. to 4:00 p.m.

Location: On Park Avenue, just past the fancy shopping district

Could the Charles Hosmer Morse Museum of American Art be the best museum in Central Florida? Well, for my money, it's hard to beat the world's largest collection of Tiffany glass. That's Louis Comfort Tiffany, the magician of stained glass who flourished at the turn of the twentieth century. The works on display here are absolutely ravishing and, if you have any interest in the decorative arts, your visit to Orlando will be poorer for not having found the time to visit this unparalleled collection.

When most people think of Tiffany glass they think of those wonderfully organic looking table and hanging lamps with the floral designs. Those are here, of course, as are some stunning examples of his large-scale decorative glass windows and door panels. But there's much else, some of which may come as a surprise.

As brilliant a marketer as he was an artist, Tiffany saw the World's Fair of 1893 as an opportunity to spread his fame worldwide. So he put his best foot forward by creating an enormous chapel interior for the exhibit. Everything in it, from a massive electrified chandelier, to a baptismal font, to intricate mosaic pillars to stunningly beautiful stained-glass windows was of Tiffany design. The surviving elements of the chapel have been lovingly restored by the Morse and displayed in a room that is entered through the chapel's original, massive wooden doors.

The faces on Tiffany's glass pieces were painted with powdered glass that was fused to clear glass, but much of the other detail and molding is created by the rich colors and tonal fluctuations in the glass itself. Tiffany is less well known as a painter, but several of his paintings, including some very deft watercolors from his worldwide travels, are to be seen here. There are also miniature glass pieces, vases in delicate, psychedelic-colored favrile glass, inkwells, jewelry, and other decorative objects.

The Morse's collection focuses on the decorative arts and is extensive, comprising some 4,000 pieces. In addition to the permanent displays, the museum dips into its collection to mount special exhibits illuminating various aspects of American decorative arts, including "vignettes," small rooms in which interior designers show off the museum's collection of furniture and decorative objects as they might have looked in the well-to-do homes for which these lovely objects were created.

Nearby: Albin Polasek Galleries, Cornell Fine Arts Museum, Winter Park Scenic Boat Tour.

Orlando City Hall Galleries

Orange Avenue and South Street, Orlando 32801
(407) 246-2221

Admission:	**Free**
Hours:	Monday to Friday 8:00 a.m. to 9:00 p.m.; Saturday and Sunday 12:00 noon to 5:00 p.m.
Location:	Just off I-4 Exit 82

The City of Orlando has a long-standing policy of supporting the arts and an extensive public collection of art, much of which is on display at City Hall. The ground floor gallery, just off the impressive entry rotunda, is used for special exhibits that rotate every three months or so. The third-floor gallery just outside the mayor's office displays selected works from the permanent collection; continue down the stairs to the second floor and see more art on display. In fact, if you wander through the building, you will see that most of the hallways are alive with art. Much of the collection focuses on Florida artists, with an accent on folk art, but some major artists with national reputations are also to be found here. More of the city's folk art collection is on display at the Mennello Museum of American Folk Art, described above.

Nearby: Lake Eola Swan Boats, Orange County Regional History Center.

Orlando Museum of Art

2416 North Mills Avenue, Orlando 32803

(407) 896-4231; fax (407) 896-9920

www.omart.org

Admission:	Adults $8, children (6 to 18) $5, students and seniors (55+) $7; more for special exhibits; **free** on Thursdays 1:00 p.m. to 4:00 p.m. to local residents
Hours:	Tuesday to Friday 10:00 a.m. to 4:00 p.m.; Saturday and Sunday noon to 4:00 p.m.
Location:	In Loch Haven Park, near I-4 Exit 85

The Orlando Museum of Art (OMA) was founded in 1924 to present local, regional, and national artists and develop art education programs for the community. Today, its handsome modern building with its arresting circular hub houses a permanent collection of nineteenth and twentieth century American paintings. There is also a distinguished collection of pre-Columbian art housed in its own gallery.

On any given day, the galleries may host a special exhibit, a selection of works on loan, and a selection of works from the permanent collection. The museum also offers regular video, film, and lecture series, most of which require an additional admission charge. Wheelchairs and lockers are provided free of charge.

A small but very classy gift shop offers a tasteful range of small art objects, reproductions, calendars, glossy art books, and artisanal works you are unlikely to find elsewhere. You can even get an Orlando Museum of Art t-shirt. There is also a small cafe with some interesting menu choices. On the first Thursday of each month, from 6:00 to 9:00 p.m., the museum throws a party with a cash bar, live music from local bands, and themed art by local artists. The $8 admission also allows entry to the galleries.

Nearby: Leu Gardens, Mennello Museum, Orlando Fire Museum, Orlando Science Center.

Osceola Center for the Arts

2411 East Irlo Bronson, Kissimmee 34744

(407) 846-6257

www.ocfta.com

Admission:	**Free** to art gallery
Hours:	Monday to Friday 9:00 a.m. to 5:00 p.m.; Saturday 9:00 a.m. to noon and whenever there is a theater performance
Location:	A mile east of Florida Turnpike Exit 244

This community-based arts organization mounts exhibits of Florida artists. Based on what I've seen, the standards for exhibition are quite high. Exhibits change monthly. The Center also hosts special events, such as a recent exhibition of work by established and emerging local artists.

In addition to presenting art work, the Center hosts a regular schedule of theatrical and musical presentations. Among these are tours by local professional performing arts groups and the productions of a local community theater group.

Polk Museum of Art

800 East Palmetto Street, Lakeland 33801

(863) 688-7743

www.polkmuseumofart.org

Admission:	Adults $5, seniors (62+) $4, students (K-12) and college students with ID **free**. **Free** to all Saturday mornings
Hours:	Tuesday to Saturday 10:00 a.m. to 4:00 p.m.
Location:	Near Lake Morton in downtown Lakeland

If you're making the pilgrimage to Lakeland to see the Frank Lloyd Wright buildings at Florida Southern College, it's worth taking a bit more time to visit this small museum. Housed in a handsome modern building with marble floors and high ceilings, the museum is notable primarily for the Taxdal Pre-Columbian Gallery, an impressive collection of ceramics from ancient American cultures ranging from Mexico to Peru. Otherwise, the museum presents rotating exhibits, some from the permanent collection, some on loan. All eras are represented, but the emphasis seems to be on contemporary art. The museum also showcases art by local students, from kindergarten through high school. Some of it is remarkably sophisticated.

Nearby: Fantasy of Flight, Frank Lloyd Wright Buildings, Water Ski Experience.

Zora Neale Hurston National Museum of Fine Arts

227 East Kennedy Boulevard, Eatonville 32751

(407) 647-3307

www.zoranealehurston.cc

Admission:	**Free** (donations appreciated)
Hours:	Monday to Friday 9:00 a.m. to 4:00 p.m.
Location:	From I-4 Exit 88 take Lee Road east and turn left almost immediately on Wymore; at the next light turn right on Kennedy for about a quarter mile

The tiny enclave of Eatonville is the hometown of the writer Zora Neale Hurston, one of the shining lights of the Harlem Renaissance of the 1920s. Her namesake museum is a small gallery hosting rotating exhibits of African-American artists from Florida and around the nation. The shows change about every six months. The museum also hosts an annual festival in Hurston's honor celebrating various aspects of African-American culture.

THEATER

Orlando and the surrounding communities have an extremely active theater scene, which is not surprising considering all the talent attracted to central Florida by the nearby theme parks.

In addition to the companies listed here, you should be aware of the Starlight Dinner Theater, reviewed in *Chapter 10: Dinner Attractions*. There are also a goodly number of community theaters. You will find complete listings of the day's theatrical offerings in the Living section of the daily *Orlando Sentinel*. The "Calendar" section of the Friday *Sentinel* contains listings for the entire week. Listings also appear in the free weekly paper, *Orlando Weekly*.

Annie Russell Theatre

1000 Holt Avenue, Winter Park 32789
(407) 646-2145
www.rollins.edu/theatre

The drama department of Rollins College holds forth in this lovely, 377-seat Spanish Mediterranean style theater, offering an eclectic season of modern classics, a contemporary musical, and an old farce or Shakespearean play. The season runs from August to April and ticket prices are a bargain — $17 to $19 a seat. The repertory is ambitious and the productions I have seen belie the fact that all the performers are undergraduates. There is also a Second Stage series presenting more experimental work and the occasional new play.

The Annie, as it's known locally, also presents touring dance companies of international renown. Pilobolus and the Paul Taylor Dance Company are among the troupes it has hosted.

Bob Carr Performing Arts Centre

401 West Livingston Street, Orlando 32801
(407) 849-2001, (407) 849-2020
www.orlandocentroplex.com

Located downtown within sight of I-4, the Bob Carr is Orlando's venue for touring Broadway shows and other high-ticket, high-attendance performing arts events. The ultra modern 2,500-seat theater hosts the **Broadway Across America Series**, presenting a season of six or seven shows for runs ranging from one week to a month. These are either touring companies of current or recent Broadway hits, or revivals showcasing a star you've probably heard of. It's mostly "feel-good" musicals, but the occasional straight play is also presented. Tickets for this series range from $40 to $70.

The Bob Carr is the venue of choice for local groups like the **Orlando Opera** and **Orlando Ballet**, described below, as well as one-night stands by comedians like George Carlin, magicians like David Copperfield, and the usual mix of pop and rock concerts.

Mad Cow Theatre Company

105 South Magnolia Street, Orlando 32801
(407) 297-8788
www.madcowtheatre.com

This is Orlando's version of New York's Off Broadway or London's Fringe. Mad Cow has moved several times over the years, each time getting a little bigger and a lot better. Their new home boasts two intimate theaters in an attractive modern downtown building. Stage Left is the larger space at 100 seats; Stage Right is just half that size. The company has now achieved professional status, employing both Equity and non-Equity performers in a ten-play season of new works and modern classics.

The selection of plays is eclectic, everything from Ibsen's *Ghosts* to *My Fair Lady*. Other recent productions include *The Laramie Project* and *As Thousands Cheer*. Although the theaters are comfortable, don't expect Broadway-style production values. The budget for these shows ranges from the minuscule to the modest. But for those with an adventuresome taste in theater-going, Mad Cow will be well worth checking out. Tickets range from $14 to $24, with discounts for seniors and students and some "pay what you wish" nights thrown in for good measure.

Orlando Ballet

1111 North Orange Avenue, Orlando 32804
(407) 426-1739
www.orlandoballet.org

From October to May, this homegrown ballet company, under the direction of Bruce Marks, mounts three-performance runs of about five ballets, ranging from "timeless classics to innovative contemporary works." They draw on a permanent company of professional dancers and a number of apprentices, occasionally presenting guest artists and visiting choreographers. Each year during the Christmas season, they present the ever-popular *Nutcracker*, in association with the Orlando Philharmonic.

Performances are usually given at the Bob Carr Performing Arts Center downtown (I-4 Exit 83). Single tickets range from $15 to $70. Call the number above to purchase tickets.

Orlando International Fringe Festival

398 West Amelia Street, Orlando 32801
(407) 648-0077
www.orlandofringe.org

If you're in Orlando during May and your tastes run towards experimental theater, you won't want to miss this theatrical feast. For 10 days, from noon to midnight, the streets of downtown and Loch Haven Park are given over to an international smorgasbord of traditional theater, cabaret, performance art, and street acts. A typical Festival will see over 500 performances by more than 50 groups from around the world. Most of the fare is decidedly adult, sometimes X-rated, but a parallel Fringe features fare for younger folks. Most of the shows are indoors, but there are some outdoor performance venues.

To attend, you must first purchase a $5 button, which serves as a sort of cover charge for the Festival's shows. You then pay an additional $1 to $10 for each show you see, although some shows are free; if you purchase tickets in advance of the day of performance an additional $1 fee is levied. The Festival is not as geographically compact as it once was, but a printed program lets you know what's coming up next and helps you plan your route from site to site. Veteran Festival-goers suggest quizzing others making the round of shows for suggestions on what's worth seeing and what should be avoided like the plague. Call the number above for the exact dates and location of this year's bash.

Orlando Opera

1111 North Orange Avenue, Orlando 32804
(800) 336-7372; (407) 426-1700
www.orlandoopera.org

Dedicated to bringing the piercing sounds of Italians in pain to Central Florida, the Orlando Opera offers a season of three mainstage productions and two minor productions. The major productions feature the heavyweights (you should excuse the term) of the opera world; Pavarotti, Domingo, and Graves have all performed here. Recent major productions include *Samson et Dalila*, *The Barber of Seville*, and *La Bo-hème*. The minor productions feature resident and studio artists. Recitals and concert performances with major artists have been discontinued but may make a comeback depending on the funding situation.

The season runs from September to May. Most performances are given in the Bob Carr Performing Arts Center mentioned earlier. Prices for tickets to individual performances range from $25 to $120; half-priced tickets are available to students with a valid ID.

Orlando Repertory Theater

1001 East Princeton Street, Orlando 32803
(407) 896-7365
www.orlandorep.com

This professional, non-Equity company is the only local troupe specializing in family and children's theater. Productions range from Off-Broadway hits to adaptations like *Bunnicula* and *A Christmas Story*. Productions are of remarkably high quality in a well-appointed and comfortable 328-seat space in a beautiful modern building that allows room for expansion. The theater is located in the Loch Haven Park arts complex that includes the Shakespeare Festival, the Orlando Museum of Art, and the Orlando Science Center.

The season runs from October through June and typically features six productions, each running for about five weeks. Performances are Fridays through Sunday, with matinees on Saturday and Sunday. Ticket prices range from $8 to $9 for children and $12 to $14 for adults, with musicals being the most expensive.

Orlando Theatre Project (OTP)

P.O. Box 536274, Orlando 32853
(407) 491-1397
www.otp.cc

This small Equity company (all of its actors are based in the Orlando area) has returned to Orlando after several seasons in Sanford to the north. OTP performs in space leased from the Orlando Rep and the Orlando-UCF Shakespeare festival in Loch Haven Park. They present primarily American plays by playwrights such as Arthur Miller and A. R. Gurney. OTP also produces original scripts by local playwrights.

The three-play season runs from October to April, with each production running for three weeks. Performances are Thursday through Saturday at 8:00 p.m. and Sunday at 2:00 p.m. Tickets are $24; students and seniors (65+) $20. Orlando Theatre Project also presents a free play reading once a year.

Orlando-UCF Shakespeare Festival

812 East Rollins Street, Orlando 32803
(407) 447-1700
www.shakespearefest.org

The Bard of Avon is alive and well in Orlando, thanks to this up and coming professional theater company whose home (renovated at a cost of some $3.1 million) in Loch Haven Park boasts three performance spaces. The 330-seat Margeson Theater features a thrust stage and plenty of theatrical bells and whistles, while the 120-seat Goldman Theater is for more intimate productions. There is also a 100-seat "black box" house for experimental shows, workshops, and readings.

The Festival (as they like to be called) is arguably the best theater group in Orlando, and the shows I have seen, including top-notch productions of *Taming of the Shrew* and *Cyrano*, have been excellent. The theater also has a very loyal cadre of performers, which means regular theatergoers have the pleasure of seeing good actors tackle a wide variety of roles over the years. Each season, the Festival presents five plays that may or may not have a Shakespearean connection. In the spring, the company presents a Shakespeare play under the stars in the open-air 936-seat Walt Disney Amphitheater at Lake Eola. One play a year is an adaptation of a classic novel written by a local playwright.

If you are in Orlando in December, don't miss their Christmas show. The Festival has made something of a cottage industry of producing offbeat alternatives to those tired old revivals of *A Christmas Carol* that so many rep companies do year after year. Some of them, like *The Trial of Ebenezer Scrooge* and *Every Christmas Story Ever Told*, are side-splittingly funny.

Throughout the season, the Festival offers PlayFest, a series of professional readings of contemporary plays in development. These events usually take place on the second Monday of the month and are free. Otherwise, ticket prices range from $12 to $38. Mainstage plays run about six weeks with evening performances on Wednesday through Sunday and a matinee on Sunday.

Pinocchio's Marionette Theater

525 South Semoran Boulevard (Route 436), Winter Park 32792
(407) 677-8831
www.pinocchios.net

Tucked away in a shopping center on the northern fringe of metro Orlando is a delightful vest-pocket marionette theater that brings timeless children's stories to life while teaching kids basic theater etiquette. Don't let the shopping center location fool you, either. The technical and artistic quality of the productions here are first rate and the miniature sets (if expanded to three times their actual size) would be the envy of most Orlando area theaters. A visit here is definitely worth the trip.

Pinocchio's is a non-profit organization and the labor of love of David Eaton, who writes most of the shows, and Pady Blackwood, a master puppeteer who worked with Howdy Doody. The set designers have worked for Disney and Universal, and it shows. The two-foot-high marionettes, which are pre-Muppet stringed puppets, are all hand-crafted for each show and costumed with the elegance and attention to detail you'd expect of much grander theaters.

The repertory includes children's classics like Hansel and Gretel, Cinderella, and of course Pinocchio. Performances are given Thursday through Sunday, with up to three shows daily. Call or visit the web site for exact times. Reservations are suggested since many shows sell out and on occasion the entire theater will be booked for a birthday. Each show runs about two to three months. At Christmas time a seasonal show is presented with more frequent performances.

Admission is $9 for adults and $8 for children 3 to 12 and seniors 55 and older. There are special rates for groups of 10 or more. Birthday parties, which include a puppet show, can be arranged for up to 18 kids. Call for details.

The Plaza Theatre

425 North Bumby Avenue, Orlando 32803
(407) 228-1220
www.theplazatheatre.com

Slightly to the east of downtown Orlando, in a renovated 60s-era movie house, the Plaza Theatre is devoted to presenting "family-friendly" live theater. Their opening show, *The Rock and the Rabbi*, an acoustic rock retelling of the relationship between Jesus and his disciple Peter, proved so popular that it ran for years. Recently, the theater booked in the long-running *Menopause: The Musical*. Just in case *Menopause* doesn't last, the *Rock and the Rabbi* production team is readying *David*, another Biblically themed show. From time to time, the theater may be rented to another show or concert.

Shows at the Plaza are presented on a rather erratic schedule. Typically there are shows on Wednesday, Friday, and Saturday at 7:30 p.m., with matinees on Saturday and Sunday. There are frequent "blackout dates," so it's worth checking the box office or web site to make sure. Tickets are $36 and up depending on location in the 860-seat house.

SAK Theatre Comedy Lab

380 West Amelia Street, Orlando 32801
(407) 648-0001
www.sak.com

In the heart of downtown you'll find the Orlando home of improvisational comedy. "Improv," as its practitioners invariably call it, involves a group of agile and quick-witted actors creating a coherent and hilarious sketch based on frequently bizarre suggestions from the audience. More often than not, SAK succeeds. Speaking of success, Wayne Brady of the TV show *Who's Line Is It Anyway?* is a SAK alumnus.

Typically, what you will see is *Duel of Fools*, which is described as "two teams of improv comedy stars . . . in an all-out battle for laughs with Olympic judges, official referees, the pink shoe of salvation, help from the audience, and free candy!!!" From time to time, they present "plays" based on improv principles, such as *Blank: The Musical* and *Suspect*, a murder mystery in which the audience gets to decide whodunit. Popcorn and soft drinks are served. Unlike many comedy clubs, SAK adheres to a strict PG policy; there's no bad language and no booze is served, making it an entertainment possibility for your hipper kids.

The SAK is open year round, Tuesday to Saturday. There is one performance on Tuesdays at 9:00 p.m. and, seasonally, on Wednesdays at 8:00 p.m. and two on Thursdays and Fridays at 8:00 and 10:00 p.m. Tickets are $15 for adults, but Florida residents with photo ID, and all students, seniors, and military personnel with ID, get in for $12. The Tuesday and Wednesday performances are by SAK's student company and are cheap at $2 to $5.

Studio Theater

398 West Amelia Street, Orlando 32801
(407) 872-2382
www.orlandotheatre.com

This intimate venue in downtown Orlando is maintained by the nonprofit Central Florida Theatre Alliance as a rental space for companies that don't have a permanent home. Among the groups that have performed here are the Orlando Black Essentials Theatre, People's Theatre, and the Oops Guys, a duo presenting what is described as "schticky gay comedy."

Ticket prices are set by the group currently using the space and range from $1.50 to $15. The web site contains not only information about what's going on at the Studio Theater but a searchable database of the entire Orlando theater scene.

Theatre Downtown

2113 North Orange Avenue, Orlando 32803
(407) 841-0083
www.theatredowntown.net

Here is another Off-Off Broadway-style theater offering mostly hip contemporary fare like *Psycho Beach Party* and *Little Shop of Horrors* and the occasional classic at moderate prices. The theater, a converted industrial building, has a 115-seat main stage with the audience on three sides of the stage. The performers are non-Equity, many of them just starting out on the stage, so the performance quality varies. The rock musical I saw there was vastly entertaining thanks to a spirited cast that made up in energy whatever they may have lacked in the talent department. Shows run for about a month with performances on Thursday, Friday, and Saturday evenings, with a Sunday matinee. Tickets are $18 ($15 for students and seniors).

Winter Park Playhouse

711-B Orange Avenue, Winter Park 32789
(407) 645-0145
www.winterparkplayhouse.org

Hidden in an inconspicuous storefront location, this Equity company specializes in small-scale musicals presented in an intimate and unpretentious space. Typical shows presented here include *I Love You, You're Perfect, Now Change*, *Godspell*, and *Pete 'n' Keely*, a cabaret-style show evoking the glamour and sophistication of the Steve and Edie era. They also do the occasional straight play like Neil Simon's *California Suite* or a one-man show about Mark Twain.

The Playhouse's season runs from September to June. Show times are Friday to Sunday evenings at 7:30 p.m., with Sunday matinees at 2:00 p.m. General admission tickets are $30 for adults, $28 for seniors (62+), and $20 for students. Matinee tickets are a bit less. Shows in their Youth Theater series are $15 for adults and $12 for children 12 and under.

FILM

Orlando has the usual quota of mall-based multiplex movie theaters offering the latest Hollywood entertainment. The typical admission price is about $7.50 to $8.50 for adults. Some theaters have lower prices ($3.75 to $5) for all showings prior to 5:00 p.m. or for one late afternoon screening each day.

The **Park Theatres** (407) 644-6000, in Winter Park, and the **Colonial Promenade 6** (407) 888-8224, in east Orlando on Colonial Drive, show slightly older films for $1 to $2.50. The "Calendar" section in Friday's *Orlando Sentinel* lists the show times of every movie showing in the greater Orlando area (which extends to the Atlantic coast) along with helpful capsule reviews.

One local film venue deserves special mention. The **Enzian Theater** (1300 South Orlando Avenue in nearby Maitland, (407) 629-0054, www.enzian.org), is the local art house. It shows subtitled European imports and the more adventuresome independent American films. From time to time, it runs special series built around a specific theme. Best of all, the films are screened in a 225-seat movie theater-restaurant. You can have a full meal, washed down with beer or wine, while soaking up culture. They serve up appetizers, sandwiches, and pizzas with a variety of toppings. Beer is sold by the pitcher as well as by the glass. A very filling meal can be had for less than $20 per person. Tickets are $6 for matinees (before 6:00 p.m.) and $8 for evening performances.

In March or April of each year, the Enzian hosts the **Florida Film Festival**, screening as many as 150 films in four venues. Many filmmakers journey to Orlando for the event and give seminars. Single tickets are $9 with discounts available when you buy packs of 20 tickets. Two shorter festivals are held in June (the three-day South Asian Film Festival) and in November (the two-day Central Florida Jewish Film Festival).

MUSIC

The Orlando music scene is far too fleeting and fluid to cover in a guidebook, but if you like your music live rest assured that you will have plenty of opportunity to indulge yourself during your Orlando vacation.

For classical music fans, there is the **Orlando Philharmonic Orchestra**, (407) 896-6700, www.orlandophil.org, which presents a dozen or so concerts each year in a variety of venues including the Bob Carr Performing Arts Center mentioned earlier. That same downtown arena plays host to the usual array of aging rock stars and pop headliners, while the local bar and club scene serves up a wide variety of musical offerings from folk, to ethnic, to rhythm and blues, to country-western. Orlando has also garnered a reputation as an incubator of teen pop groups. If your taste lies in this direction you may be able to catch some rising stars.

The best way to plug into the music scene is the "Calendar" section in Friday's *Orlando Sentinel* which lists all musical performances for the week, arranged helpfully by genre, along with a list of web sites for local bands. A "Calendar" page in the daily *Sentinel* lists that day's offerings. The free *Orlando Weekly* also has extensive coverage of the local music scene.

For those whose tastes run to classical music, the magazine *Orlando Arts*, available at museums and other cultural hangouts, lists upcoming events.

Chapter Sixteen:

Moving
Experiences

NOT ONLY ARE THERE A LOT OF THINGS TO SEE IN THE ORLANDO AREA, THERE ARE A lot of ways to see them. If walking or driving around begins to seem a bit boring, why not try some of these alternate modes of taking in the sights? There are some sights you will be able to see in no other way. Then again, some of these experiences are ends in themselves, with the passing scenery merely a backdrop.

Gathered together in this chapter, then, are the many and varied ways to get up in the air or out on the water during your Orlando vacation.

Balloon Rides

Up, up, and away in a beautiful balloon. It's a great way to start the day and, if floating along on a big bubble of hot air appeals to you, that's when you'll have to go — at dawn. The weather's capricious in Orlando and at dawn the winds are at their calmest. A number of companies offer ballooning experiences in the Orlando area, and they all operate in much the same fashion, providing much the same experience.

Typically, you make your "weather-permitting" reservation by phone; your flight is confirmed (or called off) the night before. Then it's up with the birds to meet at a central location in the predawn twilight for a ride to the launch site, which will be determined by the prevailing weather conditions.

Most balloon operators let their passengers experience the fun (or is it the hard work?) of unloading and inflating the balloon. When the balloon is fully inflated, you soar aloft on a 45-minute to one-hour flight to points unknown. Of course, the pilot has a pretty good idea of where he'd like to put down, but the winds have a way of altering plans. After landing, once the balloon is packed away, a champagne toast is offered. With photographs and certificates, the passengers are inducted into the confraternity of ballooning. Some excursions include breakfast. The whole experience takes anywhere from three to four hours.

The balloons — or more properly the baskets that hang beneath the balloons — hold anywhere from two to 20 people, with six- to eight-passenger baskets being the most common. Usually, then, you will be riding with other people. If a couple wants a balloon to themselves (a frequent request), the price goes up. A few balloon operators try to float over Disney World whenever the winds cooperate, but it's hard to guarantee. The Disney folks are (understandably) less than happy about balloons landing on their property, so pilots must plan with care. Typically, your flight will be over the less-populated fringes of the metro area.

Hot-air ballooning is not cheap (most operators accept credit cards). Figure on about $175 to $200 per adult, about $100 per child (based on age or weight), plus tax, for the brief flight and the attendant hoopla. Some operators offer kids-fly-free promotions. Special packages, such as a wedding flight, can cost upwards of $1,000. Hot air balloon operators, I have discovered, are a prickly lot, who are reluctant to provide pricing information, citing frequent fluctuations in fuel and other operating costs. So use the listing below as a starting point for your own comparison shopping.

Reservations must typically be guaranteed with a credit card and there are cancellation penalties. Many of the outfits listed below offer Internet discounts.

Despite the cost, for those looking for a very special way to celebrate a birthday or an anniversary, the ballooning experience is not quite like any other. As one brochure puts it, "the ballooning adventure will last three to four hours, the memories will last a lifetime!"

A Hot Air Balloon Ride
(407) 897-5432

www.ahotairballoonride.com

Post-flight festivities include a "special balloonists prayer," a certificate of ascension, a commemorative pin and a "sparkling beverage" toast. Helping the crew inflate the balloon is optional.

Aerostat Adventures
(877) 495-RIDE

www.balloonflorida.com

Specializing in couples-only flights, this operator offers flights near Mt. Dora and Eustis, north of Orlando, as well as flights in the Disney area. Post-flight there is a "champagne brunch."

Blue Water Balloons
P.O. Box 560572, Orlando 32856

(800) 586-1884; (407) 894-5040

www.bluewaterballoons.com

Sunrise champagne flights in the Disney area are the draw here and special "couples only" flights are offered. Free hotel pickup in the Orlando area is included in the price and owner Don Edwards limits capacity to four passengers per balloon.

Bob's Balloon Charters

732 Ensenada Drive, Orlando 32825
(877) 824-4606; (407) 466-6380
www.bobsballoons.com

Bob Wilamoski's two balloons and 100-plus takeoff and landing sites let you soar pretty much anywhere in the Orlando area; they say they'll even take off from your home if conditions are favorable. Another draw is that you can crawl around inside the balloon while it's being prepared.

Fantasy of Flight

P.O. Box 1200, Polk City 33868
(863) 984-3500
www.fantasyofflight.com/balloon.htm

This roadside attraction reviewed in *Chapter 11* now offers balloon rides. You must book at least 48 hours in advance. Fantasy of Flight is about 50 miles west of Orlando off Exit 44 from I-4.

Magic Sunrise Ballooning

(866) 606-RIDE (7433)
www.magicsunriseballooning.com

Offers the standard range of flights and amenities and the least expensive wedding package I've seen.

Orange Blossom Balloons

P.O. Box 22908, Lake Buena Vista 32830
(407) 239-7677
www.orangeblossomballoons.com

There are 25 launch sites scattered around the Orlando area. All flights include a champagne toast and an all-you-can-eat breakfast buffet served after the flight. Orange Blossom also offers wedding packages.

Painted Horizons Hot Air Balloon Tours

7741 Hyacinth Drive, Orlando 32835
(866) 578-3031, (407) 578-3031
www.paintedhorizons.com

Couples-only flights are available only on weekends. Flights end with champagne, cheese, pastries, and crackers. I'm told the couples-only flights book up fast.

SkyScapes Balloon Tours

P.O. Box 452953, Kissimmee 34745
(407) 856-4606
www.skyscapesballoontours.com

SkyScapes specializes in "couples only" and family flights. The flights culminate in a champagne brunch and party. The whole experience lasts about four hours.

Boat Rides

As you can easily see when you fly into Orlando, Central Florida is dotted with lakes, from the tiny to the fairly large. It also boasts its fair share of spring fed streams and rivers, as well as acre upon acre of swamps. It should come as no surprise, then, that the Orlando area offers the visitor plenty of opportunities to get on the water.

The signature Central Florida boat ride, of course, is aboard an airboat. These cleverly designed craft were created to meet the challenges of Florida's swamps and shallow estuaries. The pontoons allow the craft to float in just inches of water, the raised pilot's seat allows the driver to spot submerged obstacles (like alligators) before it's too late, and the powerful (if rather noisy) airplane propellers that power them let the boats skim across the water at a remarkable clip. The airboat is a raffish, backwoods sort of vehicle and it is used to give tourists a taste of what the old Florida of trappers and hunters was like. The "prey" is much the same — gators and such — but these days the only thing that gets shot is photographs.

There are other ways to cruise Central Florida's waters. One of the most popular is the pontoon boat, a flat rectangle set on two buoyant floats and designed for leisurely lake cruising. For many of Florida's lakeshore residents, they serve as floating patios; for the tourist trade, they make excellent sightseeing vessels. Central Florida even lays claim to a sort of cruise ship that takes passengers out on the broad St. John's River for an elegant dinner. All these options are listed below, along with the major airboat excursion companies.

A-Awesome Airboat Rides

P.O. Box 333, Christmas 32709
(407) 568-7601
www.airboatride.com

Cost:	Varies with the cost of gas; call
Hours:	Daily, 24 hours
Location:	Meets on SR 50 at the bridge over the St. John's River

"Captain Bruce" runs this low key operation offering private airboat tours of the extensive St. John's River ecosystem near Christmas, to the east of Orlando. The 90-minute tours are by reservation only. They offer a close-up look at alligators, bald eagles (September through May), and other denizens of this starkly beautiful landscape.

You can take a trip in the middle of the night if you wish, but you are better advised to consult with Captain Bruce on the best time to go to see what you want to see. There are two six-passenger airboats, but if you have a large group, Captain Bruce can round up enough boats to accommodate 30 people. There is a minimum per boatload, which means that if only two people go they will be charged a premium.

Boggy Creek Airboat Rides

1. 3702 Big Bass Road, Kissimmee 34744

(407) 344-9550

2. 2001 East Southport Road, Kissimmee 34746

(407) 344-9550

www.bcairboats.com

Cost:	Adults $21.95, children (3 to 12) $15.95, under 2 **free**; $45 per person for 45-minute tours
Hours:	Daily 9:00 a.m. to 5:30 p.m.
Location:	1. About 8 miles from East Irlo Bronson Highway on the north shore of East Lake Tohopekaliga. 2. On the north shore of West Lake Tohopekaliga, about 20 miles from US 192 on Poinciana Boulevard (which becomes Southport Road).

Boggy Creek Airboats operates half hour tours on 18-passenger boats that explore the shores of their respective lakes. The eastern location also covers the nooks and crannies of Boggy Creek, one of the few habitats of the endangered snail kite. On the wildlife menu for both are alligators, turtles, and a multitude of water fowl. "Private" 45-minute tours on 6-passenger boats are $45 per person. On warm summer nights, both run hour-long alligator tours by reservation only. The tab is $35 for adults and $30 for kids.

You'll find the Big Bass Road location at East Lake Fish Camp, a lovely camping and fishing resort. Several fishing guides operate from this base. You might want to consider spending a day (and perhaps a night) here.

The Southport Road location also offers an off-road Wildlife Safari Tour described a little later in this chapter.

Glades Adventures

4715 Kissimmee Park Road, St. Cloud 34772

(407) 891-2222

www.gladesadventures.com

Cost:	Adults $30, children (3 to 10) $20 for 1-hour trip
Hours:	Daily 10:00 a.m. to 5:00 p.m.
Location:	On the east side of Lake Toho

Billing itself as the "upscale alternative," Glades Adventures operates only smaller 6-passenger airboats on one-hour tours of Kissimmee's Lake Tohopekaliga. On this tour, you might spot (depending on the season) bald eagles, osprey, otters, deer, wild boar, and, of course, alligators. Two-hour nighttime alligator hunts are also available by appointment.

Back at the dock, there is a small alligator nursery, which is primarily an opportunity for tourists to touch a real live (and small) alligator. There is also a restaurant at dockside serving "Florida-style" food like gator tails, catfish, and frogs legs. Yum.

Old Fashioned Airboat Rides

24004 Sisler Avenue, Christmas 32709
(407) 568-4307
www.airboatrides.com

Cost:	Adults $40, children (3 to 12) $25, including tax; no children under 3
Hours:	By appointment
Location:	SR 50 at the public boat ramp about 45 minutes to an hour from Orlando

Captain John "Airboat John" Long runs this boutique operation from his home, specializing in private airboat tours on three six-passenger boats. Make your arrangements by phone (don't drop by the office!) and make sure you bring along lunch or a snack.

John's 90-minute nature trips are leisurely by the standards of most airboat tours. They explore a 40-mile roundtrip swath of river and swamp. There's plenty of gators and bald eagles to be seen along this remote stretch. On one side is the Tosohatchee Preserve, on the other large swaths of private ranch land. You can stop at a small island cabin or an ancient Indian mound for lunch and a great **photo op** of the boat on the water.

In the warmer months, John runs night trips in search of alligators. Gators have a reputation for being stupid but they avoid the blistering summer sun, making them smarter than the average tourist in some people's estimation.

Expect to ride with other folks, unless your party is four or more people. "Those boats burn a lot of gas," John explains. "Private tours" of one or two people are offered at $160. John doesn't allow children under three for safety reasons. Payment is strictly in cash or travelers checks; no credit cards.

Osprey Eco Tours

3301 Lake Cypress Road, Kenansville 34739
(407) 957-2277
www.ospreyecotours.com

Cost:	$45 adults; $35, children for one-hour tour
Hours:	Daily, by appointment only
Location:	From US 193 East, turn right on Vermont Avenue (also known as Canoe Creek Road); go 11.6 miles and turn right onto Lake Cypress Road

Operating on the lesser-known Cypress Lake, south of Lake Toho, this operator offers a standard half-hour ride aboard 12-passenger airboats and longer one and one and a half hour eco tours aboard 6-passenger craft. The longer tours poke into even more remote Lake Hatchineha and the Dead River in search of a smorgasbord of Florida wildlife, with gators topping the list. Night gator hunts are also available. Osprey Eco Tours provides an intercom system to facilitate quiet conversation and provides binoculars.

Rivership Romance

433 North Palmetto Avenue, Sanford 32771

(800) 423-7401; (407) 321-5091

www.rivershipromance.com

Cost:	$37 to $53, plus tax, drinks, and tip
Hours:	Cruises at 11:00 a.m. daily and 7:30 p.m. Friday and Saturday; year-round
Location:	From I-4 Exit 103, 4 miles east on SR 46

The Rivership Romance is a refurbished, 100-foot, 1940s Great Lakes steamer that plies the waters of Lake Monroe and the St. John's River for leisurely luncheon and dinner cruises. It's not quite the "Love Boat," but for a nice change of pace from landlocked dining, it will do quite nicely.

There are three-hour luncheon cruises on Wednesday, Saturday, and Sunday; four-hour luncheon cruises on Monday, Tuesday, Thursday, and Friday; and three-and-a-half-hour dinner cruises on Saturday. Live entertainment is featured on all cruises and there is dancing to a sophisticated combo on the evening cruises.

On Friday nights, they will offer up more elaborate entertainment in the form of wacky wedding parties to which you are invited. These romps, somewhat in the mold of the Off Broadway hit *Tony 'n Tina's Wedding*, use actors who roam the aisles, yell and scream at each other, and even eat at your table, all the while jabbering on in character. It can be a lot of fun, if you're in the mood.

The dinner menu is short but sumptuous and, in true cruise line tradition, the portions are generous. After starting off with salad, you can choose from Tuscan chicken breast, herb-crusted grouper, Caribbean pork, beef loin, or eggplant parmesan.

The scenery's nothing to sneeze at either. The St. John's is one of just two large rivers in the world that flow north and during the four-hour luncheon cruise, you'll get to see some 25 miles of its history-steeped shores. There's not much to see at night, of course, except for the stars, which can be spectacular on a clear night. And for the romantic couples who take these cruises that's the whole point.

Reservations are required and all major credit cards are accepted.

Scenic Lake Tours

101 Lakeshore Drive, Kissimmee 34741

(800) 244-9105

www.fishingchartersinc.com

Cost:	Adults $25, children (6 to 12) $15
Hours:	10:00 a.m. to 4:00 p.m. Monday to Friday; 11:00 a.m. to 3:00 p.m. weekends; sunset cruises by request
Location:	Departs from the Big Toho Marina on the Kissimmee waterfront

"Captain Rick" runs this friendly tour operation offering one-hour "scenic/eco tours" of Kissimmee's Lake Toho (Tohopekaliga) aboard a 24-foot, six-passenger pontoon boat. Soft drinks, water, and snacks are thrown in at no additional charge.

Bald eagles and ospreys can sometimes be spotted around the lake, but gators are more frequently sighted. Cruisers can also see the island from which Chief Osceola himself ruled over his territory.

Reservations must be made 24 hours in advance. Captain Rick also provides fishing charters for crappie and bass on the Lake.

TJ's Airboats
1550 Scotty's Road, Kissimmee 34744
(407) 846-6540

Cost:	Adults $28, children (12 and under) $23
Hours:	Daily 9:00 a.m. to 6:00 p.m.
Location:	At Richardson Fish Camp on the east shore of West Lake Toho; call for directions

TJ's runs six-passenger airboats on one-hour tours along the shores of West Lake Tohopekaliga in search of the usual wildlife suspects, including gators, eagles, and a wide variety of birds. There is an $84 minimum charge per boat, so you may have to pay extra or wait for more passengers to show up.

In the summer months, night rides are offered by appointment. These hour and twenty minute tours go in search of gators and cost $50 for adults and $35 for children with a $150 minimum.

Winter Park Scenic Boat Tour
312 East Morse Boulevard, Winter Park 32789
(407) 644-4056
www.scenicboattours.com

Cost:	Adults $10, children (2 to 11) $5, with tax
Hours:	Daily 10:00 a.m. to 4:00 p.m. on the hour
Location:	At the foot of Morse Boulevard, a short stroll from Park Avenue's fancy shops

The little town of Winter Park has 17 lakes. Thanks to the operators of these modest, flat pontoon boats, you can visit three of them on a leisurely one-hour cruise. You slip between the lakes through narrow canals originally cut by logging crews in the 1800s and barely wide enough to accommodate the tour boat. It's not quite Venice but it makes for an unusual and relaxing outing.

There's plenty of bird life to be seen on this tour and your guide will dutifully point out the wading herons, muscovy ducks, and ospreys nesting high in the cypress trees. Less frequently sighted, but there nonetheless, are alligators, some of them quite large. There's also a bit of local history to take in, from the campus of Rollins College to the palatial 1898 Brewer estate, the only Winter Park home on the National Historic Register.

But, this tour is really about real estate envy. As you glide past one gorgeous multimillion dollar home after another, their impeccably landscaped backyards cascading down to boathouses that coyly echo the architecture of the big house, you will find yourself asking, "Why them and not me? Why, why, why?"

Helicopter Tours

Small operations offering guided aerial sightseeing by helicopter pop up (and disappear) with some regularity. If the ones listed here are closed by the time you arrive, you'll probably spot new ones as you drive around the tourist areas. They all seem to offer much the same menu of tours, ranging from short two- to three-minute hops for about $15 to half-hour surveys for about $200, with children's prices somewhat less. Some offer extended trips that take in Kennedy Space Center for $400. Typically, these operators require a minimum of two adult passengers, although some require a full craft for takeoff and some offer special one-person rates. Most operators start up at 9:00 or 10:00 a.m. and continue until sunset, but call first to check.

Tip: The farther they have to fly the more expensive the trip. So if you especially want to see Universal Orlando, pick a helipad on International Drive; if Disney World is on your must-see list, try a tour that leaves from Kissimmee. You might save some money.

Air Florida Helicopters

8990 International Drive, Orlando 32819
(407) 354-1400
www.airfloridahelicopters.com
At Trolley and Train Museum, next to Race Rock

Helicopters International

5855 American Way, Orlando 32819
(866) 794-6359; (407) 903-0284
www.helicoptersinternational.com
Just off International Drive, near Kirkman Road

Legacy Grand Heliport

5069 West Irlo Bronson Highway, Kissimmee 34746
(407) 390-7502
East of I-4 Exit 64, between Mile Markers 10 and 11

Orlando Helicenter

4623 Irlo Bronson Highway, Kissimmee 34746
(407) 396-6006
www.orlandohelicenter.com

Orlando Helitours

5519 West Irlo Bronson Highway, Kissimmee 34746
(407) 397-0226
www.orlandohelitours.com
East of I-4 Exit 64, near Mile Marker 9

Universal Air Service

201 Nilson Way, Orlando 32803
(800) 433-5561; (407) 896-2966
www.universalhelicopter.com
At the Orlando Executive Airport. $1,000 an hour for up to nine people.

Off-Road Adventures

Florida's low-lying swampy terrain has given rise to a type of tourist ride not found in too many other places. Sometimes called "swamp buggies" or "monster trucks," the vehicles are custom designed all-terrain vehicles that have been created by combining an old bus chassis with huge tractor or other massive tires that can bull their way through shallow muddy swamp water. They give you a chance to see wild-life in a natural setting that Nature did not design for casual strolling.

One such ride is offered at Forever Florida, described in *Chapter 14: Gardens and Edens*. There are others closer to the Orlando action.

Boggy Creek Wildlife Safari

2001 East Southport Road, Kissimmee 34746
(407) 344-9550
www.bcairboats.com

Cost:	Adults $21.95, children (3 to 12) $15.95, under 2 **free**
Hours:	Daily 9:00 a.m. to 5:30 p.m.
Location:	On the north shore of West Lake Tohopekaliga, about 20 miles from US 192 on Poinciana Boulevard (which becomes Southport Road).

The folks who operate Boggy Creek Airboat Rides have a land-based alternative for those who'd like yet another way to catch a glimpse of what locals like to call "the Real Florida." Your ride vehicle is an old school bus, with the sides cut off and a sheltering canopy mounted on top. It all sits atop huge, cartoony tires and it takes you on a bumpy ride through a chunk of an 8,000-acre working cattle ranch that dates back to the earliest days of ranching in Florida. There are animals to be seen here that you usually miss on the airboat tours, including wild hogs, deer, raccoons, and other small mammals. Best of all are the bald eagles and ospreys that nest in the area. The guides are all drawn from local families, so they know the territory, the history, and the folklore of the region. If you're lucky, you might get to see a cattle roundup in progress, as this is still very much a working ranch.

Showcase of Citrus Eco Tours

5010 Highway 27, Clermont 34711
(352) 267-2597
www.showcaseofcitrus.com/ecotour.asp

Cost:	Adults $20, children (4 to 12) $10, $80 minimum per trip
Hours:	By appointment
Location:	Take US 192 or I-4 west to US 27, then drive north; Showcase of Citrus is on your right.

The main business of Showcase of Citrus is selling oranges and other citrus products, but as a sideline they operate one-hour "eco tours" through the groves and surrounding woods and marshes. The palmetto, oak, and pine scrub habitats here offer shelter to a variety of wildlife and the swamps feature the ever-present alligators.

Plane & Glider Rides

Although there will be plenty to see once you're aloft, these plane and glider rides are more about the experience itself than the sightseeing. If you'd like to be a little more "hands on," check out the plane rides listed in *Chapter 12: Do It!*

Fantasy of Flight

P.O. Box 1200, Polk City 33868
(863) 873-1339
www.fantasyofflight.com

Cost:	$60 to $200 per person
Hours:	Daily 10:00 a.m. to 5:00 p.m. weather permitting, October through May only
Location:	Exit 44 off I-4, about 50 miles west of Orlando

Get a look at Central Florida from a vintage 1929 New Standard open-cockpit biplane. No reservations are necessary for the $60, 20-minute flights. For $200, you can get a half hour in a 1942 Boeing Stearman PT-17 and even get a chance to take the controls. (See *Chapter 11* for Fantasy of Flight's other attractions.)

Seminole-Lake Gliderport

P. O. Box 135516, Clermont 34713
(352) 394-5450
www.soarfl.com

Cost:	$95 to $160, including tax
Hours:	Tuesday to Sunday 9:00 a.m. to dusk; closed Tuesday June, July, August
Location:	Just south of Clermont, at the intersection of SR 33 and SR 561

If you look up in the sky and see puffy cumulus clouds against a warm blue sky, it's perfect gliding weather. You might just want to pop over to the Clermont area for an air-powered glider ride. The folks at Seminole-Lake Gliderport will put you in a high-performance glider with an FAA-certified instructor, tow you into the wild blue yonder — and let you go.

The price depends on the altitude at which the flight starts and, hence, its length. A $95 flight starts from 3,000 feet and lasts 20 to 25 minutes. At $130 and 4,000 feet they'll throw in some aerial maneuvers for the 35-minute flight. The $160 flight tows you to 5,000 feet, offering a spectacular view of Central Florida on the 45-minute glide to landing.

Flights begin about 10:00 a.m., with the last flight about 4:00 p.m. Visa and MasterCard are accepted. Instruction is also offered; rated pilots can pick up a gliding add-on to their license in about three or four days.

Train Rides

Inland Lakes Railway

150 West Third Avenue, Mt. Dora 32757
(352) 589-4300
www.inlandlakesrailway.com

Cost:	Varies with ride from $12 to $60
Hours:	Wednesday to Sunday 11:00 a.m. to 8:00 p.m.
Location:	In Mt. Dora: At the corner of Third and Alexander in downtown Mt. Dora, across from the Lakeside Inn
	In Eustis: 51 West Magnolia Avenue, near Ferran Park Drive

The grandly named Inland Lakes Railway runs a numbers of excursions on vintage railway cars that will appeal to railway buffs and run of the mill tourists alike.

The **Southern Heritage Dinner Train** departs on Saturday and Sunday evenings for a leisurely two-and-a-half-hour meal on wheels cooked right on the train. Your mobile restaurant is a glistening, restored 1948-vintage stainless steel dining car, The Silver Spur. The cost is $55 on Friday, $60 on Saturday. A less expensive ($40) lunch excursion is also available on Saturday. These trips depart from Eustis.

The other major outing is the **Herbie Express**, a one hour 15 minute excursion to Tavares on vintage railway cars pulled by "Herbie," a 1942 locomotive. Along the way, a narrator tells the history of the line and fills you in on other locomotive lore. The line runs right down the middle of the road in Tavares where the train is turned around on a "wye," a triangle-shaped switching mechanism. These trips have two departures in the afternoon Wednesday through Sunday, with an additional morning departure on Saturday. The fare is $12 for adults and $8 for kids 12 and under. These trips depart from Mt. Dora.

There are other, themed outings such as the "Pizza Express" and seasonal jaunts like "The Great Pumpkin Express." Schedules, of course, are subject to change.

Chapter Seventeen:

Sports Scores

THE MILD CLIMATE OF CENTRAL FLORIDA IS AN OPEN AND ONGOING INVITATION TO THE active life. Sportsmen and women will find a wide array of choices to fit every taste and every budget. These activities are listed in *Chapter 12: Do It!*

The more sedentary among us will find enough spectator sports in and around Orlando to keep them busy for quite some time. And if you visit in the month of March, then you should by all means sample the pleasures of baseball Spring Training — even if you don't fancy yourself much of a baseball fan.

With the notable exception of the Magic, Orlando's professional basketball team, tickets to most events are easy to come by and reasonably priced.

Arena Football

Arena football is a scaled-down, indoor version of pro football. Two eight-man teams square off on a field about a half the size of the outdoor version. Adding interest to the game, six players on each team play both offense and defense. Otherwise, the rules are much the same as those for pro football. There are 19 professional arena football teams in the United States.

Orlando Predators

600 West Amelia Street, Orlando 32801
(407) 44-PREDS
www.orlandopredators.com

Season:	February to May
Where:	T. D. Waterhouse Center, 600 West Amelia Street, in downtown Orlando, just off I-4 Exit 83
Ticket Prices:	$7 to $85

Auto Racing - Dragsters, Motocross

Amateurs race for the love of it at two sets of racing venues that lie within driving distance of Orlando's main tourist areas. One is to the east of Orlando on busy State Route 50 and the other a short drive down Interstate 4 in Lakeland at Exit 38. If you're staying near Disney, it may be easier to get to the Lakeland tracks.

The Lakeland track has two distinct styles. The dirt or clay tracks (which are subject to the vagaries of the Florida weather) is where you want to be for BMX bicycles, motocross, stock cars, and four-wheel-drive Mud Boggs (modified trucks). The drag strips use a straight paved track with bleachers, including a platform for wheelchairs.

In Orlando, Bithlo Motorsports specializes in motocross, an especially exciting form of motorcycle racing featuring rugged bikes competing on bumpy dirt tracks. The drag strip in Orlando is much like that at Lakeland.

There's usually something going on at all these tracks on the weekends, with additional events on some weeknights, but it's a good idea to call the track or check online for current information.

Lakeland Motorsports Park

8100 Highway 33 North, Lakeland 33809
(863) 984-1145
www.lakelandmotorsportspark.com

> *Season:*　　　Year round, call for schedule
> *Ticket Prices:*　$10 and up, varies by race

Bithlo Motorsports

19400 East Colonial Drive, Orlando 32833
(407) 568-2271

> *Season:*　　　Year round, call for schedule
> *Ticket Prices:*　$10 and up, varies by race

Speed World Dragway

19442 East Colonial Drive, Orlando 32833
(407) 568-5522
www.speedworlddragway.com

> *Season:*　　　Year round, call for schedule
> *Ticket Prices:*　$10 and up

Auto Racing - Stock Cars

There is no major stock car track in Orlando, but fans probably won't mind traveling a short distance to get their speed fix, especially since one of the nearby tracks is the Daytona Speedway. Daytona hosts NASCAR's legendary "Daytona 500" in February. In Lakeland, a relatively short drive from Orlando to Exit 38 on I-4, is a track that operates under the ASA (American Speed Association) banner.

Daytona International Speedway
1801 West International Speedway, Daytona 32114
(800) PITSHOP; (866) 761-7223
www.daytonainternationalspeedway.com
Season: NASCAR races in February (the Daytona 500) and July; other events in other months
Ticket Prices: $30 to $230, varies by race

USA International Speedway
3401 Old Polk City Road, Lakeland 33809
(800) 984-7223; (863) 984-7223
www.usaspeedway.com
Season: January to November; 8 to 10 events a year, call for schedule
Ticket Prices: Adults $20 to $30, children under 10 $10

Baseball, Major League
Thanks to the arrival in 1998 of the Tampa Bay Devil Rays, an expansion team in the American League, Central Florida boasts its own professional baseball team. Despite the name, the team plays in St. Petersburg, not Tampa.

Tampa Bay Devil Rays
1 Tropicana Drive, St. Petersburg 33705
(727) 825-3137
www.devilrays.com
Season: April to September
Where: 1 Tropicana Drive, St. Petersburg
Ticket Prices: $8 to $260 for general admission

Baseball, MLB Spring Training
Many major league baseball teams find Florida's spring weather ideal for their preseason warm-ups. The training regimen includes a number of exhibition games in March that allow the teams a chance to limber up and practice under realistic conditions. They also give fans a chance to look over their favorite team's form and check out new players before the official season begins.

I have listed here the teams that have spring training camps within striking distance of Orlando, bearing in mind that a true fan's definition of "striking distance" could mean 100 miles. The closest teams to Orlando are the Braves (at Disney) and the Astros (in Kissimmee). The prices listed below are for the 2006 season.

I can't claim to have visited all of these parks, but I've been to a bunch. My favorites are the Astros field, for its intimacy, and the Phillies park in Clearwater, which is a model for what a modern small-scale baseball stadium should be.

If you are serious about Spring Training and would like to build a vacation around this most American of experiences, then the indispensable guide is Alan Byrd's *Florida Spring Training: Your Guide to Touring the Grapefruit League* (Intrepid Traveler, $14.95). Byrd provides in-depth, analytic reviews of every Spring Training stadium in Florida, including tips on how to get autographs and where to sit to maximize your chances of snagging a fly ball, as well as tips on where to eat and what to see and do after the game. For more information, visit
http://www.theotherorlando.com/shop/

Atlanta Braves
Cracker Jack Stadium
Disney's Wide World of Sports Complex
Lake Buena Vista 32830
(407) 939-4263

Location:	West of I-4 in the Disney complex
Ticket Prices:	$14 to $22.50

Cincinnati Reds
Ed Smith Stadium
2700 12th Street, Sarasota 34237
(941) 954-4464

Location:	I-75 Exit 210, west to Tuttle Avenue, right on Tuttle to ballpark
Ticket Prices:	$5 to $14

Cleveland Indians
Chain O' Lakes Park
500 Cletus Allen Drive, Winter Haven 33880
(863) 293-3900

Location:	Near the intersection of US 17 and Cypress Gardens Boulevard (look for the big orange dome)
Ticket Prices:	$5 to $21

Detroit Tigers
Joker Marchant Stadium
2301 Lakeland Hills Boulevard, Lakeland 33805
(813) 287-8844

Location:	South of I-4 Exit 33 about 3 miles
Ticket Prices:	$7 to $18

Florida Marlins / St. Louis Cardinals
Roger Dean Stadium
4751 Main Street, Jupiter 33458
(561) 775-1818

Location:	I-95 Exit 83, then 1 mile east to South Central Boulevard; follow traffic circle to Main Street; stadium is straight ahead
Ticket Prices:	$6 to $23

Houston Astros

Osceola County Stadium
1000 Bill Beck Boulevard, Kissimmee 34744
(321) 697-3200

Location:	Off US 192, just east of Kissimmee
Ticket Prices:	$15 to $18

Los Angeles Dodgers

Holman Stadium (Dodgertown)
4101 26th Street, Vero Beach 32960
(772) 569-6858

Location:	Take SR 60 East from I-95, turn left on 43rd Avenue, then right on 26th Street
Ticket Prices:	$15

New York Yankees

Legends Field
1 Steinbrenner Drive, Tampa 33614
(813) 879-2244

Location:	I-4 to I-275 Exit 41, Dale Mabry North
Ticket Prices:	$14 to $18

Philadelphia Phillies

Bright House Networks Field
601 Old Coachman Road, Clearwater 33765
(727) 442-8496

Location:	US 19 to Drew Street (SR 590); west on Drew to stadium
Ticket Prices:	$9 to $25

Pittsburgh Pirates

McKechnie Field
1611 9th Street West, Bradenton 34205
(941) 748-4610

Location:	I-75 Exit 220, then west on SR 64, left on 9th Street West
Ticket Prices:	$6 to $11

Tampa Bay Devil Rays
Progress Energy Park
230 First Street South, St. Petersburg 33701
(727) 825–3250
www.devilrays.com
> *Location:*   I-275 to I-175 (Exit 22), I-175 turns into Fifth Avenue South, left at First Street South
> *Ticket Prices:* $7 to $19

Toronto Blue Jays
Dunedin Stadium at Grant Field
373 Douglas Avenue, Dunedin 34698
(727) 733–0429
> *Location:*   From US 19, west on Sunset Point Road, right on Douglas Avenue
> *Ticket Prices:* $13 to $24

Baseball, Minor League
The Orlando area's two farm teams give you a chance to see some rising (and a few falling) stars in action. Many devotees of minor league baseball say it takes them back to a simpler time, before players started commanding multimillion dollar salaries. The prices are comfortably old fashioned, too.

Daytona Cubs (Class A, Chicago Cubs)
105 East Orange Avenue, Daytona Beach 32114
(386) 257–3172
www.daytonacubs.com
> *Season:*   April to September
> *Where:*   Jackie Robinson Ballpark; from I-95 take International Speedway Boulevard exit (SR 92) east to Beach, then south to East Orange
> *Ticket Prices:* $6 to $9

Lakeland Tigers (Class A, Detroit Tigers)
Joker Marchant Stadium
2301 Lakeland Hills Boulevard, Lakeland 33805
(863) 431–4142
www.lakelandtigers.net
> *Season:*   April to September
> *Where:*   From I-4 Exit 33 follow signs to SR 22 South; go south about 2.5 miles to stadium
> *Ticket Prices:* $4 to $5

Basketball

The Magic are definitely the hottest sports ticket in town. Don't be surprised if you find them sold out well in advance, especially if they are playing the Lakers or the Bulls. Still, tickets are sometimes available. You can always try your luck outside the Arena on the day of a game; someone just might have an "extra" ticket. Florida law prohibits the sale of a sports ticket for more than $1 over its face value, but scalpers have commanded from $225 to $1,000 for tickets to Magic playoff games.

Orlando Magic

1 Magic Place, Orlando 32801
(800) 338-0005; (407) 896-2442
www.orlandomagic.com

Season:	October to April
Where:	T. D. Waterhouse Centre, 600 West Amelia Street, in downtown Orlando, just off I-4
Ticket Prices:	$10 to $150

Dog Racing

Orlando itself does not boast a greyhound track, but there's one just across the Seminole County line, north of the city. It operates year round. Admission is cheap, just $1 for grandstand seats and $2 for the clubhouse. When you tire of betting on the dogs here, you can bet on dog and horse races elsewhere that are beamed in by satellite.

Sanford-Orlando Kennel Club

301 Dog Track Road, Longwood 32750
(407) 831-1600
www.floridagreyhoundracing.com/SOKC

Ice Hockey

The Florida Seals are members of the Southern Professional Hockey League and were launched in 2002, when they were known as the Orlando Seals.

Florida Seals

215 Celebration Place, Celebration 34747
(407) 343-PUCK (7825)
www.floridaseals.com

Season:	November to April
Where:	Silver Spurs Arena, 1875 Silver Spurs Lane, Kissimmee, off US 192
Ticket Prices:	$12 to $30

Jai-Alai

Jai-Alai is played on a sort of elongated racquetball court but, instead of a racquet, the players use a long curved wicker basket, called a cesta, strapped to their right hand, to catch and return the pelota (or "ball") at blinding speeds. To facilitate betting, the game is played in round-robin fashion by eight single players or two-man doubles teams. The first to reach seven points wins, with second and third place determined by point totals. Playoffs settle ties.

Reflecting the Basque origins of the game, most of the players have Basque or Spanish surnames. The action is fast and often surprisingly graceful. Points are determined much as they are in racquetball or squash. As one player (or team) loses a point, the next player takes his place. Although the program gives stats on the players, betting seems more like picking the numbers for a lottery game.

If you tire of the action unfolding in front of you, you can repair downstairs and bet on jai-alai matches in Miami or horse racing at New Jersey's Meadowlands, all of them shown on large video screens. When live games aren't being offered you can still stop by for the simulcasts of events elsewhere.

Orlando Jai-Alai

6405 South U.S. Highway 17-92, Casselberry 32730
(407) 339-6221
www.orlandojaialai.com

Season:	Live games January to March; simulcasts year-round
Ticket Prices:	$1 at the door (55 and older **free**)
Game Times:	Thursday to Saturday at 7:00 p.m.; matinees Thursday and Saturday at noon, Sunday at 1:00 p.m.

Chapter Eighteen:

Shop 'Til You Drop

SEEN ALL THE ATTRACTIONS? GOT SOME MONEY LEFT? NO PROBLEM! ORLANDO makes it easy to go home flat broke and maybe with a few genuine bargains to help convince the folks back home that you're not simply an unregenerate spendthrift. Of course, for many people shopping is an attraction in itself, bargain or no. Whatever category fits you best, you're sure to find plenty of opportunities to shop till you drop.

In this chapter I have concentrated mostly on discount shopping opportunities on the theory that, a) you can always pay full price back home and, b) your wallet can probably use the break during an Orlando vacation. Basic information about other shopping venues in the Orlando area can be found on the Internet at orlando.retail-guide.com. And don't forget all those gift shops in the various attractions described in earlier in this book.

Upscale Shopping

There's a lot more to buy in Orlando beside the gaudy t-shirts and cheap souvenirs you'll find in the theme parks. In fact, for many foreign visitors, high-end shopping excursions are a big part of Orlando's appeal.

The major upscale shopping destination is the **Mall at Millenia** (Exit 78 on I-4), a super-deluxe mall anchored by three major department stores, including Bloomingdale's and Neiman Marcus. Elsewhere among the more than 100 merchants you'll find familiar names like Tiffany, Gucci, Burberry, Christian Dior, Kenneth Cole, Jimmy Choo, and Hugo Boss. There's art, too, including the fine collectables at Lladro and Swarovski. When you're ready for a break, fine dining at McCormick & Schmicks or the Brio Tuscan Grill beckons and when your shopping day is done you can unwind at the Blue Martini, which features live entertainment. The mall's web site is www. mallatmillenia.com.

ther major shopping destination is the **Florida Mall**, Central Florida's largest, at the intersection of Sand Lake Road and South Orange Blossom Trail. It is
conveniently located between the airport and the major tourist districts, so don't be
surprised to see tour buses lined up outside. There are five major department stores
here, including Nordstrom's and Saks Fifth Avenue along with 250 other stores that
run the gamut from Abercrombie & Fitch and Banana Republic to Victoria's Secret
and Zales Jewelers. There's even a large shop devoted entirely to M&Ms candies!
There's no fine dining here, just a large food court.

For a more traditional, less frenzied shopping experience head for **Park Avenue
in Winter Park,** just north of Orlando. Here, under the shade of moss-draped live
oaks, you can stroll past upscale boutiques like the Golden Rabbit, Cody's, John Craig,
Nicole Miller and Patchington. There's also an outpost of Williams Sonoma, as well
as The Wine Room, which sells fine wines by the bottle and by the glass, using a
state-of-the-art dispensing system, the only one of its kind in Florida. There are some
terrific restaurants as well, including Chef Justin's Park Plaza Gardens. At the end of
the street is the gift shop of the Morse Museum.

Speaking of museums, don't overlook the gift shops of museums listed in *Chapter
15* as sources for one of a kind gifts for you or for that special someone. Even theme
parks like SeaWorld and Discovery Cove offer some upscale items, usually art pieces,
to lure the discriminating shopper.

Outlet Shopping

Once upon a time, "factory outlets" were just that — small shops located in or
near the factory where seconds, rejects, overruns, and discontinued lines could be sold,
at a discount, directly to the public. Factory outlets existed outside the standard retail
channels and were a classic win/win proposition: The public got a bargain and the
factory recouped at least some of its costs.

Today, factory outlets have become very much a part of the retail scene, located
far from the factory in glossy malls and often featuring merchandise specifically designed for and marketed to the bargain-hunting segment of the market. And the
words "Factory Outlet" have become a marketing buzzword used to suggest deep,
deep discounts, whether they are there or not. Some factory outlets are run directly
by the companies whose merchandise they sell. Others are run by entrepreneurs who
contract with big name companies and then set their own prices. Still others are run
by merchants who buy cheap merchandise from a variety of off-cost producers or
from brokers who specialize in overstocked and "distressed" goods. All of which is to
say that, when it comes to factory outlet shopping, the warning "caveat emptor" (let
the buyer beware) is in full force. On the other hand, I do not mean to suggest that
the outlet malls in the Orlando area are filled with shady operators out to fleece the
unwary tourist. Far from it. Most of these outlets offer excellent deals on first-rate
goods and any factory seconds or irregulars are clearly marked. Still, a wise shopper
will arrive with a clear idea of what he or she is looking for and what the "going rate"
for those items is back home.

What follows is a survey of the major factory outlet shopping venues in the Orlando area. Conveniently enough, most of them are located along International Drive in Orlando. I have listed them in the order you would encounter them when traveling from north to south along this well-traveled tourist corridor and then south to Kissimmee. The list is not meant to be all-inclusive. You may find other bona-fide outlets. On the other hand, there are many shops that use the words "factory outlet" rather loosely.

Prime Outlets
www.primeoutlets.com

Location:	5401 West Oak Ridge Road, at the north end of International Drive, in Orlando
Information:	(407) 352-9600
Hours:	Monday to Saturday 10:00 a.m. to 10:00 p.m.; Sunday 10:00 a.m. to 9:00 p.m.

Prime Outlets is the 900-pound gorilla of the outlet scene with two malls and several "annexes," including an upscale shopping area just a short hop down International Drive. The sprawling complex plays host to some 170 merchants. Stop by Guest Services first to pick up a list of today's unadvertised special bargains. Like any self-respecting mall, this one features food courts and snack kiosks to refuel the flagging shopper. There are also games and rides for the kiddies.

Orlando Premium Outlets
www.premiumoutlets.com/orlando/

Location:	8200 Vineland Avenue, off International Drive just south of SeaWorld
Information:	(407) 238-7787
Hours:	Monday to Saturday 10:00 a.m. to 10:00 p.m.; Sunday 11:00 a.m. to 9:00 p.m.

The newest entry in the outlet shopping sweepstakes boasts 110 stores representing such upscale vendors as Brooks Brothers, Armani, Versace, and Burberry, plus a central food court with its own Starbucks. Register online for the VIP Club for extra savings or to check out current specials offered by mall merchants.

Lake Buena Vista Factory Stores
www.lbvfs.com

Location:	15591 SR 535, 2 miles south of I-4 Exit 68
Information:	(407) 238-9301
Hours:	Monday to Saturday 9:00 a.m. to 9:00 p.m.; Sunday 9:00 a.m. to 6:00 p.m.

This mall of more than 40 shops is located on the well traveled state road that links I-4 to US 192. There's a small food court if you get hungry and a playground for the kids. They offer free shuttle service from nearly 50 participating local hotels.

Flea Markets

The flea market is an Old World concept. Originally the term was applied to impromptu markets, the yard sales of their day, where enterprising individuals at the frayed edge of the merchant class displayed a grab bag of merchandise, some of dubious provenance — hence the alternate term: "thieves' market." Like the term "factory outlet," the term "flea market" has evolved over the years. Today, as practiced in Central Florida, a flea market is a sort of alternate shopping mall. The market owner provides, at a modest rental, simple booths in covered arcades. The merchants are, for the most part, full-time professionals with long-term leases on their booths who differ from their counterparts in the glitzy malls only in the matter of scale.

Whereas the old flea markets of Europe held out the lure of uncovering some priceless antique at an unbelievably low price, the modern Florida flea market more often offers inexpensive merchandise, purchased from a wholesaler and offered at a price that might not be any better than you could get at Kmart. Still, savvy shoppers can find bargains here if they know what they're looking for (and at). The best bets, in my opinion, are the secondhand dealers, the craftspeople, the fresh produce vendors, and the purveyors of the sort of wacky and offbeat stuff you don't usually see elsewhere.

Whatever the drawbacks of flea market shopping, there's no denying that the atmosphere of these bazaars is a lot of fun. There's plenty of greasy and fattening food to keep your energy up and the very challenge of navigating the seemingly endless rows of wares tends to keep you going. For those who have never experienced this particular slice of Americana, I recommend it highly. For those of you who simply love the flea market experience (and you know who you are), the following flea markets should keep you busy. If you must have more, just look in the Yellow Pages in your hotel room under "Flea Markets."

Flea World

www.fleaworld.com

Location: Highway 17-92 in Sanford; I-4 Exit 98
Information: (407) 330-1792
Hours: Friday, Saturday, and Sunday 9:00 a.m. to 6:00 p.m.

Flea World bills itself as "America's largest flea market" with 1,700 dealer booths, most of which are occupied on any given weekend. There's bingo here and an amusement park next door to keep the kids occupied.

Main Gate Flea Market

Location: 5407 Irlo Bronson Highway (Highway 192) in
                   Kissimmee
Information: (407) 390-1015
Hours: Daily 10:00 a.m. to 8:00 p.m.

This market is housed in a series of long metal buildings set well back from the heavily traveled tourist strip of route 192, just east of I-4. There are over 400 booths here and a smattering of food stands, some of which offer some intriguing ethnic specialties.

OBT Flea Market

Location:	5545 International Drive in Orlando, just east of Kirkman Road
Information:	(407) 460-8375
Hours:	Monday to Saturday 10:00 a.m. to 8:00 p.m.; Sunday 10:00 a.m. to 6:00 p.m.

This bare-bones operation has space for 350 booths, but they are far from full. Look for a mix of costume jewelry, inexpensive clothing, and toys. Just across the street is the excellent **Passage To India** restaurant.

192 Flea Market

Location:	4301 West Vine Street (Highway 192) in Kissimmee
Information:	(407) 396-4555
Hours:	Daily 9:00 a.m. to 6:00 p.m.

This is Kissimmee's original flea market. Over 400 booths offer a variety of wares, including plenty of Disney souvenirs and Florida t-shirts for the budget souvenir hound. I especially like the fact that this market seems to attract the casual vendor who uses it as a sort of substitute yard sale.

Osceola Flea & Farmers Market

www.fleaamerica.com

Location:	2801 East Irlo Bronson Highway (Highway 192) between Kissimmee and St. Cloud
Information:	(407) 846-2811
Hours:	Friday, Saturday, and Sunday 8:00 a.m. to 5:00 p.m.

A little farther off the tourist track, this flea market offers more fresh produce than the others. It also has a "garage sale" section that draws folks with some junk to unload (as opposed to regular merchants). There are about 900 booths selling everything from Disney souvenirs to home improvement items to car stereos.

Visitors Market

Location:	5811 Irlo Bronson Highway (Highway 192) in Kissimmee
Information:	(407) 390-9910
Hours:	Daily 9:30 a.m. to 9:30 p.m. (to 6:00 p.m. in slower periods)

A modest market housed in a former retail location on Kissimmee's gaudy tourist strip, this one has space for 250 booths, most of which are open for business selling a wide variety of cut-rate merchandise.

Antiquing

Depending on what you're looking for, the greater Orlando area may hold some hidden treasures for the antique hound. Don't expect much in the way of fancy European antiques, but if your interest runs to American vernacular furniture of the twentieth century, you may be in luck. There are even some pieces dating to the nineteenth century to be found.

What you will find in abundance is *stuff* — Depression-era glass, weaponry, old toys (including some nifty Disney memorabilia), Art Deco and Art Moderne bric-a-brac, old orange crate labels, Highwayman art, the list goes on and on. If rummaging through aisle after aisle of assorted stuff in search of hidden gems is your idea of a great time, you will find plenty to keep you occupied.

There are a number of antiquing hotspots in the area. The toniest is **Antique Row in Orlando,** a collection of fourteen shops that runs for several blocks along Orange Avenue, just north of Lake Ivanhoe (Exit 84 or 85 on I-4). A standout here is Flo's Antique Accents (407-895-1800) for mahogany furniture of the early twentieth century. Farther afield, a number of historic downtown areas in nearby towns offer concentrations of antique stores. To the south lie **Kissimmee**, where Lanier's (407-933-5679) is the most prominent merchant, and **St. Cloud**, whose downtown is a sort of time capsule of mid-twentieth century working class Americana. To the north lies the picturesque and more upscale village of **Mt. Dora**. Here, you will find an antique mall in the downtown area and just outside town, on Highway 441, the sprawling Renniger's Antique Fair (352-383-8393), featuring over 300 dealers.

As you explore, be sure to pick up a free copy of *The Antique Shoppe*, a monthly newspaper that will point you to other antiquing destinations within easy driving distance of Orlando. It also contains valuable information on antique shows, auctions, flea markets, and collectors' clubs. The web site is www.antiqueshoppefl.com.

Index to Rides & Attractions

Free Updates

For free updates to this book and its companion volume, *Universal Orlando: The Ultimate Guide To The Ultimate Theme Park Adventure,* visit:

http://www.TheOtherOrlando.com

Other Books from
The Intrepid Traveler

The Intrepid Traveler publishes money-saving, horizon expanding travel how-to and guidebooks dedicated to helping its readers make world travel an integral part of their everyday life.

For more information visit our web site, where you will find a complete catalog, frequent updates to this and our other books, travel articles from around the world, Internet travel resources, and more:

http://www.IntrepidTraveler.com

If you are interested in becoming a home-based travel agent, visit the Home-Based Travel Agent Resource Center at:

http://www.HomeTravelAgency.com